Clock Tower Press
3622 W. Liberty Rd.
Ann Arbor, MI 48103
www.clocktowerpress.com
Corporate Sales 1 800 956 8999

Printed and bound in Canada.

10 9 8 7 6 5 4 3 2

Library of Congress Cataloging-in-Publication Data

Klein, Bradley S.
       Discovering Donald Ross : the architect and his golf courses / by
Bradley S. Klein.
              p. cm.
       Includes bibliographical references and index.
       ISBN 1-886947-55-4
Ross, Donald J., 1872-1948. 2. Golf course architects—United States—
Biography. 3. Golf courses—United States—Design and construction—
History. I Title.

GV964.R67 K54 2001
712'.5.092—dc21
[B]
2001020965

DISCOVERING

THE ARCHITECT AND HIS GOLF COURSES *by* BRADLEY S. KLEIN

DONALD ROSS

to Sterling Farmer,
because Brae Burn is a
special place.

Bradley S. Klein

CLOCK
TOWER
PRESS

ACKNOWLEDGMENTS

The book began as a straightforward biographical project. There was plenty of evidence to mine, and more than enough golf courses to visit. The two and a half years it took to research and write this volume is not a long time by academic standards for a biography. But for those tuned to the frantic rhythms of modern journalism and sportswriting, such a time frame is seemingly unending. Perhaps I undertook too much. In any case, what follows is in part a biography of the architect, partly an analysis of his work, and an account of what to do today with the substantial body of work Ross bequeathed to us. In short, this is Ross's life—his work and his legacy.

Only very late in the process of creating this book did I realize how personally vested I was in its outcome. When I started work, in March 1998, golf writing was half my life. Academic political science was the other. By the end of that year, I became founding editor of *Golfweek's Superintendent News* and left teaching altogether. Along the way, I also started taking an active interest in the day-to-day affairs of my golf club, the Ross-designed Wampanoag Country Club in West Hartford, CT, and even spent a few mornings with the maintenance staff learning how to operate their equipment. At the same time, I became a board member of the Donald Ross Society, which had been founded at Wampanoag a few years before I became a member. So the personal investments began to mount, as well as the reasons for not finishing sooner. There was ample reason, both professional and personal, to get the story right.

This book would not have been possible without years of prior work by the late W. Pete Jones of Raleigh, North Carolina. He poured his soul into accumulating, sorting, and cataloging many thousands of letters, files, maps, and notes generated during the course of Donald Ross's life. Pete's archival work provided valuable raw data that had to be sifted through. Though he died before writing any of his long-promised volume, he made it possible for others to study Ross's life.

This volume would never have come about without Khristine Januzik, curator at the Tufts Archives in the Given Memorial Library, Pinehurst, North Carolina. She patiently answered hundreds of my questions, steered documents my way that came across her desk, and was always willing to hunt for some obscure photograph or map. The Ross family also proved generous with their time. I am grateful to Ross's daughter, Lillian Ross Pippitt (who, unfortunately, died in November of 2000 before I could present her with the book), and his granddaughter, Elizabeth Shapiro, for their many hours of conversation and remembrances, including sharing with me a look through family heirlooms and memorabilia. Ross's stepgranddaughter, Elizabeth Blackinton Crawford, also shared her time. I was particularly humbled by the opportunity to overnight at Ross's vacation home at Little Compton, Rhode Island, including one memorable night during which I slept in Donald Ross's bedroom. No, he did not appear in the middle of the night, either in person or in my dreams. Little Compton, by the way, was one of eight former Ross residences I had the pleasure of visiting during my research, including his childhood home in Dornoch, Scotland.

For golf-course-oriented advice, I am grateful to a number of people. Three founding members of the Donald Ross Society—Steve Edwards, Michael Fay, and Barry J. Palm—provided much-needed encouragement, as did another Society member (and fellow Wampanoag Country Club member), Glen Rapoport. Dr. John Macleod of Dornoch provided invaluable help on historical matters pertaining to Ross's life in Dornoch; there was something peculiarly postmodern about being to able to communicate via E-mail with a man who grew up in the town before electricity arrived there. Geoffrey Cornish provided invaluable help, not least as a close reader of the manuscript. I must also offer both thanks and apologies to architect Brian Silva: thanks for his eagerness to help, and apologies for having earlier contributed to an unduly harsh climate of criticism regarding his work.

I am also grateful to Pat Corso, president of Pinehurst Resort & Country Club, and Stephen Boyd, director of communications there, for hosting a number of my visits and giving me the run of the golf facilities and resort, both before and after (but not during!) the 1999 U.S. Open. When people comment that, "such work is tough, but someone has to do it," I point out — rather defensively—that on several research trips to Pinehurst I actually left my golf clubs at home.

On matters of design, I drew heavily on the input of Bill Coore, Ben Crenshaw, Pete Dye, Tom Fazio, Ron Forse, Gil Hanse, Rees Jones, Stephen Kay, Brad Kocher, John LaFoy, Tim Liddy, Ron Prichard, Steve Smyers, Bobby Weed, Ron Whitten, and Phil Wogan. Jeff Mingay provided keen help on Canada. Brian Delacey shared his knowledge about Ross's work on municipal layouts in Boston. Paul Richards and Richard Holland were infectious in their enthusiasm for Ross's work in and around Chicago, and I appreciate their having focused my attention on the virtues of their home course, Beverly Country Club.

I am especially grateful to superintendents Greg Stent of my own Wampanoag Country Club, Paul Jamrog of Metacomet (RI), Paul Jett at Pinehurst No. 2 (NC), Pat Krickseonaitis of Essex County Club (MA), and Herb Watson of Hartford GC (CT) for their willingness to spend time with me, usually very early in the morning, explaining their craft. I also appreciate the many superintendents, club managers and club presidents of dozens of other courses who made themselves, and their facilities, available. I also want to thank Gery Krewson for his work on graphical elements, including maps and charts. He helped me confront a virulent form of computer technophobia and along the way, set up an interesting website of his own called DonaldRoss.com. I am also grateful to my own publication, Golfweek's Superintendent News, for the support shown by Ken Hanson, Dave Seanor, Anthony Pioppi, John Steinbreder, Terry Buchen, Frank Rossi and the entire editorial staff.

Help came in many forms. Jack Nicklaus kindly agreed to write a back-of-the-book blurb. The work of photographers Larry Lambrecht, Arthur Cicconi, Tony Roberts, Ralph Chermak and Dave Richards greatly enhanced the text. Longtime friend and fellow golf writer Lorne Rubenstein provided much encouragement. Details and inspiration came from Jerry Breen, Arthur Fischer, William G. Hall Jr., David Hosford, Michael Jamieson, David Joy, Gary Larrabee, Tommy Naccarato, Mike Pilo and Tom Stewart.

Divot, my dear dog, sat under foot while I wrote and kindly desisted from chewing or pawing the manuscript. Cory-Ellen Nadel, my daughter and an accomplished fiction writer of her own, now knows more than she needs to about golf course design.

Most of all, I want to thank my wife, anthropologist Jane Nadel-Klein, for her extraordinary patience. Not only did she teach me about Scottish culture and how to conduct fieldwork there. She also put up with my many research trips, incessant phone calling, and middle-of-the-night obsessing about the details of this book. During the first conversation we ever had she asked me what there was to write about golf. This book continues what has turned out to be a much longer answer than she ever expected.

FOREWORD

The mystique about Donald Ross starts with his marvelous routings. The way he set up the golf course was also impressive. When I see Ross courses, and I mean the ones he was seriously involved in, I'm amazed how he could take an old topographic map and route the holes with such variation.

Many of the Ross courses that we've heard about and that have come into national recognition were on good pieces of ground to start with. They were all on self-contained lots, where you didn't have any residential development or have to cross roads or walk around areas that you couldn't build on. When you have one parcel of ground that allows for connections from green to tee, the walks are a lot more manageable.

He was the first designer to make the opening shot play one way, then switch the kind of play needed on the second shot. Whatever he had done on the first hole, he'd flip on the second. He might set up a bunker on the right-hand side and expect you to cut your tee shot. He would then reverse that around the green and expect you to draw your approach. He did this at Seminole on the first two holes. At the first, he set bunkers down the right side and asked the player to fade the drive. The green, though, is set up to hold a draw shot. Ross switched this on the second hole, where you're supposed to hit the tee shot right-to-left, then move the ball the other way on the approach. That's also what makes Seminole's famous sixth hole so great. You have to draw the tee shot, then hit your approach left-to-right over bunkers in front of the green.

Ross also had a way of varying his par 3s. He'd put the dominant hazard on one side, then on the opposite side on another hole. So it wasn't just yardage he was changing but the kind of shot he was asking you to make. He did this a lot at Pinehurst No. 2 and it's what makes his holes there so interesting. It's not something you'd necessarily notice but you'd find yourself having to hit different kinds of shots, so you'd never feel like you were repeating yourself.

About that No. 2 course. Those greens with the crowns? I'm sorry to say it but they're not what you'd call part of Mr. Ross's style. Go down the road to Mid-Pines and Pine Needles, for example, where Mr. Ross built the greens himself, and

Opposite page: Seminole's sixth, viewed from behind. (Larry Lambrecht)

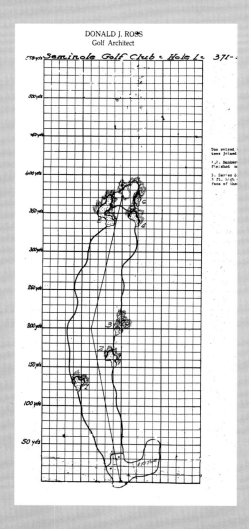

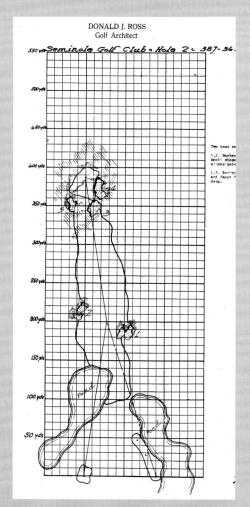

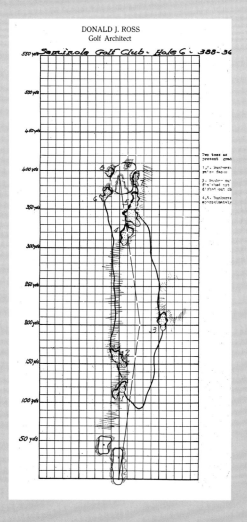

Above & middle: Ross's sketches of the first and second holes at Seminole Golf Club, Juno Beach, FL, 1929. The first hole calls for a cut tee shot and a drawn approach. The second hole plays just the opposite. (Seminole Golf Club)

Above right: The sixth hole at Seminole. A 388-yard par 4, it perfectly embodies Ross's principle of shifting demands. Favor the left side with a draw off the tee; the approach then requires a cut across a diagonally arrayed set of bunkers protecting the front of the long putting surface. (Seminole Golf Club)

you'll see more features than just crowns. That's what I think is so great about his work—that he changed what he was doing. This was unlike, for example, a Seth Raynor, who always built the same kinds of holes, good holes, certainly, like his Redan par 3, but still the same. I've been known to try to copy my hole designs from one course to the next as well. But with a Ross course, there's hardly anything that's the same from one to the next.

At Pinehurst No. 2, however, those crowned greens are not really what he did anywhere else. This is because they've been top-dressed so much that they now look like perched-up angel cakes. That's what happened with common bermuda-grass in those days. The only way to keep healthy turf on them was by top-dressing with lots of sand. Richard Tufts, who ran that place for many years, told my wife Alice and me that Pinehurst always put a lot more money into its greens—especially on the No. 2 course. They were top-dressed more often than at other courses, and the result was that they changed over the years as they became built up from the additional sand. So they're quite different today from what Ross had planned. The slopes on the greens, and the way they fall off around the edges, are probably

a lot more severe than he intended.

    That's the thing about Ross courses: for all their genius, they vary. He designed them one way, but the builders had to be really skilled at construction to interpret them correctly. It often depended on who was hired to build them. Some of his courses are good because they were built by people who got their hands dirty and made his plans come alive. Other Ross courses (I probably shouldn't say which ones) look different and are a little extreme because they were built by people who weren't very good at making sense of his sketches.

    As if that weren't enough to account for the variation, each course has its own maintenance practices, and that meant that there would be a lot of variety from one course to the next. What they all have in common, though, is that they all have good routings.

    One final thing. I often wonder what Mr. Ross would say about the game and about how his courses play today. If he were somehow to come back and watch Tiger Woods and all those kids in college hit the ball so far, I wonder if, or how, he would have changed his designs. And it isn't just in response to the men's game.

Pinehurst's putting surfaces, grassed in 1935, originally featured grade-level, low-lying entrances and were not turtle-backed. This is the sixth hole on the No.2 course. (Tufts Archives)

There are many women amateurs who regularly hit the ball farther than the pros did when Ross was doing all those courses.

In some ways, design was easier for him because there wasn't such a big difference between good players and average resort players. Ross could build a green figuring someone was going to hit a middle-iron into it, so he could contour it a little flatter or leave a little margin. But now good players are hitting *wedges* into those same greens. I wonder how he'd change his designs given the incredible distance some players can hit it—even though a lot of everyday fellows still only hit the ball 190 yards and most women don't carry the ball more than 130 yards.

Ross could also count on firm, fast fairways back then, but today's courses are much more lush. Which means it's become a different game, and the difference between midrange golfers and professionals is bigger than ever.

I've been reading Brad Klein's work for years. I got to know him when he came down to South Carolina in 1990-1991 to watch me build the Ocean Course at Kiawah Island. When he phoned a few years ago and asked me to design a golf course for his town of Bloomfield, Connecticut, I couldn't say "no" because I was afraid he'd write bad reviews about me in the magazines he works for. So I guess you could say that I now work for him (although my fee is only $1 because it's going to be a municipal golf course).

Brad has frequently told me that he wants me to keep the design simple and that I should keep in mind the way Ross designed his courses. After reading this book, I'm more certain than I used to be that there's no such thing as "a" Ross course. However, if Ross didn't have a simple formula, he certainly had a good way of going about his work. I think Brad explains as clearly as anyone could what made Ross such a genius. Donald Ross may not have had a single way of designing, but he sure had a sense of what made a golf course interesting.

Pete Dye
Delray Beach, Florida

Above: Pete Dye

Opposite page: The convex, pop-up style of Pinehurst's putting surfaces today only evolved through years of top-dressing. This is the fifth green at No.2. (Bradley S. Klein)

Introduction

The name Donald Ross carries considerable weight throughout the world of golf. That is no small achievement for someone whose main contribution to the game was as a designer and builder of golf courses and who last worked half a century ago. Most of the game's legendary figures established their reputations as great players. Ross, by contrast, never won a national championship. Nor did he compete on the professional tour. He conducted his life in relative quiet—relative, that is, to the more crass elements of media hype and consumer culture that have come to define our modern sports worlds. Instead, Ross worked a more modest landscape—that of the earth's contours. And he made his mark in an era when golf, like sports in general, was just beginning to establish itself as part of everyday culture.

He was a quiet man, resolute in his vision of the land and unshakable in his personal commitments to friends, colleagues, and family. He was by no means educated by modern standards, though he was sustained by a certain native intelligence cultivated through close association with many of the game's pioneers. Most importantly, he was born to humble origins, to a family whose strength was shaped less by wealth—for there was none—than by a steadying, religious sensibility of right and wrong.

Between his birth in 1872 in Dornoch, Scotland and his death in Pinehurst, North Carolina in 1948, Donald James Ross nonetheless managed to help reshape the face of American sports. He left behind a legacy of 399 golf courses that he either designed or redesigned—a far cry from the 600 or more that have mistakenly been attributed to him. During his heyday in the 1920s, he was the country's most prolific creator of golf courses. From 1919 through 1931, eight of the thirteen U.S. Opens were contested on layouts he had designed or redone. He also presided over the making of the country's first substantial golf resort at Pinehurst. Along the way he pioneered developments in turfgrass that dramatically altered the playing texture of the country's golf layouts. Small wonder that in December of 1947, during the founding meeting of the American Society of Golf Course Architects held in Pinehurst, Ross was named honorary president. Today, the ASGCA's highest award, presented annually, is called the Donald Ross Award.

And his work continues to inspire today. A list published annually by *Golfweek* of "America's Best" golf courses includes two separate rankings: a top-100

Above: The inaugural meeting of the American Society of Golf Course Architects, held at Pinehurst in December of 1947. From l. to r.: Billy Bell, Robert White, William Langford, Donald J. Ross, Robert Bruce Harris, Stanley Thompson, William Gordon, Robert Trent Jones, Bill Diddel, and J.B. McGovern. (ASGCA)

Right: Map of Ross designs across the U.S. (Gery Krewson)

list of Classical layouts that predate 1960, and another top-100 list of Modern courses that debuted in 1960 or later. Ross, with 22 courses on the Classical list, has 10 more than the next most honored traditional designer, A.W. Tillinghast. His 12 design credits on the 1999 *Golf Digest* list (including Congressional CC, where he added nine holes in 1930) give him one more than Robert Trent Jones Sr. and two more than Tom Fazio. His dominance is confirmed on the *Golf* Magazine list of top-100 U.S. courses as well, where his 12 design credits exceed all others, living or deceased. Despite substantially different selection methods, all three national lists affirm Ross' place in history.

Comparative Ranking of Leading Ross Courses
(INCLUDES ORIGINAL DESIGNS AND RENOVATIONS)

Course	*Golfweek*-2000 (100 Classical)	*Golf Digest*-1999 (100 U.S.)	*Golf Magazine*-2000 (100 U.S)
Pinehurst No. 2, NC	9	9	6
Seminole, FL	15	14	12
Oakland Hills (South), MI	16	10	14
Wannamoisett, RI	25	49	61
East Lake, GA	36	66	66
Holston Hills, TN	37	—	—
Oak Hill (East), NY	40	26	18
Salem, MA	41	78	96
Inverness, OH	42	29	32
Interlachen, MN	45	54	56
Congressional (Blue), MD	46	59	47
Plainfield, NJ	47	44	72
Scioto, OH	51	37	33
White Bear Yacht Club, MN	61	—	—
Essex County Club, MA	67	—	—
Pine Needles, NC	71	—	—
Franklin Hills, MI	75	—	—
Minikahda, MN	82	—	—
Newport, RI	88	—	—
Northland, MN	93	—	—
Wykagyl, NY	97	—	—
Brookside, OH	99	—	—

Wannamoisett Country Club, Rumford, RI, with its devilish 128-yard par-3 third hole. Ross designed the course in 1914 and reworked it in 1926. (Larry Lambrecht)

Just to name his most famous courses—Pinehurst No.2, Seminole, Oakland Hills, Oak Hill—is enough to induce fanciful thoughts among golfers. But it's also an awareness of his more esoteric gems—Franklin Hills in Michigan, Holston Hills in Tennessee, Wannamoisett in Rhode Island—that gets itinerant golfers thinking lovingly about the brilliance of classic course architecture which Ross championed.

If Ross himself knew that his work was legendary, he never betrayed it in his letters or in the records of his conversations and relations with colleagues. Everything he did was undertaken in his own self-restrained manner. Ross was by no means publicly celebrated. Indeed, he was no hero at all—except, perhaps, to his immediate family, who to this day revere his memory. When interviewed for this biography of her father, for example, 89-year old Lillian Ross Pippitt was almost apologetic for not realizing at the time she was growing up that her father was so well respected or that he would become famous for his achievements. "I didn't know him as a famous person," she told me. "I just knew him as Dad."

In his day, Ross was deeply respected by those who worked around him, whether in the fields of course architecture, agronomy, resort operations, or club making. Most impressive is that a half century after his death, he is revered for the boldness of his vision and for the clarity with which he designed, shaped, and built

Ross and his daughter, Lillian, in 1923. (Elizabeth Pippitt Shapiro)

golf holes. Generations of golfers are indebted to him for his having made their idle pursuit so enjoyable. And his work is still carefully studied by would-be practitioners of the trade who are searching for the secrets and principles that made his designs so enduring.

This design biography explores what made his work so impressive. If this doesn't result in a precise list of golden rules to follow, it will reveal the kind of creativity and persistence needed to create a substantial body of work. Even in golf, it is possible to have artistry. The only difference between the traditional arts and golf course design is that the creativity has to be blended with sound engineering, good agronomy and drainage, and lots of tender loving care. Ross had all those skills—plus the ability to convey it to those around him. The result is a body of work that 75 years after its apogee continues to thrill golfers and to inspire those interested in the craft of course architecture.

Unfortunately, it is no easy matter interpreting such a vast body of work. Earlier in my golf writing career, I would regularly walk a golf course and speak notes about it into a small tape recorder. "Interviewing the golf course," I used to call it, and it had its merits as a means of gaining an understanding of what the land was suggesting by its various folds and contours. I well remember a cold, wet Monday in early May of 1989, when I was forced to experience the Oak Hills East Course this way, without playing it, because that day's U.S. Open media preview round was snowed out. I've since been fortunate to have played the course twice, but actually never gained a better view of the holes than during that otherwise miserable day more than a decade ago.

For better or worse, it has not been possible to conduct an extended enough series of interviews to cover all of Ross's work. Had that been the case, the book would have been delayed even longer. What I have attempted here, however, is an interpretive biography in which I place Ross's life in the context of his own evolving design work. My interest is less on the everyday facts of his life than on how his experiences shaped his work and how, in turn, his golf courses influence us today. For that reason, I have also avoided a hole-by-hole or course-by-course narrative. The point of this exercise, after all, is not to reproduce Ross but to make sense of him for us today. In that tradition, there is an element of "how to" in this book that might actually be of some use to golfers seeking to improve their game.

I never fail to be stunned by how bullheaded many golfers can be—regardless of handicap—in playing a hole a particular way when it clearly suggests another line or angle of play. An attention to the architect's purpose is important. No bunkers or swales are there by accident. "Every contour has a story," an architect once told me. Paying attention to those stories might actually help us play better. It will certainly make the walk in the park more enjoyable, and that alone is a worthy achievement. Indeed, as far as I can tell it is the main purpose of playing golf at all.

Ross was more of a designer and builder than he was a reflective intellectual about his work. His sole musings on architecture, published in 1996 as *Golf Has*

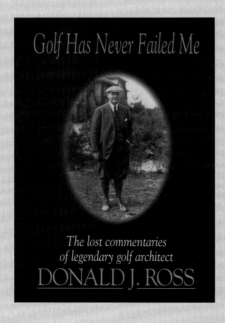

Golf Has Never Failed Me, a manuscript that Ross wrote many years ago, was finally published in 1996.

Never Failed Me, is a suggestive set of observations. They do not, however, represent the kind of boldly unified or systematic approach to the game found in parallel books by such contemporaries as Charles Blair Macdonald, Alister MacKenzie, George Thomas, or Tom Simpson. Nonetheless, Ross does betray a coherent and admirable sensibility about the game: that it should be kept simple, diverse, and enjoyable for all classes of golfers, and that architecture must draw upon the principles of links golf and adapt them to parkland circumstances.

Ross wrote in an era when handwritten letters were commonplace, and when legal and business matters were handled on the basis of exhaustively detailed correspondence. The convenience of the telephone had not yet registered its mark. In short, his was a world where the pace of communication and life was extended over space and time and there was more time for matters to unfold at a pace that enabled thought, planning, and response. How different it was from today's world of real-time communication, instantaneous responses, and electronic, web-based information.

The altered tone of contemporary life is reflected in the nature of course design. Today's design values seem governed by a certain immediacy in which first impressions of visual appeal are the standard of architectural judgment. In such a world, it is understandable, if not excusable, that the older, more enduring virtues of classic design might be considered quaint, old-fashioned and of mere historic interest.

There are many golfers today who find traditional or classic design unexciting or even boring. Their tastes, cultivated by a flashy, cover-girl approach adopted by certain glossy magazines, value the appearance of a golf course rather than its more enduring playing values. The result has been a concern to make a sudden, immediate impression rather than to build layouts that would speak to the heart of the game.

While players cannot be blamed if they find such new works appealing, the same cannot be said for architects. Amazingly, there are all too many course designers today with little tolerance for traditional works like Ross's. Not that all architects need to uphold his values in their own work. But they should at least have made a careful study, and if they find his work objectionable or uninteresting, they owe the golf world the decency of simply refusing to touch such works. Instead, too many designers today have been willing to ply a heavy hand in improving, updating, renovating, or simply changing (for its own sake) the work deeded to us by Donald Ross.

Bad enough that so many designers have never even bothered to look carefully at the classic courses. A philosophy professor unfamiliar with the works of Plato and Aristotle would never secure university employment in the field of ethics. Why, then, are benighted architects—some of them indifferent on principle to history—allowed to practice course design? Worse yet, why are they allowed a free hand by green chairmen and course owners to tinker, alter, or improve upon the traditional masters without having made a thorough study and shown respect for the genre? An attitude prevails today that sees the golf course as a piece of property that can be dispensed with or abused as the owner might desire. Yet when it comes to recognized works of art, an attitude of respect for the painter's or scuplfor's intent counsels far more caution and limits intervention to painstaking efforts at restoration. If the same attitude were more widely cultivated among golfers and within the course design industry, many regrettable butcheries of classic courses might have been spared.

To be sure, there is no licensing in the design business when it comes to judgment and taste. Market principles prevail, and if there is demand for services of a particular sort, then a designer will fill that niche—even if, in doing so, he ends up destroying classic work. But not all of the choices that clubs and officers make are informed ones. Many come by way of deference to the architect and to his presumed expertise as a practitioner, especially when he has won many tournaments on the PGA Tour and impresses by virtue of his celebrity.

In this case, some education would help. The point is to cultivate a different taste among consumers of golf courses and to promote a more refined taste that would embrace the virtues of classic design.

Today, greater respect, even awe, is beginning to find a toehold across the industry. There is a discernible movement among certain architects and among club officers toward preservation and restoration rather than toward wholesale renovation in the name of "modernization." Evidence for this can be found in the many new books devoted to classic design. There are also several websites devoted to the praise of traditional golf, and preservationist societies devoted to the work of a particular architect are having a modest if growing influence.

Many of the most egregious examples of classic golf course renovation are being viewed not as exemplary but as unfortunate, to be avoided rather than emulated in the future. To that end, many courses are beginning to peel back layers of secondary tree growth and planting. Flashed-up bunkers are being built with lower profiles. Native grasses as well as fescue are making a return. There is also evidence that the virtues of the short game in and around greens are gaining new prominence. "How can we modernize?" is not what clubs are beginning to ask. They're asking, "What can we do to enhance, preserve or restore our classic heritage?"

If the pages that follow contribute toward that appreciation, this design biography of Donald J. Ross will have succeeded. It is not that all of his work was brilliant. But much of it was thoughtful, well executed, and at times ingenious. In short, it merits careful study. Three-quarters of a century after Ross's heyday and a half a century after his death, his work continues to inspire golfers and to encourage designers on the merits of classic landforms.

Ross (center) on 10th tee (then the 11th hole) at Pine Needles in Southern Pines, NC. (Tufts Archives)

Chapter One
Child of Dornoch

TO

THE MEMORY OF

DONALD CAMPBELL

WHO DIED AT DORNOCH 2ND FEB. 1866

AGED 58 YEARS

ALSO HIS WIFE

CHRISTINA CAMPBELL

DIED AT DORNOCH 20TH NOVEMBER 1894

AGED 88 YEARS

ALSO THEIR SON AENEAS

WHO DIED AT BENIN SO. AFRICA 10TH

SEPT. 1863

AGED 24 YEARS

AND THEIR GRANDSON JOHN ROSS

WHO DIED IN LONDON 30TH MARCH 1902

AGED 27 YEARS

THEIR DAUGHTER LILY

BELOVED WIFE OF MURDOCH ROSS

WHO DIED 25 MARCH 1924, AGED 76

THE ABOVE MURDOCH ROSS

WHO DIED 4TH JUNE 1925 AGED 76

AENEAS CAMPBELL ROSS

DIED 21 FEBY. 1957, AGED 75 YEARS

A visitor to Dornoch, Scotland, eager to canvas the town that spawned one of golf's great figures, would scarcely find any evidence there of a hometown boy who made good. It was not until February of 1999 that a single marker was placed, this one a modest plaque fronting the house at 3 St. Gilbert Street where young Donald James Ross grew up. The Royal Dornoch Golf Club, where he played as a youth and later became professional, greenkeeper, and club maker, exhibits nothing that might proclaim his work there a century ago. Next door, however, in the cemetery along Golf Road, just behind the Dornoch Free Church of Scotland, the Ross family gravestone does memorialize three generations of his immediate relatives.

EARLY YEARS

Donald James Ross was born on November 23, 1872 to Murdoch Ross and Lillian Campbell Ross. Their first child, Jane, born earlier that year, had died almost immediately and Donald was conceived soon thereafter. Following Donald into the family were three brothers, Alex, Aeneas, and John, and two sisters, Jean and Christina. The two-room stone cottage draped with climbing red creeper was crowded, but no more or less so than most of the other living quarters that surrounded them. The house, on the far western end of St. Gilbert Street, sat but a block from Dornoch Cathedral (Church of Scotland) and the commercial center of town along High Street. It was a short walk to the main east-west road through town, Castle Street. The Free Church, home of the Presbyterian congregation to which the Ross family belonged, was a five minute walk to the other side of town. Along the way were Dornoch Castle, the town police station and, at the far end of the square, the Sutherland Arms Hotel. Just to the south along Church Street, behind the Free Church and not a half mile from Ross's house, was Scotland's third oldest golf links.

Donald's father, Murdoch "Murdo" Ross was a mason—a stone cutter and bricklayer. By all evidence, Murdo Ross was able to provide little more than a very modest living for his burgeoning family. Unfortunately, he also seems to have squandered much of his earnings in local pubs. Known as a man who worked hard, he had set off to the United States in his mid-twenties, leaving behind his wife, Lily, while he earned money. In the mid-1870s, Murdo found a job on a masonry crew that was working on the New York State capitol building in Albany. For this reason he was away from home during Donald's early years. The bond that formed between the son and his mother during this time proved to be a powerful one. It was the kind of strong, unquestioning sense of love and support that Donald Ross would convey later to his own child.

Upon Murdo's return to Dornoch, a rousing celebration was planned to welcome him. He missed his own party, however, after stopping off at Eagle's for a drink and not returning home until the guests had all departed. Murdo tried to convince his wife to join him in the States, but her mother, Christina Campbell was widowed and sick and Lily insisted on nursing her. Even after Christina recovered, Lillian Campbell Ross made her intentions known to her husband: she would not leave behind her family and town. So she remained in Dornoch, as did Murdo (although he may have been embittered by her refusing to leave). He certainly did not change his ways when it came to drinking.

Lily was a devoted homemaker who took particular care in conveying to

Top: The Ross cottage in Dornoch today, showing the second story expansion. (Bradley S. Klein)

Top right: Ross family gravestone at Dornoch Free Church. (Bradley S. Klein)

Above: The Ross family cottage, 3 St. Gilbert Street, Dornoch, where Donald grew up. The photo was taken in the late 1800s before the second story was added, paid for from Donald's earnings in America. (Dornoch Historical Society)

Top left: The Sutherland Arms Hotel, at town center, early 1900s. (Dornoch Historical Society)

Top right: High Street, Dornoch, ca.1900. (Dornoch Historical Society)

Above: Dornoch town map, with the golf grounds at lower right. (Dornoch Historical Society)

her six children a strong religious upbringing, including weekly attendance at the local Free Church.

It was here that young Donald Ross acquired both his sense of religious commitment as well as an enduring love of music. Services at the modest chapel took place without accompaniment—organ music in the chapel being strictly forbidden by the dictates of Free Church Presbyterianism. Instead, parishioners took turns cueing in the psalms and Gaelic hymns by singing, or "presenting," them to the rest of the congregation. Donald enjoyed the task, and churchgoers seemed to have enjoyed (or tolerated) his voice as well. His mother especially encouraged him—except on Sundays, when even whistling was prohibited at home. Donald, meanwhile, took up with the local bagpipers band.

The Free Church originated in 1843 during a mass secession of ministers and parishes from the Church of Scotland. Scots Presbyterians are known for being dour. They have an outlook that is very stern and serious and they disapprove of such frivolities as dancing and singing—to say nothing of golf—and they are quite strict about the Sabbath as a day limited to holy activities. All of this applies with even more force to the Free Church and its members.

Donald's piety in church does not appear to have been matched by a devotion to schoolwork. By all accounts, he was an indifferent student at the local Dornoch School at both the primary and secondary levels. At the age of 13, he earned a temporary suspension from school for a prank involving a female student's pigtails and an inkwell. His adolescent effort also earned him a good smack on the nose by his teacher, which resulted in one of Donald's nostrils being so badly injured that for the rest of his life he suffered impaired breathing.

If he shared his mother's religious commitments, he also shared his father's predilection for the practical arts. By the age of 14, Donald, like most young teens in those days, was done with his studies. It was time to earn a proper living, and so he took up an apprenticeship in town under master carpenter Peter

Murray. An avid golfer as well as a skilled craftsman, Murray enjoyed an arrangement with Dornoch Golf Club whereby he built the wooden boxes containing sand at each teeing ground. (Before the advent of the wooden teeing peg, custom had it that the drive was played with the ball perched upon a small mound of dirt. The box on each tee that held this sand, and from which the caddies fetched the sand for their players, is the origin of the term "tee box.") This was surely not the only example of how the woodworking skills that the young Ross acquired would prove of considerable help when his vocational interests turned, as they soon did, to golf. The fine art of club making seemed a perfect outlet for his handicraft.

By all appearances, the world in which Donald Ross grew up afforded remarkable freedom and security. The whole town of Dornoch provided a certain intimacy in which everyone knew everyone else. Plus there was a wondrous sense of adventure to be had in exploring, as Donald did in his youth, the great fields of farmlands that stretched out to the north. He became an inveterate walker from those early days. Perhaps it was also here, or from his mother's vegetable garden in

Free Church, Dornoch, where the Ross family worshipped. Just behind it were the cemetery and the golf course. (Bradley S. Klein)

the backyard, that he acquired what turned out to be another lifelong interest—this one in gardening. There was a small garden behind the house where Lily grew lettuce, turnips, beans, and gooseberries for the family table. Fresh fruit was a treat in those days. The only time of the year an orange might be enjoyed was at Christmas. A typical main meal in the evening consisted of hot or cold meat or fish, potatoes, a garden vegetable, and often a huge bowl of soup. Always, there was soup.

Beyond his penchants for hiking and gardening, Donald was also a keen observer of local farm life. At one point, he admitted to a particular fascination with plowing contests among the farm hands. In his midteens he was also a member of the town's rifle squad that won the regional Caledonia Trophy.

For all its quaintness and surface charm, Dornoch was, like any town, the product of historical and cultural forces that helped shape popular outlooks. A brief survey of them will establish a context, not only for the town in which Ross grew up but also for his character and his view of the world. It might also help explain the virtual neglect that Donald Ross has received in his hometown. Small Scottish towns have never been keen about celebrating their own, least of all someone who was rather an outsider. As much by personality as by position in society, Ross was very much the quiet observer rather than a leader or strong public presence. He was, after all, at root more of a working man than from the elite. His family were "incomers" rather than native to Dornoch. Plus he was a member of the dissenting Presbyterian Church rather than the Episcopalian congregation, or Church of Scotland, which gathered at Dornoch Cathedral. As famous as he was to become in the States, at home he remained little more than a local carpenter in overalls.

DORNOCH TOWN

Dornoch is a coastal town some 145 miles north of Glasgow center. It sits in the lower corner of Sutherland County, where the Dornoch Firth empties into the North Sea. Unlike many of the settlements scattered along the eastern shore of the Scottish Highlands between Inverness and John O'Groats, however, Dornoch is not a fishing village. Not being blessed (or cursed, as the case sometimes has seemed) with a harbor, the town's economy was never dependent on the vast fleets of small boats that headed out to sea for herring and cod. A small fishing village, Embo, was located just to the north. Dornoch's economy and workforce, however, were necessarily diverse and not bound by the seasonal fluctuations of the fishing trade. The town enjoyed relatively steady prosperity as a market center for much of the surrounding countryside. As a county seat it enjoyed a measure of well-being out of proportion to its modest size. That good fortune was reflected in the town's distinctive architecture. Sandstone quarried locally near the Evelix River proved to be substantial building material; its distinctive solid gray look gave the town's buildings an impressive visage. Instead of the ramshackle structures of a small village, one could see in Dornoch evidence of durable strength. This was especially visible in the thirteenth century cathedral that towered over the town, and in the darkly imposing old bishop's residence—Dornoch Castle—that sat at the town center.

The town was also isolated, and therefore self-contained. The nearest big city, Inverness, was 64 miles away by road. There were no bridges (as there are today) across any of the three intervening firths—Beauly, Cromarty, or Dornoch. In Donald's youth, the nearest rail link was seven miles to the north, over a man-made rock causeway called The Mounds that separated Loch Fleet from the freshwater areas to the west. From there, visitors to this Highland outpost would disembark, then reload onto a mail coach for the journey into town. Not until 1903 was a direct rail link made between The Mounds and Dornoch.

A stretch of water, the Kyle of Sutherland, even cut off Dornoch from its nearest neighbor to the south, the burgh of Tain. Though the town centers are only five miles away across the water, the sole road linking them required a trip west through Bonar Bridge—a journey measuring 28 miles each way. For years the isolation contributed to Dornoch's charm, at least for those willing to undertake the journey.

Fishwives' Race, Dornoch Games, February 29, 1904.
(Dornoch Historical Society)

Dornoch had been endowed as a bishopric in the thirteenth century and received its charter as a Royal Burgh from King Charles I in 1628. Together, these legacies created a strong English presence: the first owing to frequent exchanges of church officials from other bishoprics to the south; the second owing to the privileges enjoyed by merchants in their trade with the locals. To some extent, the town was characterized by a basic split between the more English-speaking and established Episcopalian congregation and the more Gaelic-oriented group of peasantry and laborers associated with the dissenting Presbyterian Free Church.

Complicating matters was a certain historical resentment, embodied in the image of Dunrobin Castle in the hills to the north. Here at the ancestral home of the Duke of Sutherland was a visible reminder of the Highland Clearances of the late eighteenth and early nineteenth centuries. During this period, the Duke, like many other Scottish Highlands and Islands landowners, evicted many of his tenants in order to clear the land for sheep grazing. These evictions were brutal, frequently involving violence. Donald Ross grew up surrounded by people who still seethed with their memory of the Duke's betrayal of his own people.

As a market center and royal burgh, Dornoch proper had not been the site of direct aggression. But the unrest played no small part in uprooting vast populations in the surrounding countryside and created a certain lingering cultural resentment. The Disruptions of 1843, as it was called, involved a dissenting movement of crofters and fisherfolk. The mass secession of ministers and parishes from the

Church of Scotland leading to Free Church Presbyterian ("Free Kirk") congregations was especially popular in the Highlands. Thus arose the religious body to which the Campbells of Dornoch and, in turn, the Ross family, belonged.

Both the Church of Scotland and the Free Kirk Presbyterians were founded on Calvinist doctrine. The doctrine stated that everyone was predestined by God, either for salvation or damnation. Accordingly, people read the Bible for themselves, in the vernacular language, in contrast to the priestly hierarchy of Rome and its monopoly of Latin scripture. The Calvinist tradition rejected transubstantiation and the idea of authority without merit. Christ was understood as the only head of the church, and so ritual sacrament was limited to baptism and communion. Those who were predestined—or "elected"—to be saved were obliged to demonstrate their worthiness through attention to hard work, a strict moral code, and constant Bible study. They also placed a strong emphasis upon education, and there was a strong belief that a talented and energetic young man could go far in life, even if he came from humble origins.

The Free Kirk breakaway movement in 1843 saw many Highland and coastal congregations leave the established Presbyterian Church for an even more austere version that rejected the patronage of landowners. Virtually no members of the upper class supported this middle and working class reform movement.

DORNOCH LINKS

Meanwhile, the game of golf flourished. Indeed, the sport flourished as a common domain where historical animosities, real and perceived, took a back seat while citizens engaged in the singularly pleasurable activity of chasing a ball across open linksland.

Dornoch was ideally suited for golf. Records suggest that the game was played along its beachfront at least as far back as the year 1616. As with all of the classical Scottish golf courses, Dornoch's layout emerged along the receding coastal sand at the foot of the raised marine platform, or "links." Here, on fertile sand reclaimed from the receding glacial sea cover, hybrid fescue and marram grasses rooted themselves and spread. The hearty turf proved impervious to salt air and sea winds. The best native fertilizer in the world was available in abundance in the form of animal droppings, rotting seaweed, and crushed seashells. Nor could there be a better surface landscape than the wild hummocks, hills, and swales that had been shaped by eons of winds and tides. There was no need to build anything like a sand bunker. The leeward side of a natural ridge or mound provided all the shelter an animal could hope for, and it was here, under the constant treading of cattle and wildlife, that there emerged those unturfed areas that became sand hazards.

Writing in 1630, Sir Robert Gordon, tutor to the House of Sutherland and county historian, proclaimed the virtues of the setting: "About this toun, along the sea road, ther are the fairest and lairgest links (or green feils) of any pairt of Scotland, fitt for Archery, Goffing, Ryding and all other exercise; they do surpasse the feilds of Montrose or St. Andrews."

No earth needed to be moved, no plantings to be made. Players simply stroked the ball from one spot to the next. Eventually, paths of play developed. Sand bunkers were not built; they evolved where local golfers habitually gouged out the turf or where native animals, seeking shelter from the weather, had created sandy hollows.

At some point in time, probably around the middle of the nineteenth century, the old Scottish links were lengthened and updated for play to accommodate increased traffic. The development was made necessary by the enhanced performance of the mass-manufactured gutta-percha golf ball, which in the mid-nineteenth century had replaced the old handmade "feathery" (concocted from a boiled-down hat-full of duck or goose feathers that were then stuffed into a leather pouch). Still, the basic sites remained very much as they had originally been found. A few wheelbarrows of dirt were hauled from here to there, and some flattening and rolling of surfaces was needed to achieve a rough version of putting surfaces. The game's tradition was to utilize available land—all of it, it must be noted, in the public domain—and to run the holes through natural dunes and features.

Complementing these natural conditions was the town's northerly location. At 58° north latitude, the town of Dornoch was blessed with seemingly endless daylight at midsummer so that even a working lad could put in a solid day's labor and still have plenty of time left for a round of golf. Of course, the downside of being able to play golf in midsummer from 4 a.m. to 11 p.m. is that winter light is painfully fleeting. But here, too, Dornoch's geography aided the game's development. There would be cold winds, and the occasional blanket of snow, but a deep frost was unknown, so golf could be played year-round. For many years, a highlight of the club's competition calendar was a New Year's Day match that pitted citizens from the east and west sides of town.

Dornoch Golf Club was formally incorporated in 1877, but it was not for nearly another decade that enough subscriptions could be raised to fund the actual design of a golf course. A driving force throughout the club's early years was John Sutherland. He accepted the reins as club secretary and treasurer in 1883 and stayed onboard for 58 years. When he took over at Dornoch, the club's income was all of £6 for the year. By 1901, the club was

John Sutherland, longtime secretary and treasurer of Dornoch Golf Club, putting at his home course, ca.1900 with Ross next to him. The course did not acquire its "Royal" designation until 1906. (Dornoch Historical Society)

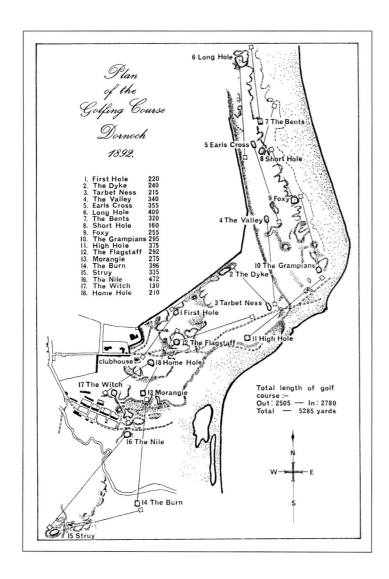

Plan
of the
Golfing Course
Dornoch
1892.

1. First Hole   220
2. The Dyke   240
3. Tarbet Ness   215
4. The Valley   340
5. Earls Cross   355
6. Long Hole   400
7. The Bents   320
8. Short Hole   160
9. Foxy   255
10. The Grampians   295
11. High Hole   375
12. The Flagstaff   292
13. Morangie   275
14. The Burn   396
15. Struy   335
16. The Nile   472
17. The Witch   130
18. Home Hole   210

Total length of golf
course :—
Out : 2505 — In : 2780
Total — 5285 yards

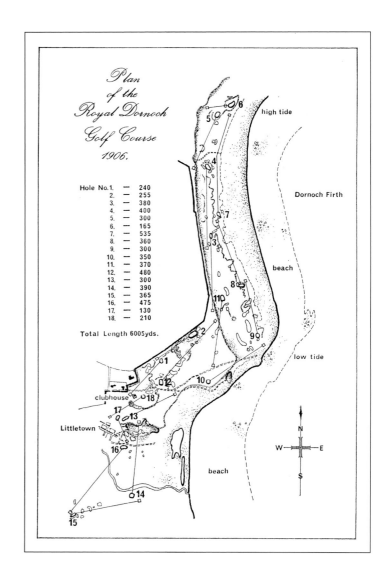

Plan
of the
Royal Dornoch
Golf Course
1906.

Hole No.1. — 240
2. — 255
3. — 380
4. — 400
5. — 300
6. — 165
7. — 535
8. — 360
9. — 300
10. — 350
11. — 370
12. — 480
13. — 300
14. — 390
15. — 365
16. — 475
17. — 130
18. — 210

Total Length 6005yds.

generating over £250 annually. Inflation alone doesn't explain the club's good fortune. Sutherland worked closely with the longtime town clerk Hector Mackay in assuring that the burgh's interests flourished with the club's. As public land, the links were subject to municipal control. If land was needed to expand the golf ground or if citizens needed to be encouraged to keep their cattle from grazing on the course, the town's modest offices could be relied upon. Sutherland, besides working closely with his good friend Mackay, also served as an agent who secured local housing for the growing number of visitors who came for the summer.

The golf club's reputation was enhanced by considerable work done on the course. Fourtime British Open champion Old Tom Morris arrived by invitation at Dornoch in 1886 to lay out nine proper holes out of the paths that had long been played. His fee was paid from donations made by members. The work was evidently successful because Morris returned in 1892, this time to fashion a full 18-hole course. The result was a 5,285-yard layout, with the first six holes heading out toward the beach of Embo Bay and running under the headland, roughly following the ground of the present first five holes of Dornoch's current Championship Course. Holes 7-12 then headed back along the primary dunes line and up the cliff, approximating the routing of what are now holes 12-16 and 18. The last six holes of the Old Tom Morris layout occupied ground south of the clubhouse that has since been taken up with the opening and closing holes of Dornoch's second course, the Struie.

There was no capacity to irrigate the turf. There was no need, either, because the weather took care of that. A greenkeeper's equipment consisted of little more than wheelbarrows, spreaders, rakes, shovels, and hand cutters.

Every account of the golf course at the time extols the raw native beauty of the setting. The links were dotted with thick green gorse—"whins"—that flowered a brilliant gold in springtime. Darker patches of purplish and brown heather also adorned the grounds, and everywhere could be seen the dense wispy stems of the native broom plants. It helped that the natural setting was so wondrous, on a sandy headland that tumbled into the sea and offered panoramic views. From "High Hole," No. 11 on the old golf course, a clear day revealed the lighthouse at Tarbat Ness nine miles to the east. It was sometimes possible to see clear across Embo Bay and the Moray Firth all the way to the coast at Lossiemouth. Looming to the west were the rolling slopes of the Highlands, and to the north, the Caithness coast and Dunrobin Castle.

The firm sandy conditions and howling winds at Dornoch produced a distinctive local swing suitable to the course's shot-making demands. It was best to

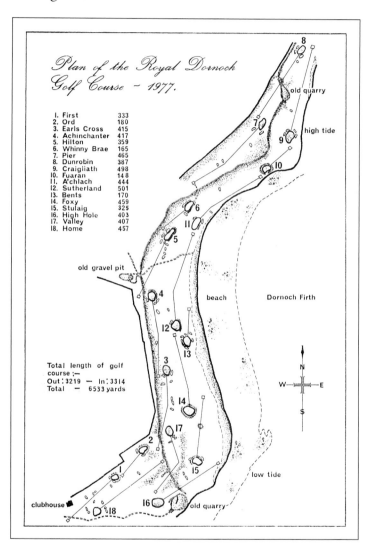

Opposite page and above: Three maps showing the evolution of Dornoch Links—1892, 1906 and 1977. (Royal Dornoch Golf Club)

Above: Dornoch's fourth hole, "The Valley," and Embo Bay. (David Joy and Ewing & Co.)

Right: Ross teeing off at the 130-yard 17th hole, "The Witch," in 1894. (David Joy and Ewing & Co.)

Opposite page, top: Dornoch's 14th hole, "Foxy," an unbunkered 445-yard par 4 with a classic plateau green. From 40-50 yards away, the firm, elevated green can be approached with almost anything—putter, bump-and-run mid-iron—except a lob wedge. (Bradley S. Klein)

Opposite page, bottom: Dornoch's 15th hole, "Stulaig," is a 319-yard par 4. This view from the beach shows the proliferation of native seaside grasses. (Bradley S. Klein)

keep the ball flighted low. The combination of hickory shafts and gutta-percha golf balls did not make it easy to play a bold aerial game anyway; yet even decades later, after the advent of the modern rubber-core ball and steel shafts, Dornoch's signature swing remained discernible. When Donald Ross learned the game, the prevailing swing called for a wide stance, with the right foot drawn back to keep the position closed at address. The ball was also kept well forward of center in order to sweep it rather than strike down upon it. The result was a low draw that made for precisely controlled shots, especially into the wind. It was swing technique to which Donald Ross would always adhere.

In those days Dornoch's meager resources were not wasted on a lavish clubhouse. Writing in the 1970s, longtime club member and part-time historian Donald Grant fondly recalled that primitive structure behind the first tee as a

"simple, old tin-roofed bungalow with its front verandah supported by that memorable row of six knotty, pinetree boles, well varnished, and only golf club lockers within." The membership was drawn from every social class of citizenry. Golf on the links being much a public affair, the game was open to all comers. There were not, as in many other prosperous Scottish towns to the south, rival golf clubs springing up to represent this or that group of artisans or tradesmen. The only limitation on access was a ban on Sunday golf.

Caddies were plentiful—drawn from the local stock of youth, both male and female. Donald Ross was among them from his childhood days. The adoption of the golf bag in Scotland around 1890 made the caddies' task considerably less clumsy than in an earlier era when they had held the clubs loosely about their bodies. In their spare time the caddies enjoyed the run of a makeshift six-hole course on some rough ground just behind the first tee. Donald first played the game with a discarded left-handed iron. He then switched to a right-handed cleek, which he gripped with his hands crossed. When the shaft of that club splintered, the youngster struck a deal with a local carpenter. If Donald would paint two barn doors, the carpenter would give the club a new ash shaft. Perhaps the youngster underestimated the work (or else clubs were more valuable than he thought). Twelve days later, after working four hours a day, the barn doors had three coats of paint and Donald had his repaired cleek. Or so he thought. After playing only two holes at the links, the club head broke off from the shaft.

At Dornoch, caddying was considered just a step above an idle person. It was encouraged only as a youthful engagement. To make it easier to manage the caddies, and also to prevent drawing labor away from local employment, the club limited caddies to under 15 years of age. It was a useful form of golfing apprenticeship and allowed youths to learn the game's etiquette. Upon reaching their caddie retirement, the young men (but not, apparently, the young women) became eligible for club membership.

The arrival in town of someone as famous as Old Tom Morris brought out many interested parties. Reportedly among them when Old Tom showed up for the first time in 1886 was young Donald Ross, already 13 years old and smitten with the game. By the time of Morris's return in 1892, Ross, a serious student of both greenkeeping and clubmaking, was under the watchful eye of club secretary John Sutherland. Donald must have taken a keen interest in Morris's handiwork. The very next year, with Sutherland's blessing, Donald Ross headed off to St. Andrews where he apprenticed to Old Tom as keeper of the greens. The former carpenter's assistant also honed his clubmaking skills in David Forgan's shop just up the street from the first tee.

Ross returned to Dornoch in November of 1893, then spent the following golf season apprenticing again, this time at Carnoustie. Then came the commission of a lifetime. In November of 1894 he was hired by John Sutherland to serve as head professional, clubmaker and greenkeeper at his hometown course of Dornoch.

Most of his work there involved clubmaking and repair. Ross worked out of a small shop (all of 15 by 12 feet in size) that was newly created for him just a few steps north of the old clubhouse, alongside the first tee. There was just enough room inside for an assistant, and for a while Donald's younger brother Alex, born in 1879, served in that capacity after his forced retirement from the caddie ranks.

In his shop, Ross had the use of two vices set on a long workbench. He fashioned wooden shafts, hammered away at metal clubheads, and tended to ailing gutta-percha golf balls by (partially) melting and remolding them. Visitors were enamored with the sights and smells of the young craftsmen at work. Scattered about Ross and his assistant were wood shavings, a glue pot, leather wraps, hand saws, and files of all sizes and shapes, plus persimmon heads and metal blades stamped with the familiar marking: "Hand forged made in Scotland." During the four months of peak golf season, May through August, Donald's attention was turned primarily to club repair and to maintaining the greens. Of course, he also had his hands full presiding over the youthful caddie ranks. It was only during the slower winter months when Ross was able to concentrate on his clubmaking. His imprint, "D.J.Ross, Dornoch" came to be valued as the imprimatur of a craftsman. His early—if brief—training as a carpenter must have helped him in his newfound trade. While social life at the club centered on the modest clubhouse, it was the work shed that drew the interest of keen golfsmen. Incidentally, the tiny building that housed the club repair operation was torn down in 1909 to make room for

Opposite page and top: Old Tom Morris at St. Andrews in 1894, a year after Ross apprenticed there.

Above: Old Course at St. Andrews, 1894.

Right: The "Road Hole" (17th) at the Old Course.

Below: David Forgan's club-making shop in 1895, St. Andrews, where Ross apprenticed two years earlier.

Above: Carnoustie GC, 1895, a year after Ross apprenticed there. (David Joy and John Carr)

Left: Ross (left) at Dornoch, late 1890s. (Dornoch Historical Society)

Dornoch's new clubhouse. The old pavilion, meanwhile, was then adapted to serve as the pro shop and stood its ground until collapsing in 1973.

Ross also acquired a thorough knowledge of greenkeeping. From his modest shop, besides running the club repair and golf operations, he also supervised his grounds staff of two. When additional labor was needed, women from the nearby fishing town of Embo were recruited for picking weeds and trimming back the whins. Mr. Sutherland also took an active interest in turf maintenance. Though not formally trained, the esteemed club secretary made a thorough study of agronomy. Moreover, he was well connected and knew whom to rely upon. In 1890, for instance, he began a fruitful collaboration with the head gardener at nearby Skibo Castle, Hugh Hamilton. It was one thing to tend lush lawns and beds of annuals and perennials, quite another to translate those skills to the links. For the job, Hamilton and Sutherland devised a particular form of top-dressing that was then applied to Dornoch's plateau greens. The results were impressive. So much so that in 1903 Hamilton left his position at Skibo to become head greenkeeper at St. Andrews.

For all of his stature as a golf professional at northern Scotland's most treasured links, Ross was still very much a local lad, living at home, walking to work, and taking his customary strolls out on the links before reporting to his shop each morning. His salary as greenkeeper was £30 per year, and though he drew no payment from the club as golf professional, his share of the pro shop concessions and teaching fees resulted in a far better wage than an average working man—close to £100 ($500) per year by 1898.

Given his close relationship to his mother (and his father's well-known tendency to squander his own pay), Ross must surely have been contributing generously to his family's support. In a small town such as Dornoch, the bonds that tied him to his working brethren were strong. For example, in February 1898, at the start of his fourth year as golf professional at Dornoch, 25-year-old Donald Ross was welcomed into the ranks of St. Gilbert Masonic Lodge No. 790 Dornoch. The proclamation notes that "bearer brother Donald James Ross was duly entered an apprenticed past fellow craft and raised to the sublime degree of master mason." Yet membership in such a lodge conveyed a social connection rather than a professional one.

When it came time for his own needs, Ross was apparently willing to delay—even when it meant putting off his own marriage for years. While shopping in a High Street grocery store in 1897, Donald Ross met Janet Kennedy Conchie. Born in March 1866 and therefore six and a half years older than Ross, she was among seven children born to James Conchie and Grace Wilson Conchie. The family lived in the Scottish lowlands town of Moniaive, just above the border town of Dumfries. Janet, barely five feet tall, was working as a nanny and had accompanied her two young charges on holiday to Dornoch. It was there, while running an errand, that she met the young golf professional. Donald was quickly smitten with the petite woman. Yet their engagement lasted seven years, during which time Ross

Dornoch Golf Club ledger sheet showing pro shop revenues for August of 1898. The names "R. W. Willson & Mrs. W." appear on the third line from the bottom.

left for the United States in March 1899 to establish himself. Janet, meanwhile, worked as a family nurse and au pair. He wrote her lovingly during his self-imposed exile but did not return until November 1904 to claim his bride. They were married the next month in Moniaive. By that time, Janet's mother was so ill that the ceremony had to be conducted at her bedside.

What was behind Ross's departure for the United States? To be sure, it was hardly unusual for a turn-of-the-century Scotsman to seek his fortune abroad. In Donald's case, the sojourn was undertaken at the suggestion of an American visitor to Dornoch.

Among the guests who registered for play on Saturday, August 23, 1898, were "R.W. Willson and Mrs. W." They were in the middle of a journey to Britain that was scheduled to last from July 20 to November 1. With 164 members that year, plus only 127 visitors, the club's income for all of 1898 amounted to £220. The fees the Willsons paid, £1-2/6, represented a not-inconsiderable share of Dornoch's intake for the entire year. This suggests that they purchased extended privileges to the course. Whatever the duration of their stay at Dornoch, there is no doubt that the visit proved of monumental significance in the life of the club's young golf professional.

Robert Wheeler Willson was professor of astronomy at Harvard University. Born in 1853 in West Roxbury, Massachusetts, he graduated from Harvard in 1873 and went on to serve his alma mater, first as a faculty member, then as a member of its administrative board, for some four decades until his death in 1922. During that fateful visit to Dornoch, he spent time with Donald Ross. The game of golf was just beginning to establish itself in the United States. It was common for golf professionals to be recruited from abroad, especially from Scotland, to take up careers in the States. Willson, who had just become a charter member of the fledgling Oakley Country Club in Watertown, Massachusetts, 7 miles west of downtown Boston, suggested that Ross consider coming over. Ross was interested in the opportunity, and it certainly didn't hurt matters that the preliminary talk of $60 per month, plus 50 cents per lesson, would guarantee Donald considerably more money than he was currently earning. It isn't clear from accounts of their conversations at Dornoch whether Willson officially offered Ross the head pro's post at Oakley—or, for that matter, if Willson was even deputized by his club to do so. But if he were interested enough to come over to the States, Willson said, Ross should call upon him at his house at 64 Brattle Street in Cambridge.

On March 13, 1899, Donald Ross drew the last of his salary from Dornoch Golf Club: £10 at £1 per week. Within a few days, he was off to the New World.

Dornoch Golf Club ledger sheet for early 1899 shows an entry for March 13 to "D.J. Ross, Greenkeeper salary to date £1 per week = 10." It was his last pay from the club before he set out for America. (Royal Dornoch Golf Club)

Chapter Two
Settler in the New World: Oakley and Essex

When Donald Ross arrived in the New York harbor in early April of 1899 he had, among his meager possessions, a small gray address book. Penciled across the cover under his name was the address "St. Gilbert Street, Dornoch." Within a few weeks of arriving in the United States, he was to scratch out that location and replace it with a new one, "Oakley G Club, Watertown, Mass."

He hadn't come with much in tow: a suitcase in one hand, his golf clubs in a canvas bag in the other. There was barely enough money to cover transportation for the steamship over from Glasgow to New York. Upon disembarking from the boat, he walked from the pier to Grand Central Station and booked himself a coach ticket on the express train to Boston. The fare was a little more than he had budgeted for, so he found himself late on a Sunday afternoon in Boston facing his first night in the New World, with all of two dollars in his pocket. Luckily, he had written down Professor Willson's phone number: Cambridge 877. Perhaps somewhere along the way it also occurred to Donald Ross that the Harvard professor's possession of a home telephone marked him as someone of considerable social status. In any case, Ross phoned him from the train station and was happy to hear that he had, if he wanted it, a place to bed for the night.

The walk from South Station across the Charles River to 64 Brattle Street was all of four miles. Not an arduous trek perhaps, but for someone who had just endured a transAtlantic crossing and a five-hour train ride it could not have been a pleasant stroll. Surely not with a suitcase and set of golf clubs in tow. But such were the tools of the trade of this newcomer, and as with many other immigrants to the New World it would prove enough for starting up a new life.

Of course, food would help. Ross had been sparing of his meager funds along the way, so by the time he arrived at Prof. Willson's doorstep that evening he was simply famished. The professor, perhaps not accustomed to the parsimonious ways of a migrant, welcomed Ross effusively, but offered nothing more to eat than a glass of milk and a tiny sandwich.

OAKLEY

The following day Ross and the professor went over to the grounds of Oakley Country Club, four miles to the west in the adjoining town. The club, chartered on February 16, 1898 as Cambridge Golf and Country Club and then renamed on November 15, sat on a huge glacial drumlin called Strawberry Hill that overlooked Cambridge and all of Boston. Even today, after a century of suburban and urban expansion, the setting alongside Belmont Street is impressive owing to the long views of the entire region. The highest point of the golf course grounds, where the clubhouse is situated, is at an elevation of 400 feet. From there, it is still possible today to peer into downtown Cambridge and to survey the Boston harbor. There were few trees on the 90-acre site when Ross arrived, so the views stretching from the northeast to the south were virtually unimpeded. Boston's outline, punctuated by the State House dome and the Custom House tower, provided a dramatic back-drop to the golf ground. One can only imagine the strange mix of country and metropolis that confronted Ross's eye as he surveyed his new haunts. As for the golf course, Ross was far from impressed. On his first visit he saw little more than muddy, snow-patched fields. This was hardly the sandy links to which he had been accustomed in Scotland. On the contrary, Oakley had been chosen as a golf course for its location, not for its soil. Its boulders, gravel, and heavy clay soil were hardly the stuff out of which to fashion classical golf holes. It was, Ross later recalled, "an impossible problem."

Facing him was an 11-hole course laid out by members Willie Campbell and Richard Dana. Campbell, a native of Musselburgh, Scotland, was no slouch of a player, having placed sixth at the inaugural U.S. Open in 1895 at Newport Country Club. The holes were located entirely on lowlands, and thus drained very poorly. Nor was routing them a simple matter, owing to the old farmhouses, stone walls, and jagged property lines that defined the cramped site.

Surely, Ross's skills at both greenkeeping and clubmaking were what rec-ommended him to his new employer. His first official day of employment was on April 18, and he quickly set to work on rebuilding the golf grounds. A basic sketch depicting what was called the "New Course" was drawn up by civil engineer and surveyor Walter C. Stevens of Melrose, Massachusetts. It announced that the new routing would be open for play by October 1, 1900. Ross set to work with a crew that numbered as many as 50 laborers. But typical of such early efforts, there were many delays that slowed down the work. Indeed, while Oakley's members con-tinued to play their golf and to attract newcomers to the game, the new course was not completed until the 1901 season.

The new 5,901-yard, Oakley course, Ross's first design/build undertaking, was a bit constricted. A number of holes had to be squeezed in with a shoehorn. Owing to the irregular tract, it followed a routing that might be considered unusual today but which was not at all uncommon in an era when the game was far from

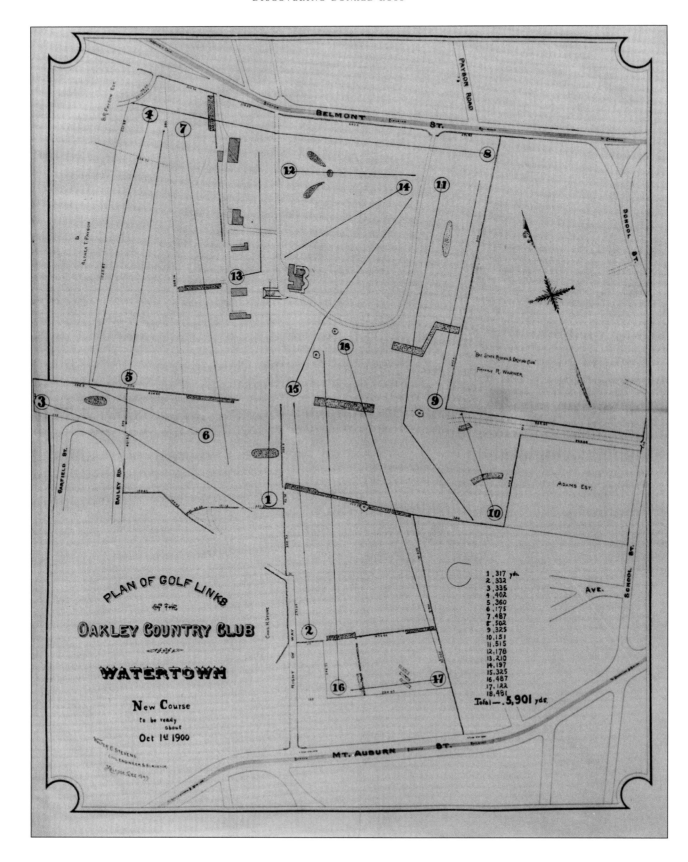

standardized. The layout included six holes in the 122 to 210 yard range, six holes that measured 317 to 360 yards, a 402-yarder, and five more that were 481 to 515 yards. While it would be tempting to call this a par 71, it must be said that par was a far less significant figure around the turn of the century, when popular parlance referred to standard "bogey score." In essence, bogey was understood as the score shot by an imaginary opponent who was playing well—hardly a scientific account, but perfectly adequate to the spirit of the game and of the era's handicap system. Bogey score at Oakley was 83, broken down into two bogey 3s, three bogey 3.5s, two 4s, three 4.5s, three 5s and five 6s.

From the second green, golfers walked along a 200-yard wooded path through adjoining property that brought them to the third tee. The fifth hole featured a deep punchbowl green set in a hollow that was six feet below the surrounding playing surface. To protect players on the green from players on the fairway who couldn't see them, club officials planted a 30-foot-high flagpole on the mound behind the green. The pole served not only as a directional device but as a semaphore that players would reset as they finished out the hole.

Such were the normal practices of golf design in Ross's early days. Blind holes were thought sporting, and it was not unusual to see holes arrayed in such a fashion as to require crossover shots. Oakley's eighth hole, a long par 5 ("bogey" 6), ran parallel to a major avenue, Belmont Street, on its left. This was also the main driveway for the entrance road to the golf club. The tee shot, partially blind over a man-made mound, crossed this driveway at a 90° angle.

Oakley's most unusual hole was the 13th, a long par 3 ('bogey' 4) of 210 yards in an era when only a professional could drive the gutta-percha ball that far. The hole was nestled into a series of natural mounds, and the green was tucked behind an elm tree, just beyond an old farmhouse, and squeezed in between squash courts on one side and greenhouses on the other.

Such was the distinctiveness of the golf course upon which Donald Ross did his first serious design and construction work.

Some changes were made in the routing of the New Course in 1909-1910, presumably by Ross. Chief among these was removal of the quirky 13th and abandonment of some holes on the back nine when property was sold off to buy new land to the west. Other changes were made to the golf course in 1915, five years after Ross last worked there. Still, a visitor today to the 6,029- yard, par-70 Oakley layout can experience 11 holes that are basically attributable—in location if not entirely in contour—to Ross's handiwork. The holes currently numbered 1-5 and 10-15 owe most of their current shape to his efforts, as do the present 6th, 8th and 17th greens. As in all such cases, much change has intervened. How much of it is "natural" and how much is due to human intervention cannot be easily answered owing to the character of such transformations. There are, for example, far more trees (and taller ones, too) than in Ross's day. Is the presence of oaks, maples, and conifers an entirely natural alteration? Or does one attribute that to natural intrusion,

Opposite page: Plan for the golf links at Oakley Country Club, Watertown, MA, Ross's first sustained involvement in the design and construction of a golf course, 1900-1901. (Oakley Country Club)

deliberate planting practices, or deliberate decisions—or "nondecisions"—by generations of green committees and superintendents?

The club's early records, for example, reveal an ongoing in-house debate about tree management. The original site included a fair number of large oaks and a few maple trees as well. The gradual construction of a new course on top, or adjacent to, the existing one, entailed continual tinkering with the holes. Moreover, in those days, golf courses were not completed in one fell swoop. They evolved over time, often painfully slowly, and it was not uncommon for fairways to be rolled and sown or bunkers to be cut months or even years after a green was in play.

Membership at a distinguished club like Oakley meant that its patrons wanted to partake of the outdoors—thus its designation as a "country club." It is not surprising, then, that members watched carefully over their countrified retreat and scrutinized every move. Small wonder that in 1903, Oakley's governing body entertained a motion "that no tree having a diameter of six inches or more within a distance of six feet from the ground be hereafter cut down without a vote to that

Oakley's heavily treed ninth hole, with Boston in the background. (Bradley S. Klein)

effect passed by the board of directors." In this case, the motion was ultimately tabled. Yet the issue would not go away, as evidenced by a resolution passed on December 23, 1903. It cannot be said of Oakley's board that it was taking a bold stance or exercising leadership when it declared, "Voted, that the tree situated at the end of the 14th hole, which was recently struck by lightning, and which is practically dead, be cut down."

The early fascination with trees did not, for better or worse, extend to conditions of course maintenance. The same held true for an entire generation of early American courses. These were layouts where the most important component of the maintenance regime was the natural "mowing" that sheep provided.

The introduction of underground watering systems, sometimes as early as the mid-1920s, often not until the 1950s, has surely facilitated lush, greener turf. But it has also added considerably to subtle changes in the soil profile whereby organic matter tends to develop and cause the site to not drain as well as it originally did. The golf ground is also subject to more water flow from surrounding plots—owing to waves of suburban building development, road construction, and parking lot paving—which has the cumulative effect of eliminating natural drainage areas and forcing water, in a manner of speaking, to seek the open ground offered by remaining parks and golf courses. In brief, the golf course gets mushier, and the texture of native (or artificially created) landforms loses its shape due to erosion and settling.

In Ross's day, with some 300-400 members at the club, the total number of rounds played at Oakley per year would have been around 8,000. There was little weekday golf in those days, certainly not until the summer. For the half of the club membership that resided in Boston, a trip to Oakley was part of a day-long outing. This made casual after-work golf all but impossible. To be sure, the club was only five minutes by foot from the B&M Railroad station and therefore accessible by electric car. But the practice of an afternoon round only arose very gradually in American golf culture and was not at all standard in the first decade of the century. Most of the play at Oakley took place during the summer. Blue laws also held down golf on Sundays—at least, that is, until Oakley member Matt Hallowell, while serving as attorney for the city of Medford, issued a legal opinion that golf was not properly defined as a game or sport but rather as an ambulatory exercise or promenade. By October of 1909, the club found it necessary to hire a starter to look after the first tee on Sundays.

Oakley's greens were of native soil. As was the practice for decades, they were pushed up and then contoured for surface drainage. The native soil was poorly percolating, and there is evidence of subterranean clay drainage pipe having been installed early on around the greens. Worms were a constant problem, and at one point the club expended as much as $100 per green to get rid of them. This was a considerable part of the club's maintenance budget, which annually averaged from $5,000 to $7,000 for the first decade of the 1900s. The sum would have included construction and improvement costs on the new, evolving golf course.

It is not clear whether, and to what extent, Ross's early responsibilities included greenkeeping. By the end of the decade, however, Oakley had its own golf course superintendent, with Ross's duties for 1909 described "as golf instructor, maker of clubs and seller of balls."

There are no records of his golf club sales, which suggests that Ross owned and operated that part of the equipment franchise independently. But by the turn of the century, golf balls were being mass-produced and the golf professional was retailing them in his shop. Small evidence that the game of golf was still struggling to establish itself, at least at Oakley, are found in notations about club revenue. In 1903, the club took in $158 in cigar sales, but only $104 for golf, racquet, and tennis balls. Not until 1905 did cigar sales take a back seat in terms of revenue.

Swing sequence of Ross, ca.1900. (Tufts Archives)

With its offerings of golf, tennis, and racquetball, Oakley was very much the prototypical country club. There were bedrooms available on-site at $1 per night, plus a charge for heating fuel. Arriving members were "requested not to leave their horses at the door in charge of house servants." There were stables provided for such purposes, though by the end of the century's first decade a vigorous debate ensued concerning the disposition of automobiles. It seems that among the perennial problems of country clubs back then was inadequate parking space.

Oakley's clubhouse, converted from an old estate building, dominated the site and its vigorous entertainments. There were lavish dinners, balls, and weddings, as well as rumors of a private liquor stock that was said to lubricate the club's leisure life.

Unlike the game in Scotland, golf in the United States was entirely a private affair, open only to the upper-middle and privileged classes. Oakley's fees reflected this bias. In 1905, for example, members paid $50 for initiation, plus $50 annually for families and $40 for individuals. This was in an era when a common laborer's monthly wage was $50 and Henry Ford was revolutionizing work life by offering rates of $5 per day. Visitors to the club were allowed to play if signed in by a member. For them the rates were 50 cents for the day, $3 per week, and $12 for a month. Caddies were paid 30 cents for 18 holes if carrying a single bag, and 45 cents for doubles. They were not paid in cash, however, but by chit.

During that era, Oakley was not alone among country clubs in allowing independent women of certain status to join as full members. Widows and unmarried women paid the standard initiation fee plus $30 for the year, and at least one woman served on Oakley's house committee in 1905. Ross himself was attentive to developing distaff golfers, and among his charges during his tenure from 1899 to 1910 were three fine women golfers: S.E. Russell, L. Underwood, and Charlotte Harding.

Perhaps an early high point of Ross's stay at Oakley was the exhibition round he played there in the fall of 1900 with Harry Vardon. This was, however, an era in which the golf professional did not enjoy an exalted status and was certainly not considered a vital part of the club's social life. Nonetheless, Ross seems to have continued in the tradition he started at Dornoch by cultivating a highly professional staff. He recruited his younger brother, Alex, to spend the 1900 season as an assistant before he moved on to become head pro at nearby Brae Burn Country Club in Newton. Among his other staffers was Eugene ("Skip") Wogan. Skip began as a caddie and shag-boy for Ross in 1907, then graduated to the pro shop before moving on to a distinguished career as a New England club professional and course designer. Fred Low, who had apprenticed under Archie Simpson at Carnoustie, served with Ross in 1908 (and was later to return as golf professional in his own right in 1937).

The club's reputation grew steadily. Oakley had joined the United States Golf Association in June of 1899 and signed on with the United States National Lawn Tennis Association in February of 1902. Links were so strong between

Harvard University and Oakley that the varsity golf team had the run of the course. In 1903, the club became a founding member of the Massachusetts Golf Association, and in 1905, Donald Ross, representing Oakley, won the inaugural Massachusetts Open—shooting 320 over four rounds with the old gutta-percha ball. In 1909, the last full year of Ross's affiliation with Oakley, the club hosted the Massachusetts Open. Donald didn't win but brother Alex did, making it the fourth of five consecutive state titles he claimed (1906-1910). This was not a modest achievement, but it paled somewhat in comparison to the U.S. Open title he won in 1907.

Donald himself enjoyed fair success as a golfer, at least until he reached the age of 40. By 1911 he had switched over to the rubber-core Haskell ball (as had everyone else in competitive golf) and won the Massachusetts Open title again, this time at The Country Club in Brookline, with a four-round total of 309. The victory meant that a Ross—Donald or Alex—won every Massachusetts Open from 1905 to 1911. Donald's record at Pinehurst's North-South Open was also impressive, although the fields there lacked the depth of his state championship. Ross took the North-South in 1903, 1905, and 1906, and was runner-up five years running, from 1907 through 1911. Nor was his play limited to local or regional events. He also played in seven U.S. Opens, with his best finish a fifth place in 1903 at Baltusrol Golf Club in New Jersey.

Soon after he had established himself at Oakley, Ross sent his mother in Dornoch considerable evidence of his newfound success. It was $2,000, a stunning sum in those days, equal to about three years' average wage. In *Golf Has Never Failed Me*, a collection of short essays that Ross wrote between the two world wars but which was not published until 1996, he says that he sent the money home the same year he left Dornoch for the United States. Perhaps this is true, though it is impossible to imagine how he could have amassed so much in only nine months while also covering his expenses. Oakley club records for the year 1899 show that he was paid $850. It's an impressive amount, but not sufficient for sending a $2,000 surplus back home. Interestingly enough, it is not until 1909 that his pay at Oakley for "golf services" exceeded $1,000 for the year. Still, he was able to generate income from other sources—including the sale of equipment. But it is difficult to understand how he could have accumulated such a surplus without the considerable boost derived from his affiliation with Pinehurst, which did not start until late 1900.

In any case, the funds, whenever they did arrive, must have been a godsend to his mother. She used it to add a second story to the family house on St. Gilbert Street. The workmanship proved first-rate. Likely, Murdo did it himself. Most of the old houses in town were expanded by stacking brick on existing stone walls, then covered over by roughcasting. An addition usually consisted of small rooms on the second floor around a narrow staircase. That was not the case at No. 3 St. Gilbert, however, where the house was built up with sandstone blocks and has reasonably sized rooms and a wide staircase in between. Lily was obviously grateful for her eldest son's generosity. In appreciation, she named the house after the club that had first employed him in the U.S. The two-story structure is still known today as "Oakley Cottage."

Ross returned to his native Scotland in November of 1904. A month later, he finally married Janet. After arriving back in America, the newlyweds set up housekeeping at 31 Bartlett Street in Waverly, Massachusetts.

Now comfortably ensconced in his post at Oakley, he was able to free himself each winter and spend November through April at the Pinehurst Resort in North Carolina. A meeting at the Medford, Massachusetts home of soda fountain magnate James W. Tufts had set Ross on his way down south each winter as overall director of golf operations. The affiliation (explained at length in the next chapter) considerably boosted his regional reputation. With a flourish of prose typical of sportswriting for the era, *Spalding's Official Golf Guide* for 1905 describes Ross as "a prince of a good fellow, one of the most popular pros in the country, and is there to stay as resident pro having taken unto himself a better half and built her a palatial home within a full drive and a mashy pitch of his favorite course."

Oakley thought enough of Janet—and of its professional—that on May 14, 1906, it voted "that the full privileges of the golf course to be extended to Mrs. Donald J. Ross and that the secretary notify her to this effect."

On October 18, 1909, their only child was born. Lillian was named after her paternal grandmother. Six weeks later, the infant accompanied her parents on their winter visit to Pinehurst. In the summer of 1910, the Ross family made its first journey back to Scotland. An announcement in a Boston paper testifies to the new-found celebrity that Ross enjoyed. His voyages were now grist for the society pages:

> *Donald Ross, professional of the Oakley Country Club and of Pinehurst, is to go abroad a week from today on the steamer Columbia, sailing from New York. He will be gone three months, returning to Boston on the steamer Canadian, which leaves Liverpool Sept. 3. While abroad he intends to play most of the leading courses and not only that, but to make a study of them, seeing for himself their best features and seeking information from members, greenkeepers and others about their construction, upkeep and other details. Being a student of the game of golf, as well as a fine exponent of how it should be played, Ross takes the keenest interest in all of these questions. He will spend a month in Dornoch and Mrs. Ross will have a long visit, with the chubby Ross baby, with her mother and other members of her family.*

In between a month each at Dornoch and Moniaive with family, Donald found plenty of time for golf. Not every stop was for purposes of study, however. During the 1910 visit, he also returned to St. Andrews and the Old Course to play in the British Open. The former apprentice greenkeeper and club maker finished in a very respectable tie for eighth, his total of 309 only 10 strokes behind winner James Braid.

1910
St Andrews
Winner J Braid

J Braid, Walton Heath	**76**	**73**	**74**	**76 299**
Alex Herd, Huddersfield	78	74	75	76 303
G Duncan, Hanger Hill	73	77	71	83 304
L. Ayton, Bishop's Stratford	78	76	75	77 306
J Robson, West Surrey	75	80	77	76 308
W Smith, Mexico	77	71	80	80
E Ray, Ganton	76	77	74	81
P Kinnell, Purley Downs	79	74	77	79 309
DJ Ross, Oakley, USA	78	79	75	77
TG Renouf, Manchester	77	76	75	81
TP Gaudin, Worplesdon	78	74	76	81
PJ Gaudin, Fulwell	80	79	74	78 311
Tom Ball, Bramshot	81	77	75	78
JH Taylor, Mid Surrey	76	80	78	78 312
M Moran, Dollymount	77	75	79	81
WL Ritche, Walton Heath	78	74	82	79 313
F MacKenzie, St Andrews	78	80	75	80
H Vardon, South Herts	77	81	75	80
J Hepburn, Home Park	78	82	76	78 314
Tom Williamson, Notts	78	80	78	78
Mr John Ball, R Liverpool	79	75	78	82
A Massy, La Boulie France	78	77	81	79 315
J Rowe, Ashdown Forest	81	74	80	80
Capt CK Hutchinson, Honourable Company	82	74	78	82 316
W Binne, Burntiland	80	76	77	83
C Roberts, Woolton	81	73	79	83
WG Reid, Banstead Downs	78	83	77	78
J Sherlock, Slough	77	81	80	79 317
E Foord, Burnham & Berrow	80	77	79	81
H Riseborough, Halifax	75	81	80	81
W Auchterlonie, St Andrews	79	76	79	83
G Whiting, Criccieth	80	81	80	77 318
WJ Leaver, Worsley	79	81	77	81
G Daniels, Cardross	77	81	78	82
WM Watt, Dirlton	74	82	78	84
F Collins, Llandudno	77	82	76	84 319
W Toogood, Ilkley	80	81	74	85 320
R Jones, Wimbledon Park	81	80	80	80 321
JD Edgar, Northumberland	80	81	80	80
Peter McEwan, Southport	80	79	80	82
P Rainford, Llangammarch	81	79	78	83
Willie Park, Musselburgh	81	78	78	84
WI Jeffries, Hallowes	79	76	81	85
CH Mayo, Burhill	80	79	82	81 322

Ross finished tied for eighth at the 1910 British Open on the Old Course at St. Andrews, Scotland. (David Joy)

Lillian Ross at the centennial celebration of Oakley Country Club in May of 1998, when this painting of her father was unveiled. (Oakley Country Club)

ESSEX

Perhaps it was the financial burden of having to support a child. Or it simply could have been that 11 years at Oakley had begun to wear thin and it was time, as the saying goes, to change the scenery. Whatever the motive, Ross made a big decision during the 1910 golf season. He left Oakley, the club that had recruited him from Scotland, and signed on as head professional at the Essex County Club, 30 miles to the northeast.

According to the definitive *History of the Essex County Club* by George C. Caner, Jr., which I follow closely here, Essex had been founded in 1893 as a summer retreat for wealthy Bostonians. Many of its founding members hailed from The Country Club, a *(the)* prestigious blue-blood club in town that had been one of five founding members—along with Newport, Shinnecock Hills, Chicago Golf Club, and St. Andrew's in New York—of the United States Golf Association in December of 1894. That same year, 1894, Essex and The Country Club even shared the services of Willie Campbell as golf professional—the same man who would lay out Oakley's first golf course. Oakley had not been far behind The Country Club, but its grounds were cramped and the club lacked the sporting repertoire of its counterpart in Brookline. The Country Club had a racetrack on-site, ice-skating on its own ponds, an expansive golf course, tennis courts, shooting and archery grounds, and indoor curling. Plus it had a more prominent membership, many of whom summered on the North Shore.

Among them was George F. Willett, who had come over to Oakley to take golf lessons from Donald Ross. Like many members of The Country Club, Willett spent his summers golfing and sporting 30 miles up the coast at Manchester-by-Sea. The sport season there ran from Memorial Day to Labor Day, considerably shorter than at Oakley. Families would arrive on the Boston & Maine Railroad line. For some families, regularly scheduled service would not suffice to meet their standards, so they pooled resources and secured a private train, the "Flying Dude," to shuttle them back and forth. A number of families made the trek aboard their yachts, which they would sail into Manchester's modest but well-protected harbor. Their destination was the Essex County Club, one mile inland, on 160 acres of rolling land sitting atop the town's aquifer. It was a fascinating tract, what with its heavily wooded areas interspersed with exposed ledge and vast deposits of sandy soil. Standing in the center of the property was the three-story Shinnecock-style, split-shingle-roofed clubhouse. Loyalties at the club were equally divided between golf and lawn tennis. The golf professional at Essex, Joe Lloyd, had won the 1897 U.S. Open. Perhaps more impressive was Essex member Margaret Curtis, who in 1908 claimed women's national titles in both golf and tennis. With less success—though with considerably greater girth—were the efforts of President William Howard Taft, who made frequent use of his honorary membership at Essex during his presidency (1909-1913). When Taft was visiting, his summer White House was set up in nearby Beverly.

Ross first saw the site in 1908, when Willett brought him there to oversee a complete redesign of the club's existing golf course. Essex had gone through several earlier nine-hole incarnations, the last one in 1896 having been laid out by the assistant professional, Tom Buntal. The 2,580-yard layout hosted the 1897 Women's National Amateur Championship, but by 1900 it proved inadequate to the growing demands of the members. Adjoining parcels were acquired, leading to an 18-hole, 5,722-yard golf course that traversed hilly, rocky terrain. This, too, would prove insufficient, not only because of the severe demands of the routing but also because the advent of the rubber-core Haskell ball had rendered many of its features obsolete. Empirical evidence of the longer ball can be found in the results of women's long-drive contests held a decade apart, on opposite sides of the great ball divide. Caner reports that in 1897 at Essex, club member Madeline Badman claimed the long-drive contest when she hit her "guttie" 137 yards, 6 inches. In 1907, another Essex member won the Women's Amateur long-drive competition. Margaret Curtis (who had driven her "guttie" only 101 yards in 1897) used the rubber-core ball to full advantage by driving it a winning 220 yards.

For all the talk about classic golf design being an art form carried out in the field, Ross set to his task with the help of a meticulous civil engineer named Charles Fritz. Working entirely by free hand, Fritz prepared a stunningly detailed topographic map. The map, drawn to an unusual scale of 1 inch = 80 feet, illustrates one-foot vertical contours throughout the 156 acre property. Ross's design superimposed the holes upon this map and then a construction crew, including in-house labor, spent some seven years implementing the plan on a piecemeal basis. To be sure, there was much ad hoc work done in the field. But there is no doubt that Ross's work included careful coordination of the routing and position of fairways with the contours as indicated on the map. The location of greens was indicated on the map by small squares, and then the construction crew, with Ross supervising some of the work, shaped the surface contours accordingly.

Construction was bone-crushing work for the Irish laborers who rebuilt Essex. Large rocks had to be blasted, harnessed by derricks or pulley-and-rope, then dragged away on horse-drawn sleds. Blind holes were less a strategic choice than a matter of adopting to the topography and to the limits of human engineering.

The process at Essex, and Ross's design work in general, formed the basis of Henry Leach's dispatch in the (London) *Evening News* of December 6, 1912, under the wonderful headline: "Nature Altered to Suit Golf: The Man who is Blowing up America." Citing a letter he received from an American golf enthusiast, Leach wrote:

> *Towards noon, when we might be somewhere about the thirteenth or fourteenth hole, a great roar and crashing sound came from the other side of the course in the locality of the fifth hole, and, looking towards it, there was to be seen a rising cloud of smoke with*

Topographic map of Essex County Club, October 1909. (Phil Wogan)

masses of earth and splintered rock being hurled high into the air. . . .

The truth is that golf at Essex, as elsewhere in the country, is undergoing a great and wonderful transformation, regardless of cost, regardless of the magnitude and seeming impossibilities of the task, regardless of everything, but caused by the insatiable desire of the American golfer to have courses as good as they can be.

To satisfy this desire he is everywhere pulling Nature to pieces and reconstructing her, doing his work most deftly and skillfully, and with a fine eye for pleasing effect. At the finish you might think that save for the putting greens and bunkers, it was all the simple work of nature herself in her gentler moods, smooth swards for rocks, and chaste glades where forests were. . . .

In the Eastern States many of the courses have had to be carved out of virgin forests. Tens of thousands of tons of rocks have had to be blasted, and hundreds of acres of swamps have had to be drained before the fairways could be laid and sown with grass. Such work is having to be done now for the extensions and improvements, and it is being most wonderfully done. . . .

Here at Essex . . . Mr. Ross is superintending all the operations, of course. He thinks out his construction schemes in a Napoleonic way, and he is going about America blowing hundreds of acres of it up in the air, and planting smooth courses on the leveled remains.

By necessity as much as by choice, Ross relied upon the native contours to give Essex its creaky, otherworldly character. Perhaps another routing might have avoided blind shots, though given the native contours of the property it is impossible to imagine how. In any case, Ross's layout simply incorporated them. Consistent with prevailing thinking of the day, such holes were never considered to be "unfair." Indeed, for a devout, God-fearing Presbyterian, there was no such thing as unfair. There was life, and golf was no small part of it, so that a golfer simply accepted the fate that luck—or grace—bestowed.

The work dragged on, with Ross and the club completing a few holes each year. Though Ross himself left as golf professional after the 1913 season, he made several return visits before finally completing the redesign in 1917.

To an unusual degree, the 6,308-yard Ross course is intact today. There have been a few changes, including the relocation of one green—the present 17th—and the shifting of several tees. And the sequence of holes has also been substantially altered—to create two loops of returning nines, rather than a truncated links-style ordering that Ross planned. But the shape of the holes is for all intents and purposes identical, thereby making Essex County one of the few pure Ross gems to be found in all of golf.

Ross kept only two holes from the 18 he found when he got there—the present 13th and 16th. The rest is his cre-

Soil sifter used by Ross at Essex County Club, 1910-1917. (Bradley S. Klein)

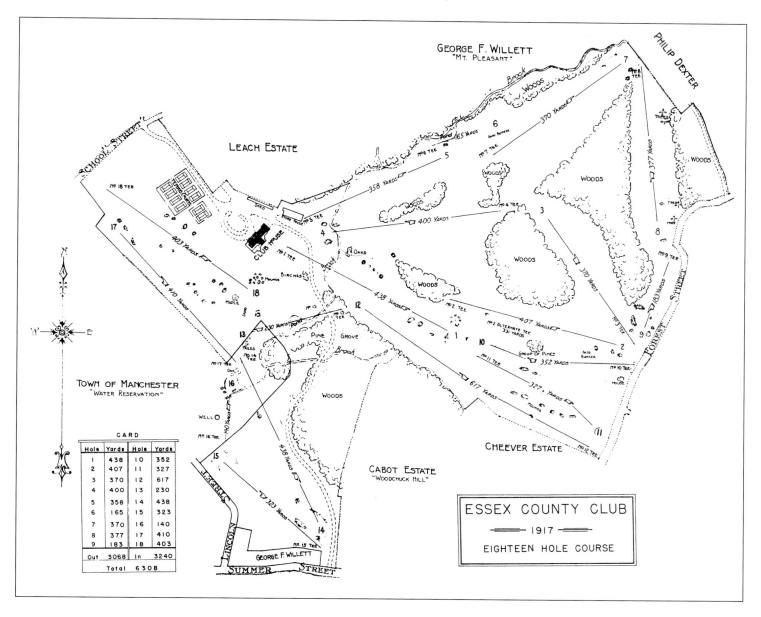

GEORGE F. WILLETT "MT. PLEASANT"

PHILIP DEXTER

LEACH ESTATE

TOWN OF MANCHESTER "WATER RESERVATION"

CABOT ESTATE "WOODCHUCK HILL"

GEORGE F. WILLETT

CARD			
Hole	Yards	Hole	Yards
1	438	10	352
2	407	11	327
3	370	12	617
4	400	13	230
5	358	14	438
6	165	15	323
7	370	16	140
8	377	17	410
9	183	18	403
Out	3068	In	3240
		Total	6308

CHEEVER ESTATE

ESSEX COUNTY CLUB
— 1917 —
EIGHTEEN HOLE COURSE

ation. The current third hole was shockingly long for its day—a 617-yard par 5—and it is followed by an equally gargantuan par 3 of 230 yards to a vaulted green set above a massive open wound of sand. To this day, the 11th hole remains the most artfully sculpted of all the holes at Essex. The green, some 165 yards away, is pinched on the fade side by a lovely set of bunkers and is perched sharply above another bunker that clings ominously to a slope on the left.

The current 14th hole, measuring 183 yards, originally called for a blind cut shot over the corner of a wooded rock slope. In subsequent years, the tee has been nudged to the left to enhance visibility—perhaps at the price of distinctiveness. When it comes to demanding shot-making at Essex, nothing surpasses the uphill par-4 17th hole (originally Ross's third). The hole climbs some 50 feet and the original

Essex County Club after completion of Ross's work, 1917. (George C. Caner Jr. and Essex County Club)

Above: Essex County Club, first hole, with green protected by mounds. (Phil Wogan)

Opposite page, top left: Essex County Club's fourth hole (Ross's 13th), a 230-yard par 3 with a distinct back-to-front cant. (Phil Wogan)

Opposite page, top right: The ninth hole at Essex CC (Ross's 18th), with mounds in front of the relatively level putting surface. (Phil Wogan)

Opposite page, middle: Essex County Club, 18th hole (Ross's 4th hole), ca.1920. (George C. Caner Jr. and Essex County Club)

Opposite page, bottom: Essex County Club's 18th hole today. The trees have grown and the hollow short and right of the fairway has been filled in. (Bradley S. Klein)

green was tucked on a sheer outcrop, just behind a large mound. The second shot was completely blind. In 1927 a new green, somewhat less punitive, was created short and left of the original.

Here was a demanding golf course, with trees overhanging a number of holes, sharp rocks intruding upon the line of play, and vast open pits of sand, such as the one that protected the 16th green. Of course in those days the ground was kept firm, owing to the absence of any automatic irrigation and to the presence of native seaside grasses that grew tall, hard, and brown. Many of the bunkers were deep, and there was no such thing as being able to keep grass on the greenside wall of a bunker. Finally, the green contours were all perfectly formfitted to the native terrain. Surrounding mounds and immovable hillocks would be blended into the surface contours of the putting greens so that each green seemed a natural extension of its surrounds. To be sure, there were also some obviously contoured putting platforms, such as that devilish 11th green. But there were no distinct decks or terraces. Because all of the greens were built with surface drainage in mind, their slopes and contours created "movement" in many directions without ever looking forced. The fairways and greens also utilized diagonal slopes, thus accentuating the line of play so that properly played shots would be rewarded while slightly off-line

shots would be punished. Far more than Oakley, Essex displayed Ross's strategic genius as well as his understanding of maintenance considerations in fashioning ground contours. All of the shapes most conducive to the ground game also facilitated surface drainage. This marriage of sound golf and sound greenkeeping was to characterize Ross's subsequent design mark.

During the three years he spent at Essex, Donald, Janet, and young Lillian took up residence in a modest two-story wood-framed cape house on Forest Street, behind what is the present 14th green/15th tee. For Donald, it was a pleasant 1,000-yard stroll westward each morning to work. The job required his full attention during the busy summer season—Memorial Day to Labor Day. He maintained a tiny club-making shop on the grounds.

While at Essex, Ross also developed a modest club-making factory in the town center of Manchester at 33 Beach Street. It was on the second floor of the old Manchester Electric building, diagonally across from the train station. There, Ross and his crew manufactured clubs that were sold under the Ross name through John

Ross and his family lived in this house behind the 14th green at Essex County Club while he was golf professional there, 1911-1913. (Bradley S. Klein)

Wannamaker's sporting goods firm in Philadelphia. Most of the clubs sold at Pinehurst under Ross' name were also built right there in the shop. Among the assistants in the club-making enterprise was Skip Wogan, whom Ross had brought along from Oakley. Wogan spent six winters at Pinehurst (1910-1916) with his mentor, and after Ross left he stayed on at Essex County Club for 44 years as professional and grounds superintendent.

Essex was a glorious sports club, prominent throughout the world for its fine tennis and golf. Walter J. Travis, the game's Grand Old Man, dropped by frequently to play. During Ross' brief reign, Essex was a busy venue, hosting the 1910 Massachusetts Open (won by Alex Ross), the 1911 state Amateur, and the 1912 U.S. Women's Amateur (member Margaret Curtis's third national title).

Donald J. Ross, five foot eight inches tall, of medium build, blue eyes, and thin brown hair, was making his mark upon the golf world. The former greenkeeper in overalls from Dornoch had come a very long way. He was well established as a head professional, first at Oakley, then at Essex, with a winter affiliation at Pinehurst that helped further spread his name.

Indeed, it was soon after he began work at Oakley that he would take up the directorship of a resort operation at the other end of the Eastern seaboard. This new position would make him something of a national and, in time, international golf celebrity. At the time of his arrival in the America in 1899, there had been a fledgling golf project underway in the barren sand hills of North Carolina. Only 18 months after alighting nearly penniless from that boat in New York harbor, the soft-spoken, devout Scotsman was becoming a figure of some significance in the golf trade.

Skip Wogan, an assistant to Ross at Oakley. He came to Essex with his mentor and became the longtime professional and superintendent. (George C. Caner Jr.)

Chapter Three
Pinehurst

Putter Boy, the caricature originally drawn by Frank Presbry for an advertising campaign (ca.1906-1911), became closely associated with the Pinehurst Resort. (Tufts Archives)

The emergence of Donald J. Ross as the country's most respected and prolific golf architect corresponded with the rise to prominence of the Pinehurst Resort. In truth, each largely depended upon the other for its respective status as a focal point of the American golf scene. Ross served as golf professional, club manager, and resident course designer at Pinehurst and saw it through its early days. Had it not been for his expertise and strength of vision, there is every likelihood that the resort would have followed the fate of dozens of other big-name interwar golf resorts that did not survive the difficulties of the Depression era.

FOUNDING

Pinehurst Resort owes its unlikely beginnings to the inspiration of James Walker Tufts (1835-1902). An apprentice apothecary in the Boston area, he parlayed an early interest in soda fountains into a major business success. By 1862 he was building and marketing the Arctic Soda Water Apparatus, a curious device combining a marble façade, a cooling chamber, pipes beneath, and adorned with silver-plated fixtures. It quickly became a staple appliance in small food service shops throughout the United States. By 1891, the country's four major soda fountain suppliers merged, with Tufts becoming president of the newly formed conglomerate, American Soda Fountain Company.

With money and time on his hands, Tufts, a philanthropist at heart, decided to turn his life to doing good works. So he started up a health resort, in part because his own fragile condition had required frequent rest cures, much of it spent on ocean voyages or on frequent trips to Florida. The clientele he had in mind were those with serious health problems, including consumption—what today is known as tuberculosis. The conventional wisdom of his day was that the disease was communicable in its advanced forms, but that in its earlier stages it could not be passed on via casual contact. A good friend of his, the Unitarian minister Dr. Edward Everett Hale, was a prominent Bostonian, author of the *Man Without a Country*, and president of the Lend a Hand Society.

It was through Hale and a number of intermediaries that Tufts learned about the curative powers of the North Carolina sand hills. The area, situated at some 600 feet above sea level, had three main advantages: a warm, dry climate without stagnant waters that might breed diseases; the salutary effects of what locals called "pine ozone" (the balsamic scent of pine trees, said to be beneficial to weak lungs); and plenty of inexpensive land. Plus there was a nearby rail line, assuring easy access to the Northeast. The day after his son Leonard's wedding on June 14, 1895, James W. Tufts headed south to inspect the proposed site. Upon his return a week later, he startled his family with the announcement that he had launched plans for a health resort. Soon he would have full control over a 5,980-acre parcel. The purchase price was $7,400, or $1.24 per acre. Most people who knew him thought his plan a folly.

His land was in Moore County. It straddled the area between the coastal plain of eastern North Carolina and the upslope of the Piedmont Plateau leading westward to the Blue Ridge Mountains. Scotch Presbyterian immigrants had settled the area in the late seventeenth and early eighteenth centuries and had been able to squeeze a living out of the land by farming corn, tobacco, and peaches, as well as the vast native stores of longleaf pines. The land used to be heavily timbered but had been clear-cut to provide wood for the resin, tar, and turpentine industries that had provisioned the world's naval fleets during the nineteenth century. As a result of the intensive cutting operations, the land was all but denuded. The northern half of Moore County had exposed clay that was arable. But in this, the lower section of the county, the clay had been submerged under a layer of white quartz sand that reached a thickness of some 300 feet. This was the region that locals called the "Pine Barrens." It was an appropriate description of the land. In an unpublished manuscript covering the early days of Pinehurst, James W. Tufts' grandson, Richard S. Tufts, later reported that the soil was so devoid of nutrients "that when a man was buried it was necessary to plant commercial fertilizer under him in order to afford some prospect of his being able to rise on the Day of Judgment."

In pursuit of his health resort, James W. Tufts toyed with several names, including "Sunalia" and "Pinalia," before settling on Pinehurst. Local residents meanwhile began referring to it as "Tuftstown." For all his hesitation before settling on a name, Tufts had no trouble calling in qualified people to help him. In the case of the town's layout, that meant the country's leading landscape architecture

James Walker Tufts (1835-1902), founder of Pinehurst, NC and its resort, here playing croquet. (Tufts Archives)

firm: Olmsted, Olmsted & Eliot of Brookline, Massachusetts. The company had been founded two decades earlier by famed landscape architect Frederick Law Olmsted. He had designed New York City's Central Park in the 1850s (with Calvert Vaux) and had gone on to fashion urban green spaces, including parks, college campuses, and estate grounds throughout the Midwest and Northeast. Olmsted was a proponent of using outdoor landforms for moral improvement. Beautification and aesthetics were part of his attempt to counteract the effects of urbanization and industrialization. Olmsted was a genius at creating natural-looking landforms, building a sense of protected space, and sculpting areas where strangers could converge without feeling overwhelmed. Among the firm's many projects was the mammoth Biltmore Estate in Asheville, North Carolina. Olmsted had just completed its arboretum. By the time Tufts called at the OO&E office in Brookline on June 20, 1895, however, the elder Olmsted was in the early stages of dementia and had ceded most design work to his younger associates. Tufts nonetheless met with the elder Olmsted, and the firm agreed to undertake the land plan for $300.

Frederick Law Olmsted did not make a site visit to Pinehurst. OO&E first worked on the basis of engineering plans drawn by local surveyor Frank Deaton. On July 6, 1895, the firm produced an ink-on-linen map drawn to a standard scale of one inch equaling 100 feet. Owing to irregularities in the original land survey, however, a redraft was needed, this one requiring a site visit. On September 24, a representative of OO&E made his inspection of the would-be town. Warren H. Manning, landscape architect in charge, had been with the firm since 1888 and would stay a total of eight years. In fact, it was his work on Pinehurst that would help him launch a successful independent career as a landscape architect. More importantly, his meticulous attention to the refinement of Pinehurst's land plan over the next four decades would endow the town with the unmistakable feel of a transplanted New England village. During much of that time, he worked with locally-based horticulturalist Otto Katzenstein in devising a meticulous planting program. Within the first decade of Pinehurst's existence, nearly a quarter of a million seedlings were introduced, transforming the area into a blooming wilderness of longleaf and loblolly pines, magnolia, holly, and pin oaks. Flowering trees and bushes also abounded, and dogwoods, azaleas, crepe myrtle, and fruit trees ensured a constantly changing tableaux of color.

Manning's drawing, delivered on November 27, 1895, portrayed a modified radial layout, with the town square at the center, surrounded by successive curvilinear arrangements of commercial buildings, private homes, and open fields for sports. The focal point of the plan was the 100 acres of town center, with a 20-acre oval arrayed in the center, a modest inn (The Holly Inn) at its north end, and the market district concentrated along the western edge. A huge hotel, to be called The Carolina, was envisioned to the west of the inner circle.

Tufts did not waste any time, hiring a work crew of 175 laborers for a furious few months of construction. By the end of that first year, the 43-room

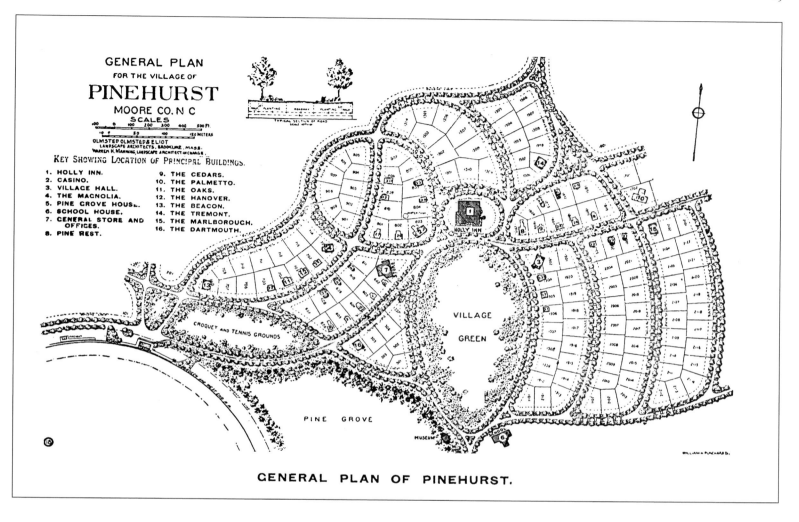

GENERAL PLAN OF PINEHURST.

Holly Inn was completed. It presided over the new town and sat at the head of the village oval. Several boarding houses were also completed that first year, including the Magnolia and the Palmetto. A two-story department store was erected at the town center. Groceries, soft goods, and household items were available on the first floor; upstairs were living quarters for seasonal staff working at the resort. Over a dozen private residences destined for rental were also built in town by the end of 1895. There was nothing haphazard about the construction work. A measure of the engineering can be found in the first-rate sanitation system; an underground sewer system linked all of the new buildings.

As for social life, the focal point of Pinehurst activity was the Town Hall. Its stage and 300-seat auditorium, plus meeting rooms on the side, were well used for everything from theater productions to religious services. Also crucial in the life cycle of the town was the misnamed "Casino," which in fact served as the dining commons for those on modest budgets. Today, the Casino is home to a real estate firm.

1895 plan of the village of Pinehurst by the Cambridge, MA firm of Olmsted, Olmsted & Eliot, as drawn by Warren H. Manning. (Tufts Archives)

Above: Pinehurst Village under construction, 1895, including a cottage (left) and the Casino (right). (Tufts Archives)

Right: Holly Inn, 1896, a 43-room hotel at the town center. (Tufts Archives)

Ever the optimist, James Tufts circulated an open letter to Boston area physicians on November 22, 1895:

Enclosed find pamphlet relating to the new town of Pinehurst, to which I desire to call your attention.

My choice of a location in North Carolina was made after careful consideration, and the evidence appears conclusive that the place selected is eminently adapted to benefit invalids.

In order to secure the best possible results, I desire to obtain the co-operation of medical men who may send such tenants and guests as will help me to accomplish the purposes for which the town is established.

While it will be evident that my work is of semi-philanthropic character, yet I desire it to appear in the light of a business enterprise, also that it may attract only a refined and intelligent class of people. Physicians are best qualified to judge not only of the physical condition, but also of the financial status of those who require a change of climate, and I trust that the benefits which may result from my undertaking will be furthered by their personal

The Casino in 1896 was actually the town's dining commons. (Tufts Archives)

interest in making it successful.

I desire to avoid admission of those in advanced stages of consumption, and think the profession will confirm my impression that such patients are usually better off at home.

Tufts had also worked out favorable travel rates via steamship liners linking Boston, Providence, New York, Baltimore, and Washington to Portsmouth, Virginia. The boat ride from Boston required 38 hours. Portsmouth was a nine-hour train ride down to Southern Pines, a town seven miles below Pinehurst. Direct rail linkage was also available from the Northeast on the Seaboard Air Line, with the overnight ride from New York to Southern Pines a trip of 662 miles that took 16 hours.

Plans called for the fresh "ozone" of Pinehurst to attract visitors for a seasonal winter cure. The official season ran from November 1 to April 30, with the resort and town all but locked up during the sweltering summer months. Cottages were made available for weekly, monthly, or seasonal rental, and included room for servants to set up housecleaning and cooking. Those of more moderate means could stay in a boarding house or the Holly Inn. Tufts' plan was to attract a well-mannered, intelligent clientele, a group that, in the past, might not have been able to afford—much less even to contemplate—such extensive comforts. As one early promotion announced:

The aim is to establish a health resort adapted to the needs of people of refined taste, who require the beneficial effects of a winter in the South, but cannot afford to pay the usual high price for accommodations. Those whose health is impaired must have such comforts and conveniences as they have at home. They must have plenty of good, nourishing food, well cooked; with pleasant surroundings, interests, amusements, occupations and agreeable companions . . . Pinehurst is not a sanatarium for invalids, but a health resort for the weary and overworked.

No land is sold, for the reason that the ideal results at which the owner aims can be assured in no other way.

Care is taken in the selection of an orderly and refined class of guests. No liquors are sold.

This was to be a unique company town, one run on a not-for-profit basis. Yet for all the philanthropic aspirations behind the project, the bills would have to be paid and a balance sheet maintained. This would require room-and-board rates that would greatly limit the potential field of resort guests. A proposed list of "expenses for two people spending 13 weeks at Pinehurst" called for a minimum of $165, covering a suite of two rooms at the Palmetto Inn with all meals at the Casino, to a maximum of $466 for the rent of a large house, all meals at the Casino, a maid's salary and fees for laundry, linen, ice box, and firewood. In 1895, $165 was half a year's average wage. Plus only a small sector of the populace could imagine taking 13 weeks off from work. For all the claims about drawing a middle-class populace, Pinehurst was always to be a decidedly upscale undertaking.

Leisure activities were to include horseback riding (for which Tufts provided a huge stable), bridle paths, and racetracks south of the town. Playing fields to the west, just below the proposed site of the Carolina Hotel, were also intended for the game of "roque," a close cousin of croquet, and an activity that had become popular in the Southeast. Space was also allocated for several tennis courts, and extensive target grounds would also provide a place for trapshooting and archery.

The presence of clients with pulmonary illness had a discouraging effect, however, upon the healthy patrons, some of whom decided to avoid Pinehurst for fear of contracting illness. Medical opinion on tuberculosis was also changing rapidly. Within two years of the town's opening, it became clear that the consumptives posed a risk—if not to the burgeoning town's people, then at least to its economic success. On June 1, 1897, Tufts published a "Note to Consumptives," advising them to avoid his new town. "The interest of the many whose health requires that they spend the winter at Pinehurst must not be sacrificed for the few who carry in themselves the danger of contagion." Advertisements promoting the resort subsequently carried a proviso to the effect that "consumptives not received at Pinehurst." A generation later, during Prohibition, the public would (mistakenly) look upon such a warning as a declaration of public abstemiousness—a dry town—rather than as talk about restricting access by tuberculars. But back in 1897, the change in policy toward those with tuberculosis was already indicative of a subtle shift in the resort town's market position. Pinehurst began emphasizing its leisure amenities rather than its medically curative properties.

Establishing Golf

In the fall of 1897, Pinehurst's third season, Tufts noticed some resort guests playing a strange game over open ground. Quite spontaneously and without forethought by the town founder, guests had found their way onto a dairy field south of town where they were using thin, wooden-shafted clubs for hitting little balls toward flagpoles. James W. made a note that there might be a future for the game in his town of Pinehurst.

By February of 1898, a nine-hole course had been fashioned on the dairy field, just to the east of the train line to Southern Pines. Dr. Leroy Culver, a patron of Pinehurst, was responsible for overseeing its design and construction. Over 100 sheep kept the 60 acres of ryegrass closely cropped. The course, measuring 2,391 yards, was routed in a counterclockwise loop on the ground currently occupied by the beginning and concluding holes of Courses 1 and 4. The original nine ranged from 116 yards to a sporting 496 yards, and standard "bogey" score was considered to be 35. In an era of hickory shafts and gutta-percha golf balls, such distances were not, of course, considered skimpy. In December of 1898, the *Pinehurst Outlook* (begun October 15, 1897) reported that Mr. Charles A. Adams had established a record score for the nine holes in shooting 58. Sadly for him, the record did not last long. The very next week, Mr. George W. Butts turned in a 53.

James W. Tufts had a new amenity to tout, and he lost little time or enthusiasm doing so. Not himself a golfer, he nonetheless recognized the game's physical and moral benefits and saw them as consistent with the overall ambiance of a resort property devoted to complete recovery:

Hazards on the Pinehurst golf course, ca.1900, included 3- to 4-foot high mounds running perpendicular to the line of play across the rough-hewn fairway. (Tufts Archives)

> *Everybody can play it—some excellently, others indifferently, still others very badly, but all enjoyably. It keeps the player out in the open air; it keeps him moving over wide spaces; it exercises all his muscles and all his wits. It is an ideal sport for the maintenance of bodily and mental health.*
>
> *Golf experts and all those who cherish the hope of becoming such, will find excellent opportunity to indulge in the game at Pinehurst.*
>
> *Mr. John Dunn Tucker, a well-known professional golfer, will have charge of the links and his services as a teacher will be available.*

So popular did the course become that a clubhouse was erected to service the many guests now drawn to the game. When it opened on January 13, 1899, the wooden, two-story structure offered a generous veranda on all four sides, plus an outdoor stairs leading to a second-floor lookout, from which guests could view most of the golf grounds. Inside on the first floor were separate changing rooms for men and women. A fireplace warmed those who lounged about in the reception room, and the golf professional had use of a small workshop on one side of the building. The building, while crammed to the gills, served the golfers until 1922, when it was torn down and replaced on the very same site by the building that, in expanded form, continues to serve Pinehurst's golfers today.

In January of 1900, a year after the clubhouse opened, Pinehurst patrons found themselves with the run of a newly expanded golf course, now 18 holes, measuring 5,203 yards. The original nine holes had been folded into a more considerable layout that stretched out farther to the south. This is the course that, with much modification, exists today as Pinehurst No. 1. Although far from the original coastal linksland of Scotland in terms of native landform, the golf course at Pinehurst could, with some justification, be referred to as a "links." The soil was firm sand, and native wiregrass provided a functional replacement for the tawny fescue and dunes grasses so common on classical Scottish tracts.

Unlike its Scottish counterparts, Pinehurst's new layout did not sport native bent or fescue greens. Nor, for that matter, would the coarser forms of rye that were prevalent along the eastern seaboard take hold in the nutrient-starved sandy soil. The hot summer months proved too taxing for such grasses so Pinehurst instead offered common Bermuda fairways and roughs and sand putting surfaces, 60 feet in diameter. After each group played out, a caddie would use a mat that was left nearby to drag the oiled, sand putting surface clear for the group behind. It was also common in winter for golfers to drive from matted platform tees, so firm could the nearly turfless teeing areas become in cold weather. Bermudagrass tees would not be established at Pinehurst until 1928; bermudagrass greens would not arrive until seven years later. Maintenance in the first decade of the new century was limited to the occasional swath cut by a horse-drawn gang mower. There was no irrigation water available for tees or fairways. Grassed areas were firm, sandy, and patchy, and what grass cover there was went dormant all winter—not that anybody back then worried about a golf course not being green.

These were the conditions that British golfing great Harry Vardon confronted during a four-day exhibition at Pinehurst in March of 1900. This was the first of what would become a widely-used strategy for drawing national attention to the Pinehurst Resort. By then, Vardon had won three (of what would turn out to be a career total of six) British Open championships. His presence attracted much

Pinehurst's first clubhouse, 1899-1922, provided intimate, well-used quarters for golfers, caddies, and casual viewers. (Tufts Archives)

interest and helped establish Pinehurst's credibility as a golf property. His best score was a 71—not bad, considering the fact that the weather was so cold that photographs of his play show spectators buttoned up in winter coats, scarves, and gloves. Equally impressive was that with wooden-shafted clubs and the old guttie, he drove the ball as far as 240 yards. Nor did he seem to have trouble adjusting to the sand greens. Vardon managed just over 32 putts per round—1.8 strokes per green.

Around the turn of the century, Pinehurst Resort hired most of its management from summer season northern properties. Indeed, the affiliations of prominent staff members with established northern properties were publicized in order to boost Pinehurst's reputation. It spoke highly of the up-and-coming resort that its winter management had been recruited from such prestigious facilities as the Hotel Weirs in New Hampshire, Hyde Manor in Vermont, and the Red Lion Inn in Western Massachusetts. This same policy would guide James W. Tufts in his selection of a golf professional. The two-year association with John Dunn Tucker (from Stockbridge Golf Club in Western Massachusetts) having lasted until the end of the 1899-1900 season, it was now time to secure a golf professional whose stature could serve as rallying point for a game whose popularity was just beginning to develop.

Because his summer home was in Medford, Massachusetts, just north of Boston, Tufts had several acquaintances who played golf at Oakley Country Club. On the basis of their recommendations, Tufts invited Ross to his house in 1900 and offered him work at the resort, to commence that winter season. The initial arrangement involved serving as golf professional, including running the club, managing the caddie corps, stocking the professional's shop, and club making. The growth of Pinehurst was so rapid, and Donald's skills so considerable, that other duties quickly accrued. Ross would soon find himself involved in golf course design and construction and maintenance, duties he variously shared with Pinehurst's superintendent of courses, Frank Maples. But first, he had to get there.

Ross headed down by train in early December, arriving on the fifth. The next day he went out to the golf course and shot an 80. He took up quarters with other bachelor staff in the rooms above the downtown department store, diagonally across the street from the Holly Inn, in what is now office space above a haberdashery. In those days, an electric trolley line linked the town center to the golf course clubhouse a mile to the south. Like other employees and many of the resort guests, Ross took his meals downtown at the Casino.

Pinehurst's newly expanded 18-hole layout didn't suffice to meet the demand for golf. The game was proving so popular among guests that in the summer of 1901, Pinehurst Resort created an additional nine-hole loop that was laid out on ground north and east of the clubhouse. This modest loop of holes was very likely the first design work at Pinehurst undertaken by its new golf professional, Donald Ross. On this and all other work done at the time, there are no surviving plans or drawings of the design, in all likelihood because there never were any to begin with. During the summer when the new layout was under construction, Ross was up north at Oakley, not at Pinehurst. This short layout, all of 1,275 yards in length, occupied the area presently taken up by the 1st, 17th and 18th holes of what would soon become the famed No. 2 Course.

The experiment of bringing Ross down for the season evidently proved a success. For the next winter season, Donald arrived with his brother Alex in tow. As the November 15, 1901 issue of the *Pinehurst Outlook* announced in an article boasting of its 27-holes of golf, "The links this season will be in charge of Messers Donald and Alex Ross, the well known Scotch professional players from the Oakley Club, whose services are available as teacher."

Early photos of the No. 2 Course show a rough and tumble series of images, with waist-high chocolate drop mounds called "Pyramids" providing a most unusual course hazard. They comprised uprooted rocks or tree stumps covered with topsoil. These oversized anthills seem to have quickly given way to scraped mounds and scruffy wiregrass, with the turfgrass splotchy and scarred. Only a few trees were scattered about and they barely provided any separation for landing areas. Perhaps color images would have shown something more recognizable to a modern eye, but such is the aura of black and white imagery that it immediately relegates landscapes and people to the appearance of a distant and long bygone era.

With the debut of the No. 2 Course in late 1907, Pinehurst vaulted to the front ranks of the country's golf resorts by virtue of being able to offer a second full 18-hole layout. The course—in every way a product of Ross's direct responsibility—also cast him as a designer to be reckoned with because of the success he

The Pyramids of Pinehurst, from the Pinehurst Outlook, *January 31, 1902. These "chocolate drop" hazards were either on course No. 1 or the new nine of Course No. 2. (Tufts Archives)*

The Pinehurst Outlook.

PINEHURST, MOORE COUNTY, NORTH CAROLINA

VOL. XIII, No. 6.   SATURDAY MORNING, JANUARY 8, 1910.   FIVE CENTS

THE NEW AUCTION BRIDGE

Mr. Becker Predicts That it Will Practically Supplant Present Game.

First Played in London in 1905 it is Now Invading America and Catching on Everywhere.

"AUCTION bridge will, I believe, practically supplant the bridge we are now familiar with," says Mr. C. L. Becker, one of the country's best known whist experts, who is at The Inn for the winter after his annual custom, "mainly because of its fascinating variety and novelty. First played at the Bath Club in London in 1905 and having its origin in India, it has rapidly increased in popularity until it is now invading America. Boston was first to take it up, something like a year ago, and it is most played almost exclusively in the Tennis and Racquet and Somerset clubs and claiming attention among devotees of the game everywhere.

"The game is clearly set forth in an article by Arthur Loring Bruce in a recent issue of *Ainslee's* which I feel sure will prove of interest to THE OUTLOOK's readers in view of the great popularity of the game here."

OBJECTIONS TO BRIDGE.

Before at all proceeding to analyze the game of auction bridge, or "auction," as it is certain some day to be called, we must pause for a moment and consider why bridge has been displaced at all. What was its weakest point? Where was it vulnerable? How could it be improved upon? The answer is obvious. The dealer and his partner had too great an advantage over the non-dealers. Not only could they declare, irrevocably, the trump that would help them the most, but they could, in the event of their both having poor hands, practically shut out their adversaries by declaring a spade.

All this sort of thing was naturally very annoying to the nondealer. The dealer's advantage was altogether too great. At all other well-regulated card games, the dealer is not so favored. In poker, the dealer has virtually no advantage at all. In old-fashioned whist, the turned card is only an infinitesimal help to him. In piquet, the nondealer has considerbly the best of the bargain, but in bridge everything and everybody must stand aside and favor the dealer wherever they may.

There is another vital objection to bridge. It is often a trifle too certain. The element of the unknown is hardly strong enough, particularly in trump declarations. A hand with seven clubs to the three top honors is almost certain to score two or more by cards in clubs. A heart make with six fairly high hearts and an outside ace and king is, even before a card has been led, almost sure to score the odd or better.

Still a third disadvantage in bridge is the fact that the dealer's partner is prevented from declaring a better suit just because the dealer has already declared. How often, at bridge, have we seen the dealer declare diamonds, when dummy could have infinitely improved the dealer's situation by declaring hearts. It seems to me that a third of all original heart makes could have been improved by dummy's jumping in after the declaration and declaring no trumps. In such cases, the dealer very often has the hearts and dummy has strength in the other suits; but, just because the dealer has murmured the word "hearts"—hearts it must remain, for all time, and to the brink of eternity.

The last objection to bridge is that one cannot bid for the trump. The bidding element, which is so fascinating in such card games as skat, solo whist, five hundred, nap, auction pinochle, etc., etc., is entirely missing in bridge.

Now, all four of these weaknesses in

the game of bridge have been rectified in auction. Auction is nothing more than bridge, without these radical defects.

First of all, let me say that the game is except for a few details, exactly like bridge. I shall assume, in the following pages, that my readers are all familiar with the game of bridge—its laws, etiquette, leads, declarations, honor values, and system of scoring. The rules of bridge must be applied by my readers to *all* auction situations not specifically dealt with in this article. I shall allude to the player who plays the hand as the *player*, his partner as the *dummy*, the leader as the *leader*—he is always to the left of the player—and to

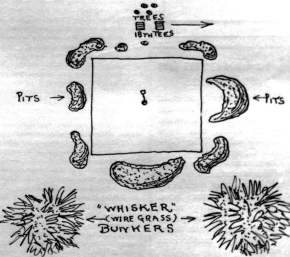

THE DEADLY SEVENTEENTH.

The superb trapping of the new eighteen-hole golf course has attracted international attention. This detail plan of the seventeenth is typical of the general scheme.

the leader's partner as *third hand*.

HOW AUCTION BRIDGE DIFFERS.

Auction differs from bridge chiefly in the matter of bidding for the right to play the hand. The dealer, having looked at his cards, must make a declaration—he is the only one of the four players who *must* declare—that is to say, he must agree, or contract, to make at least the odd trick in no trumps, or in any one of the four suits. He cannot at once pass the make to dummy, as in bridge. The leader may now pass the dealer's bid, i. e.: declare himself as being satisfied, or he may double, i. e.: make the dealer's bid of, let us say, one spade trick, worth four below the line,

(Continued on Page 2)

FOUR-BALL FOURSOME TIE

Dr. M. W. Marr and W. R. Tuckerman Win Gold Medals in Play-off.

Excellent Handicapping Bunches Field in Second Tournament of Tin Whistle Schedule.

MEDAL play handicap four ball foursomes, combined scores, rounded out an interesting afternoon in the second of the Tin Whistles tournament program, excellent handicapping bunching the field closely and a tie resulting for first between Dr. Myron W. Marr of Dorchester, and W. R. Tuckerman of Washington, whose allowance was twenty-three, and S. H. Martel, Jr., of Montreal, and C. B. Hudson of New Suffolk (19,) at one hundred and sixty-six each; Dr. Marr and Mr. Tuckerman winning the gold medals offered in the play-off.

Next in order came W. C. Johnson of New York and D. G. Mackay of Passaic, N. J., (24,) one hundred seventy-one, H. W. Ormsbee of Fitchburg and J. D. C. Rumsey, New York, (22,) one hundred seventy-two; J. R. Towle of Chicago, and J. S. Linsley of Lenox, Mass, (20,) one hundred seventy-four; J. B. Moore of New York, and J. E. Kellogg of Fitchburg, (37) one hundred seventy-five; R. J. Clapp of Glastonbury, Ct., and T. J. Check of New York, (21,) one hundred seventy-six; E. A. Guthrie, St. Augustine, and C. H. Matthiessen of New York, (18,) one hundred and seventy-six; H. W. Priest of New Castle, N.H., and P. L. Lightbourn of Bermuda, (24) one hundred seventy-seven; A. L. Creamer, North Conway, N. H., and Spencer Waters, of New York, (20,) one hundred and eighty; Leland Ingersoll of Cleveland, Ohio, and F. E. Beldon of Hartford, (21,) one hundred and eighty-one.

THE SCORES BY ROUNDS:

Dr. M. W. Marr	29	61	52	113	29	93	}	166
W. R. Tuckerman	3	39	37	76	3	73		
S. H. Martel, Jr.	10	46	48	94	10	84	}	166
C. B. Hudson	9	47	44	91	9	82		
W. C. Johnson	6	46	43	89	6	83	}	171
D. G. Mackay	18	57	49	106	18	88		
H. W. Ormsbee	11	51	46	97	11	86	}	172
J. D. C. Rumsey	11	46	51	97	11	86		
J. R. Towle	12	51	50	101	12	89	}	174
J. S. Linsley	8	47	46	93	8	85		
J. B. Moore	25	52	56	109	25	84	}	175
J. E. Kellogg	12	53	50	103	12	91		
R. J. Clapp	10	52	47	99	10	89	}	176
T. J. Check	11	47	51	98	11	87		

(Concluded on Page 11)

enjoyed before so distinguished a group of visitors, both amateur and professional. Interestingly, Walter J. Travis, in a 1920 article in *American Golfer*, claimed credit for turning a dull, lifeless No. 2 Course into a well-bunkered strategic gem. Back in 1906, he said, he convinced Leonard Tufts, James Tufts's son, and then Ross, of the merits of his plan. This was no small boast, though there's no evidence to confirm his account—and none, as well, to refute it.

The 1907 incarnation of No. 2 played to 6,023 yards, with a standard bogey score of 80, though a modern golfer might recognize its par as being closer to 72. Thirteen of its holes remain today basically as Ross conceived them in terms of character, contour and hazards: the first, second, and the entire string of the eighth through 18th. The present third, sixth, and seventh were fashioned in 1923, and the fourth and fifth were added in 1935. Along the way, a number of holes were taken out of rotation, to be plowed under or incorporated into the No. 4 Course. Remnants of No. 2's old, abandoned holes and their ground features can still be spotted today by a visitor to the No. 7 Course, who will be able to discern overgrown areas and hollows along land adjacent to the No. 2 layout.

Opposite page: The new par-3 17th hole at Pinehurst No. 2, as seen in the January 8, 1910 issue of the Pinehurst Outlook, *is basically the same hole that exists today, although the "pits" have been enlarged and joined into more shapely bunkers. (Tufts Archives)*

Above: Greenside at Pinehurst No. 2, ca.1920. Note that the bunker has been hand-raked but not tended to during the days play. The sand putting surface only has a small amount of contour. (Tufts Archives)

Even with its sand greens, Pinehurst aroused trepidation. But it was not because of water—the only such hazards were inconsequential farm ponds incorporated in front of the old 10th and 16th tees. The primary task at No. 2 was keeping the ball in play and fashioning recovery shots off all the surrounding pine straw. Plus the bunkers. This was, after all, an era prior to the advent of the sand wedge with its heavy flange (1930s). Until then, landing in a bunker really was a penalty and it required both skill and luck for a proper escape.

No. 2 was quickly regarded as a stern challenge. Visitors loved its demands, and it proved adaptable to the demands of tournament golf, both amateur and professional. But it also was a bit much for regular guests, whose basic reason for an extended stay at Pinehurst was to enjoy themselves rather than suffer. This was particularly the case for female and elderly golfers, and for golfing neophytes.

As is often the case with golf, the addition of a course to meet burgeoning demand does not so much sate the market as encourage more play. This was exactly the situation with No. 2. Within three years, guests at Pinehurst had the run of a No. 3 Course, this one located to the west, across the railroad line and state highway. The course was situated on more rolling terrain than Pinehurst's other courses and incorporated two returning nine-hole loops, each routed clockwise.

The course was an instant success, and a particular favorite of women. Less punitive than No. 2, it offered small, elevated greens and bunkering that was pulled back so there were few intruding sand hazards that had to be negotiated. The fairways canted and doglegged, but were wide, and the only irrevocable hazard were two ponds on par 3s, though in each case the holes were routed so that the ponds sat much closer to the tees than to the putting surfaces. Nor were there any out-of-bounds to contend with, another reason why golfers loved it. Sadly, the course has

Opposite page: A crew member prepares to smooth a sand green. Until the conversion to bermudagrass greens in 1935, laborers at Pinehurst waited at the putting surface for groups to finish, then smoothed the green by dragging a damp, heavy rug across it. (Tufts Archives)

Above: Ross tees off at Pinehurst, ca.1930. Notice the sparse turfgrass cover and the sand teeing grounds. (Tufts Archives)

been picked apart over the years, with nearly half of its original holes eventually incorporated into the No. 5 Course in 1961. The current routing of No. 3 includes nine holes that date back to Ross' handiwork: the third through 8th, and the 14th, 15th and 18th. These are, by far, the most compelling holes on the No. 3 Course in terms of subtle contours, the use of native slopes, and fore bunkers that appear much closer to the target than they really are.

By this time, Pinehurst golf was flourishing, the regulars having formed their own Pinehurst Country Club in 1903, housed in the ramshackle, two-story wooden clubhouse. A men's association was formed in February of 1904 and took the name of the Tin Whistles. Local lore attributes the group's name to the signal used for summoning the surreptitious attendant at the whiskey supply stashed by the 12th tee of the No. 1 Course—this in a dry town where such activities would

Opposite page: Ross putting at Pinehurst, ca.1930. This small, circular sand green has a natural pitch that matches the native ground. (Tufts Archives)

Below: The Tin Whistles in 1904. The men's golf club at Pinehurst included Ross, sitting just left of center at the top of the stairs. (Tufts Archives]

have been strictly, if inadequately, prohibited. As is often the case, however, the truth is less exciting than the legend. The name actually derives from a group of scallywags portrayed in a just-published political novel by Alfred Henry Lewis, *The Boss and How to Rule New York*. Club members, having received a signed copy of the book from the author, obviously identified with the inner workings of the Tammany Hall machine.

The women of Pinehurst golf who formed their own association in February of 1909 showed, by contrast, that they were made of nobler elements. Their name, Silver Foils, was intended to evoke the more precious material with which they would "foil" their male counterparts. Like their male alter egos, the Silver Foils maintained a steady stream of competitions. In the interest of inclusiveness and encouraging sociability, most of these events included net handicap events with multiple flights, with some competing female members receiving as many as 50 shots per round.

The Silver Foils, 1914. Among the members of the women's golf club at Pinehurst was Mrs. D.J. Ross (far left). Daughter Lillian stands just to the right. (Tufts Archives)

A trolley line already linked the town to Southern Pines. Starting with the 1905-1906 season, direct service was made available (two trains a day in each direction) that linked Washington, D.C. to Pinehurst. Local trolley service continued for two years, tying together the hotels, golf club, administration offices, and market district along one convenient line.

After founder James Walker Tufts died in 1902, his son Leonard, born in 1870, was entrusted with the club presidency alongside his duties as head of the Pinehurst Corporation. Ross, meanwhile, assumed the post of club secretary while continuing his work as "directing superintendent" of the golf courses.

Not even a third course proved adequate to growing demands. In one day alone in early 1914, the resort accommodated 510 golfers. What with expansion of the Carolina Hotel to fully 350 rooms by this time, plus additional lodging at the Pine Crest Inn, Holly Inn, and elsewhere in town, the resort's three golf courses were supporting a vast assemblage. And it was not only hotel guests, but townspeople and Pinehurst employees.

By 1916, employees had access to their own 9-hole golf layout, a forerunner to the No. 4 Course on ground to the south of the clubhouse and between No. 1 and No. 2. Hotel trade slowed somewhat during World War I, but soon thereafter the town was again abuzz with visitors, and employees were forced to concede their course to resort guests and Country Club members during the November to late-March season.

By 1923, Pinehurst sported four impressive 18-hole golf courses, each the handiwork of Donald Ross and his head of construction and maintenance, Frank Maples. The courses ranged in length from 5,919 yards at No. 1 to 6,479 at No. 2, with the No. 3 and No. 4 tracts falling in the middle in terms of length. There were only two teeing grounds per hole in those days, and owing to the dry, sandy soil conditions even these could not be grassed until techniques were developed in 1928. Grass greens came later, with the first three greens of No. 2 not able to cultivate bermudagrass until 1934, and the rest of that course getting grass greens the following year. Grass greens on the No. 1 and No. 3 courses arrived during each of the subsequent two seasons. Despite its national reputation as a golf resort mecca, in fact Pinehurst was the last of the country's major golf hotels to develop workable grass greens.

PROMOTING GOLF

Pinehurst rarely overlooked a chance to trumpet its golf. The resort managed to produce a succession of events that would yield promotion, if not news, running the gamut from professional and amateur competitions to staged exhibitions with noted figures. It is doubtful, however, if the resort ever hosted a more distinctive event than the moonlight golf contest of Tuesday, January 9, 1906, when Donald Ross went up against New York-based golf professional Jack Jolly at 8 p.m. under a full moon. The idea for the competition had been born on the veranda of the Holly Inn the previous Saturday night. The precise amount of liquor needed to inspire the scheme is not mentioned in any account, but within 20 minutes of the idea being announced, a committee of distinguished gentlemen had raised $40 in purse money and gotten the two principals to agree. To ensure the proper weather conditions, the ritual sacrifice of a chicken, a quail, and a sparrow hawk was made, apparently to good effect. At the appointed hour, Ross played his tee shot down the first fairway of the No. 1 Course. Two forecaddies lined each side of the holes to facilitate location of the golf balls by sight (and sound). Amazingly, the match took

Page 82: Overhead map of Pinehurst's four courses in 1923. The ninth and tenth holes on No. 2 were replaced by new fourth and fifth holes in 1935 to give the layout its present routing. (Tufts Archives)

Page 83: Aerial photo of Pinehurst during the 1950s. The new fourth and fifth holes on the No. 2 Course can be seen at top left. (Tufts Archives)

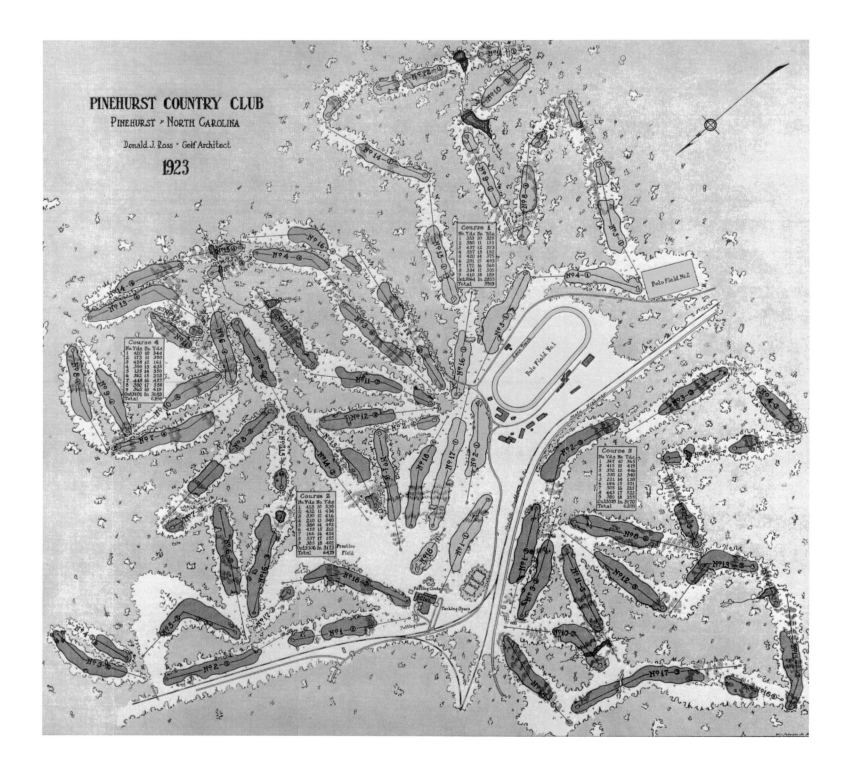

The 18th green on No. 2 in 1929. The sand green is in
the location of the present grassed putting surface.
(Tufts Archives)

all of two hours, with Ross winning 5 & 4 and completing his full round in 93 to Jolly's 88. It seems that the players had little trouble hitting long shots, but that putting in the strange light upon sand greens proved particularly troublesome. Not surprisingly, the *Pinehurst Outlook* got a front-page, three-column story out of the event: "...unquestionably the most novel and unique match in history." The event proved two important things: winters in Pinehurst were fine for golf; and the folks who ran the resort could milk anything for news.

In its early days as a fledgling resort, Pinehurst's founders and promoters acknowledged the resort's debt to the home of golf, and along the way oversold itself by referring to the property as "America's St. Andrews." A measure of the success it enjoyed and of the vast distance, both as a development and in terms of reputation, that James Tufts's visionary property had come can be gleaned by the fact that some 15 years later, other resorts were claiming the Pinehurst mantle for them-

selves. The opening issue of the *Pinehurst Outlook* for the 1913-1914 season con-
tained a by-now-familiar self-congratulatory piece titled "Reputation on the Move"
in which the anonymous author pointed out that a California golfing resort styles
itself "The Pinehurst of the Pacific." Also noted is the parallel claim made by mil-
lionaire hotelier Henry S. Hale on behalf of his Balsams Resort in far northern New
Hampshire. So intent was he on making his White Mountain retreat "The Summer
Resort Pinehurst" that he would go on to hire Ross to design the hotel's featured
18-hole Panorama Golf Course. Pinehurst, less than a generation after its founding,
had become a brand name. The same envied market position would be enjoyed by
its visionary golf professional and "directing superintendent," Donald J. Ross.

Luminaries also visited the golf courses, their periodic exhibitions chronicled by the newspaper and their laudatory comments then disseminated as further
evidence of Pinehurst's deserved reputation as a haven—*the* haven—for golf. When

*Night golf at Pinehurst, January 9, 1906. Jack Jolly
(center left) versus Donald Ross (center right). The
twosome completed their round in two hours under a
full moon. Ross won 5 & 4. (Tufts Archives)*

reigning U.S. Open champion Francis Ouimet came down in January of 1914 for a week-long visit, his exploits during two rounds a day were dutifully chronicled on the front page of the local weekly, as were his admiring words about the courses. Interestingly, Donald Ross outplayed Ouimet in a featured match, shooting 72 to the amateur's 77. It seems that Ouimet had trouble adjusting to sand greens, though this would not stop him, as the paper proudly announced, from returning later in the season for the North and South Amateur. Ouimet, as it turned out, had to make a considerable swing adjustment to get his approaches to stay close to the pin. The conventional strategy to approach shots was to run the ball in on a low trajectory, but the springy and, at times, resilient bermudagrass defied predictability regarding how the ball would react upon impact. The ideal seems to have been an approach that landed just short of the sand green surfaces (the ability to hit high, lofted irons at exact distances was still decades off in terms of swing technique, yardage markers, and reliability of equipment). Considerable adjustment was thereby needed, not only in strategy and swing plane but also in putting technique. When he returned for the 1914 North and South Amateur, Ouimet spent 10 days practicing just to get accustomed.

Pinehurst's North and South Amateur, an annual match play event since 1901, has enjoyed a solid national reputation second only in longevity to the USGA's national amateur championship. The tournament, originally held on the No. 1 Course, moved to No. 2 in 1909, where it has continued to be played each year in the late spring. A distaff counterpart was added in 1903 and has continued to be a part of Pinehurst's annual golf calendar.

One prominent player who proved reluctant to make the adjustment to Pinehurst's sand greens was U.S. Amateur and U.S. Open champion Robert Tyre ("Bobby") Jones. He made his first playing visit to Pinehurst in 1917 at the age of 15, before he had ever won a national title, but he never competed in the North and South Amateur. Nor did he return until 1932—after he had retired from competitive golf—and it was for a social visit rather than a tournament. While he had pleasant enough things to say about golf at Pinehurst, it was not an appreciation that transplanted itself into regular visits.

Toward the end of the century's first decade, it became customary for the North and South Amateur champion to be taken aloft in Lincoln Beachey's biplane for a flyover of Pinehurst. Mr. Beachey was an accomplished pilot, and no golfers seem to have been lost in the process. But when Chick Evans claimed the title in 1911, he came back from his obligatory airplane ride acknowledging second thoughts about whether his victory had been worthwhile. Interestingly enough, he never won the title again despite frequent appearances in the North and South Amateur.

Equally important to Pinehurst's promotional efforts was its annual professional event, the North and South Open. The tournament began as a three-person exhibition in 1902, with Alex Ross's 75 taking a small purse that was raised on the spot from spectators. The tournament proper was not officially started until the next year. Donald Ross claimed his first North and South Open title with a score of 147 that was good enough to top a field of about a dozen players. The tournament was still small enough in 1904 that only 14 competed, 12 of whom turned in scorecards. Alex took the $100 first prize with a 152, with Donald tying for fourth and earning $10 for his two-round score of 154. The next year Donald put on an impressive display, managing a winning total of 146 that included nothing but 3s, 4s, and 5s for his 36 holes. He won the North and South Open again in 1906 and tied for first with his brother in 1907, the last year the event was held on the No. 1 Course.

Thereafter, Ross's finishes show a modest but discernible slide. However, he was competing against stronger fields each year. Such was the growing reputation of Pinehurst Resort that it was able to recruit professionals of national

Alex Ross, 1907 U.S. Open champion. (Tufts Archives)

standing to spend a few days there. It certainly helped that they enjoyed free run of the golf grounds and hotel, and had their transportation paid as well. Indeed by 1915, Ross, as manager of the country club, was urging Leonard Tufts to offer some of the big name pros several hundred dollars each in appearance money just to play in the event. While celebrity amateurs like Ouimet, Evans, and Travis couldn't be compensated for their time, professionals could be. Ross himself spent considerable time negotiating with prominent golf professionals to come down for a few days of exhibition matches with the intent of generating favorable national press. He used his contacts freely in an attempt to land prominent players, whether for a specific exhibition or to play in one of Pinehurst's many competitions.

The practice seems to have worked, because Pinehurst attracted increasingly impressive fields. When the 42-year old Ross finished sixth in the 1915 North and South Open, the five people ahead of him included three recent U.S. Open champions: Alex Ross had the 1907 U.S. Open to his credit; he was followed by Francis Ouimet (1913) and Walter Hagen (1914), with Jim Barnes and Jock Hutchinson just ahead of Donald.

That was the last year of Donald's contending in the North and South Open. By 1917, the tournament was played at 72 holes, and by 1920 the tournament—in spite of the sand greens on the No. 2 Course—had achieved the status of a regular stop on the pro golf circuit rather than a mere exhibition event. Ross, however, was by now no longer convinced that paying these fellows for their time actually benefited the resort. He grumbled that the pros habitually overestimated their marquee value and had priced themselves out of the market. "I do not think the professionals have as much advertising value as they think they have," he wrote. Ross preferred to roll the money into the purses and use them to attract stronger fields. Befiting PGA policy, the North and South Open—though never an official tour event—abandoned the habit of paying competitors' expenses and put that money into the overall prize fund. By the late 1920s, the North and South was a fixture on the fledgling PGA circuit and it continued to draw press attention and prestige to the resort until the last rendition of the tournament, held in 1950.

Even when his competitive days were behind him, Ross maintained an active presence at the events and regularly spent time with the game's big names. Pinehurst's legendary practice area, "Maniac Hill," was unusual even on the tour circuit for its suitability to long afternoons of beating buckets of balls. Ross regularly worked the practice tee, visiting with the fellows and chatting them up over swing technique, equipment

Opposite page: Leonard Tufts (left) and Ross (right) in 1926. (Tufts Archives)

Below: Ross presents Horton Smith with the award for winning the 1937 North and South Open. Paul Runyan looks on. (Tufts Archives)

developments, and the game's inside news.

As Ross turned his attention away from outright competition, the Country Club began to occupy a considerable share of his attention. Indeed, the amazing thing about professional life in the period spanning the First World War was that he was able to establish himself nationally as a notable course architect while managing to preside over day-to-day operations at one of the country's most active golf resorts. Nor was his affiliation the kind of billboard variety so common among today's professionals, who routinely accept six-figure fees annually for token representation involving little more than wearing a shirt and hat bearing the hotel's logo and playing three Monday rounds with important clients.

By the mid-1920s Pinehurst was hosting 10,000 resort guests annually and accommodating nearly 100,000 rounds on its four courses—a number that surely ranked it among the busiest golf facilities in the country. Rates for the 1926-27 season were $3 for the day, $12 for the week, $35 for a month and $75 for the season. A revealing measure of social practices of the era regarding average length of stay was that for the 1926-27 season, the Country Club recorded 64% of its revenue from weekly green fees.

Ross managed to negotiate his way through an extraordinary amount of minutiae as part of his everyday responsibilities at the Country Club. Although he had a telephone in his office and another one at home, the preferred method of handling all matters was via detailed correspondence. Ross's "In" and "Out" boxes were subjected to a steady stream of concerns, all of which had to be acknowledged, then documented, via letter. In some cases, the chain of correspondence would reach absurd proportions, with letters acknowledging receipt of a check generating a response to confirm receipt of the acknowledgment.

Ross at Pinehurst No. 4, ca.1927. (Tufts Archives)

Chief among Ross's responsibilities was handling requests—actually denying requests—for discounted golf, whether at reduced rates or with the fee waived altogether. It is no exaggeration to say that in the face of such recurring pleas, even when accompanied by a merciful appeal to penury or bad luck, Ross, the parsimonious Scotsman, dug his heals in and resisted. In short, he was reluctant to offer discounts for golf at Pinehurst. Much of his correspondence back and forth to management in the 1920s concerned attempts by various local parties—state workers, local officials, suppliers of goods to the hotel—to play golf on the cheap. Ross was consistent in rebuffing such efforts. "If we do this," he wrote on August 13, 1924, "there is no saying where it will end."

The same could be said for his spirited claims that club facilities should be offered to all under the same conditions. Even when his own affiliated group might have benefited, Ross held to a principle of charging equally across the board. In 1929, for example, Ross and Richard Tufts exchanged letters over whether the local Kiwanis Club and American Legion were to continue being charged $150 for fundraising dances in the clubhouse while the Moore County Shrine Club paid only $50. Tufts made the suggestion that they all pay the discounted price. Ross, who was affiliated with the Shrine, took a different tact. After pointing out that with the much smaller Shrine Club, "every cent we made went to a very worthy fund for crippled children," he argued that the Kiwanis Club and American Legion were much larger, better able to support charitable work, and could therefore afford the higher price. "However," he concluded, "if you think the Shrine Club should pay the same price as the others, we will charge them also $150.00 for the night."

Parsimonious as ever, Ross was not one to squander funds on publicity just to make an appearance if he thought the expenditure would not produce a return. He turned down as wasteful an offer to take an ad out in the souvenir program for the 1929 U.S. Open at Winged Foot Golf Club. "I do not think it amounts to a row of pins," Donald wrote to Richard Tufts on March 12 in rejecting the idea of placing the ad. "I have had advertising space in those books for a number of years and I do not think it helped me a particle. It is a scheme worked out by the club in the hope of making some money to defray the expenses of the tournament and leaving a profit in the club treasury. I really do not

Above left: The Carolina Hotel. (Tufts Archives)

Below: Richard Tufts (left) and Ross. The younger Tufts, who went on to become USGA president in 1955-56, had a more comfortable working relationship with Ross than his father, Leonard, did. (Tufts Archives)

think it would be of any benefit to Pinehurst to take an ad in this souvenir book."

Pinehurst achieved its exalted position through a careful and sustained strategy of drawing the game's luminaries to the Sandhills region. Businessmen were attracted not only by the promise of the weather and the golf, but also by the opportunity to spend moderate temperature winters in the company of their social equals. It helped matters that the Country Club arranged a seemingly endless series of competitions involving both male and female members, with the results trumpeted regularly in the *Pinehurst Outlook*. As every sports editor of a newspaper knows, the way to win reader loyalty is not through national coverage of major events but through slavishly adoring attention paid to the achievements of local figures, especially at the amateur levels so that readers can see their own names and those of their friends and kin in print. Such was the approach apparently taken by the *Outlook*—no surprise, really, since this was less a general interest newspaper than an in-house bulletin of good cheer designed to reinforce a sense of community among inhabitants of what amounted to a company town. When necessary, the club hired out-of-town journalists to write laudatory travel pieces, though sometimes the journalistic results were less than desirable. The feeling, apparently, was that good press was important enough to cultivate, even to buy. Careful attention was taken to getting the tone right. In November 1927, for example, Leonard Tufts scolded the distinguished *New York Times* golf correspondent Lincoln Werden for a piece he had done on behalf of Pinehurst slated to appear in a magazine. Tufts wrote that:

> [T]he enclosed bit of Pinehurst Golf Lore is so very badly done that I hardly know where to start to make suggestions for change. There are more misstatements, and damaging statements as far as that is concerned, than I thought possible to put into one article. . . .
>
> Then you say it is a typical paradise except for the fact that the courses are too hard. That is a nice slam. Time is short and I suppose you will have to dope this out some way and let it go on but it certainly is a mess and it is going to cost us $225 and a bunch of misstatements like this put across. Correct the worst of them and let it go.

Overseeing Pinehurst's marketing was a New York based advertising executive named Frank Presbrey. He had first offered his services to founder James Walker Tufts during the resort's pioneer days, and ended up deploying his peculiar penchant for promotions over the next four decades. Among his many schemes was the creation in 1905 of the American Golf Association of Advertising Interests, whose annual meeting brought together industry heads from golf, travel, and writing to—where else?—Pinehurst. The resort quickly learned from such efforts that holding business meetings was a profitable way of drawing clientele, and of filling empty hotel space during the very beginning and end of the regular season. Presbrey also served as a founding figure of the United States Seniors Golf Association in 1917, and organized the first of Pinehurst's senior events for men in 1921.

Presbrey's promotional acumen found an ally that year when Bob Harlow came to Pinehurst as golf correspondent for the International News Service and the *New York Herald Tribune*. Harlow wrote a number of favorable dispatches, and after serving stints as Walter Hagen's manager and then as tournament director for the PGA of America during the early growth days of the professional Tour, Harlow returned to Pinehurst, this time in 1937, to direct publicity operations for the resort. It wasn't enough that his praising articles appeared in nearly every issue of the *Pinehurst Outlook*. Soon, he purchased the paper outright and tried to make a go of it as an independent publication. Ultimately, Harlow's penchant for golf journalism won out. In 1947, Harlow started a news weekly, *Golf World*, devoted exclusively to the game on a national and international scale.

Air conditioning would not come to the Pinehurst hotels until 1958. In Ross's day, the resort was only open from late October through early May. The courses also shut down for repair and recovery, with only one layout—not the No. 2 Course—at the Country Club and another at Southern Pines held open for summer play.

Pinehurst marketed itself like no other golf property. The readily identifiable "putter boy" character quickly became associated with the resort. Posters and advertisements featuring the diminutive fellow with the big grin appeared in newspapers, train stations, and travel magazines. The ads portrayed him with golf clubs slung over one shoulder and a modest suitcase in tow with the free hand, hauling off on a train or steamer from some major eastern city to Pinehurst. The image conveyed ease of travel, a carefree attitude about life, and the simple boyish comforts of life down at Pinehurst. Of course the depiction of southern Blacks (they were not yet called African-Americans) in these posters was unmistakably degrading. It was part of a generally widespread cultural attitude of racial insensitivity and prejudice.

Town life at Pinehurst, after all, was organized around the comfort of guests. This entailed carefully limiting access of minority populations. Rules governing the village oval park, for example, made it clear that white people alone were welcome there. Blacks could walk through it but could not sit down on park benches. An exception, however, was made for those women acting as nurses and nannies for the town's white families.

Accompanying such proscriptions was a standard clause in deeds covering property transferred within Pinehurst town limits:

The Pinehurst Putter Boy, with the racial stereotype of the smiling black caddie nearby. (Tufts Archives)

(4) The party of the second part, their heirs, assigns or lessees shall not permit said premises to be occupied by a Jew or Negro, after five (5) days notice in writing by the party of the first part or its legal representative, nor convey nor lease to any person of Jewish or Negro descent or lineage.

Ross himself was very much a social creature rather than a rebel, and so it is neither surprising nor scandalous to say that, along with so many others, he shared rather than repudiated the conventional prejudices of his day. It was, for example, more a matter of conventional discourses rather than an expression of some deep-seated rage for Ross to write, as he did on August 27, 1925, to Leonard Tufts, that "Miami is crowded with Jews and many of the best people are leaving the more prominent resorts . . . to get away from the undesirable element which the real estate boom has brought into the state."

When it came to the area's Black population, or at least that share of it in which Ross had a working relationship, he seems to have devoted himself in an impressive, if utilitarian, manner. All of the caddies at Pinehurst were Black, and part of his extensive responsibilities at the Country Club was to oversee their work conditions. In this, he worked with the caddie master. But Ross's position came with more authority than merely assigning bag toters to players each day. In 1922, it was Ross who had to make sure that the caddie master checked the crew for smallpox. And when questions arose in 1924 as to the resort's compliance with child labor laws, it was Ross who had to negotiate with the state's Child Welfare Commission. At one point, he visited school officials in nearby Taylor where the

A Pinehurst caddie tends to his golfer as the rest of the corps looks on. (Tufts Archives)

Black community all lived; only students with passable grades were to be approved for caddying, while delinquents would be denied access altogether. Ross also spoke out on behalf of a cut-rate caddie restaurant near the clubhouse. Against management concerns that it wasn't making a profit, Ross argued—persuasively, as it turned out—that the value of the provisions made it easier for Pinehurst to attract a reliable caddie corps and that this benefit outweighed any financial losses that were incurred. Ross consistently argued on behalf of upgraded caddie quarters, and in 1928 even built a separate shed for female caddies. For their own safety they were to be kept apart from the male caddies, and the expectation as Ross expressed it was that their bag carrying services would be offered only to women guests at Pinehurst.

Ross's instinctive conservatism can be seen in his treatment of women as well. Toward the distaff side of the profession he was cool, even suspicious—although, it must be said, no more so than any other proper gentleman of his

Above: The Pinehurst caddie yard showed clear evidence of a racial divide between caddies and the managers and golfers. (Tufts Archives)

Left: The Pinehurst caddies provided their own music between rounds. (Tufts Archives)

PINEHURST COUNTRY CLUB

PINEHURST, NORTH CAROLINA

DONALD J. ROSS
SECRETARY-TREASURER

WRITTEN FROM

Newton Centre, Mass.,
October 5, 1925.

Mr. Richard S. Tufts,
Pinehurst, N. C.

Dear Richard:-

      I have your favor of September 28th, enclosing
a letter which you received from Mrs. Baldwin and also one
from Miss Johnstone. My opinion is that Miss Johnstone
wouldn't make a living in Pinehurst. It is hard enough now
for the teachers we have there to make ends meet and my candid
opinion would not to engage her as an instructor. I do not
believe even the women would hire her and certainly the men
wouldn't. Her best scheme is to try and get connected with some
hotel in Florida who has a short nine hole course and where they
couldn't afford to pay a recognized professional of any standing.
I knew of another **woman in Cleveland** who took her place as a
golf professional and she made a howling failure of it.

      Strange to say I have had some correspondence
with Mr. Baldwin, husband of the lady who wrote you, with reference to the laying out of a nine hole course in Concord.

      Mrs. Ross and I sent a wedding gift to Mrs.
Tufts, addressed to Meredith, N. H. and I am wondering whether
you got it. I hope it has not gone astray, so if you will please
advise me whether **or not you did** and someone would forward it
from Meredith after you left.

      I am astonished to hear that the fairways are so
good considering the very dry year you have had in Pinehurst.
Irving Johnson wrote me several times this wummer telling me of
the very trying conditions. It kind of worried me for **awhile**
until Frank Maples wrote me telling me that everything looked
pretty good.

      I hope to get down pretty early this year and
are looking forward to seeing you all. I trust you are all very
well and with my kindest regards.

          Yours very truly,

          Donald J. Ross

DJR/N

day. Witness the time he was asked to evaluate Richard Tufts's inquiries on behalf of two women who made requests regarding employment at the Pinehurst resort. "My opinion," he wrote to Richard Tufts on October 5, 1925 from Newton Centre, Massachusetts, "is that Miss Johnstone wouldn't make a living in Pinehurst. It is hard enough now for the teachers we have there to make ends meet and my candid opinion would be not to engage her as an instructor. I do not believe even the women would hire her as an instructor and certainly the men wouldn't. . . . I know of another woman in Cleveland who took her place as a golf professional and she made a howling failure of it."

If Leonard Tufts thought he could get his way concerning a seemingly minor personnel change at Pinehurst Country Club he did not know Donald Ross as well as he should have. On one notable occasion, the president of Pinehurst wrote to complain about two porters at the country club whose demeanor was alleged to be below standard. Along the way, Leonard Tufts betrays a certain cultural stereotyping regarding Ross's countrymen that could not have escaped Donald's discerning eye.

May 10, 1924

Mr. Donald J. Ross
Pinehurst, N.C.
Dear Donald:

In spite of your and my regard for Willie Wilson and Alex Innes, I am sure, from the complaints I have heard this year, that we ought to replace one of them with a more cordial person.

I have been told over and over again by people who go up to the desk that they go there with a smile and with pleasurable anticipation, and all the joy and happiness that they feel on entering the club is lost after their contact with Willie and Innis. This, of course, is not true of those who have been down here for any length of time and who know these two men.

It is a principle of an American hotel that a man should be smiled upon and made to feel at home upon arrival. It is the principle, as I see it, of all Scotchmen that upon meeting a stranger they shall freeze and show no enthusiasm. It is a sort of national diffidence.

I know that in order to encourage the new guest and add to our numbers we should replace Innes with someone who has a smile. Why not put a fellow like Nelson in? I am not speaking of him as the ideal but he is a little more cordial, I believe, than either Innes or Willie.

You know the majority of the people today are not accustomed from childhood to clubs. Most men, especially those who come here, are people who have made their own way in the world and they are not entirely familiar nor at home even yet in club life.

Yours very truly,
Leonard Tufts

Leonard could scarcely have considered the depths of personal affiliation that Ross had for these two. Willie Wilson and Alex Innes were old friends whom

Ross had personally hired. Indeed, Innis was himself from Dornoch and had played golf there with a younger Donald. Ross's written reply, dated two days after Leonard's letter, was typed—to be sure, not incidentally—on Ross's own stationery rather than that of the Pinehurst Country Club. He claims to have had no "knowledge of any criticism of either of these two men. On the contrary," the letter continues,

I have heard innumerable compliments paid to their courtesy and ability. Criticism must be expected as long as there is a Country Club. When it ends, failure is certain. Constructive criticism is always helpful and sensible men will accept it as such, and I feel sure that if Mr. Wilson or Mr. Innes were aware that anything they did was subject to reasonable criticism, they would be anxious to remedy it. I know them as honest, capable and courteous men, always working for your and the Club's interests, the kind of men I feel proud to be associated with, and the more I see of other Clubs and their organizations the prouder I am of our own.

Ross was laying the groundwork for such a principled defense of these two men that, as he made clear, his own reputation was on the line as well. "On the assumption that I was to have charge next season, I made a verbal agreement with Mr. Wilson and Mr. Innes to return next November and unless I have knowledge of some good reason for their not being engaged, in fairness to them and myself, I cannot break my word."

All of which is prelude to a dramatic position that Ross takes. If Leonard Tufts is serious about removing the men in question, he will have to do it, in effect, over Ross's body. "To relieve the Pinehurst guests of the embarrassment of having to be greeted by gentlemen of the type of Mr. Wilson and Mr. Innes, the simplest way would be for you to engage another man to take my place as manager."

A principled stand indeed, and it was enough for Leonard Tufts to abandon his schemes for getting rid of the offending men. It was clear that Pinehurst's operation was more dependent upon Donald Ross than upon anyone else.

So valuable had Ross become to the Pinehurst Resort that he was even allowed to set himself up as a competitor of sorts to the resort. On May 15, 1920, Ross extended his domain to off-course matters when he became a hotelier by buying the Pine Crest Inn. It was a rambling, creaky old wood frame hostelry in Pinehurst with 40 guest rooms. Even then, it never quite stood square, with its interior construction just slightly awry—right angles of anywhere from 87 to 93 degrees, depending on the heat and humidity. Actually, he and his good friend James MacNab were co-owners. Ross, who had most of the equity backing the mortgage, was not involved in day-to-day management of the Inn; that was left to MacNab and his wife, Isabel Cheney MacNab. The Pine Crest, located just behind the middle of town, sat along Dogwood Road behind the more prestigious Holly Inn. The hotel was a rather quiet place in those days. Pinehurst was a dry town, after all, so dinners and nightlife there were not nearly as lively (nor as lucrative for the proprietors) as they were subsequently to become. That the Inn ran as little more than a shoestring operation is evidenced in the occasional demands by Pinehurst Inc.'s legendary Scrooge-like treasurer, a fellow with the Dickensian name of I.C. Sledge, for payment of overdue utility services and various town assessments. Sledge was not much of a diplomat, and both Ross and MacNab complained in writing to Leonard Tufts about the treasurer's acidic tone. Whatever wiggle room that Ross was allowed by Pinehurst Inc. in running the Pine Crest operation did not extend to a credit line.

All the while, Ross's keen sense of the business climate proved an asset to the Tufts family. His perceptive letters from the field showed a wide-ranging interest as he evaluated the resort competition. These were skills that not only benefited the Pinehurst operation but his design outfit as well.

> *Pinehurst Country Club*
> *Pinehurst, North Carolina*
> *Donald J. Ross*
> *Secretary-Treasurer*

February 9, 1926

Mr. Leonard Tufts:

On my last trip South the two resorts which are unquestionably having the most successful business this year are Bellair and Augusta and in neither place do they make any particular effort to get the first-class players in their tournaments. They are quite indifferent to them and certainly those two places cater to as nice a people as visit the South.

Bellair a week ago had seventy-five more guests than it had on any previous year on the same date. The Bon Air Vanderbilt had every room taken and my information is there is not a room to be had for the season. The Poinciana two weeks ago had fewer people than it had on the same date last year. The Flamingo was full. The Nautilus was only one-half full. The Miami Biltmore at Coral Gables was just opened and could not accommodate very many people but the situation in Miami is this. The high class hotels are having difficulty in filling their rooms. The medium class hotels, night clubs and cabarets are having an excellent business all due to the fact that the race track in Miami is bringing there an undesirable and sporty class of people.

The land speculation boom in Florida is ended. Building and improvement operations in all the large developments are cut down to minimum and there are many more sellers than buyers of land all over the state. My information is that there have been several failures already particularly among the poorly financed operations and it is believed generally among the substantial business men of Florida that a house cleaning among the real estate operators

Top: The co-owners of the Pine Crest Inn during the 1920s and 1930s. James McNab (left) and Ross are pictured in 1934 in one of photographer John G. Hemmer's typically sharp images. (Tufts Archives)

Above: The 40-room Pine Crest Inn, just behind downtown Pinehurst. (Tufts Archives)

has started and only those well financed and honestly operated can survive.

I think the movement that has drawn people to the South will before long react very favorably to this section and I have a stronger belief than ever that when all is said and done the Middle South is the ideal place in which to live.

Yours very truly,

DJRoss

Nor did Ross's involvement as local hotelier end his interest in business opportunities. In 1928, he was offered a permanent agreement with Augusta CC in Georgia to help it in conducting club affairs. Richard Tufts reluctantly agreed on October 5, adding that he hoped this would not endanger Pinehurst's use of him for promotional purposes. Ross argued that the clientele was different enough so that there would be no conflict, and that indeed it might well have a positive effect on resort trade there. The agreement, though taken up, proved short-lived.

So important had Ross become to operations that by the 1924-1925 season he was Pinehurst's highest-salaried employee, with a rate of $6,500 for his six and half months, plus $678.86 in commissions from sales at the Country Club. Only a Mr. E.G. Fitzgerald, manager of the Carolina Hotel, drew a higher compensation, nearly $14,000, though almost all of his pay was commission for room and conference sales he negotiated. Ross was thus drawing a higher wage than any officer of the company, including treasurer I.C. Sledge, who received $5,439 in salary and commissions for his 12-month contract, and director of maintenance and course construction Frank Maples, whose 10-month salary plus commissions for various projects totaled $3,730.

Interestingly, Ross's income for 1925 can be easily estimated. Figuring 22 new course designs at $2,000 apiece plus one remodeling at $1,000, plus a percentage of the construction costs, and then adding in his Pinehurst income, it becomes clear that Ross was grossing on the order of $60-70,000 annually at his peak in the mid 1920s. That would make him one of the top earners in the game and among the elite in all of American sports.

Six years later, as the Depression took hold, Ross's relative status at Pinehurst remained unaffected. His $6,000 salary still topped the list, though his commissions for the 1930-31 season were down to all of $231. The only two Pinehurst employees who received greater compensation—all of it by way of commission work on a per assignment basis rather than salary—were Gould B. Martin, who took in $18,438 as head of publicity, and photographer J.G. Hemmer, who received $10,592 for his work.

For all its fame within the golf world, however, the Pinehurst property never truly enjoyed prosperity. Much of its revenue was plowed back into an ongoing series of projects. The real estate side of the business had never been planned as a source of capital—James W. Tufts's original vision was to operate at a self-financing level, with the result that property in town always remained under the firm control

of the Tufts family. The result was a permanent condition of financial uncertainty. One representative letter dated just before the onset of the Depression suggests the precariousness of the situation Pinehurst—and Donald Ross—faced.

Richard Tufts (left), Ross, and Pinehurst treasurer I.C. Sledge (right), 1942, in another Hemmer photograph. (Tufts Archives)

> *May 17, 1929*
> *Mr. Donald J. Ross*
> *Dear Donald,*
>
> *We have a rather serious situation to face this summer. As you know this spring we intended to put an addition on to the Holly Inn but unfortunately the money rates were so high, due to the New York speculation, that we gave this up.*
>
> *Since then our business has been very poor as you know and instead of coming out with about our usual profit, we will probably end up the year with a profit of only about two-thirds of what we have been making. In fact I shall be surprised if we do as well as that.*
>
> *This makes it very, very important for us to keep down our new work this year to*

the very minimum. We have got to do something to talk about so we are putting on a small addition to the dining room at the Carolina, fixing up the help's dormitory and rest room at the Holly Inn and moving the Gun Club.

I am asking you therefore to do not one penny's worth of work over there more than is necessary. We will, of course, have to build 18 new tees at the least on account of the talk that was made and what we told the Board of Governors. And Richard [Tufts] thinks it is necessary to put grass tees at all of the four 18 hole courses, but as soon as this is done I hope you will tell Frank [Maples] to cut down to the smallest possible maintenance force and not do any more work. And if you think it feasible I certainly wouldn't put them all in but this I will leave to yours and Richard's judgment, but if you can put one in for $4.95 and put in a good deal better one for $5.00, use only the $4.95 variety. Let's not be too artistic. And don't put in any more traps or change around any more holes.

The difficulty with this business is, we never know for sure what we can do until the hotels are closed for, as you know, we spend all of our profits each year in improvements.

Very truly yours,
Leonard Tufts

For all the financial constraints at Pinehurst, Ross and course superintendent Frank Maples managed to keep tinkering with the design and the grassing plan. Constant experimentation with bermudagrass—at one point Ross claimed that the best ground for a test plot was the front lawn of the Holly Inn—finally yielded acceptable results in 1935. For the first time, golfers at Pinehurst No. 2 could play on tees and greens that were fully grassed. The final step in the evolution of the modern routing of Pinehurst No. 2 came that same year when the present par-5 fourth and long par-4 fifth holes were created, replacing the old par-4 ninth and tenth holes. Each of the new holes was distinctive for bold bunkering and the clear delineation of angles of approach. The course, which had played to 6,126 yards, par-70 in 1918, and 6,479 yards, par 71 in 1923, was now fully prepared for the era of the sand wedge and steel-shafted clubs with a par of 72 and back tees totaling 6,879 yards.

Below: Pinehurst Country Club, 1936, showing the two practice putting greens in the foreground and the 18th hole of the No. 2 Course to the right of the clubhouse. (Tufts Archives)

Opposite page: Program cover, 1936 PGA Championship at Pinehurst No. 2. (Tufts Archives)

The efforts of Ross and the Tufts family culminated with the PGA Championship being held at the No. 2 Course on November 16-22, 1936. In the 36-hole match-play final, Denny Shute defeated Jimmy Thomson 3 & 2.

Surprisingly in those days, including during the PGA Championship, the new 467-yard fifth hole was played as a par 5 and the eighth hole, only one yard shorter, played as a par 4. In subsequent years, the pars on the two holes were reversed for everyday play. For tournaments, both play as par 4s. Today's professionals who find the dogleg-left fifth hole the most challenging on the course can take some solace knowing their troubles were anticipated by Ross, who had intended it to be a par 5.

Map of Championship Course, Main Automobile Routes
and Principal Points of Interest in the Village of Pinehurst

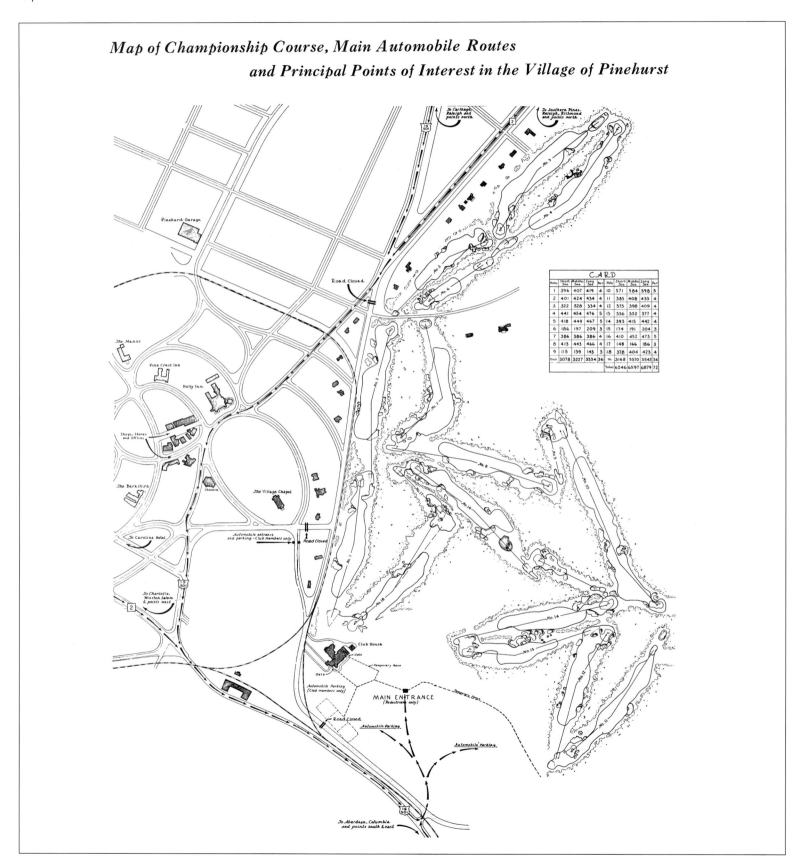

		CARD									
Hole	Short Tee	Middle Tee	Long Tee	Par	Hole	Short Tee	Middle Tee	Long Tee	Par		
1	396	407	419	4	10	571	584	598	5		
2	401	424	434	4	11	383	408	433	4		
3	322	328	334	4	12	375	398	409	4		
4	441	454	476	5	13	336	352	377	4		
5	418	449	467	5	14	393	415	442	4		
6	186	197	209	3	15	174	191	204	3		
7	386	386	386	4	16	410	452	473	5		
8	413	443	466	4	17	148	166	186	3		
9	115	139	143	3	18	378	404	423	4		
Out	3078	3227	3334	36	In	3168	3570	3545	36		
					Total	6246	6597	6879	72		

Opposite page: Map of PGA Championship course, Pinehurst No. 2, 1936. (Tufts Archives)

Left: The new fourth hole on the No. 2 Course, a 476-yard par 5, as seen in 1936. Note the low-lying contour of the green and its grade level perimeter. (Tufts Archives)

Below: The fifth hole on No. 2 as seen today. The par 4 measures 463 yards from the blue tees and 485 yards from the gold markers. (Bradley S. Klein)

Chapter Four
Master Builder

The offers kept pouring in and it allowed Ross, for the first time in his career, to begin to be selective about the design assignments he was offered. In a June 13, 1921 letter to Leonard Tufts, Ross conveyed the position in which he now found himself. "I have already this year laid out nine new eighteen hole courses and have had many more applications which I was not able to consider for lack of time, all of which goes to prove that catering to the American love of outdoor life is becoming a leading and important business."

CAREER EVOLUTION

Donald Ross was only 13 years old when Old Tom Morris made his first visit to Dornoch in 1886. Whether the youngster accompanied the famed course designer around the links in the company of club secretary John Sutherland is today a matter of speculation. What is certain is that the effects of Old Tom's handiwork made their impression quickly in the transformation of the links. It was not long before Ross himself was taken under Sutherland's wing to study and practice green-keeping. By 1893, when Ross was sent off to study with the master at St. Andrews, Old Tom Morris had established his reputation throughout Great Britain as a course designer.

By the time Ross joined him at St. Andrews, Old Tom had moved beyond the old practice of staking out a golf course one day and playing it the next. In 1893, for example, Old Tom undertook a considerable project at Luffness New, 25 miles east of Edinburgh. Construction took several months, and the opening was delayed a full season to ensure the holes were in proper condition. In what might well have been the first example of its kind in Scottish golf, the club listed the exact distances from the tees of the many man-made bunkers and ditches that dotted the course.

It is unlikely that Ross would have accompanied his master to the grounds

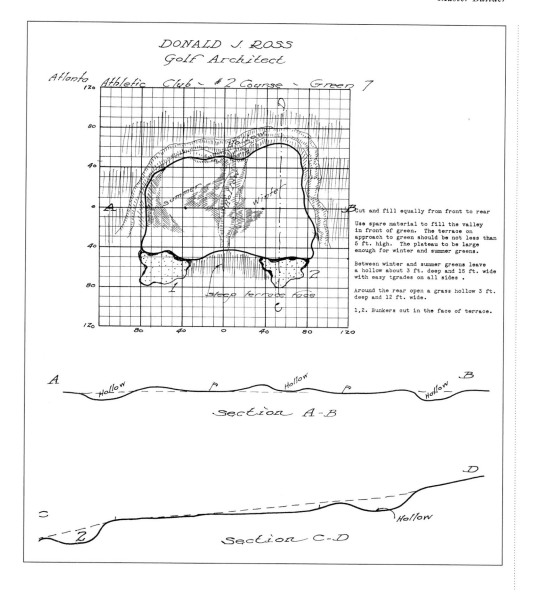

DONALD J. ROSS
Golf Architect

Atlanta Athletic Club ~ #2 Course ~ Green 7

Cut and fill equally from front to rear

Use spare material to fill the valley in front of green. The terrace on approach to green should be not less than 5 ft. high. The plateau to be large enough for winter and summer greens.

Between winter and summer greens leave a hollow about 3 ft. deep and 15 ft. wide with easy tgrades on all sides.

Around the rear open a grass hollow 3 ft. deep and 12 ft. wide.

1,2. Bunkers cut in the face of terrace.

Section A-B

Section C-D

of Luffness New, but there is no question of Ross's having been on site in 1894 as Old Tom was creating the New Course at St. Andrews. Early on, Donald Ross was getting a complete education in the art of golf course design, construction, and maintenance. Though John Sutherland would allow him precious little opportunity to maneuver the links at Dornoch, by the time Ross set up in the New World, there was no one to hold him back from applying his knowledge to the land.

Yet he might have overindulged himself. Some time toward the end of his career, Donald Ross was asked by one of his design associates what, in retrospect, he would have done differently in his design practice. Ross told Ellis Maples, son of Pinehurst's director of maintenance and construction Frank Maples, that he now realized he had taken on far too much work and that he should have only accepted as many assignments as he could have personally supervised.

Sketch of seventh green, Atlanta Athletic Club, No. 2 Course, ca.1925. Note the double putting surface, one for winter and one for summer. It's approximately 13,000 sq. ft. in size and divided by a huge swale 3 feet deep and 15 feet across. (Tufts Archives)

Ross is often credited with as many as 600 courses. In fact, the most reliable number is 399—though there may well be a handful of others he did for which no reliable evidence has turned up. The total number of projects he worked on was 457—including about 72 where he did subsequent work on a course he had already worked upon or the work did not materialize into a completed project. The precise numbers are difficult to determine, but they are as close as the evidence allows one to specify. In any case, by sheer volume alone those 399 courses comprise an extraordinary body of work, especially because Ross undertook it in an era when travel was not a matter of hopping on an airplane and dropping in on a course for a morning or afternoon—as is the case too often today.

Ross was an inveterate train traveler. In his 40-plus years of designing, he plied his way up and down the east coast and into the Midwest and South with a fervor that belied his modest nature. For all his traveling, however, it actually appears that he was able to make personal visits—even if only one—to no more than two-thirds of his course portfolio. Leeway, however, must be allowed for unconfirmed casual site visits, as well as the unavoidable incompleteness of the historical record governing his lifework. The fact remains that aside from his personal involvement, he was very good at delegating work to trusted associates. Even here, as we shall see, travel and budget limitations did not always allow for comprehensive oversight, and rarely did it allow for sustained on-site management. But he was able to forge a body of work of admirable consistency and quality, largely because he recruited and maintained a small but very talented corps of associates.

His ability to manage what, by the 1920s, had became a virtual empire of golf course design and construction, became the prototype of contemporary management techniques whereby name architects would farm out vast numbers of projects. This alone represented a fundamentally modern method of business administration. It also entailed a subtle if decisive shift in the nature of golf course architecture: from a highly individualized craft to a more business-oriented form of work in which a paper trail of design sketches became paramount. Varieties of terrain, the limitations of earthmoving equipment, and the constraints of budgets and fees, however, still meant for Ross that the resulting courses adhered more to the contours of native land than to some cookie-cutter pattern of an assembly line.

Ross's distinctive genius came from being trained in the earlier mode of golf course design *and* adapting himself toward the newer style of what might well be called mass production. In this sense, his work method bridges two eras. He was schooled in the classical craftsmanship of an art that hewed the land. Yet the scale of his undertaking relied upon techniques of high volume output in which efficiency and coordination of schedules were paramount.

Throughout his work, Ross's golf courses were to embody a particular vision and brilliance. This has allowed many of them to stand out 75 or more years after their inception. Nor did his work remain static or formulaic. A close appraisal reveals a modest if discernible evolution that, at the risk of oversimplification, might even be interpreted as falling into phases or stages. His early work includes a number of quirks or oddities that, while distinctive, appear to be the result of certain design and construction limitations. It's not that Ross should be faulted; rather, these works, built basically between 1900 and 1918, suggest a designer who was conscious of certain site limitations and who was struggling to accommodate his designs within them. In many cases, he was able to compensate for constraints in the routing with bold and creative putting surfaces. During this period he experimented with or deployed a number of unusually shaped bunkers that by no means can be said to look formulaic or predicable. This period might be termed his "Formative Era." Among the representative works from this era that remain in relatively pristine

French Lick Springs (IN) Golf Course routing plan.
(French Lick Springs Golf Course)

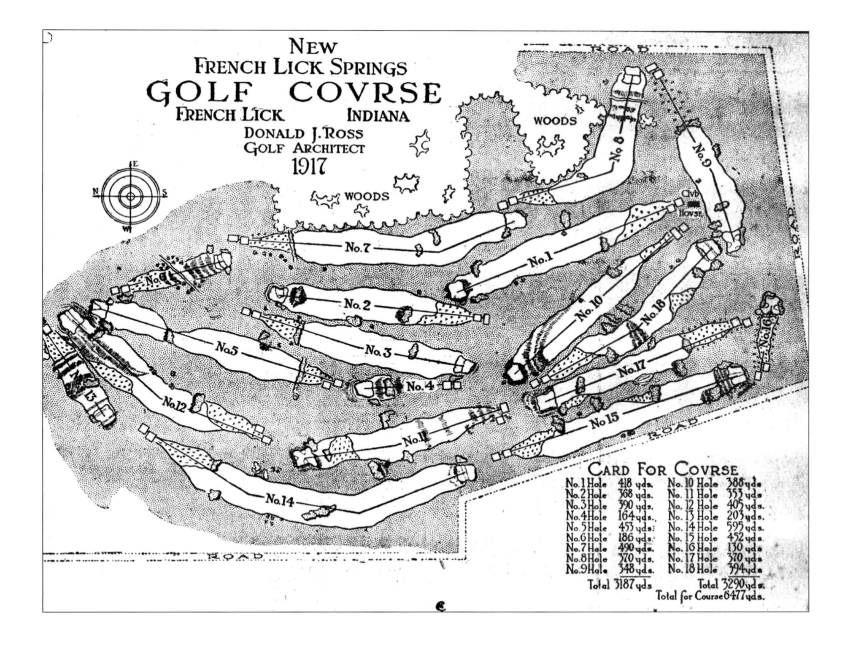

NEW
FRENCH LICK SPRINGS
GOLF COVRSE
FRENCH LICK   INDIANA
DONALD J. ROSS
GOLF ARCHITECT
1917

WOODS

WOODS

CARD FOR COVRSE

No.1 Hole	418 yds.	No.10 Hole	388 yds.
No.2 Hole	368 yds.	No.11 Hole	353 yds.
No.3 Hole	390 yds.	No.12 Hole	405 yds.
No.4 Hole	164 yds.	No.13 Hole	203 yds.
No.5 Hole	453 yds.	No.14 Hole	595 yds.
No.6 Hole	186 yds.	No.15 Hole	452 yds.
No.7 Hole	490 yds.	No.16 Hole	130 yds.
No.8 Hole	370 yds.	No.17 Hole	370 yds.
No.9 Hole	348 yds.	No.18 Hole	394 yds.
Total 3187 yds		Total 3290 yds.	
		Total for Course 6477 yds.	

Right: Mountain Ridge Country Club, West Caldwell, NJ, 1929. Ross's elegant routing starts and ends each nine at the clubhouse and provides support ground for parking, tennis, caddies, a practice area, and the green-keeper's quarters. (Ron Prichard)

Below: French Lick Springs (IN) Golf Course, eighth hole, 370-yard, par 4, with a 7,200 sq. ft. green traversed by a three-foot ridge and falling five feet behind. (French Lick Springs Golf Resort)

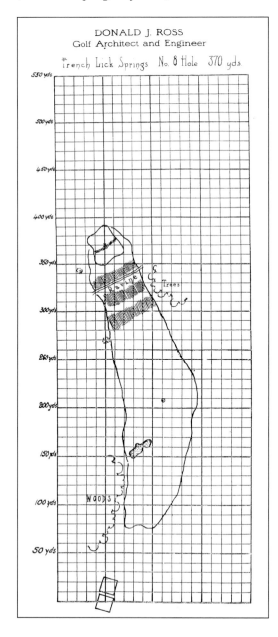

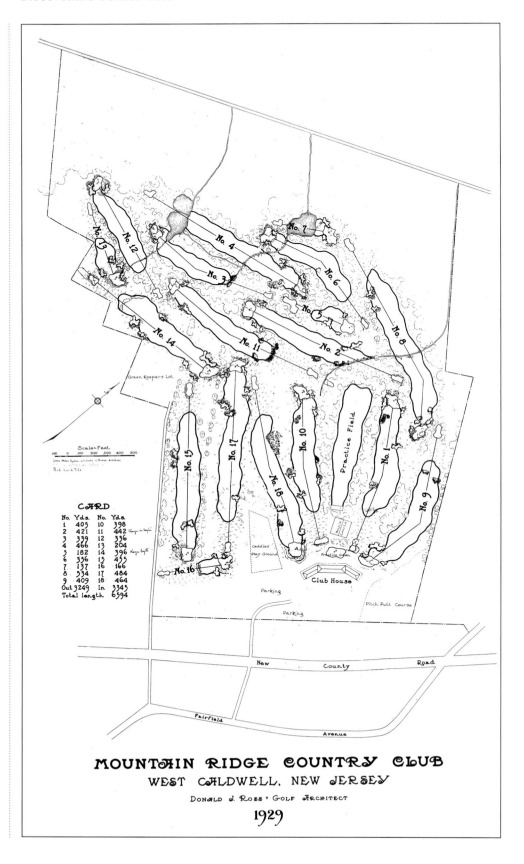

form today are Essex County Club (MA), Rhode Island Country Club, Wannamoisett Country Club (RI), Brae Burn (MA), White Bear Yacht Club (MN) and French Lick Springs Golf Course (IN). These courses were cultivated around a gnarly look, with abrupt mounds, often containing piles of rocks gathered on site. The putting surfaces offer steeply graded contours, and there is a tendency for the green complexes to embody sharply graded outslopes rather than smooth, flowing lines.

After World War I, Ross developed a more mature, flowing style in which features were more carefully integrated—"floated out," in the parlance of construction shapers, whose task it would become to "tie in" contour lines that adhered to natural topographic features. This work was greatly aided by his hiring of design associates Walter B. Hatch and J.B. McGovern. Ross's plans also became more technically adept thanks to the professional engineering and drafting provided by Walter Irving Johnson, who came on board in October 1920. The lines are smoother, more economical, and incorporate more mechanical construction equipment such as tractors, steam shovels, and mechanized plows. The most dramatic improvement came in terms of fairway preparation and shaping, so that the entire course could be more closely integrated. Again, at the risk of oversimplification, we can call this his "Mature Phase." Representative works that still embody these features would include Broadmoor Country Club (IN), Franklin Hills (MI), Holston Hills Country Club (TN), Salem Country Club (MA), Seminole (FL), and Mountain Ridge (NJ).

These works of the 1920s are more elegant, with smoother transitions from fairway into the green and fewer bunkers but more strategic in nature. There is a certain grace to these layouts, reflected in the more carefully fashioned contours of the greens and their positioning so that they were visible from a standard area of approach. Ross was also more meticulous in matching green position and contouring to the length of the shot. There is a clear relationship of proportionality governing the matchup of green severity with length of shot.

Ross's workload, the busiest in the country through the 1920s, quieted dramatically the last 15 years of his life. What work that did come his way was sporadic, and done with greater concern for economy of production than for aesthetic effect. Again, at the risk of considerable oversimplification, this can be termed his "Functionalist Phase"—a concern more for playability and maintainability than with a particular aesthetic or strategic effect. His works during this era really bridge two different modes of building. In the 1930s his work, such as it was, consisted largely of municipal projects that were impressive feats of construction. After World War II, when prosperity and an incipient golf boom were in the making, Ross found more

Mountain Ridge's 13th hole, a 204-yard par 3. (Larry Lambrecht)

Raleigh (NC) Country Club, the last course Ross ever did. He made a site visit in late 1947 to secure approvals. The course was completed by J.B. McGovern and Ellis Maples after Ross' death in April of 1948. (Bradley S. Klein)

work—for two years or so, until his death in April of 1948. The few projects he designed throughout this era do not readily show the same attention to detail of his Formative and Mature phases. How could they, as Ross was limited in his travels, and he had also slowed down physically and mentally owing to aging and declining health? This was work almost entirely taken up by J.B. McGovern, with assistance by Frank Maples's son, Ellis. That Ross's work was in such good hands helps explain the substance and elegance of Raleigh Country Club (NC), the last course he ever did.

Early Field Work

He was capable of some inventive techniques. The blasting required to create playable holes at Essex proved to be a familiar, if expensive, method. The real problem came in hauling such material away. Before the advent of huge mechanized earthmovers and steam shovels, it took massive effort to dislodge rocks and stones that had been blasted out of the ground. One reliable strategy was to gather the materials together and bury them in the form of huge mounds, often covered with dirt and grassed with native long fescue or tawny field grasses. Ross was scrupulous in avoiding the chocolate drop look used by an earlier generation of penal-oriented designers, much of whose work proliferated obstacles rather than defined strategic lines of play. Ross's genius, early on, was to incorporate difficult sites and make use of what some might have considered constraints.

At Brae Burn Country Club in Newton, MA, Ross's reconstruction of an existing 18-hole layout was constrained by a clubhouse that sat on a rise, with its back pinched by a road. The site featured considerable elevation change (steep slopes some 20-30 feet high) rather than land that flowed gradually up and down. Ross solved the problem of routing in a number of ingenious ways. Since there was only enough room for a two-hole corridor onto, and out of, the central golf grounds, these, naturally, became the first and last holes. They played from, and returned to, a dramatic upslope and offered a generous sense of the journey as it unfolded, from beginning to end, and ended. Rather than force long holes onto awkward terrain, Ross utilized a strategy that would inform the rest of his work; utilizing par 3s and short par 4s for the steeper land, and saving the longer 4s and the par 5s for the open, more meadow-like ground.

Brae Burn's first three holes comprise a succession of wonderful short par 4s that have scarcely changed since their 1912 inception. The first hole, only 337 yards and downhill, plays from a terrace in front of the clubhouse and offers a generous but well-bunkered fairway, and a small, tightly sloped green on the far side of a rocky creek bed. The second hole, all of 304 yards, winds left around a rocky hill and presents a frightening little second shot to a domed green surrounded by tiny, deep bunkers. The scale and slope of the bunkering and the putting surface replicate the overall terrain of this demanding little hole. On the third tee, golfers face

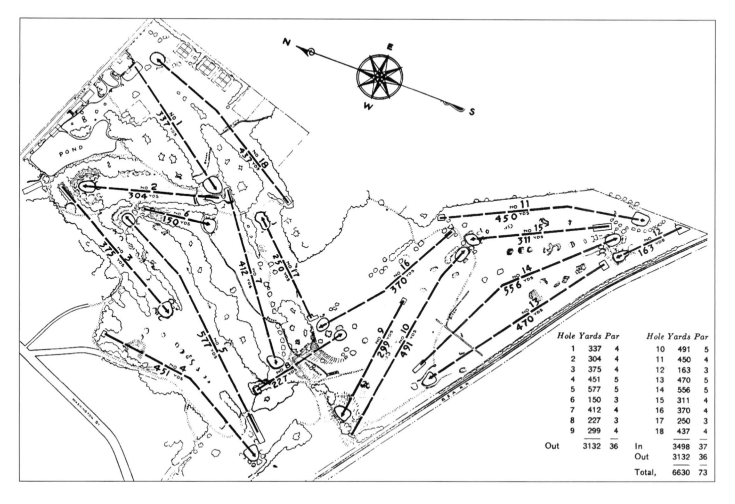

Hole	Yards	Par		Hole	Yards	Par
1	337	4		10	491	5
2	304	4		11	450	4
3	375	4		12	163	3
4	451	5		13	470	5
5	577	5		14	556	5
6	150	3		15	311	4
7	412	4		16	370	4
8	227	3		17	250	3
9	299	4		18	437	4
Out	3132	36		In	3498	37
				Out	3132	36
				Total,	6630	73

a somewhat longer par 4 at 375 yards. But here, too, the green, though broader in form, sits atop a precipitous rise and demands a crisply played approach.

For a course that starts with such nominal intimacy, there is nothing undersized about Brae Burn, not even at its present length of 6,630, par 72. It was surely considered a demanding layout in its day. The USGA liked it enough to conduct the U.S. Open there in 1919, and the course held up well enough so that Walter Hagen and Mike Brady (by then, the golf professional at Oakley Country Club) tied at 301. The playoff did not produce lower scoring, with Hagen's 77 good for a slim one-shot margin of victory.

Brae Burn in 1919 was the first of 21 U.S. Opens to be held on Ross-designed or redesigned layouts. That string included 8 of the 13 national championships held between 1919 and 1931. Ross undertook minor modification of Brae Burn prior to the 1928 U.S. Amateur there. He took the land devoted to the old par-4 12th and par-3 13th holes and converted them into their present incarnations of a par 3 followed by a par 5. While the routing has basically remained since 1912, the land has become far more heavily treed than in Ross's day. Recent efforts to prune

Top: Ross's routing plan for Brae Burn Country Club, West Newton, MA, modestly revised from 1912. (Brae Burn Country Club)

Above: Brae Burn Country Club's second hole, an uphill 304-yard par 4 to a small green pinched by sand and mounds. (United States Golf Association)

them back have opened up some of the ground features to the way Ross had originally built them. What a visitor learns today from a close look at Brae Burn, however, is the ability to make use of a very demanding site. Not that every hole is brilliant. Indeed, the par-4 16th hole, a rather short par 4 of 370 yards, betrays the limits of entirely naturalistic routing, with its fairway that cants some 10 degrees from right to left, enough so that virtually any full shot from the tee winds up in the same low pocket of ground on the left. Only a major cut and fill operation would have alleviated such an awkward fairway. It was not the kind of operation that anyone would have contemplated in Ross's day. The occasional unfortunate slope is the price to be paid for living with the terrain, and judging by the rest of Brae Burn it was, and is, a worthy price.

In 1911-13, Ross was balancing his time, with his winters committed to Pinehurst and his summers to Essex. He was still playing competitively when the design assignments multiplied, with his work focused on New England.

The year before his work at Brae Burn, Ross had gone to Cuba for several weeks and laid out the Country Club of Havana. The par-73 course (6,073 yards) quickly became the focal point of the island republic's golf life, and continued to host prominent tournaments for both wealthy tourists and professional golfers until its demise after the 1959 Cuban Revolution, when it was allowed to go fallow and ultimately plowed under to make room for industrial development.

A kinder fate has been bestowed upon Rhode Island Country Club in Barrington, on a coastal site where the Providence River empties into upper Narragansett Bay. Ross's original 18-hole work there also dates back to 1911. How much of Ross's design remains is a matter of speculation, though there is virtually no change from a well-preserved 1931 plan documented by local engineers Leighton T. Bohl and William R. Benford that hangs in the club's creaky clubhouse. The waterfront setting would seem to have suggested a links-inspired layout, but as Ross's subsequent notes make clear, the site posed some difficult issues. There are "some features of British seaside courses," he reported, with "sand dunes covered with bents" and an "endless supply of sea sand." A visitor today might wonder why the course is essentially oriented inland, on land away from the sea and on the upland side of the clubhouse. Only the last four holes are across the access road and located on the coastal side of the site, and even here, the parcel closest to the shore is reserved for a practice range rather than golf holes. The answer comes in Ross's comment: "control of tides difficult." The area most desirable for golf from an aesthetic standpoint was prone to flooding.

Rhode Island Country Club nevertheless remains a fascinating if overlooked example of early Ross work. A massive bunker complex dividing the first and second fairways displays sand in convex rather than concave form. The twisting, uphill 349-yard par-4 third hole calls for a layup short of a steep upslope, or a full-bore drive that carries it altogether. And the 169-yard par-3 fifth hole offers a green complex that is classic Ross: a raised fill pad, with the dirt hauled in from

the surrounding area, and bunkers built into the base of the platform. This was to become his classic form: elevated fill pad, with the bunkers built low into the upslope surrounding the putting surface.

The abiding interest of Ross's work in those days is how he fitted the holes to the native contours and placed his bunkers in low-lying areas where the ball was likely to run out and settle. This was very much based upon ground game principles rather than on modern aerial considerations. Such was the case at White Bear Yacht Club in White Bear Lake, MN, on the far northeast side of St. Paul. White Bear Yacht Club was the first of half a dozen Ross ventures in the Land of 10,000 Lakes. He was there in 1912 to lay out a nine-hole loop on the north side of the lake, between the St. Paul & Duluth Railroad line and Stillwater Road. Ross returned in 1915 to expand the course to 18 holes. He created holes on the far side of Stillwater Road that enabled White Bear Yacht to enjoy two returning nines, with each side making a road crossing. The bunker surfaces were laid low rather than flashed up, with many of them placed in the run-up area well in front of the greens or along the deep side of the fairway landing area. If the 1912 holes have a far more rolling character,

Top: The 313-yard par-4 sixth at Rhode Island Country Club in Barrington. (United States Golf Association)

Above: Rhode Island Country Club's 169-yard par-3 fifth hole. The putting surface is a classic raised fill pad with bunkers built into the base. (Bradley S. Klein)

Detail of 1915 surveyor's plan for White Bear Yacht Club, White Bear Lake, MN, shows the 14th hole at the top, a dogleg-right par 4. Bunkers are indicated by darkened areas. The hole, measuring 342.7 yards, includes a second shot across a low-lying area marked "sand and grass mounds." (White Bear Yacht Club)

it's simply Ross responding to the more severe ground features of the area near the golf house. The second set of holes is more expansive owing to the softer flow of the terrain. And once again, there was that inverted bunker feature, this time in the middle of the fairway on the dogleg right 14th hole, a 336-yard par 4. As with Rhode Island Country Club, Ross lifted the sand up atop mounding to create something of a vertical hazard.

Among those who enjoyed life at White Bear Yacht Club were F. Scott Fitzgerald and his wife, Zelda, who spent the summer of 1922 on the grounds. Zelda played golf and both of them drank and carried on furiously, to the point where they were asked to leave the grounds by September. Before they left, however, Fitzgerald wrote a short story set at the club called "Winter Dreams." It was published in December of 1922 and served as a prototype for *The Great Gatsby*.

A FULL-TIME ARCHITECT

By the early 1910s, Ross was sharing his design duties with two different assignments as golf professional. Winters were devoted to Pinehurst, while from early April through mid-October he reported to work at Essex. Both clubs afforded him time for travel, but against the measure of a growing design trade the constraints must have been considerable. He had, for example, no new design work in all of 1908 and 1909. But from 1910 through 1913, he was completing five to six new designs annually.

In at least one documented case Ross took on the construction work of a layout designed by another, far more famous architect—H.S. Colt. The club was Old Elm, a very private men's club in Highland Park, Illinois, just inland from Lake Michigan on the far north side of Chicago. Colt's hand-printed notes from April 27, 1913 provide a brief introduction to hole-by-hole sketches of a course that in routing and bunkering has remained essentially intact to this day. Indeed, it is one of the very few courses of its era not to have become overrun with pines, cedars and firs— or hardwoods, for that matter. The routing is intimate enough that as many as seven of the planned 61 bunkers served double duty collecting shots for adjacent holes.

Ross, then 40 years old, apparently made a strong impression on Colt, though not in one crucial respect. Witness one paragraph in his field notes introducing the hole-by-hole drawings:

"Douglas Ross, whom I met for the first time & with whom I am most favorably impressed, made notes of everything & if given a free hand will I am sure carry out the work in a natural & excellent manner."

In 1913, Edward E. Babb of the Boston Athletic Association was playing a round of golf at the old Mt. Tom Course in Holyoke, MA with Lewis Wyckoff, a coprincipal in the paper manufacturer, White & Wyckoff. After the round, Wyckoff expressed dissatisfaction with the quality of the course. When Babb mentioned that he knew of a man in the Boston area uniquely qualified to undertake design work, Wyckoff was interested. Soon, Ross was on his way out to look at the Mt. Tom Course. It was the start of a business, friendship, and family association that would involve both men for the rest of their lives.

Ross appears to have completed the 1913 golf season at Essex County Club. Whereas he had shared teaching duties during his first two years there with Skip Wogan, Essex brought on board Matthew Campbell in 1913 to assume the major teaching burden. The reduced commitment was a portent. Essex would be the last northern golf club Ross would be affiliated with as golf professional. Increasingly, his design work occupied his attention away from Pinehurst. The visit to Wyckoff in Holyoke precipitated a major move for Ross. He would essentially become a full-time designer. There is even some suggestion in the admittedly circumstantial evidence that Wykcoff staked Ross to his new design career, included paying for a new home/office in Holyoke. Whatever the exact financial terms of Wyckoff's support, Ross moved his family to Holyoke for the summer of 1914. His local affiliation was strong enough that the next year he began a term at Mt. Tom Golf Club as green chairman. From Holyoke, Ross accelerated his travels, doubling his output from any previous year: six new layouts, six remodels, and three additions in 1914.

Among those new layouts was Wannamoisett Country Club in Rumsford, RI, just east of Providence. The site was cramped, and many of the tees seemed to back up upon property boundaries, but Ross managed to create one of his most efficient routings with as diverse a set of putting surfaces as he would ever produce. The design was started in 1914 and took two years to bring to fruition, at a construction cost of $22,800. When he returned a decade later, he kept the hole corridors and green surfaces and concentrated on deepening the bunkers and bringing more of them into play for longer drives. Upon completion of the new plans, Ross sent

Right and opposite page: Wannamoisett Country Club, Rumsford, RI. The greens at the 399-yard par-4 10th (left) and 200-yard par-3 12th (right) show the remarkable diversity of this layout's putting surfaces. Ross did the original design in 1914 and reworked it in 1926. Upon completion of the new plans, Ross sent the sketches to his draftsman, W.I. Johnson, with a note: "This is the best layout I ever made, a fine course on 100 acres of land, no congestion, fine variety." (Bradley S. Klein)

his field notes to his draftsman, Walter Irving Johnson with a note. "This is the best layout I ever made, a fine course on 100 acres of land, no congestion, fine variety."

The move to Holyoke also occasioned Ross to sit down and draft a series of brief essays that would eventually comprise his posthumously published book, *Golf Has Never Failed Me* (1996). It is likely that these observations were intended as a modest manifesto of sorts, an attempt to establish himself as an authority on the subject and thus a marketing device for his own burgeoning business.

In June of 1914, Ross came to West Hartford, CT. The membership of Hartford Golf Club was looking to move some of its existing golf course north across Albany Avenue while reworking the rest of the layout. Ross's plan for the new holes involved laying 900 feet of 24-inch gauge railway track, then using three 4 x 6 foot platform cars for shuttling dirt around the site. The club must have been in quite a rush to complete the plans because it contracted with a local supplier on December 23rd for the makeshift railway line. Ross apparently made several return visits over the next few years to complete the work—which today is still visible on the otherwise much-changed course in the form of holes four, five and six, the 14th green and the present 15th tee and fairway, plus an old par 3 at the far southern end of the present course which is kept up for tradition's sake but is only played as a temporary replacement.

Interestingly, Ross's design plans for Hartford Golf Club include two-dimensional blueprints of the holes at the course he worked on, but not of the new ones he built from the ground up. Subsequent documentation of these plans, drawn up on grid paper with 30-foot squares, are remarkably detailed and come replete with his standard instructions for construction. Their detail suggests they were done around 1918 or perhaps soon after by Ross's new hire, Walter B. Hatch. The drawings do not include perspective accounts of the holes, nor are there any topographic

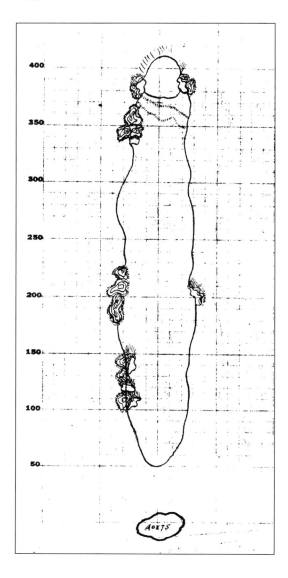

Above: Ross's plan for Hartford Golf Club's first hole, 1914. It shows a 385-yard par 4 with extensive mounding and bunkering in the primary landing areas and additional hazards well short of the green. (Hartford Golf Club)

Right: In 1946, Ross's new plan for Hartford Golf Club (now 27 holes) showed dramatically reduced fairway bunkering. The first hole, now stretched to 445 yards, offers much less reliance upon hazards. (Hartford Golf Club)

cross sections. These were not always in evidence in Ross's design work career. Indeed, Hartford allows us to an unusual degree to see the maturation of Ross's work. His design plans from the mid-1910s reveal a multiplicity of bunkering options, whereas a plan he prepared after a site visit in 1946 (the actual drafting undertaken by his associate J.B. McGovern) are much richer in detail. They include cross-sections and perspectives, and are also much more sparing in their bunkering. There is also far greater instruction for every aspect of course construction: clearing, drainage, turf cultivation, seeding and planting, and the irrigation system.

The differences had as much to do with the nature of course development and construction as with Ross's own abilities. In laying out the Bay Course at Seaview Golf Club in Absecon, New Jersey in late 1914, Ross completed a detailed set of hole-by-hole drawings. The two-dimensional sketches, done on his standard 10 yard x 10 yard grids, carries the heading "Donald J. Ross, Golf Architect, Holyoke, Mass." There is no indication of any associates. What is indicated is an

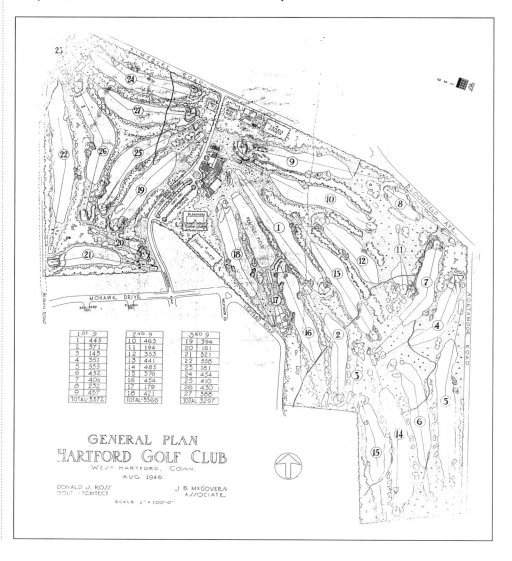

inventive set of holes over rather flat land. The paths from tee to green are interspersed not only with a variety of bunker shapes (both large waste-type areas as well as deeper pits) but also with sandy mounds and grassed mounds from 4 to 7 feet high. An article the February 1915 issue of *Golf* Magazine discusses the 280-acre Seaview property and devotes considerable space to play on the marsh-side, sandy layout. No mention is made of the architect. There is much discussion of the greens, including their punchbowl, terraced, and convex (saucer-shaped) surfaces. But it is also clear that while the course was open for play, it didn't have any bunkers. These were to come later. Indeed, a close look at Ross's plans for the holes shows that many of the features indicated are themselves revisions of existing hazards and mounds. Moreover, the writing alongside each hole is not Ross's handwriting. In short, the drawings are not of Ross's original layout, but drawings of the course when it opened. The sequence of course development allowed for considerably more latitude in construction, sometimes with crucial features added months or even years after opening. These were truly works in progress.

Hartford's 481-yard 16th hole, following bunker restoration by Stephen Kay. This is how it looked for the 1996 U.S. Mid-Amateur. (Bradley S. Klein)

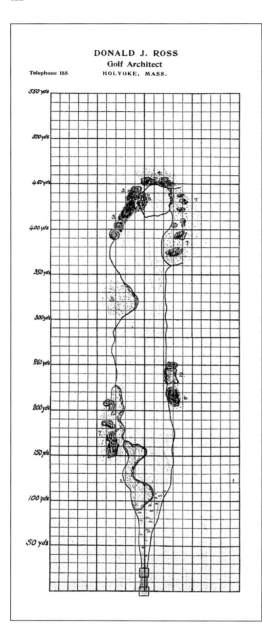

Seaview Golf Club, 1914. Ross' plan for the long 430-yard par-4 second hole on what is now Seaview's Bay Course called for deepening the existing sand pits and running a serpentine fairway around them. Note the 4- to 7-foot high grass mounds short and left of the green. (Marriott Seaview Golf Club)

Opposite page: Exmoor Country Club, Highland Park, IL. Cross hazards were commonplace on Ross's work here from 1914 to 1916. (Exmoor Country Club)

CHICAGO

Ross quickly flourished—to the point where "Douglas" was taking work from Colt in the Chicago area. In 1913, for example, the year he was designing Old Elm, Colt was engaged by another club in Highland Park. Exmoor Country Club wanted him "to go over our course and to make plans and suggestions for its betterment." It is not known what happened to Colt's proposal for Exmoor's 5,880-yard layout (designed by H.J. Tweedie in 1901-02). But in 1914, Exmoor turned to Ross to undertake a thorough remodeling that resulted two years later in the opening of a 6,502-yard, par-72 layout.

Other area clubs, both new and prospective, lined up quickly. Within a 10-year period, 1913-1923, Ross built or renovated nearly a dozen courses in metro Chicago. The spurt of activity and the frequency with which he had to be in town ultimately gave rise to reports that he had an office in the city. But if so, there is no direct reference to it in any surviving letters and no address on stationery or working documents (such as blueprints and sketches). On the basis of all available evidence, it can be confidently stated that Ross was working very much on his own, or only with casual arrangements with foremen hired for discrete jobs and without benefit of a local office in Chicago.

At Oak Park Country Club in the city of Oak Park, Ross created a links-style layout replete with split or alternate fairways and cross bunkers. The site was low-lying land alongside the Des Plaines River. The soil, predominantly clay, was on the heavy side and drained poorly, but Ross deliberately avoided using a densely wooded six-acre copse on the east-central side of the property and allowed his huge bunkers with moderate faces to create the strategy (along with a burn that was an element on more than half of a dozen holes).

Ross was on site at Oak Park and finished his layout plans on July 18, 1914. Construction, overseen by a W.J. Matthews, led to the first nine opening the following July 3, and the second nine debuting on May 31, 1916. A vast, prairie-style clubhouse reminiscent of Frank Lloyd Wright's work soon graced the site. However, its location some 200 feet north of where Ross assumed it would be led to a modest resequencing of the front nine holes to simplify the walk—and perhaps to avoid the awkwardness of a first hole that Ross had routed into the morning sun. One dramatic hole, the 390-yard par-4 seventh (now the fifth), incorporated the brook on a long diagonal line from left to right. Mature oaks lining the left side effectively forced golfers to the right, from where they would have to cross the stream again on the approach.

One of Ross's more inventive creations was the 403-yard, par-4 15th. It offered a split-fairway option around a massive bunker that bisected the landing area. Changes suggested by Ross himself in October of 1921, however, led to a much revised 14th hole and abandonment of the double-fairway 15th. What started as evidence of an unusual double-option defined by a serpentine bunker became

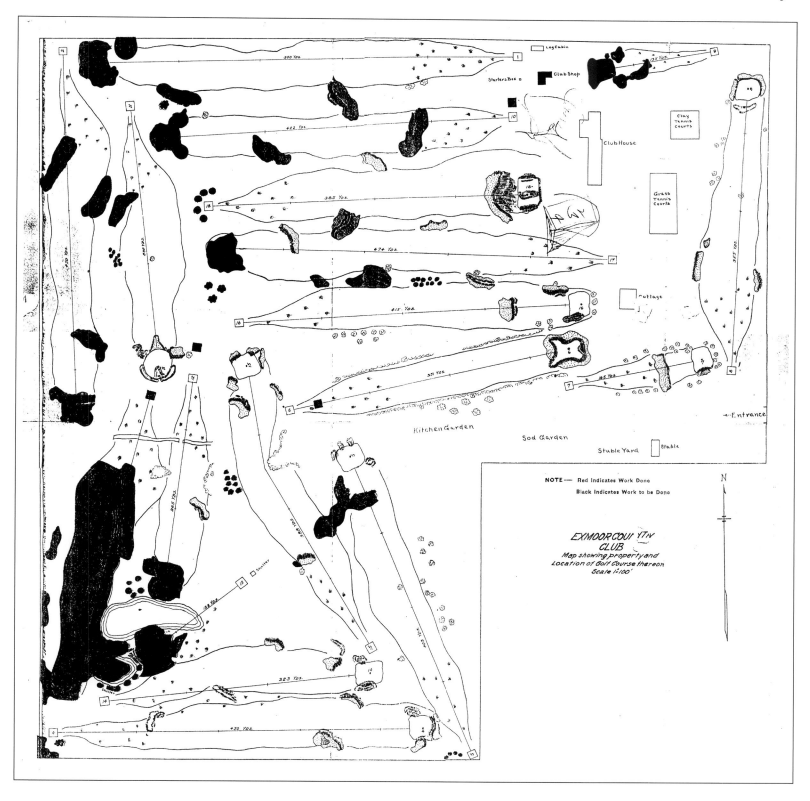

Right: Oak Park (IL) Country Club in May of 1931, looking east, with a smattering of recent tree plantings and a six-acre copse of mature hardwoods on the far side. (Oak Park Country Club)

Below: Oak Park Country Club in October of 2000, viewed from the same angle. The effect of heavy tree growth is obvious. (Ralph Chermak)

transformed into a far more conventional pathway to the green flanked by small, circular bunkers.

While working on Exmoor and Oak Park, Ross also redesigned Skokie Country Club in Glencoe, on the north side of Chicago. The club was founded in 1897, with the course having evolved from a member-designed 9-hole layout to a full 18-hole layout by Tom Bendelow in 1905 that measured 6,115 yards. Ross was commissioned in 1914 to remodel the course. His extensive renovation work, which debuted the next year, produced the course that hosted the 1922 U.S. Open, won by 20-year-old Gene Sarazen. The Ross version was substantially altered in 1938 by William J. Langford and Theodore J. Moreau. This was necessary because the club gave up a parcel on the north side for real estate development while enjoying a net gain through land acquisition on the southwest side. Of Skokie's current routing, just over half the course—holes 1, 2, 8, 10, 14,15, 17,18 and the last half of No. 7—can be said to be Ross's work. As Skokie presently undergoes an extensive restoration program, the membership and architect Ron Prichard face the

Skokie Country Club, Glencoe, IL, 1922. Skokie was the site of that year's U.S. Open. (Skokie Country Club)

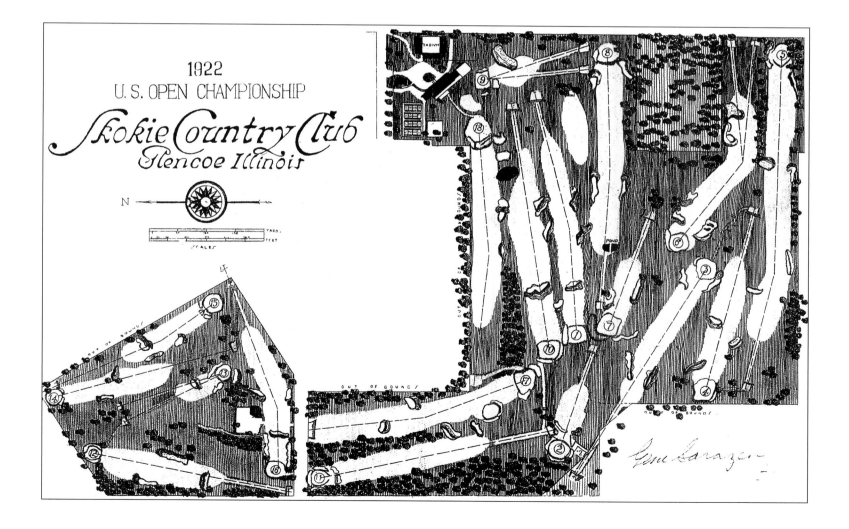

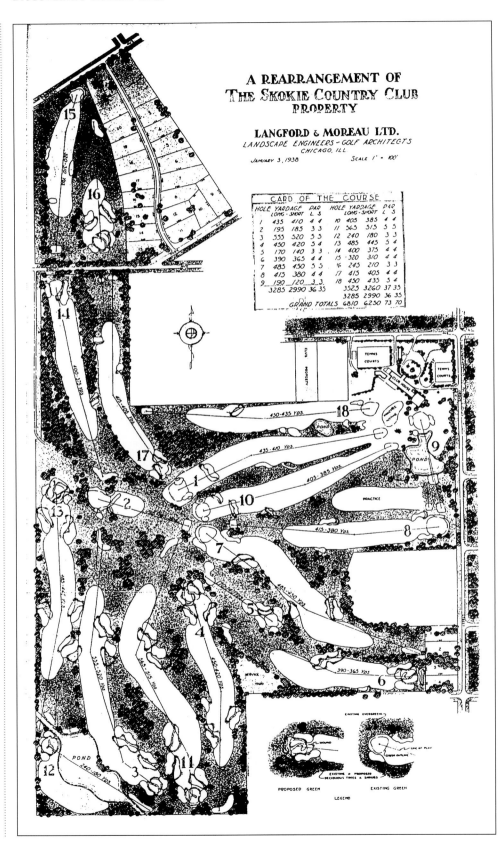

Skokie in 1938, as redesigned by William J. Langford and Theodore J. Moreau. The architects utilized additional land to the south and southwest. (Skokie Country Club)

intriguing issue of two distinct design styles, one overlaid upon the other. In this as in all restoration work, the effort involves a substantial degree of interpretation and creativity in deciding which (hybrid) style to adopt.

In nearby Highland Park, Ross designed Bob O'Link Golf Club in 1916. His 6,348-yard layout featured two returning nines, the outgoing side arrayed on the southeast side of the property and the incoming side set on the northwest half. The fairways were wide enough and so unencumbered by trees that nearly a dozen bunkers served double duty on adjoining holes. This is a far cry from the densely treed layout that exists today. Indeed, little remains of Ross's design work following three separate waves of renovations, the first involving major work by H.S. Colt

Skokie was virtually devoid of trees when the 1922 U.S. Open took place. (Skokie Country Club)

Above: By 1997, Skokie had become a densely planted parkland layout. The view here is to the northeast toward the clubhouse. The club is now undergoing a restoration program, overseen by architect Ron Prichard, and 400 trees have already been removed. (©Tony Roberts)

Opposite page: Bob O'Link Golf Club, Highland Park, IL. Ross's 1916 design was essentially replaced during a 1925 renovation by Harry Colt and Charles Alison. It was common for Ross to build fairway bunkers that served double duty on adjoining holes. (Tufts Archives)

and C.H. Alison in 1925 that kept only a handful of the original Ross's fairway corridors and green sites. The layout was also subjected to an ambitious tree-planting program, largely overseen by superintendent Bob Williams during his reign at Bob O'Link between 1955 and 1976.

In 1918-1919, three miles south of Bob O'Link, Ross designed an 18-hole layout at Northmoor Country Club in the town of Ravinia. His work is well-preserved, not only in a period-piece blueprint of the original design but also in the fact that the club preserved the original holes during a nine-hole expansion in 1965 on land to the southwest that included an area marked off ominously by Ross as "Skokie swamp." Ross's 6,511-yard design was largely arrayed in north-south fashion. Both nines ran out and back from the clubhouse and required a crossing of Clavey Road—in those days a dirt road, but now a busy four-lane highway. Today, the original front nine is split between Northmoor's Red and White nines. The Blue nine has preserved Ross's back nine in excellent form. What his 1919 design plan shows as bunkers are now easily seen in the land as dramatic hollows and scooped-out areas. Many of these intended fore-bunkers in front of tees were likely never filled with sand. A January 2000 tree survey revealed 1,632 hardwoods and evergreens on the grounds—a far cry from the virtually open field that Ross

worked upon. Yet his distinctive landforms are still in evidence. Despite its heavy clay soil base and its lack of much elevation change—only 10 feet in all—Northmoor provides compelling evidence of fascinating ground game features.

There isn't anything low-profile about the land on which Beverly Country Club sits. This Chicago layout 11 miles southwest of the downtown Loop includes the highest point in Cook County (at the second tee), as well as 40 feet of elevation change. For years, it was claimed that Ross designed this layout in 1908—almost five years before any other work of his in the region. But historical research by club archivist Paul L. Richards and others has now shown that this attribution is misleading, and that while the club and golf grounds enjoyed their inception that year, Ross's work almost certainly did not ensue until at least 1919.

The rectangular 157-acre site, a mile long and one-quarter mile across, lay on a north-south axis between 83rd Street and 91st Street, with Western Avenue on the east side and the B&O Railroad tracks on the west. A ridgeline of glacial deposit formed an upslope that traverses the ground and formed a natural basin for what was once known as Lake Chicago. Much of the site consists of well-draining sand—a rarity in Chicago.

Resident golf professional George O'Neil laid out the original course in 1908. He either had the help of Tom Bendelow or Bendelow made some subse-

The 1918-1919 routing plan for Northmoor Country Club in Ravinia, IL. (Northmoor Country Club)

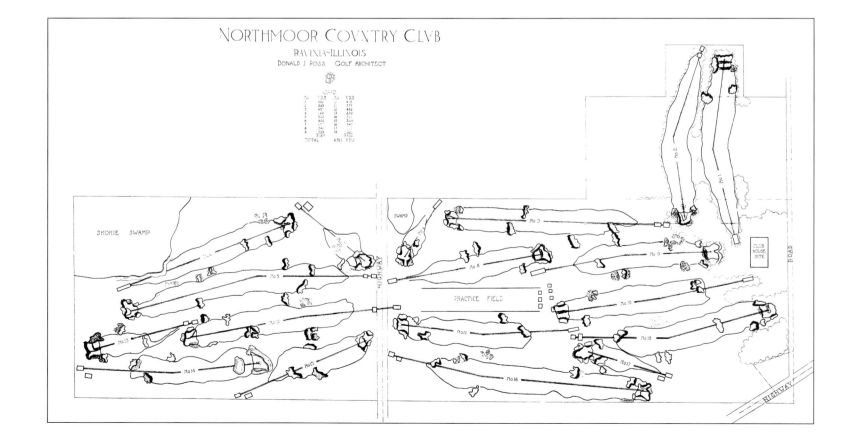

quent suggestions for alterations. There is, perhaps, some outside chance of Ross's involvement at Beverly prior to 1919, but if so, there is no mention in any area golf publications. A clubhouse fire that Beverly suffered in 1917 may have destroyed the chain of evidence pointing to earlier Ross plans or work. In any case, a running record of Beverly's proceedings only begins in January of 1919. Ross's name first appears under the date of March 4, 1919, when mention is made of "contemplated alterations on the links as outlined by Donald Ross." That and subsequent references over the next five years confirm the fact that Ross's involvement came a decade or more after the layout was opened and that the work he did consisted of considerable modification. Moreover, the work was not done all at once; it appears to have been undertaken in at least two stages, with the bulk of it completed by 1922 and some subsequent work in 1924-25.

When Beverly hosted the 1910 Western Open, the course played to 6,050 yards—a length bolstered considerably by a 600-yard third hole and a 565-yard 11th hole. For the 1931 U.S. Amateur, a rendition of the golf course that exists today was in shape and measured 6,702 yards. Unfortunately, there are no drawings or sketches of either the original Beverly layout or of Ross's plans. The only detailed contemporary drawings of Beverly came not from Ross but from Chick Evans in 1931-32.

The Ross version of Beverly played to a par of 71, with five par 3s and four

Not all of the areas at Northmoor that were originally designed for short-carry bunkers were filled with sand, but the swales nonetheless remain in place today. (Bradley S. Klein)

Right: The front nine at Beverly Country Club in Chicago, April 1930. Note the unusually large, pig-eared bunkers. The tiny road at the lower end of the photo— 87th Street—was expanded into a four-lane thoroughfare in 1932. A straight wall of poplar trees lines the right side of the par-5 second hole. (Beverly Country Club)

Opposite page, top left: Beverly Country Club, front nine, October 2000. Trees have grown in dramatically. (Ralph Chermak)

Opposite page, top right: Beverly Country Club, back nine, 1931. The par-4 13th hole, played over a large cross bunker, is at the lower end of the photo. (Beverly Country Club)

Opposite page, bottom: The back nine at Beverly Country Club, October 2000. The cross bunker on the 13th (below) has been removed. (Ralph Chermak)

long, demanding par 5s. The course was extraordinary for its reliance upon length in the par 5s: they averaged 568 yards. The shortest of the par 5s was the 545-yard second hole. Chick Evans's 1932 "topographical plan" of the course shows a feature that is highly unusual for Ross: a string of five pearl bunkers on the left side of the tee shot landing area. It is not clear if Evans was working from Ross's original drawings or whether he was presenting what amounted to a proposed revision. In any case, the bunkers do not appear in either of two aerial photographs taken in the early 1930s. The 568-yard seventh hole demanded an uphill tee shot to the top of that transverse ridge and brought the short hitter within all-too-easy reach off the tee of three traps built into the upslope. The 590-yard 11th hole, only slightly

longer but still in the same place as the one from the O'Neil layout, was legendary in Chicago golf circles for its uphill blind tee shot to a tree-lined fairway that dog-legged left, away from the train line that flanked the right side of the hole.

As with many older, blind holes, the drive on the 11th hole was eventually softened. In 1955-56, the crowned section of the fairway 150-yards off the tee was leveled and the tee raised to make the landing area visible. As much as Ross might have regretted such a move, he would have been far more upset about a very substantial change to Beverly in 1932, when the county extended 87th Street through the very heart of the golf course. An early plan—whether it was O'Neil's or Ross's is not clear—had called for a modest internal driveway along that path to be used by club members and staff. Beverly was already divided evenly, with the front nine on the north side of 87th Street and the back nine (and clubhouse) on the south. The establishment of what became a four-lane road is not something most golf courses can withstand. In Beverly's case, it required relatively minor modifications, primarily a foreshortening of the first tee and ninth green. "Unless absolutely necessary," wrote Ross in *Golf Has Never Failed Me*, "don't for a minute consider a property divided by either a street or a railroad. The very intent of a golf course is to get away from just such things."

Despite the road crossing, Beverly has stood up well. The club's routing has remained intact since the 1920s. Both nines sport a similar formation: each comprises a twin, counterclockwise loop that returns to the clubhouse relatively late in the sequence. On the front nine it's the seventh green, on the back it's the 15th

The 558-yard second hole at Beverly Country Club. The string of five pearl bunkers on the left were part of Chick Evans's 1932 "topographical plan" but were not actually installed until the fall of 1999. (Bradley S. Klein)

green. Only a single two-hole sequence—numbers 11 and 12, the longest and the shortest holes, respectively—is routed in the same direction. Despite an altered green or two and some undue bunker work in the 1980s that softened the definitions of the bunker edges, the club retains its character. Indeed, like many vintage Ross layouts, it has sought to deepen its Ross heritage by an ambitious program of restoration. The string of pearl bunkers on the second hole were installed, some trees have been removed, and a coterie of several highly motivated and ambitious members has helped educate other members about the club's architectural heritage. Recently, designer Ron Prichard has been retained to oversee a master plan that is oriented around restoration. Plans call for recapturing lost hole placements, regaining lost fairway areas through a tree removal program, and rebuilding the bunkers so that they will sport the classic look of low-lying concave bottoms and turfed walls that lead down to the bunker floor.

Perhaps Ross's most idiosyncratic design in the Chicago area was Ravisloe Country Club in Homewood, 20 miles southwest of downtown. The course dates to a 1901 layout by James Foulis Jr. (1896 U.S. Open champion) and his brother Robert. Ravisloe was updated twice—by Aleck Bauer and Robert White, then by Willie Watson—before Ross was brought on board in 1916. Ross's plan took four years to implement and yielded a layout that is virtually intact today in terms of routing, but not in bunkering.

An aerial photograph of Ravisloe from the early 1920s shows a remarkable sprinkling of bunkers throughout the layout, perhaps 200 in all, though not all are

Ravisloe Country Club, Homewood, IL, early 1920s. An extraordinary photo of the multiple bunker styles on this most unusual Ross design. (Ravisloe Country Club)

Ravisloe's first hole, with a flashed-up fairway bunker half hidden in the woods. (Bradley S. Klein)

visible in the photograph. The first hole, a mid-length par 4, has six oval bunkers across the entrance about 15 yards short of the putting surface. There appear to be about 20 bunkers—most of them of the pot variety—on the second hole. The seventh hole (on the left side of the photograph) features a dozen or so long, snaky bunkers down both sides of the fairway. A necklace of half a dozen bunkers circles across the 17th fairway well out of the reach of most drives.

Over the years, Ravisloe, like many Ross courses in the Midwest and Northeast, has become a heavily treed layout with only a few dozen large, circular bunkers. In some cases, the trees overhang or even block the bunkers and there is scant evidence on the ground of the links-style scattershot bunkering that used to characterize the course.

TECHNIQUES IN THE FIELD

Ross's plans for a 1915 reconstruction of the Mount Washington Golf Course in Bretton Woods, NH reveal a number of interesting aspects of his work. The plans, laid out on hole-by-hole drawings depicting 30 ft. x 30 ft. grids, show greens ranging in size from 5,000 sq. ft. up to 8,100 sq. ft., with an average size of 6,345 sq. ft. There appears to be a rough correlation between the overall size of the green and the distance of the hole, with some adjustment made in size for accommodating uphill shots as opposed to downhill shots. Most of the putting surfaces are rectangular in shape. To the extent that there is irregularity in configuration, there is, without exception, a section of 3,600 square feet in the heart of every green.

His par 4s and par 5s are marked with an "X" at the 200-yard mark, indicating what course designers call the "turn point" of the hole. Most of his fairway bunkers are located just short of this point, indicating that Ross anticipated a drive of 175-180 yards in the air to carry his fairway hazards. The 200-yard mark indicated the strategic and visual focal point of his golf holes. From this vantage point Ross would organize how the hole would play and how its various features would present themselves to golfers. He would subsequently adjust this point—as far as 250 yards—depending on terrain and the relationship of the teeing ground to the fairway. But in 1915, it appears that 200 yards would suffice as the measure of an extremely proficient driver of the golf ball.

Ross's plans came with specific construction details, indicated in telegraphic form. "Pits cut in face of slope finish 4' 6" deep." "Build flat irregular undulation, 2 to 3 ft. high rear of green." His putting surface plans, at least at Bretton Woods, offered precious little detail, with nothing more than "Build new green adding three undulations shown. Undulations should be about 18 inches high and at least 20 ft. wide at the base." There was some topographic relief shown, in the form of a cross-sectional vertical profile delineating the change from point A to point B as indicated on the hole-by-hole maps. Sometimes this would simply indicate the horizontal axis across the middle of the green and include surrounding swales and mounds. Or the cross section would indicate the shape of the fill to be piled on for creating a desired mound or bunker face. In this rudimentary but illustrative manner, Ross would provide his era's equivalent of a rough grading plan.

In 1916, Ross explained the routing process in an interview he gave to a Chicago reporter named Paul R. Leach on the occasion of designing Bob O'Link Country Club in Highland Park. "To begin with I walked over the land with sketchbook in hand for two days before ever laying a stake. I could see propositions here and there, but I had to take cognizance of such things as alternating with the wind; taking advantage of the lie of the land for long and short holes, presenting every possibility as I saw them; wasting no ground, making no holes overlap or conflict;

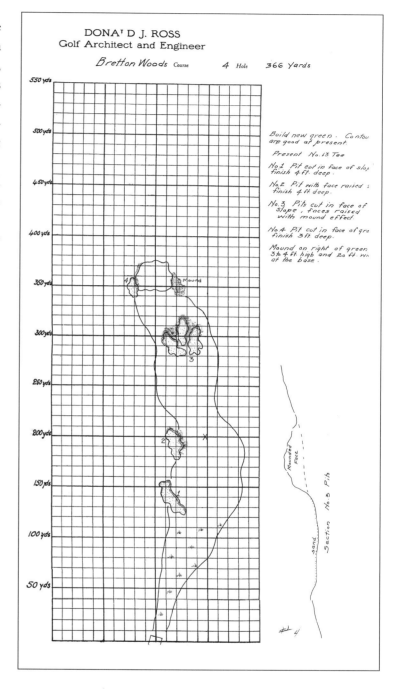

The fourth hole at Bretton Woods GC, Bretton Woods, NH, 1915. (Bretton Woods Golf Club)

staking out my hazards with an eye toward their usefulness not only on one hole but to help for another."

For all of his skill with land, Ross also proved adept in his own way with the press. Not that there was anything disingenuous about his representations. Indeed, he appears to be giving his journalistic audience the one commodity it valued above all else during an interview—quotable material. That this resulted in an almost formulaic praise of the property could only have thrilled a client as well as establish the groundwork for financial success on the part of would-be members. A 1915 trip

1915 layout of Cedar Rapids (IA) Country Club. Ross's routing had the short par-4 eighth hole playing through a defile to an area in proximity to the fourth and fifth greens. (Cedar Rapids Country Club)

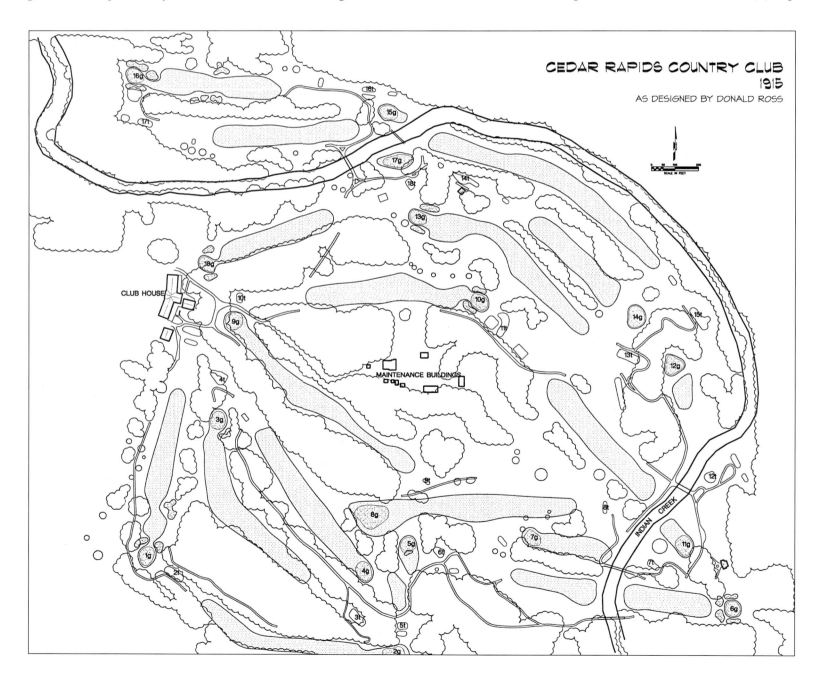

to the Broadmoor Hotel in Colorado Springs was Ross's first extended venture out beyond the immediate Midwest. Along the way, he made fleeting site visits to what would become the Cedar Rapids Country Club in Iowa and Shawnee Country Club in Topeka, Kansas—the only Ross courses to appear in those respective states.

When he arrived in Colorado Springs, Colorado, Ross characteristically pronounced the Rocky Mountain site of the new resort as ideal for spectacular golf. "I am very favorably impressed with the prospect for one of the very best golf courses in the country at Broadmoor. The opportunity there is exceptional. The

Cedar Rapids Country Club, 2000. New seventh and eighth holes and a lengthened ninth were the 1989 work of architect Bob Lohmann, who had earlier added irrigation ponds. (Cedar Rapids Country Club)

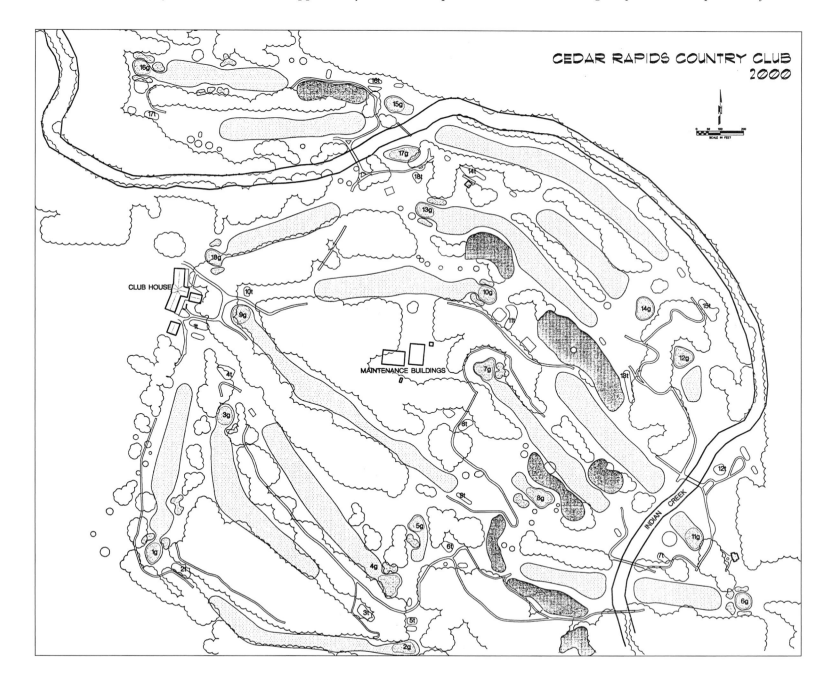

soil is first class and really needs only water to make first class turf." Often he would focus on an aspect of the design that would make good copy because of its inventive, if not ingenious, nature. At the Broadmoor, he announced, all the tees and greens for the course would be visible from the main hotel building.

The list of projects steadily grew. Ross had to do little to solicit new work. Many requests for his services came personally from guests at the Pinehurst Resort. He was riding the wave of the post-World War One construction boom. Not only were new courses opening at prodigious rates, but facilities with nine-hole layouts or a rudimentary 18-holes increasingly turned to Ross and his colleagues who were masters of the newfound craft of golf course architecture.

This was no Sunday afternoon walk with 18 stakes for greens. As Ross wrote in 1919 when preparing for a visit to Banff Springs, Alberta:

My usual method of procedure is to mark with permanent stakes on the property, the location of tees, centre line of fair-greens, size and shape of bunkers and outline of putting-greens. I submit a working plan for each hole, giving approximate depths of bunkers, contours of putting greens, and the outline of fair-greens. The club then furnishes me—free of charge—a surveyors plan of the property on which is indicated the exact centre of each tee and putting-green. From this plan I prepare and submit a general plan showing the complete layout.

Ross did dozens of courses in and around the Great Lakes. He was constantly journeying through Cleveland, Detroit, Chicago, and Minneapolis. Along the way he made fine use of native contours that had been carved up during the glacial period; the uplift of glacial till and the soft layers of topsoil atop them proved ideal landforms for golf.

A classic case in point can be found at Inverness Golf Club in Toledo. The basic charm of the layout derives from the fact that it sits on a lovely piece of rolling terrain. The club's visionary was Sylvanus P. Jermain, known in his day as the father of Toledo's city park system. In 1903, he and a group of prominent townsmen took the trolley line west to the far end of Dorr Street, walked another 300 yards, and settled upon a gently rolling 78-acre site for what they envisioned as a recreational social club. Bernard Nichols designed a nine-hole course on land whose natural contours had been fashioned 12,000 years earlier by a glacier. By 1907, the original 3,098-yard layout was expanded to 18 holes.

Ross arrived in 1918 for a total revamping, including the use of newly acquired land to the south. Actual construction was entrusted to Inverness's own greenkeeper, and the work was completed in time for Inverness to host the 1920 U.S. Open. The genius of the course lay in its routing over and around a ravine and drainage ditch named, appropriately enough, "Inner-Ness." Ross made wonderful use of the resulting 20-foot deep natural swale that looped across the north half of the site. For the most part his fairways crossed these natural dunes perpendicularly, so that tee shots and approaches were played to natural plateau landing areas.

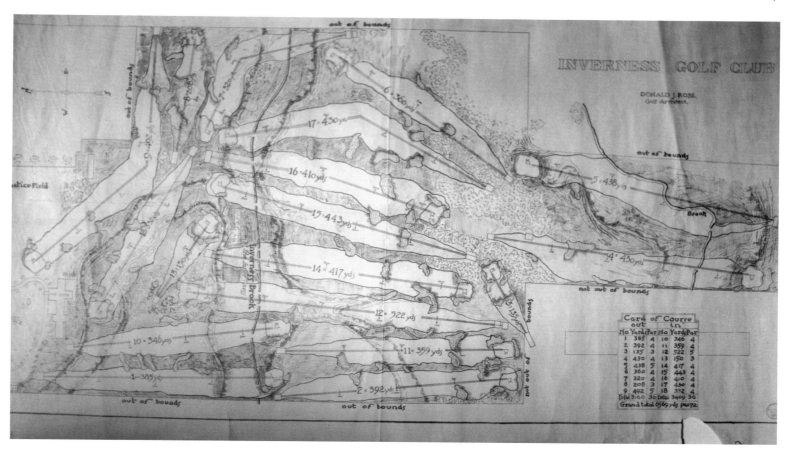

Above: Ross's 1919 routing plan for Inverness Golf Club, Toledo, OH. (Tufts Archives)

Left: Inverness Golf Club, where the long par-4 fifth hole of Ross's original design (now the seventh) master-fully incorporates a brook as a diagonal fairway hazard. (United States Golf Association)

The 18th at Inverness Golf Club. This 354-yard par 4 is one of the shortest finishing holes in championship golf. (Bradley S. Klein)

There was great variety in the 4-pars. The old seventh, at only 320 yards, sharply doglegged left around a stand of American elm trees to a 4,000 sq. ft. green that fell six feet from right to left.

One oddity of Ross's Inverness is that the last five holes are all par 4s. In fact, the 14th through the 17th—each measuring over 400 yards—are lined up like parallel sausage links. Yet each requires completely different shot-making and angles of approach. It was a design style that Ross emulated with equal sophistication at Metacomet, in East Providence RI, a 1921 layout where the last six holes are parallel par 4s. As with Inverness, the holes derive their character from their subtle incorporation of native slopes and the setting of the approach into the greens along a diagonal ridgeline that works its way into either bunkers or other slopes.

At both Inverness and Metacomet, Ross concludes a string of demanding, 400-yard+ par 4s with short par 4s in the 350-yard range. At Inverness, gears suddenly downshift at the 354-yard 18th hole when golfers face a minuscule green set adrift in a sea of bunkers. Wise players will lay back on the tee shot and then try to

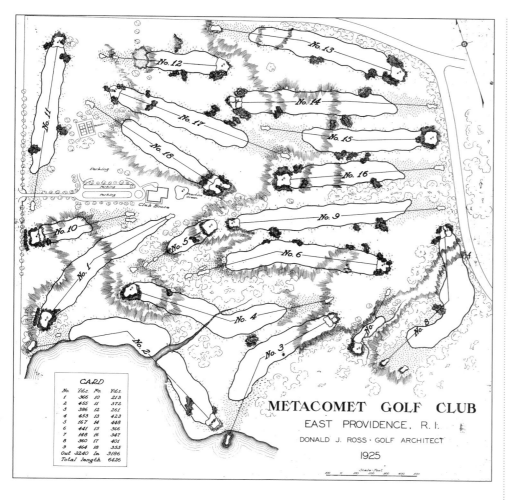

Above: Metacomet Golf Club, East Providence, RI. Ross's efficient routing continually brings golfers back to the clubhouse area. (Ron Prichard)

Left: The 18th at Metacomet Golf Club shows the basic Ross style of a raised fill pad for the green with bunkers built into the base. (Bradley S. Klein)

hit a dart of an approach shot. The slightest deviation leaves a confounding chip. Indeed, the safest miss here just might be the front bunker, as Bob Tway well knows from his famous sand shot in 1986 that won him the PGA Championship.

For the year 1921, Ross completed 33 new courses. In the decade from 1919 through 1928, he created an astonishing number of golf courses—208, or two-thirds of the new courses he would design and build in his entire 45-year career. During that same period, the United States saw the opening of some 1,400 new golf courses, of which fully 15% were Ross layouts. Plus, he was busy with remodeling and course additions. Clients lined up at his door, and many of them paid a premium to jump to the top of a backlog that reached two to three years between inception and completion of a project. It was period of unprecedented creativity in the craft of American golf course architecture—an era that has come to be known as the Golden Age of Golf Course Design. Alister MacKenzie, Charles Blair Macdonald, A.W. Tillinghast and George Thomas Jr. were also at their creative peak, but no one even approached Ross in terms of productivity. His was the most dominant market share of design activity the golf world has ever known. He became, in fact, course design's first brand name. A front-page advertisement in *the Augusta Chronicle* for Sunday, March 7, 1926 made the case in a promotion for Forrest Hills, "the South's most exclusive estate."

"Why Donald Ross. . . Instead of someone else?
The dean and master of all golf architects
It had to be Ross!
When Forrest Hills was conceived—the best, and the best only, was planned.
That is why Donald Ross is building the golf course."

ASSOCIATES

Ross moved about the country alone, armed with his plans, a detailed travel schedule, and a close reliance upon the Western Union for telegraphing his associates.

He was on his own as a designer until 1916, devoting himself to course architecture the year-round while limiting his duties as a golf professional to the Pinehurst Resort from late fall to early spring. Gradually, his design portfolio expanded to the point where, in 1916, he took under his wing a full-time collaborator, J.B. McGovern, worked out of Wynnewood, Pennsylvania, 15 miles northwest of downtown Philadelphia. With his hire, Donald Ross & Associates was born.

To this day, little is known about McGovern. He appears to have been satisfied with working quietly, behind the scenes, assisting his senior colleague on dozens of jobs in the mid-Atlantic, Northeast, and Midwest. McGovern, interestingly enough, along with Ross, was one of the very few course designers to make it through the combined ravages of the Depression and World War II with their careers intact. When the American Society of Golf Course Architects held its first

Opposite page, top: Walter B. Hatch (1884-1960) was Ross's trusted associate on projects in the Northeast between 1916 and 1933. He worked out of North Amherst, MA, and is pictured here in 1910. (David Hosford)

Opposite page, bottom: Walter B. Hatch, ca.1950s. (David Hosford)

annual meeting at Pinehurst in December of 1947, McGovern and Ross were among the 13 charter members.

Two years after McGovern was hired, Walter B. Hatch joined Ross & Associates. Hatch, born in 1884 in Brockton, MA, studied at what was then called Massachusetts Agricultural College (now the University of Massachusetts at Amherst). He graduated from there in 1905 with a major in landscaping and a minor in engineering. He spent just over a decade undertaking a variety of landscape projects throughout southern New England, including the design of several cemeteries. While at work in Providence, RI, he happened to meet up with Donald Ross. "It's not that I had such a great love for the game of golf," Hatch later told an interviewer. "But in 1918 the profession of designing golf courses was in its infancy and I thought it was a great opportunity for me. So I guess it was opportunism rather than the game itself that lured me." Indeed, it certainly wasn't Hatch's love of golf that mattered. He played indifferently and infrequently. What counted was his capacity as a landscape architect who could work with topographic maps in more sophisticated ways than could Ross, who was still relying upon simple two-dimensional plans and draft notes in a notepad he carried with him in the field.

Along the way, Hatch had to develop a certain tactfulness to negotiate the world of golfers—including some wealthy and powerful ones—who thought that playing skill or business success translated into design ability. "Some of those golfers had some rather crazy ideas for designing a course," he said. "The problem was to sympathize with their ideas and at the same time let them know as diplomatically as possible how impractical they were."

Hatch worked full-time for Ross from 1918 until 1933. His base of operations was North Amherst, MA, from which he maintained a furious travel schedule that saw him engaged in 28 states, the Canadian provinces of Ontario, New Brunswick and Nova Scotia, and the island republic of Cuba. It remains unclear to what extent he was a salaried employee of Donald J. Ross & Associates and to what extent he was paid independently on a consulting basis. In the early 1920s his fee was $75 per day, half of what Ross charged. For laying out a complete 18 holes, Hatch charged $1,500. Ross's fee was $2,000. For all of the business and income generated during the decade, there obviously was not much left by the time the Depression hit. In a 1930 note to the home office in Pinehurst, Hatch wrote of some much-needed sketches. "I hope you will be able to send these soon as I can not send them a bill until they have the plans and I am BROKE. Let me know when they are sent."

Hatch's association with Ross ended in 1933, when the Depression knocked the bottom out of the golf market. Hatch retired from the design trade, then spent four years working for the U.S. Department of Interior as supervisor of two Civilian Conservation Corps encampments in the Boston area. In 1937, he settled down in North Amherst and took a job in the town water department. From 1950 to 1954, he was the town's tax collector. Between 1933 and his death in 1960, his involvement with golf was limited to the design of two rudimentary nine-hole layouts, one in town and the other a few miles north in Greenfield.

It is often said about Ross that at the peak of design operation in the 1920s, he presided over perhaps the country's largest landscape contract operation, with upwards of 3,000 men employed on his jobs. There is a modicum of truth here, although it must be clarified that such an army was by no means on his payroll. The fact is, Ross ran an extremely lean operation, with never more than handful of employees on his own payroll. Most of the work, especially the labor-intensive construction, was farmed out to independent contractors, who themselves did the hiring and handled wages. The key as far as Ross was concerned was centralizing control through his field staff, to which end Hatch performed admirably as he went from site to site. His responsibilities included scouting out potential sites, preliminary surveys and routings, walking and staking center lines, overseeing construction, grassing and growing-in, and working with established courses to tweak them—or rebuild them—as needed.

It was an enormous responsibility, especially because Ross was spending so much time in Pinehurst on the business side of his design operation that he had to delegate most day-to-day work to his associates.

Among the most important hires Ross ever made was Walter Irving Johnson Jr., a licensed professional engineer who joined the design operation in the fall of 1920. Ross himself was not much of a sketch artist. His early drawings of courses were functional and two-dimensional, capturing perhaps the rough outline of the image or hole he sought, but unskilled in the representational qualities of perspective and three-dimensionality required to create sound working drafts. It was Johnson who poured over the sketch work. He also added two skills that had heretofore evaded Ross's capacity, and which, in retrospect, limited his design work.

For one thing, Johnson could work with engineering plans such as blueprints and cross-sectional topographical analysis in ways that gave a more precise view to the holes under construction. Many of the telling drawings depicting elevation changes and vertical crosssection set upon graph paper that are now part of the Ross archives emanated from Johnson's drawing board. Ross could interpret topographic maps and work with them in the field, but not until Johnson came along could Ross translate his holes onto such detailed engineering-scale plans.

Moreover, Johnson could express himself in artistic perspective that showed bunker depth, green slopes, and surface contours. The drawings of seven different Ross bunker styles (see p. 239), for example, were Johnson's handiwork. The elegant yet economical lines of his drawing conveyed in basic terms the kind of holes that a shaper or contractor could strive for, and it allowed Ross more control over his final product.

Johnson was born in Medford, MA, graduated from high school in Oak Park, IL in 1913, and earned a degree in civil engineering from Rensselaer Polytechnic Institute in Troy, NY in 1917. He spent World War I flying in England

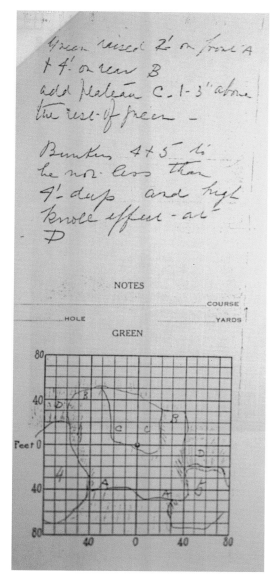

From field notes to finished plans; two stages in the evolution of the fifth green at Oyster Harbors Country Club in Osterville, MA, 1927. Ross's rough field notes (above) and the more refined version (left) as completed by Walter Irving Johnson. (Stephen Kay)

and France with the Army Signal Corps. After hiring on with Ross in October of 1920, he lived in Newton Centre, MA, within walking distance of the design office (and Ross's home) at 1032 Centre Street.

Wherever Ross took up residence—in Newton Centre, later in Little Compton, RI, or each winter in Pinehurst—Johnson was near at hand, in some cases sharing residences or living in an adjoining building to facilitate their work. It was Johnson who would pour over his drafting board, crafting his three different sets of plans: a 1 inch = 100 feet scale of the entire course, two-dimensional overhead ("footprint") views of each hole and each green and surrounds, plus cross-sectional analyses of vertical transitions of the hole from tee-to-green, as well as the putting surface and surrounding bunkers. In many cases, John prepared five full sets of such plans per project: one for Ross's files, and the others intended for the course owner, the contractor, the course superintendent, and the club itself.

Not surprisingly, the reliance upon Johnson for technical drawings corresponds to a broadening of Ross's architectural vision—from the highly improvised field work of blind holes, abrupt mounding, and circuitous paths around rock ledge and stone, to a more broadly flowing, strategic approach in which his bunker pattern got more deliberate rather than scattershot and penal. He used fewer bunkers and he placed them more carefully where well-struck golf balls were likely to land.

There were, to be sure, other factors in the transition—better construction budgets and the advent of mechanical construction devices, the steam shovel among them. But with Johnson on board, the planning process because qualitatively more sophisticated and efficient. Ross's volume of output rose accordingly.

Johnson's singular solo effort during his years with Ross was on a new nine holes for Potowohmut Country Club in East Greenwhich, RI. Otherwise, he stayed by his mentor's side—literally—though the last few years appear to have been under part-time employment because design work had all but disappeared. By 1934, Johnson had taken a full-time job as an engineer with the City of Boston. It was there, from 1933 through 1938, that he undertook his last and most impressive work under Ross's name: George Wright Golf Course. It was a vast public project carried out with the help of federal Works Public Administration labor and capital. During World War II, Johnson became chief engineer at Quonset Naval Air Station in Rhode Island, and after the war dabbled in course architecture on a very limited local basis. Upon his death on April 20, 1973, he left behind scant documentary evidence of a life partly lived at the center of the country's most prolific golf design business.

Eric Nelson was the longtime personal secretary to Donald Ross who succeeded him in 1946 as club manager at Pinehurst Country Club. Born in 1899 in Quincy, MA, he had contracted rheumatic fever in his youth and had been sent down by his family to Pinehurst in 1913 in hopes that the curative air would heal him. He thrived that first season, returned the next year, and soon landed a job in town as assistant bookkeeper at the Berkshire Hotel. Despite never having had more than a grammar school education, he was bright enough to learn accounting. In his late teens he took his newfound skills down the street to the Pine Crest Inn. When Ross took over the next year as co-owner of the Inn, he was so impressed with Nelson's managerial abilities that he brought him over to the Country Club. Nelson served there as secretary-treasurer to the club, as well as secretary for Donald Ross and Associates, Golf Course Architects. From roughly late April to late October each season, Nelson would also preside in New England—first in Newton Centre, then for a while in North Attleboro before Ross moved his summer office to Little Compton, RI in 1925—as manager of day-to-day operations of the design shop. He handled all inquiries, managed debits and credits, and made it possible for Donald Ross to leave matters behind while on his constant train junkets in the field. He was a master of the train schedule, and constantly juggled frantic telegrams advising him of last minute modifications. "Plans were subject to change without notice" was the operative slogan. What held true for the

design crew held true for the Ross family as well when it came to travel plans: "If you have a problem, call Eric."

Always properly dressed, often sporting a bow tie, the bespectacled, thin-haired Nelson was respected by all who worked with him. He was also a keen golfer, and despite—or perhaps because of—his constant presence at the club, was so well regarded among the Tin Whistles that they elected him as club captain for a term. He was an especially steadying influence on Ross, both in the golf shop operations at Pinehurst and upstairs over the shop in the architecture office.

Nelson was responsible for running day-to-day affairs at the club, including dealing with members and guests as well as making tournament arrangements. He kept the shop stocked with equipment, negotiated with suppliers, and maintained a furious stream of correspondence with resort officers, town officials, and clients throughout the country. In an era when telephones were a well-established presence in businesses and homes, there was still a strong residual tradition of committing matters to paper. Often a trifle issue would involve half a dozen letters back and forth. Nelson, aided by a personal typist, seems to have maintained a two-day turnaround on almost every piece of mail crossing his desk. Though never involved in drafting or drawing any course design plans, his name appeared on thousands of written documents that passed through the office. While many hundreds of these letters can be found in files at the Tufts Archives in Pinehurst, a far

Ross and his Pinehurst associates, ca.1931. Front row, left to right: John Capello, Eric Nelson, Bert Nicoll, Ross, Frank Maples, William Wilson, Alexander Innes, Aneas Ross, (Mitchell?). Back row, left to right: Ellis Maples, James McNab, Joe Capello, Roy Bromson, Tom Naile, Clarence Lyman, Donald Currie, George McLeod, William Agnew, Jack Williams, Ted Turner, True Chaney, John Fitzgerald. (Tufts Archives)

Frank Maples (1886-1949), longtime director of grounds and maintenance at Pinehurst and Ross's construction supervisor, was a pioneer in turfgrass and fertilizer experimentation. (Tufts Archives)

greater number of them were destroyed. Upon Ross's death in 1948, Eric Nelson himself burned the great bulk of letters and financial records. In doing so, he was following instructions of Ross's attorney, Shorty Carr.

Upon Ross's retirement from active management of the Pinehurst Country Club in 1946, Nelson was appointed his successor. He served in that post until 1960. Later, he proved influential in creating the town's Given Memorial Library. In 1975, he was given a testimonial dinner and made a lifetime member of the Tin Whistles. It was not, however, an honor he was able to enjoy for long. After returning home from the fete, he went to sleep and died during the night.

While McGovern and Hatch did much of Ross's work in the Northeast, Midwest, and mid-Atlantic regions, it was left to a longtime Pinehurst employee named Frank Maples to oversee work at the resort and throughout North Carolina. Born October 12, 1886 in Pine Bluff, NC, the heavy-set Maples called upon the Pinehurst Resort in 1902 in search of work. He was hired onto the maintenance crew and eventually became director of grounds and maintenance, where he stayed until his death on November 8, 1949.

His cramped, nervous handwriting suggests someone ill at ease with the world of letters. But put him on a golf course and Maples became a wizard of warm-season turfgrass cultivation and course construction technique. Given the constant meddling of Leonard Tufts into every imaginable detail of maintenance, Maples was required to maintain a voluminous correspondence. He was subject to a succession of hectoring, obsessively detailed letters from Leonard Tufts regarding every dime spent, each loose mower blade, and each spare minute that a crew member might have spent wandering about rather than working. Interestingly, the correspondence between Ross and Maples is far more limited—suggesting that they didn't need to document their working relationship and could get along just fine by word of mouth and during their frequent walks about the grounds. Perhaps it helped that Frank Maples was not a Ross employee. His salary was drawn from the Pinehurst Resort and from a number of other local properties that hired him seasonally, or for particular jobs. Such was the ease and mutuality of the relationship between Ross and Frank Maples that when it comes to Pinehurst No. 2, Ross's acknowledged masterwork and the course to which he devoted himself more than any other, there exists not a single drawing or plan of the holes as they evolved. It was all improvised in the field, with Frank Maples at Ross's side.

How valuable is a course superintendent? It took some time for the Tufts family to appreciate Maples enough to hire him full-time, year-round. As late as 1924 he was only on board part-time, with the resort paying him $125 per month plus half the purchase price of a car. At the same time, Maples was also tending to Southern Pines Country Club for $50 per month. Somehow, he also found the time to build tennis courts in Aberdeen and Southern Pines, and to tend to residential yards, among them Ross's, for which he was paid additionally on a piecemeal basis. A May 1924 letter by Pinehurst Inc. official G.M. Cameron to Leonard Tufts suggesting an effort to secure Frank Maples's services full-time for the resort came with a cautionary observation:

> *I do not know just how would be the best way to trade with him, as you remember last year I spoke to you about the amount of work he was doing outside of Pinehurst, and at the time it was your feeling that if we tried to close down on him too tight that Mr. Ross, appreciating his worth in directing the building of golf courses, might hire him to go elsewhere to work for him, but I am sure that we should have some arrangement with him whereby he would spend all of his time here from the time we close the golf courses until all of the new work and repairs are done to the courses.*
>
> *I will try to find out from Southern Pines just what arrangements they have with him without his knowing about it and I think we would then be in a better position to know just what salary it would take to get him all of the time.*

Soon enough, Maples's pay was raised—to about $250 per month. Also, for the first time, he was put on a commission that paid him five percent of the Country Club's annual profits—an additional $500 on top of his salary. By 1929 he was making $325 per month, plus another $1,000-$1,500 annually. It made him, as Richard Tufts noted in a letter to Donald Ross, "one of the highest paid men in our employ." By 1942, Frank Maples's salary of $1,000 plus $500 per month and an additional $3,852.42 in commissions made him the resort's second-highest paid employee. Only Ross received more. Maples actually made more than Richard or Leonard Tufts.

Frank's compensation was only fair, because he was responsible for keeping the Pinehurst layouts in good shape. The native sandy soil proved ideal for drainage but less than suitable for establishing reliable turf, especially bermudagrass that would withstand the close cropping appropriate for greens. The greens had to be amended with a 4-inch layer of loam to provide a suitable growing culture. Turf establishment was complicated because the bulk of the golf season was in the winter months, when common Bermuda would go dormant. Numerous experimental turf plots were established near Maples's maintenance area and around the clubhouse, with tests run on samples of redtop, Italian rye, Kentucky bluegrass, Canadian bluegrass, and timothy. As mentioned earlier Ross reported that the best growing medium for winter grass appropriate to greens was on the front lawn of the Holly Inn. Not even resort guests were spared the sight of frequent agronomic tinkering.

Maples was constantly fashioning fertilizer recipes, usually at the behest of Leonard Tufts, who was himself not shy about requesting advice from experts all over the country. Lime was often used to get the (otherwise) naturally alkaline soil up to a pH level of around 7. A standard organic fertilizer compound would include 10 parts cotton seed meal, 10 parts fish scrap, and 1 part muriate of potash, to be applied three times a year—except during the early Depression years, when cutbacks were necessitated at all the Pinehurst properties. Among the organic by-products that found their way onto experimental plots and into sheds for curing prior to application were horn and hoof, Peruvian bird guano, dried blood, cow manure, sewage sludge, and decomposed tobacco stems. All that was missing was eye of newt. Maples, like any good superintendent in those days, was not averse to tinkering. Among his fertilizer compounds was an inorganic mix that included 40% (by weight) sulfate of ammonia, 38% phosphoric acid, and 22% sand. Tests were often made on the golf courses themselves, with one side of a fairway subjected to one fertilizer and another side treated differently, with the results subsequently monitored.

Ross, trained as a greenkeeper, maintained a keen interest in these experiments. His field notes and construction plans contain detailed instructions on turfgrass cultivation and fertilization. He also kept abreast of efforts to organize superintendents nationally. Though he did not attend the first meeting of the National Association of Greenkeepers of America (a forerunner of today's Golf Course Superintendents Association of America) at Sylvania Country Club, Toledo, Ohio, on September 13, 1926, he did send that group's founding father, Colonel John Morley, an encouraging letter a month later. Ross had worked with Morley while

Opposite page: October 17, 1926 letter from Ross to Colonel John Morley on the founding of the National Association of Greenkeepers of America. (Tufts Archives)

Below: Sprigging bermudagrass, ca.1930. (Tufts Archives)

DONALD J. ROSS
GOLF COURSE ARCHITECTURE AND CONSTRUCTION
LITTLE COMPTON, RHODE ISLAND

ASSOCIATES
WALTER B. HATCH
N. AMHERST, MASS.
J. B. McGOVERN
WYNNEWOOD, PA

October 17, 1926.

Mr. John Morley,
Youngstown Country Club,
Youngstown, Ohio.

Dear John:-

I have read most carefully the prospectus you have drawn
up of the National Association of Greenkeepers of America. It would
be a splendid thing for golf in general if such an Association could be
organized on the lines you suggest. As I have said before and I again
repeat that the greenkeepers as a whole are a very intelligent and honest
class of men.

The wonderfull developments of golf in this Country is
largely due to their unselfish efforts and hard work in improving the
golf courses and making it possible for players to enjoy the game to the
fullest extent. I congratulate you on your work as a greenkeeper of
outstanding ability and with leaders of your type an Association would
unquestionably be a great success, not only from the standpoint of the
members but also from the Clubs who employ them.

With my cordial regards.

Yours very truly,

Donald J Ross.

Reel greens mowers, ca.1937, Pinehurst. (Tufts Archives)

doing design work at the Youngstown (OH) Country Club in 1921, where Morley was greenkeeper. "It would be a splendid thing for golf in general if such an Association could be organized on the lines you suggest," wrote Ross.

By the end of Maples's tenure at Pinehurst, the resort settled upon a regimen of bermudagrass fairways, tees, and greens, with fairways and greens overseeded with rye in the fall. One ton of organic fertilizer was applied per acre annually, and the greens were maintained at one-fourth of an inch. The greens were regularly top-dressed, and over the years there may well have resulted a bit of "doming" whereby Ross's original contours were altered by the buildup of sand. This would have raised the greens marginally at least a few inches, perhaps as much as a foot, and exaggerated somewhat their convex shape. How much of this happened, to what extent, and when it occurred, however, are all matters of speculation that can never be documented owing to a lack of detailed drawings, blueprints, and images of the original greens when they were grassed (on No. 2) in 1935.

Maples was to leave a considerable greenkeeping legacy. His first son, Ellis Maples (1909-1984), trained in both course construction and maintenance and became a prominent designer in his own right after World War II. A second son,

Fairway gang mower, ca.1935. (Tufts Archives)

Henson (1917-1980), followed in his father's footsteps as director of grounds and maintenance at Pinehurst (1940-1970). A grand nephew, Palmer Maples Jr. (b. 1932), was prominent enough as a superintendent that he became president of the Golf Course Superintendents Association of America in 1975. Three of Frank's grandsons became superintendents: Joe Maples (b. 1929), Gene Maples (b. 1945) and Wayne Maples (b. 1948). Another grandson, Dan Frank Maples (b. 1947), went into course design, served a term as president of the ASGCA, and maintains an active practice today out of his office behind the old theater building in the middle of Pinehurst's town center.

Alex Ross, six years Donald's junior, contributed to the family golf lore primarily as a player and club professional. He had come over from Scotland in 1900 and worked with his brother as a teaching professional. His victory in the 1907 U.S. Open at the Philadelphia Cricket Club confirmed his already solid reputation as a competitor, and when Donald Ross began working a 36-hole project at Detroit Golf Club in 1916, Alex was recruited as head professional, a post he held for 29 years.

The next of the Ross brothers, Aeneas, born in 1882, was a bit of a loner in the world. He served as construction foreman on several of his brother's jobs, most

prominently Salem Country Club in Peabody, MA in 1925. When his niece, Lillian Ross, Donald's only daughter, took a trip to Scotland in 1932, Aeneas accompanied her. But he never returned, and he spent the last 25 years of his life virtually penniless and something of a sad figure in Dornoch. Donald helped support him, and even held accounts and securities in his name, which were on occasion needed to settle debts accrued by Aeneas. He did no golf course work in Scotland, however, and appears to have eked out a pittance of a living as a casual farm laborer until his death in 1957.

After World War II, Donald Ross worked on a number of courses with William F. Gordon (1893-1973). One of the lesser-known members of the Philadelphia School of Design, Gordon had been a course construction superintendent for Carter's Tested Seed Company before joining the design firm of Howard S. Toomey and William F. Flynn in 1923. After a wartime stint seeding airport fields for purposes of camouflage, Gordon emerged as an independent course contractor with sufficient stature to be included (along with Ross) among the 13 charter members of the American Society of Golf Course Architects in 1947. Only then did he begin his professional collaboration as a builder of several Ross-designed courses, including Alamance Country Club, Burlington, NC, in 1946. After Ross's death in April of 1948, Gordon served as construction contractor for a number of J.B. McGovern's courses. The two evidently built up a close relationship, and upon McGovern's death in February of 1951, his widow invited Gordon to go through McGovern's papers and memorabilia. Among the salvaged documents was Ross's unpublished manuscript, *Golf Has Never Failed Me*. William F. Gordon's son, David F. Gordon, (b. 1922), a course builder and designer of his own who partnered with his father after 1953, finally was able to arrange for publication of the book in 1996. A century after leaving Dornoch, the last of the master builder's works was finally in place.

Maples family. Angus Patrick Maples (just right of center in photo) built and maintained Mid Pines and Pine Needles. He is shown with his family in 1937 on the third tee at Pine Needles. His grandson, Palmer Maples Jr. (front left) went on to serve as president of the Golf Course Superintendents Association of America in 1975. From left to right: Palmer Maples Jr., Alma Maples Morrison, Gilbert Maples, Donald Morrison, Newsom Maples, Angus Patrick Maples, Nancy Lee Maples, John Maples, Jean Maples Ripper, Elsie Lee Patria Maples, John Morrison. (Tufts Archives)

Chapter Five
On the Road

*A*n 8 mm film from 1928 that was converted to video shows Donald Ross on site during construction of Aronimink Golf Course in Newton Square, PA, a suburb on Philadelphia's west side. Unfortunately, the architect appears for only about 15 seconds out of the entire four-minute film. The site of the course is rough, with many large trees, considerable rocks and the occasional old farm building or shed. Some motorized equipment can be seen: a steam shovel, tractors, small trucks—including a dump truck—but no bulldozers or earth scrapers. It appears that most of the feature work is being done by horse-drawn pans. A tractor pulls a wheel harrow, but the seed spreaders are hand-pushed. A large hardwood, some 85 feet tall and about three feet in diameter at the base, is taken down in two laborious steps: first by an axe-wielder who hews an incision; then by a long cross saw handled by two men. Bridges with concrete footers are laid over streams. A main irrigation pipe some 6-8 inches in diameter is placed in the ground. Laborers, with their shirtsleeves rolled up, are knee-deep in water constructing a main drainage line with cone-shaped tile fitted one into the other. There is nothing easy or natural about the process of preparing such land, least of all upon such a rugged site. Yet the contours being shaped have not been created by massive cuts and fills. Beyond the clearing and removal work, the work is more like massaging or fine-tuning what is already there. The site is rolling; at times steep. Eventually it will make for stellar golf ground, but only after extensive work.

Midway into the film, Ross appears on screen. He is making a site visit, and appears in a three-piece suit with a carnation or handkerchief in his left coat pocket. He wears a modest tam. He is the man in charge and walks about with confidence, at one point with his thumbs on the inside of his sweater vest and his hands turned outward. As he confers with a group of construction supervisors, Ross holds a notebook in his left hand and a lit pipe in his right. All around him equipment is swirling and laborers are hard at work. At one point, a single-engine airplane (brand name "The Monocoupe") can be seen rolling away with a man in the back seat. It might well be Ross, about to survey his design of Aronimink from the vantage point of the air. Perhaps the man who traveled the country only by train occasionally relied upon the airplane to keep track of the routing and clearing.

TRAVELING MAN

His schedule was a whirlwind of train rides, dinners with prospective investors and—most importantly of all—site visits. Typical was an itinerary of 1920, as noted in Ross's own diary:

Sept.   11-17: Kenosha, Wisconsin, Elks Club
         Saturday: Great Northern Hotel, Chicago
         18-19: Muskegon, Mich., arrived 6:45 Sunday via Pere Marquette
         19-22: Bloomfield Hills, Mich.
         23: Brookside CC, Canton, Ohio

Often his travels would occupy him for a month, such as his schedule for October 1924:

Oct.   1: Belmont CC, Belmont, Mass.
         2: Oakhill CC, Fitchburg, Mass.
         3: home in Newton Centre, Mass.
         4-5: c/o Mr. E.E. Carley at The Biltmore Hotel, New York City
         6: with Lillian at Emma Willard School, Troy, N.Y.
         7-11: Seneca Hotel, while working on Oak Hill CC, Rochester, N.Y.
         12-13: traveling
         14-18: New Bern CC, New Bern, N.C.
         18-19: traveling
         20-21: "reaching home, unless advised to the contrary"

Telegrams flew back and forth to Pinehurst and to his family. From Washington DC he sent his daughter a telegram: "Birthday greetings and much love. May see you Monday. Home tonight. Daddy." If he did return to Troy to visit his daughter, it was in the midst of another trip because Ross arrived at Pinehurst on November 1 to begin another golf season.

From the comforts of a stately downtown hotel like the 14-story Hotel Tuller in Detroit, he would often find time in the evening to pen a letter on house stationery. The only quiet moments came during train trips, when Ross would put down his newspaper or magazine—he was not much for reading books—and stare out the window at the fleeting landscape.

Once in town for a site visit, he would do his customary walk-through of the land, meet with the owner and the construction team, and grant a brief interview with a local newspaper reporter (apparently starry-eyed, too, if one is to judge by the prose that came out a day or week later). The banner story would likely draw the interest of yet another aspiring golfer looking for a club to join.

"Famed Golf Course Architect Finishes Laying out the Links For Oconomowoc Country Club," blared the *Milwaukee Journal* on Nov. 20, 1915.

> *The greens are of good size, all are natural except four, which had to be partly made. Provision is made for moving the teeing ground for each hole forward if conditions demand. Three-fourths of the bunkers have been designed so that these will be completed before the course, which has been plowed, is sowed to grass. In this way they will have the appearance of being natural formations instead of artificial, an ideal toward which Mr. Ross always strives.*
>
> *No 'Cop' Bunkers.*
> *There are no 'cop' bunkers and no 'chocolate drops,' these being considered out of date. Not a foot of tile will be necessary for the drainage of the ground. The soil is a clay, which will have to be built up to a greater fertility to obtain the best results. A large bed of peat will be used to build up the putting greens. A large area of sandy loam will also be utilized.*
>
> *The construction work will be carried on with strict reference to the contours of the course, so that the effect will be that of improved landscape design. Later, landscape decorations of trees will be added. The work will be pushed forward this fall as long as the weather permits, and will be taken up again early next spring. It is intended to have the course open for playing in 1917.*
>
> *Mr. Ross has not forgotten winter sports. He has discovered that the knolls at the first and tenth holes will make wonderful toboggans. For skating, provision will be made to keep the ice clear on adjacent lakes.*

Opposite page: Dear Irving :

Arrange to send in hurry 2 sets of Blue Prints—as I don't knew yet who is to be the foreman there. Communicate with Frank, as to when to send and to whom. Foreman ought to have 2 sets. General plans will be along soon.

Have settled Fords and Rackhams jobs. So we have started with Smith + Matthews already here. Also Mae & Walles.

I leave in the morning (Sat. 8:50 — a.m.) for Duluth. Arr: there 8 a.m. Sunday.

All well, & as busy as possible. Regards to Mrs. J and yourself.

Yours DJR (Tufts Archives)

Right: Telegram, November 16, 1928, 10:06 p.m. The job to build a golf course for the University of Michigan eventually went to Alister MacKenzie. (Tufts Archives)

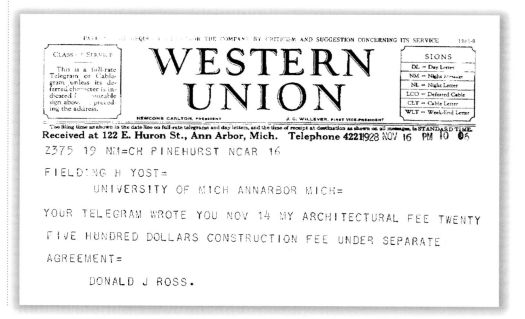

ABSOLUTELY FIREPROOF

ADDRESS ALL BUSINESS COMMUNICATIONS TO HOTEL TULLER

HOTEL TULLER

European Plan

COR. PARK, ADAMS AND BAGLEY AVES.

TULLER HOTEL CO.
O. C. FROMAN
MANAGER

DETROIT MICH

Dear Irving:

Arrange to send
Mr. Henry. 2 sets of Blue
Prints. as I dont know just
who is to be foreman there.
communicate with Mac, as
to where to send and to whom.
foreman ought to have 2 sets.
General Plan will be along
soon —

Have settled Fords & Rackhams
Jobs. so we have started them.
Smith & Matthews already here.
also Mac & Waller.

I leave in the morning (Sat.
8.50 A.m.) for Duluth. am.
there 8 A.m. Sunday.

all well, & as busy as
possible. Regards to Mrs. J and
Yourself from D.R.

OAK HILL

Opposite page: Oak Hill Country Club's East Course, Pittsford, NY, 1924. The 13th hole, a 574-yard par 5, was bisected by a pond in the fairway landing area. The two-tiered putting surface was fitted into a natural slope by cutting 3 feet from the back of the green, raising the front 2 feet, and creating a cross slope 1.5 feet high. "Green must form a saucer shape from all sides so as to fit the present surroundings," Ross noted. (Tufts Archives)

Below: Oak Hill, East Course, 13th hole, following renovations by Robert Trent Jones Sr. in 1955. He removed Ross' fairway bunkering and took out the cross slope in the green. (Bradley S. Klein)

Ross came to Rochester in May of 1922 to address the membership of the 21-year old Oak Hill Country Club, then considering a move from its cramped, in-town setting on the Genesee River to a 355-acre tract in the southeast suburb of Pittsford. He told the club he was struck by the rolling terrain and by the possibilities of the stream, Allen's Creek, which meandered through the east side of the lightly treed site. Ross presented his plan the next year for two fine layouts. The East Course measured 6,538 yards; the West Course came in at 6,503 yards. Construction and grow-in took two years and cost $167,000. Ross (actually Hatch) commandeered 165 laborers, including 54 horse-drawn teams, as well as six tractors and two steam shovels. According to club records, some 200,000 cubic yards of dirt were moved. Drainage required installation of 16 miles of tile, while irrigation entailed five miles of cast iron piping. Two modest ponds were created on the East Course, one of them fronting the par-3 11th hole and another, rather unusually for Ross, was placed smack in the middle of the fairway of a par 5—the 574-yard 13th.

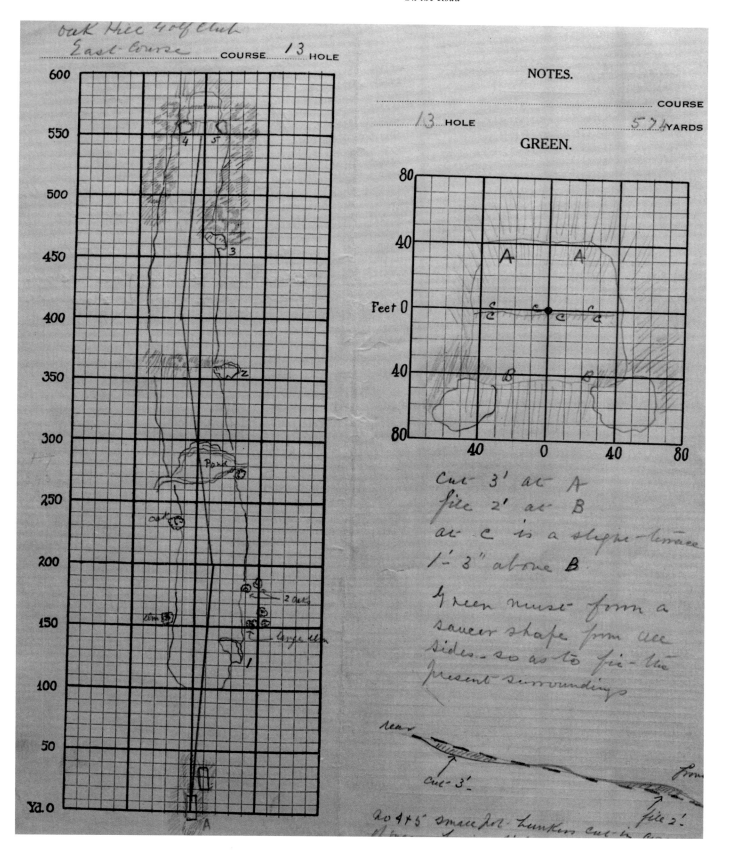

NOTES.

COURSE

13 HOLE *574* YARDS

GREEN.

Cut 3' at A
fill 2' at B
at C is a slight terrace
1'-3" above B.

Green must form a
saucer shape from all
sides — so as to fit the
present surroundings

Ross' instructions were to "remove soil below depth of present creek and form a pond 33 yards wide from 267-300 yards" from the back tee.

BERESFORD (PENINSULA)

In the summer of 1922, Ross undertook an uncharacteristic journey out West where he worked on only one course. Beresford Country Club, subsequently named Peninsula Golf & Country Club, in San Mateo, California, was just south of San Francisco. It would turn out to be his sole layout west of the Rocky Mountains.

Ross first spent three days in Los Angeles. Perhaps there was a bit of "wanderlust" because he arrived without any formal appointments or rounds scheduled and seemed simply intent on touring the town and seeing the area's golf courses. Ross later reported feeling putoff by the hotel staff that proved unable to orient him toward a golf game anywhere. Not a good sign, he thought, for the golfing tourist. Eventually, he got his bearings, largely because of renewed acquaintance with an old Scottish friend, Charlie Orr, who had helped design Wilshire Country Club. In addition to visiting Wilshire, Ross saw Annandale, Los Angeles Country Club, Pasadena, and Rancho Golf Club. He then headed up the coast and arrived at the Beresford course on Monday, July 24, 1922 for what would be two full weeks. Toward the end of his West Coast swing, Ross was also expected to tour the Del Monte area in the company of friend and fellow architect Robert Hunter, though it is not clear this tour ever materialized..

At the time, Ross was so backlogged with work that there was a two- to three-year gap between his signing on to a project and the actual commencement of work. How, then, did Beresford entice Ross to make the long trek out West? Money might well have been a factor. An account in the *San Francisco Chronicle* ("Donald Ross, Famous Golf Architect, Has Arrived at Beresford Club") reported Ross's fee as $4,000 for two weeks of on-site consulting, plus all travel expenses. The amount was impressive, even for Ross, whose standard per project fee was $2,000. The prospects of a windfall for what amounted to a working vacation must have been tempting indeed. The schedule was not overwhelming, not by Ross's standards, whose regular workweek on the road consisted of serial visits, one day per city, along a stretch of several hundred miles. This time, Ross could take one of his beloved train trips and simply relax for days at a stretch. Ross was now a widower, after all (Janet had died of breast cancer in February), and the idea of spending a month out West away from Pinehurst and Newton Centre and the empty bedroom must have been a welcome prospect. Interestingly, enough, a newspaper dispatch from September 1, 1923 ("Beresford To Open New Golf Links on Sunday") claims that Ross's fee might well have been even more substantial. The club is said to have "offered" Ross the astounding fee of $500 per day for 21 days of work— $10,500 in all, plus all expenses. This report, which has become the basis of

Opposite page: Ross's plan for Beresford Country Club, San Mateo, CA, 1922 (now called Peninsula Golf & Country Club). The nines were subsequently reversed. (Peninsula Golf & Country Club)

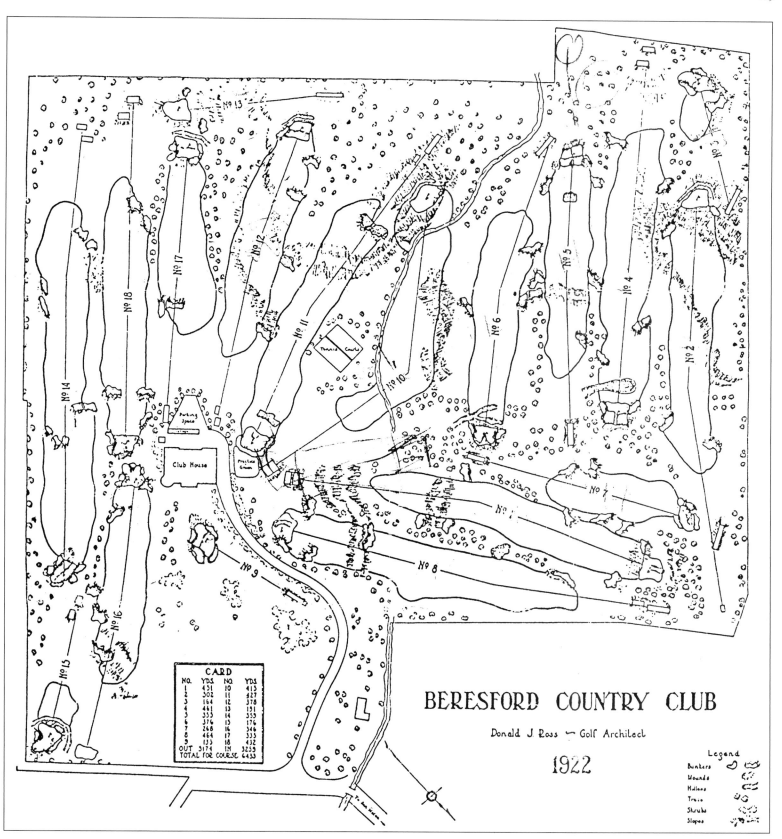

CARD

NO.	YDS	NO	YDS
1	431	10	415
2	502	11	527
3	164	12	378
4	441	13	151
5	533	14	553
6	376	15	176
7	266	16	346
8	464	17	335
9	133	18	432
OUT 3174		IN 3255	
TOTAL FOR COURSE 6433			

BERESFORD COUNTRY CLUB

Donald J. Ross — Golf Architect

1922

Legend

Bunkers
Mounds
Hollows
Trees
Shrubs
Slopes

club lore and is repeated as fact to this day, can be questioned on several accounts, not the least being the ambiguous nature of an "offer." Official club records are inconclusive, though the club's (otherwise) excellent history claims Ross visited in 1923, when in fact he was there a year earlier. The truth is that Ross was being paid for his time and for a design plan, but not for any actual construction work, which did not proceed on the grounds until the following year. It is difficult, therefore, to accept the accuracy of the higher fee given the limited nature of Ross's work there in 1922.

Beresford was the Bay Area's Jewish club, a country club founded in 1911 by a class of golfers (and their families) who were denied access to established facilities in town. Club president Walter W. Stettheimer, with whom Ross stayed during his work at Beresford, had arranged for Ross's services. The club had recently acquired a 40-acre parcel for expansion and wanted to rebuild its golf course.

Ross's 1922 sketch shows a compact, 6,433-yard, par-73 golf course with two returning nine-hole loops. The order of the nines was later reversed, but Ross's original design is unique among his layouts for having started with back-to-back par 5s. Walks between greens and tees were very short, and the overall layout was so intimate in its configuration over the 95-acre site that five greens were laid out immediately around the clubhouse.

Construction work was begun in the spring of 1923 and undertaken by longtime club manager Ed Lyden. Somehow, he managed to negotiate the creation of the new golf course on land that overlapped with the old course, all without a significant disruption of play. The new course was basically ready by September of 1923, but owing to the normally wet winter season, club officials decided to delay final opening until the spring of 1924. The heavy clay soil proved less than ideal because it drained poorly.

Opposite page, top: Beresford's long par-4 11th in 1925. It's now the second hole. (Peninsula Golf & Country Club)

Opposite page, bottom: Honoring Donald Ross: A plaque at Peninsula G & CC. (Bradley S. Klein)

Below: Beresford, 1933. This aerial shows the old 14th green at bottom, with the 16th green above it and the short par-3 ninth to the right of the clubhouse. (Peninsula Golf & Country Club)

Beresford's greens were planted with a new strain of creeping bentgrass. To ensure a steady supply of water during the summer, Ross and Lyden designed two large on-site reservoirs capable of storing 300,000 gallons.

Sparse stands of Canary Island pines, live oaks, eucalyptus, and redwoods dotted the Ross layout, enough to create a sense of separation without infringing upon lanes of play. Three holes at Beresford quickly became favorites of area golfers. The seventh (now the 17th) was a short par 4, originally only 268 yards, that funneled through a tightly bunkered fairway to a green even more snugly protected by sand. The short, par-3 ninth hole, a mere 133 yards, was especially dramatic because its tiered, closely guarded green sat

directly under the rear windows of the clubhouse. And Beresford's 10th, a sharp dogleg left of 415 yards, offered a diagonal green set on a hillside above a stream bed. Subseequently, these holes have all undergone change. The 17th has been lengthened and its bunkering has lost much of its early, harrowing character. The short ninth was taken out of circulation in the mid-1950s to make room for a new club entrance road and parking lot. And the old 10th—eventually becoming the first—was altered dramatically by Robert Trent Jones Sr. in 1964 when he reduced the dogleg and lowered the green.

DONALD J ROSS
MASTER ARCHITECT
THE PENINSULA GOLF & COUNTRY CLUB

Named "Golf Course Architect of the Century" by his peers, Donald Ross was responsible for the original design and redesign of over 400 golf courses in his life time. His work also includes Pinehurst #2, Seminole, Inverness and Oakhill. The Peninsula Golf & Country Club, founded in 1911 as the Beresford Club, remains the only Donald Ross designed course (1922) on the West Coast of the United States.

Above: Peninsula's second hole today, a 424-yard par 4. (Bradley S. Klein)

Opposite page: Par-4 eighth hole at Charles River Country Club, Newton Centre, MA. (Arthur Cicconi)

Charles River and The Country Club

Ross didn't have to travel far to fulfill some of his assignments. Some of his lasting works were created right in his own backyard, among them Charles River Country Club in Newton Centre, which Ross did in 1921. The course occupies three separate parcels divided by road crossings. The front nine has a more open, meadowy feel, but the back nine winds through some rough, rocky terrain. The par-3 14th hole incorporates a ravine where players walk across a 100-yard long wooden bridge to get from tee to green. Ross, who lived only three miles away on Beacon Street at the time, enrolled as a charter member and retained his affiliation for the rest of his life. It was the only American club membership that he paid for himself.

That same year, Ross completed plans for a second 18-hole layout at The Country Club in Brookline, MA. The drawing, dated October 25, relies upon five-foot topographic contour lines and is presented on a scale of 1 in. = 300 ft. The proposed new layout would have been located to the northeast of the existing 18-hole course, the one where Francis Ouimet had won his 1913 U.S. Open title and which exists intact today as the members' regular tract. Ross's plan would have called for a change only in the existing 15th hole, which was to have been shortened and

moved to the right nearer to the clubhouse. This shift would have enabled the new course to start and end by the front part of the existing 15th fairway, just short of the entrance road. For better or worse, Ross's plans were shelved. When the design team of Howard C. Toomey and William S. Flynn added nine holes to The Country Club in 1927 while renovating its full 18-holes, none of the new holes resembled what Ross had sketched out.

BIRMINGHAM

With the demands mounting on his time, it might be a year or more between some of Ross's field visits to far-flung sites. Consider Ross's work at the Country Club of Birmingham, in Alabama. In 1922, the club was considering a move from its downtown Lakeview site to a 284-parcel site in the Shades Valley section of town just south of Red Mountain. Ross had been invited to visit by club president Dr. A. Buckner Harris and ended up spending 10 days, accompanied by McGovern,

Opposite page: Ross's 1921 plans for a second course at The Country Club in Brookline, MA. The design, never implemented, would have required shortening the original 15th to make room for the new course to the north. (The Country Club)

Below: Birmingham (AL) Country Club routing, 1923. Ross's plan for the 36-hole facility is a classic fan-shaped sequence, with seven greens arrayed adjacent to the clubhouse. (Birmingham Country Club)

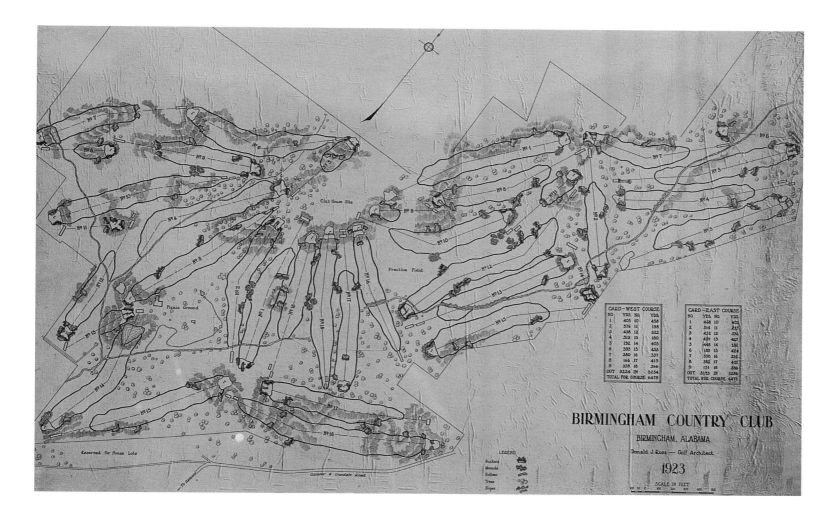

walking the site and laying out golf holes. His visit culminated in a special meeting on Saturday, December 9 at which Ross spoke. A lengthy account of the meeting was carried in the next days' *Birmingham News*. Zipp Newman's article was headlined "Country Club's new golf course can be made into one of America's finest, says D. Ross."

I have laid out two course measuring between 6,400 and 6,500 yards to be known as the East and West Course [sic]. The East Course is laid out in two loops of nine holes, while the West Course is a circuit of 18 holes. Each course is an entirely different type. The East Course is laid out on fairly flat land, but not so flat as to be monotonous. There are water and other type of hazards. The putting greens will be located in hollows and on hills, so there will be plenty of diversity, requiring the use of every club in the bag. If work is started in January the course will be ready for play in June, 1924.

He was impressed with the site's potential and thought its clay loam soil easily workable. For all the basic virtues of the East Course, Ross went on to suggest that his proposed West Course would sit on more interesting terrain and provide a sterner test. His version of the routing, however, was not quite borne out in the splendid linen drawing McGovern subsequently prepared and that now hangs in the clubhouse lobby. The map, dated 1923, shows two sets of returning nines. The routing is ingenious because the land, laid out in a broad butterfly with the clubhouse atop the center, is only about 500 yards deep, yet Ross managed not only to get all four nines to return to the clubhouse but fitted in a total of seven greens around it, five of them immediately visible below the veranda that looks over the grounds.

Ross's construction schedule proved optimistic. Construction on the East Course did not start until 1924, so the 6,479-yard, par-72 layout didn't officially open until the 1926 golf season. The West Course, only one yard shorter but playing to par 71, was another two years in the making. Its more rolling terrain and broader slopes over far more ground made for a more demanding test. If the chief hazard of the East Course was a stream, Watkins Branch, slithering through six holes, the West Course derived its solidity from bolder slopes and steeper features. Ross, by the way, made two follow-up visits to Birmingham in 1928: the first on February 17, the second came during an ambitious two-week swing in late-September/early October that saw him visit Cleveland, Detroit, Chicago, Indianapolis, Birmingham, and Atlanta. By then, however, his attention was no longer exclusively on the Country Club's 36 holes. A breakaway faction of the membership proved so determined to have its way with a Southern Colonial style clubhouse design that when the majority settled on English Tudor, they left the club to form their own—the Mountain Brook Club—a little farther to the south. They also achieved their plans, both in terms of clubhouse design and in the form of a Donald Ross golf course. It opened in 1929.

WINCHESTER

Dating Ross's work is not always an easy matter. Consider Winchester Country Club, 12 miles northwest of downtown Boston. One hundred twenty acres are in the town of Winchester and 50 acres are in the town of Arlington. A number of sources, including the influential *The Architects of Golf* by Geoffrey S. Cornish and Ronald E. Whitten, as well as the Ross Society's own data book, mistakenly attribute the design to Ross in 1903, which, however, would make it Ross's first independent design outside of Oakley or Pinehurst. In fact Ross was not hired until 1916, at which time he was asked to renovate and expand a nine-hole layout that Scotsman Alex Findlay had completed in 1902. There were many delays, and Ross's comprehensive plan for a new 18-hole layout was not completed until 1925.

It was a very difficult site, and the later date of Ross's work there is suggested in his contour work, which incorporated native swales and slopes but did not offer the craggy, heavily-mounded look seen on so much of his earlier work. The chief problem at Winchester was engineering a suitable routing for a parcel of land that sloped well over 130 feet from west to east. Ross's innovation was to terrace the holes so that they ran parallel to one another along the same contour line. The holes are thus arrayed along a northwest-southeast axis, and while there's plenty of movement to the fairways, they nonetheless have the overall appearance of being slotted into the side of a steep slope. Like any good architect would have, Ross saved the par 3s for the steepest or most constricted terrain. He also was not afraid to shift rhythms rather abruptly in order to make the holes worthy. A back nine stretch of par 3, par 5, par 5, par 3 is followed by an unusual finish of 4, 4, 4, 4, with each hole longer than its predecessor. So powerful was the resulting crescendo that the Massachusetts Golf Association later selected them as the toughest finishing holes in New England.

Winchester's terracing effect is most dramatic on the 13th hole, a par 5 of some 500 yards that features a highly unusual bunker complex in the middle of the fairway and within reach of the tee. Ross used it to divide two distinct fairways, an upper one to the right and a lower one to the left. The bunkers provide such an unmistakable aiming point that golfers often fail to notice that the upper fairway to the right is 30 feet above the lower. So conspicuous are the bunkers that their left sides—in a manner that Pete Dye would not have found unusual—look like they're suspended above the lower fairway. The effect is strategically brilliant: strong players fly the bunker with a draw and thus can scoot the ball down the upper slope with hopes of getting on the green in two; higher handicappers will opt for the safer low road, which in any case offers no chance of getting the second shot home. Should a player really launch a drive down this easier path, the ball will kick far left and get stuck behind mounds and trees.

Interestingly enough, Ross returned to Winchester in the midst of the Depression in 1935 to tweak a few holes. Among the adjustments was to fill in a

swamp that had to be carried on the tee shot at the short par-4 fifth hole. Ross simply used a bulldozer to push dirt down the hill from the left side of the seventh hole. Along the way he created a gracefully arced little par 4, and he was able to do so because in those days there were no environmental regulations prohibiting such matters. In fact, there was no such thing as a "wetland." It was just a swamp, and treated accordingly—as a nuisance. No wonder Ross was able to create such wonderful routings; there was no one standing behind him saying, "You can't do that." Today's architects work under very different conditions, and if their designs call for annoying forced carries across water hazards it is often less because they love such obstacles than because they are prohibited from filling in wetlands. An earlier day had its design virtues, although the unfortunate result in terms of ecology was that many valuable habitats were sacrificed in the process.

SALEM

Few of Ross's courses have held up as well as Salem Country Club in Peabody, MA. It represents his design vision and detail in an extremely mature way, enough so that the layout—which hosted the 1932 U.S. Women's Amateur, the 1954 and 1984 U.S. Women's Open, and will host the 2001 U.S. Senior Open—is virtually unchanged from the one designed and built in 1925.

  The land was not easy to work. Hardwoods covered much of the site, and while some of it was open pastureland, there were rocks everywhere. Donald's younger brother Aeneas served as construction foreman and presided over a 300-man crew, 40 teams of horses and 10 tons of dynamite. According to club historian Gary Larrabee, lumberjacks from Maine cut down 1,000 cords of wood. Some of the rocks were used to create foundations for the clubhouse and to undergird the parking lot. Rock was also incorporated into the base (subgrade) of tees and bunkers, thereby providing both elevation and subsurface drainage. The course was outfitted with a full irrigation system. Five months after construction began, the water was turned on and the turfgrass grew. Salem's course construction committee was so impressed with Aeneas's efforts that it honored him with a gold wristwatch and an invitation "to visit us often and play on the course."

  Ross's routing of the par-72 course (6,619 yards from the back tees) relies upon two returning nines, each arrayed in a counterclockwise loop. Somewhat unusual for him, the nines do not occupy contiguous ground; instead they cross over in the middle. The bunkering is restrained; only 54 in all, and many of them are suggestive of the line of play rather than intruding upon a likely landing area. The holes make lovely use of the natural slopes, and each green seems to present a different set of challenges in terms of angle and contour. They are anything but domed surfaces. Ross was mindful enough of basic drainage that he knew not to tip his greens simply from back to front because that would leave the approach areas

Opposite page: Par-3 ninth hole at Winchester (MA) Country Club. (Arthur Cicconi)

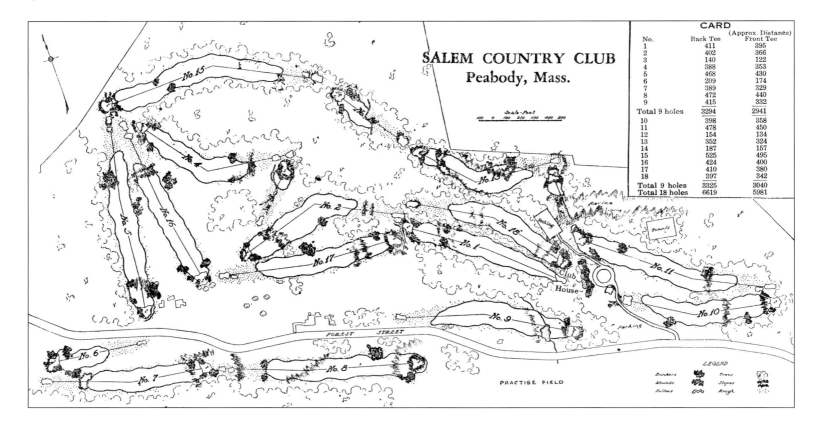

No.	CARD Back Tee	(Approx. Distance) Front Tee
1	411	395
2	402	366
3	140	122
4	388	353
5	468	430
6	209	174
7	389	329
8	472	440
9	415	332
Total 9 holes	3294	2941
10	398	358
11	478	450
12	154	134
13	352	324
14	187	157
15	525	495
16	424	400
17	410	380
18	397	342
Total 9 holes	3325	3040
Total 18 holes	6619	5981

SALEM COUNTRY CLUB
Peabody, Mass.

Above: 1925 routing plan for Salem Country Club, Peabody, MA. (Salem Country Club)

Right: Salem's 352-yard par-4 13th hole. (United States Golf Association)

Opposite page: Salem's 13th hole today. (Arthur Cicconi)

wet. Instead, he created out-slopes to the sides and rear so that each green has distinct if not severe contours that continually create compelling interest in the shot.

The effect is nowhere more dramatic than at the famous par-4 13th hole, a 352-yard uphill hole that remains as challenging and frustrating today as it must have been when it debuted three-quarters of a century ago. A huge bunker on the right sets the tone; it isn't in play, but it forces the golfer to select an angle to the crumpled, S-curve fairway that avoids the second fairway hazard. The green is perched up, with the rise exaggerated thanks to a pair of bunkers well short of the green that enhances one's sense of the elevation change.

PINE NEEDLES

Ross's involvement with the Tufts family in the North Carolina Sandhills area did not end with the Pinehurst Resort. Even with four courses in operation at the resort by 1921, there was interest in further development. Consequently, the family acquired an extensive parcel four miles to the east, in Southern Pines. The land, straddling Midland Road, was more heavily wooded than the original Pinehurst site and required extensive tree removal for course construction. Ultimately, two adjoining courses were created: Mid Pines Golf in 1921, and Pine Needles Golf Club in 1928. Both were designed by Ross and in each case the construction coordinator and greenkeeper was Angus Patrick Maples (1882-1958), Frank's older brother by four years.

Mid Pines was part of an extensive new golf resort that offered more modest (and affordable) accommodations than Pinehurst. The front nine was built on low-lying land that included significant wet areas—wetlands by today's standards, though in Ross's day they were just bogs to be filled or culverted. Many of the green surfaces are located on natural rises, and there is a certain vertical abruptness to their appearance.

Across the street, Pine Needles, built seven years later, has a more elegant flow. The land was drier, and more expansive. The feature shaping showed greater flow and integration with existing ground features. Was this an example of Ross's acquired sophistication, or the result of more refined earthmoving and shaping tools that allowed for more ambitious construction?

Extensive documentary photography from Pine Needles verifies that making features look natural requires tremendous skill and hand labor.

Construction at Pine Needles. (Tufts Archives)

Left: Blasting at Pine Needles, 1927. (Tufts Archives)

Below: A tractor-driven plow hoeing fairways. (Tufts Archives)

Right: Scraping out bunkers at Pine Needles and else-where in the 1920s required careful coordination among laborers and horses. (Tufts Archives)

Below: Feature shaping. Note the finish work on the fairways – with a wooden board. (Tufts Archives)

Opposite page, top: Hand sprigging the rough grasses. (Tufts Archives)

Opposite page, lower left: The Pine Needles Lodge in 1928. Later on it was a hospital and a monastery. (Tufts Archives)

Opposite page, lower right: Working the bunkers. (Tufts Archives)

The 13th at Pine Needles, a 189-yard par 3. (Bradley S. Klein)

HOLSTON HILLS

One of Ross's best-preserved designs can be found at Holston Hills Country Club in Knoxville, Tennessee, a layout he did in 1926. He had been to Knoxville in 1910 to do original design work on Cherokee Country Club and returned to the area in 1924 when he ventured 40 miles to the northeast to the town of Bean Station. There, in the middle of the 2,800-acre Tate Springs Resort, he converted a 9-hole layout into an 18-hole course that opened two years later. But the resort, replete with mineral spas, a 150-room Victorian hotel, and one of the largest swimming pools in the state, suffered financially. The hotel did not survive the Depression and was demolished in 1936. The creation of Cherokee Lake by the Tennessee Valley Authority flooded part of the land in 1942. The golf course was then split in half by a new roadway, Route 11W and eventually fell into disuse.

Holston Hills, by marked contrast, has flourished. Designed and built by Ross in 1926, it has reached as high as No. 37 on *Golfweek* magazine's list of "America's Best Classical Courses." The property, on the far east side of Knoxville, is straddled by the Holston River and is arrayed in a broad, fan-shaped formation,

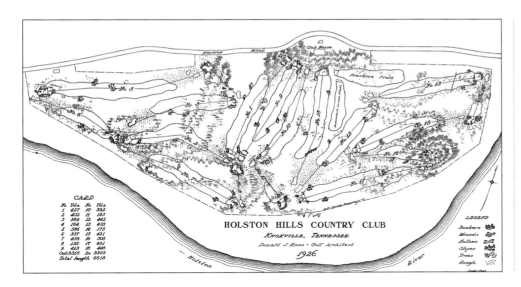

Left: 1926 routing plan for Holston Hills Country Club, Knoxville TN. (Holston Hills Country Club)

Below: Aerial of Holston Hills, ca.1935, looking east across the lightly treed grounds. The par-5 7th hole is at right center. (Holston Hills Country Club)

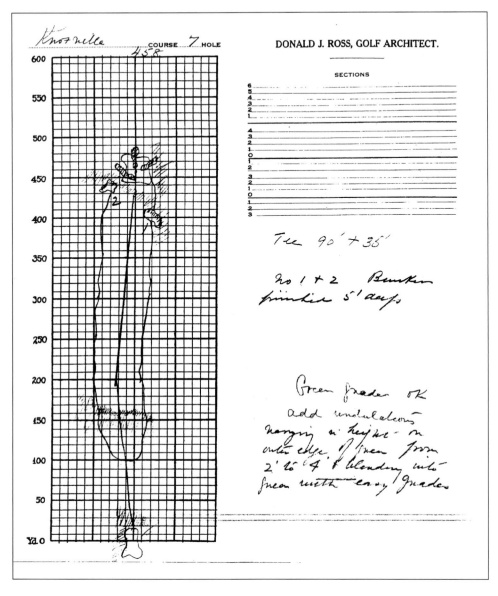

The seventh at Holston Hills was originally sketched by Ross as a straightforward 458-yard par 5 with no fairway bunkers or other hazards to deal with on the tee shot. (Holston Hills Country Club)

with both nines returning to the clubhouse that sits on an upslope along the long, north side of the property. With the first, ninth, 10th, and 18th holes all unfolding in parallel formation on a north-south axis from the clubhouse, Ross made it clear in his notes to his associate, Walter Irving Johnson, that there be adequate safety margins. "Between the 200 yds mark on 1 & 9 there should be 80 yds. I moved the centre line of each a little bit." The precaution was all the more important on what was essentially a treeless, site. Greens averaged 80 feet by 80 feet. A detailed map of the entire grounds shows a par-72 course measuring 6,618 yards and includes room for both a practice field and an "instructor's lesson field." The routing is notable for its efficient use of the 140-acre parcel. Yet within three years room had been found (based on evidence from a 1929 scorecard) for an additional 300 yards, so that the course played from 6,301 to 6,993 yards and without any out-of-bounds.

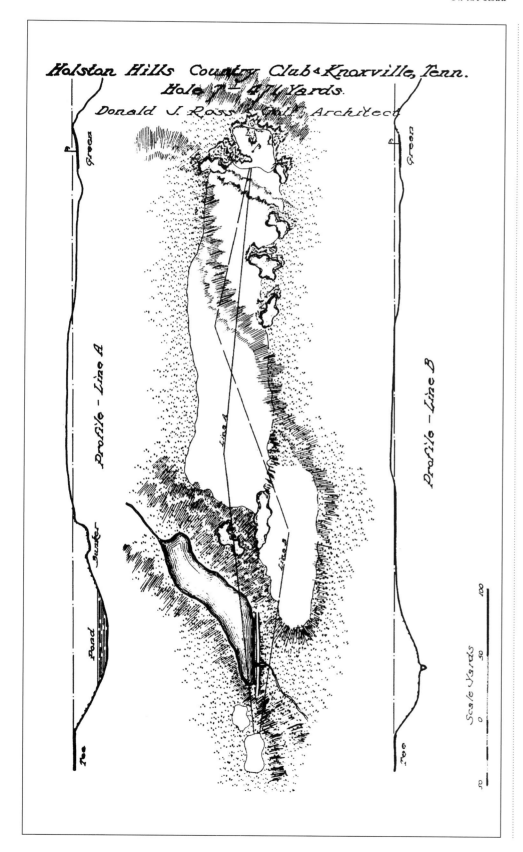

Holston's seventh upon completion in 1928, as depicted in W.I. Johnson's as-built sketch. The 471-yard par 5 offered optional tee shot routes divided by bunkers. There is also a much more demanding second shot than originally conceived. (Holston Hills Country Club)

WATERBURY

Few sites ever caused Ross more trouble than the Country Club of Waterbury in Western Connecticut. The site was tight, rocky and, on the upper part, boggy. Construction began in May of 1927 to replace an existing layout. The new course, after considerable modification of the ground, opened on September 15, 1928. The construction superintendent was Charles Baskin, who would stay on as head green-keeper for 34 years. Ross managed to make the 6,329-yard, par-69 course play longer than its length indicated by locating back tees in such a way as to bring the upslopes of fairways into play on many landing areas. Construction, as Ross noted in a handwritten message to Walter Irving Johnson, was a nightmare. "Irving: Enclosed you will find the holes on Waterbury C Club. Where no holes are given the present holes are to be used—the topo plan shows shape of greens & location of bunkers. It's a hell to build—rock & more rock—big fills and cuts—and most new holes through dense rocky woods—it's about a 100 thousand dollar job."

Country Club of Waterbury (CT). The par-69 course had only one par 5, the 451-yard ninth. Ross's 1926 plan included very few fairway bunkers. (Tufts Archives)

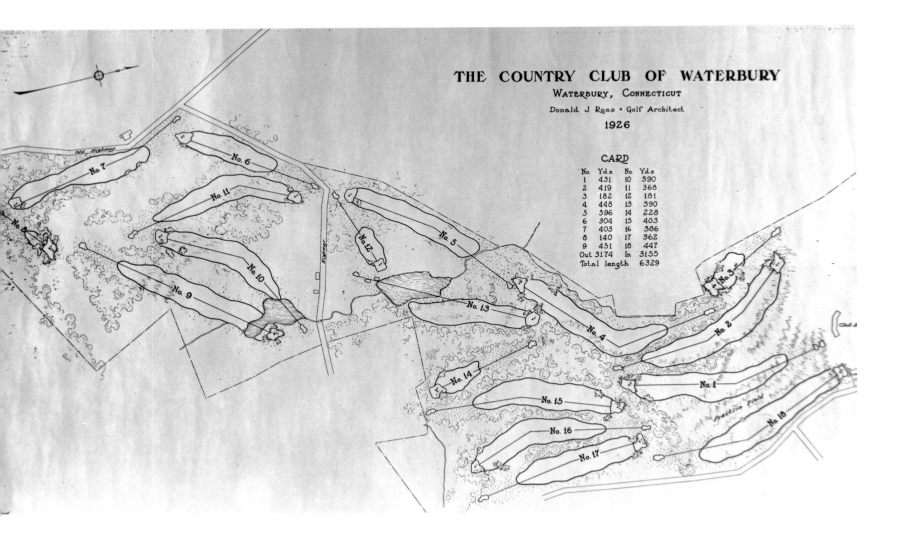

THE COUNTRY CLUB OF WATERBURY

WATERBURY, CONNECTICUT

Donald J. Ross • Golf Architect

1926

CARD

No.	Yds.	No.	Yds.
1	431	10	390
2	419	11	368
3	182	12	181
4	448	13	390
5	396	14	228
6	304	15	403
7	403	16	386
8	140	17	362
9	451	18	447
Out 3174		In	3155
Total length	6329		

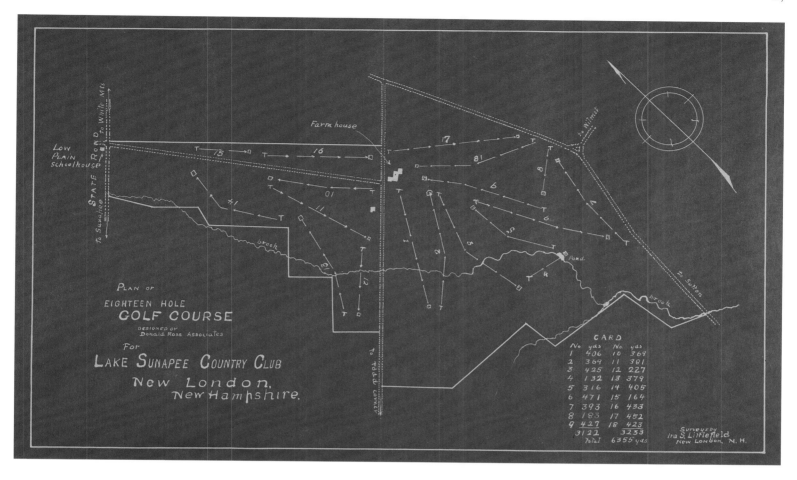

LAKE SUNAPEE

Ross's 1927 surveyor's sketch of Lake Sunapee Country Club, New London, NH. (Lake Sunapee Country Club)

Lake Sunapee Country Club in New London, NH, is one of Ross's least appreciated layouts. The private club sits on a 213.5-acre parcel in the center of the state. The par-71 layout, originally 6,355 yards, sits at 1,125 feet above sea level on a south slope facing Mt. Kearsarge. The location protected the grounds from the north wind and allowed for relatively good growing conditions and fine playing conditions well into foliage season. Ross spent several days in the area in 1927 to select the land from among seven proposed sites. The front nine was built in two months and opened July 3, 1928. The second nine was finished later that year and opened in June of 1929. Jerome Lewis of Plainville, CT served as construction foreman. His biggest headache was drainage; eight carloads of drain tile had to be brought in at a cost of $89,000.

When the course opened, the whole state only had 59 courses, and 46 of them were nine-holers. The setting, layout, and maintenance—the early budget for greenkeeping alone was $15,000 annually—immediately made the course a favorite in the state. Much of the tone of the place was established by Henry J. Homan, Lake

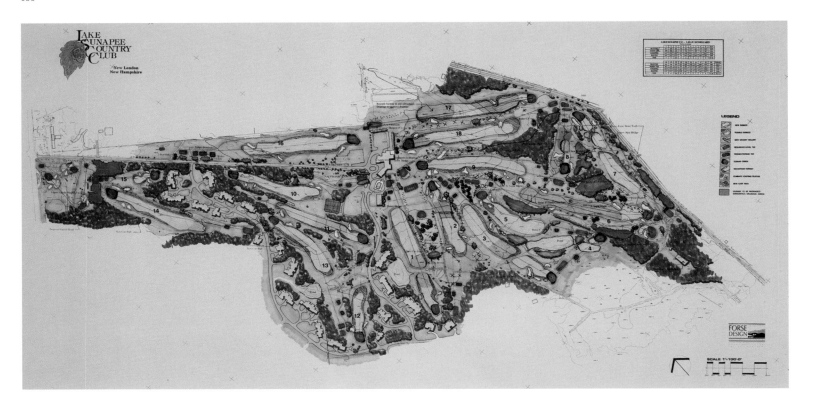

Lake Sunapee restoration plan under architect Ron Forse, 2000. The plan calls for extensive tree removal, reconstruction of all bunkers, recapturing lost green surface, and bringing back native roughs. Notice how the short carry bunkers in the fairways (holes 2, 8-11, 16-18) are being kept in place. (Lake Sunapee Country Club)

Sunapee's first golf professional, manager, and greenkeeper. Even when the Depression slowed play down and threatened Lake Sunapee with bankruptcy, course conditions excelled, especially the greens. They had been planted with a Washington strain of bentgrass, and then had been converted to Velvet bentgrass as an experiment in the 1930s by greenkeeper (and future New England course architect) William Mitchell.

Homan eventually acquired the course in 1945, and it has remained in the family ever since. His grandson, Doug Homan, who took over the property in 1985, is now undertaking a massive restoration effort under the supervision of Uniontown, PA-based architect Ron Forse. Some 1,200 trees are slated for removal, many of them non-native spruce. Green surfaces, most of which have shrunk by 20-30% over the years, will be brought back to full size—a task that calls for removing the bluegrass and Poa annua that have taken over the perimeters and sodding them back to Velvet bentgrass. Bunkers whose faces had become flashed up to show a sheer, exposed surface are being folded back down with a sodded vertical slope and planted with fescue. The bunker floors will not be level, however; they are being reestablished in a gentle bowl formation, the way Ross designed them. This saucer shape allows for visibility from the approach area and enables golf balls that roll in to settle at the bottom. This more traditional look also makes good maintenance sense, as it reduces the amount of sand exposed to washouts. Interestingly, Forse is not moving the original carry bunkers (many of them only 100-175 yards from the middle tees) any further out. In some cases he is actually unearthing them, along with other fairway hazards that had been removed over the years. Lake Sunapee is therefore a case of pure restoration, with the intent being to bring this unheralded New Hampshire gem back to its glory days.

SEMINOLE

Ross couldn't have known it at the time, but his 1929 work at Seminole Golf Club in Juno Beach, Florida, would turn out to be his last great original course design. It was also the last course he ever laid out alongside the ocean. The setting for this low-lying stretch of barren, windswept sand was just above North Palm Beach, on a spit of land between the Intracoastal Waterway and the Atlantic Ocean.

Ross was awarded the Seminole contract partly because of his renowned reputation, but also because his bid was considerably lower than that of another architect who had made a misguided play for the job. Sadly, the name of that unfortunate competitor has been lost to us; club records are silent on the issue. It would be interesting to learn the name of this architect who proposed leveling the massive 40-foot sand ridge that would ultimately give Seminole its distinctive character. In an area known for its lack of elevation, such a landform was to be treasured rather than destroyed. Ross did not share the idea of taking down the ridge and using the soil to fill the low areas of this site; this would have made the tract no different than 100 other Florida layouts. His instincts for using the native lay of the land would not allow him to entertain so grandiose an earthmoving project as moving 100,000 or so cubic yards of dirt. Nor would his sense of modest (i.e., proper) budgets indulge such a prospect. Quite to the contrary, he used the ridge to bold effect, making it a central point of the routing. Indeed, the genius of the two returning nines Ross planned for Seminole is that each one twice visits the highest point of the ridge—at the far northwest corner of the property. The result is that fully four greens and four tees are situated atop it, without in any way creating a sense of undue crowding. On the contrary, visitors to this day revel in the long views of both the ocean and the entire golf course afforded them from this unique vantage point.

A team of 180 men labored 60 hours per week at 25 cents per hour to complete the construction work. They cleared palmetto trees with machetes and then had mule teams drag

Seminole Golf Club, North Palm Beach, FL. The 183-yard par-3 fifth hole, as sketched by Ross. The plans called for the five greenside bunkers to be at least 4 feet deep. His green markings mistakenly reverse the positions of "A" and "B." (Seminole Golf Club)

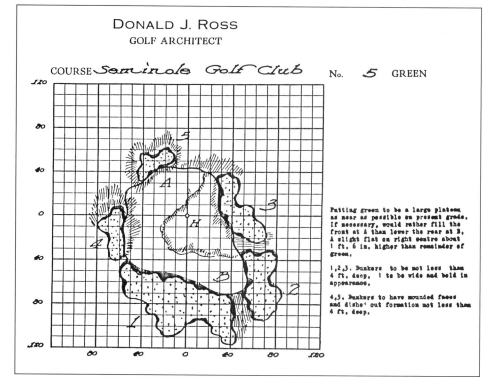

The Golfers Dream—the ingeniously desig[...]
course of the Seminole Golf Club with its pictur[...]
house shown near the white line of the brea[...]
the Atlantic.

Seminole Golf Club as viewed in 1929 in the only remaining aerial photograph of the original course. Note the wide fairways and scruffy bunkers. (Seminole Golf Club)

away the trunks. The earth was reshaped with slip pans, and all the greens elevated in classic linksland fashion. The major problem was building up the low areas. Most of the golf ground was a mere two feet above sea level, and so shallow was the soil that the spines of the holding ponds he dug out were only a few feet deep.

Ross's engineering skills proved handy at Seminole because he was faced with the major issues of how to capture irrigation water on-site *and* forestall flooding from tidal surges. While dynamiting some cap rock to move soil, he had come upon an artesian water flow that appeared to be a good irrigation source. Absorbing tidal surges from Little Lake Worth that adjoined the property on the south side was a different problem. The trick was to design an irrigation system and pumping facility that would keep freshwater circulating over the golf course while steering salt water through a system of streams and shallow ponds that he was forced to dig.

Ross, an inveterate reader of self-help magazines and how-to journals, drew upon an idea he had seen in a recent issue of *Popular Mechanics*. He installed a water pump that would empty into Little Lake Worth on the south side of the property, to the right of the par-5 ninth hole. This would help draw down the water level through the ponds and allow the course to drain, especially at times of heavy rain or during high tides. The idea was to control the water flow in both directions so that when Little Lake Worth filled up, it didn't threaten to back up onto the golf course. By this means, he could control the flow of water in both directions. In fact, he was able to direct enough saltwater through the pond system that the course developed a vibrant marine life.

Ross splashed Seminole with 187 bunkers—perhaps only Ravisloe in Chicago had more. With the wind howling and the Atlantic splashing ashore just

Seminole's fifth hole today. Dick Wilson had flashed up the sand at Seminole in 1947. Architect Brian Silva brought back the turfed faces in 1996. (Bradley S. Klein)

beyond the dunes along the eastern flank of the golf course, the visual effect of all that sand was to make the course look like waves were breaking across it. The bunkers also have a powerful strategic effect since they help protect lines of play no matter which direction the wind is blowing. In Ross's days, only a few palmetto trees dotted the landscape. Separation of the holes was created by that one dramatic central dune, as well as by the many ponds and water courses that traversed the property. Playing the site, a golfer would never sense that the holes occupy all of 105 acres. That's because the course presents an expansiveness, owing to its openness to the elements, that belies its spatial intimacy.

There is also something gracious and timeless about Seminole's clubhouse, with its pink stucco walls and Spanish Mediterranean architecture, replete with a walled courtyard. Plus, there could not be a more inspiring locker room—with its vaulted ceiling and six-foot-high wooden lockers arrayed around the perimeter of a single room. From the day Seminole opened on January 1, 1930, the entire facility was rightly praised as a stunning architectural achievement.

GOING PUBLIC

Seminole was to be Ross's last great private golf course. The Depression took its toll, not only on the market for new courses but also on the market for existing layouts. Only a handful of courses were commissioned over the next 15 years. Moreover, the expansion of existing 9-hole layouts, which had comprised fully one-third of Ross's work in the decade after World War I, had also proved unfeasible in the new economic climate. From 1925 to 1929, course construction in the U.S. had been growing at an average annual rate of 12%. For 1930, the increase was 8%, and a number that was not likely reached again for nearly another two decades. According to one detailed account of the U.S. golf market in 1930 (Conrad H. Roser, "Golf Course Design and Construction," in *American Landscape Architect*, 1931), the overwhelming majority of clubs were in the private sector. Equally revealing was the persisting dominance of 9-hole facilities over 18-hole facilities. Despite a healthy expansion of 9-hole facilities into full 18-hole courses since World War I, nearly 6 in 10 American courses were 9-hole layouts.

1930:	total number of U.S. courses:	5,856
	18-hole facilities:	2,414 (41% of total)
	private clubs:	1,919
	public and daily-fee:	423
	9-hole facilities:	3,442 (59% of total)
	private clubs:	3,300
	public and daily-fee:	142

Opposite page: Seminole's 17th hole, a 175-yard par 3 along the dunes fronting the Atlantic Ocean. (Larry Lambrecht)

The spurt of construction in U.S. facilities had greatly overextended the supply of private layouts to meet the demands of a population. Increasingly, after the stock market crash of October 1929, the country could no longer sustain the kind of luxury represented by country club life. Municipalities, meanwhile, appear to have turned their attentions to construction of public works, including highways, bridges, tunnels, parks, and sports facilities. The point was to provide gainful public employment through government-sponsored programs while providing valuable recreational amenities that citizens could utilize at little direct cost.

Ross, always with an eye on the promotional side of his craft, championed the cause of public golf. "There is no good reason why the label 'a rich man's game' should be hung on golf," he wrote in *Golf Has Never Failed Me*. "The development of municipal golf courses is the outstanding feature of the game in America today. It is the greatest step ever taken to make it the game of the people, as it should be. The municipal courses are all moneymakers and big moneymakers. I am naturally conservative, yet I am certain that in a few years we will see golf played much more generally than is even played now."

The press picked up and ran with this populist sensibility, as the following headline from the *Asheville* (NC) *Citizen* proclaimed on February 22, 1923: "Municipally Owned Golf Courses Needed Here Says Donald Ross On Arrival." The article, which paraphrases rather than quotes Ross, trumpets the cause of a municipal layout for "the Mountain Metropolis" of Asheville as a stimulant to the tourism trade. Ross was apparently making a pitch for a future project because he was in town on this occasion to work with local landscape gardener C.D. Beadles refining the Biltmore Forest Course, that was then under development.

Two years later, Ross arrived in Wilmington, North Carolina to start plans for that city's municipal layout. This visit was also announced by the local paper, with the article affirming the role that such a project would have on making Wilmington more attractive to out-of-town visitors. "It is the consensus of opinion of almost all that a municipal course will go a long way toward drawing winter and summer tourists . . . " Namedropping would play no small role in the promotional effort. The news item reports that R.C. Cantwell, Wilmington's commissioner of public works, "says that for the lovers of the golf sport to know that the links have been layed [sic] out by Mr. Ross is a tremendous advertisement in itself."

The next year, 1926, Ross set to work at Manikiki Golf Course in the town of Willoughby, Ohio. This is a layout that Ross planned for the old Hahn estate in 1926; it was then deeded over to the Cleveland Metropolitan Park District in 1964. Ross was certainly here during construction, and he returned for the opening festivities in 1928. On-site construction was handled by one of his lesser-known Midwest associates, George Alves, but the routing looks and feels more like Ross. Each nine occupies its own contiguous ground rather than being overlapped or interlocked. The land itself offers some interesting elevation changes, and instead of the holes set at right angles to one another there is a continuing alteration of twists and turns in the orientation of one hole to the next. Characteristic of Ross routings is that there is precious little land between a green and the next tee. Manikiki's greens are almost all set on natural plateaus (another hallmark) though they are also somewhat smaller than average—closer to 4,000 sq. ft. than the 5,500 sq. ft. (60 ft. x 100 ft. oval) that is more normal for Ross. The bunkers, meanwhile, are often set back 10 or 20 yards from the greens so that they create the illusion of being closer when in fact there is some workable distance in between. But these bunkers all offer flashed-up sand, and their shapes are very saucer-like rather than lower-lying ovals with flat bottoms. Surely this is something that evolved, probably through erosion of the bunker walls and through years of players excavating sand that remained on the formerly turfed walls of the trap. In one very sad concession to modernity, there is the obvious installation of a paved cart path over the entire length of the course—from the first tee to the last green. Not itself terribly odious, except that in several cases the small amount of land between adjacent holes forced the cart path between the fairway and a flanking bunker.

One of his more ambitious municipal plans was a proposed 54-hole facility for the city of Savannah, Georgia. The 800-acre site, five miles south of downtown, had been donated by the Bacon family and specified for public recreational use. Two courses were ultimately built and opened for public play in 1929 but one of them ceased to exist after World War II. Today, however, the remaining layout, the 6,430-yard, par-72 Bacon Park Golf Course, is a thriving daily-fee facility. Course conditioning has suffered somewhat, but interestingly enough, the most serious drainage and agronomic problems have occurred on a nine-hole loop added in 1985. Ross, it seems, knew what he was doing with the site when he routed his 18 on the higher ground around a flood channel called Casey Canal. The new nine sits on mucky land 5-12 feet lower and in the floodplain. Whenever there's a heavy rain, the new holes turn to near mud.

TRIGGS, PONKAPOAG AND GEORGE WRIGHT

Three major municipal projects of the 1930s in New England confirmed Ross as a friend of daily-fee golfers: Triggs Memorial Golf Course in Providence, Rhode Island (1931), Ponkapoag Golf Club in Canton, Massachusetts (1932), and George Wright Golf Course in Boston (1938). There was nothing cheap or second-rate about their construction, and for years they served as powerful reminders of the quality work that public-minded bodies were capable of when the consensus to do so existed.

Triggs was built on the west side of Providence, on the grounds of the old Obadiah Brown Homestead. The undertaking was part of a comprehensive park ground that included eight tennis courts, two baseball diamonds, a football field, a full-length golf practice field and a 9-hole children's pitch-and-putt course. The bigger course was not shortchanged either; the par-71 layout measured 6,551 yards over a rolling, sparsely treed site that offered 70 feet of elevation change. The routing of the two returning nines was elegant and intimate: the outgoing nine traced out the figure of a heart; the incoming nine turned back on itself like an amoeba. Two streams meandered across the eastern side of the property and came into play on half a dozen holes. A farm pond at the lowest point on the site sat in front of the 16th tee. Construction costs were not low for the era: around $100,000 in all. When Triggs Memorial opened in the spring of 1931 it quickly assumed a premier place among New England municipal layouts.

A year later, Ross's design for 18 holes at Ponkapoag Golf Club in Canton, Massachusetts, opened for play. The public course, undertaken by Boston's Metropolitan District Commission, was located 14 miles south of downtown and was ultimately expanded in two subsequent phases (1938 and 1956) to 36 holes. Ross's original handiwork is evident today as the front nine of Course No. 2 and holes 1,2,9,10,14,15,16,17, and 18 of Course No. 1. Not surprisingly, Ross selected the best uplands and avoided the areas for wetlands soils. His greens are gently tipped toward the line of play, with many of them displaying the telltale crown at the back that was Hatch's trademark. By contrast, the 1938 greens all betray the same look of three framing mounds. The contrast with the original putting surfaces is marked, as is the soil for these newer holes, which in nearly every case were the peaty wetlands that Ross knew to avoid. The final nine, done by longtime Ponkapoag greenkeeper Samuel S. Mitchell, has a broad, well-defined look that suggests the use of earthmoving equipment as well as some know-how on the part of its designer/builder.

Ponkapoag could not have been an ambitious undertaking in terms of site constraints. There was enough ground to maneuver a reliable routing without having to revert to expensive blasting or plating. The same, however, cannot be said for Ross's other Boston-area public project during the 1930s. "City Duped on New Golf Links, Say Councilmen: Hyde Park Land Called 'Swamp' and 'Quarry'" ran a headline in the *Boston Herald* of February 10, 1931. One anonymous critic of the project dismissed it as "the worst piece of rascality ever put over under the guise of unemployment." Councilman Robert Gardiner Wilson Jr. of Roxbury was quoted as saying that "Donald Ross, the engineer engaged in laying out the course, who recently promised to develop it into 'the best course in the country' had character-ized the same land, a few years ago, as 'not appropriate for golf.'" Ross was evi-dently so incensed by the councilman's comment that in his personal scrapbook, he penciled in "Who said?" next to the offending quote.

The course in question would come to be known as George Wright Municipal. Wright, a former Boston Red Stockings baseball player and then a prominent sporting goods proprietor, had known Ross since just after the turn-of-the century from winter forays to Pinehurst. An advocate of Boston municipal golf, Wright had been influential in the creation of the city's first municipal layout, Franklin Park, in 1890. Ross, who did some redesign work at Franklin Park in the early 1920s, was recruited by a group of wealthy Bostonians in 1928 to plan an exclusive club in the Hyde Park/West Roxbury section of town in southeast Boston. The private project fell through when the Depression set in, but Ross's planned layout was revived in 1931, this time for a public layout. The project would drag on to become one of the most complex construction jobs in American golf—public or private. Initial budget estimates of $225,000 quickly doubled when the full extent of the rocky site became apparent to engineers. Expenditures on the 158-acre site totaled $1 million, making it the country's most expensive public layout. The project was initially funded by the federal Emergency Relief Administration and then continued by the Works Progress Administration, eventually employing as many as 1,000 laborers at a time on the job. The manager of the project was Walter Irving Johnson, Ross's former engineer, who was now working for the Metropolitan District Commission. Johnson was not one to flaunt the expenditure of money. In fact, he attempted to make it look as if he had been frugal. "A road builder," he said, "spends $10,000 on a stretch of road and wants it to look like he spent a million. A golf course builder spends a million and wants it to look like an investment of $10,000."

Newspapers documented the massive earthwork required to blast through the ledge and to clear and fill marshland for the holes. Streams had to be culverted under fairways with 30-inch pipes. Budget items included $109,000 for 72,666 cubic yards of earth to be spread up to six inches deep over two-thirds of the course. Excavating 10,000 cubic yards of the ledge required 30 tons of TNT and cost $30,000. Moving another 40,000 yards of rocky earth cost $40,000. Laying 8,000 feet of irrigation pipe cost $12,000. The course was equipped with an unprecedented number of quick couplers—130 in all—to provide up to one inch of water per hour. Drainage alone ran to $25,000. Building the parking areas cost $10,000. Bridle paths cost $2,000. Upwards of $200,000 was spent on constructing and furnishing a spacious, brick Norman-style clubhouse (replete with 315 full-length lockers) that helped make George Wright a public golf landmark when it opened on April 23, 1938.

It was the first course in the country to be surrounded by artificial means—a combination of rock wall and wire fencing that gave it a modicum of security. The par-70 course, which stretched to 6,820 yards over difficult terrain, drew rave reviews from everyone who played it. A season's pass was $35, the daily green fee was $2. Head professional William E. Taylor did not draw a salary; his income was derived entirely from pro shop sales and lesson fees. The course was nominally public, but the clientele was disproportionately upscale. Photos of the course before World War II show many large black sedans parked by the clubhouse. The availability of country club-style facilities for a small percentage of what exclusive club memberships would cost was surely an allure. The clubhouse's Great Hall held a steady stream of proms and weddings.

The golf course was notorious for both its raw beauty and terror, with

George Wright Municipal Golf Course, Boston. The 170-yard par-3 17th hole. (Bradley S. Klein)

sharp falloffs, rocky outcrops, and marshlands presenting dangers to every golfer. No course Ross ever did required more work to get it to fit the land. Even today, a visitor has the sense that the holes were squeezed, hammered, and imposed upon the land. In Ross's day the fairways were generously wide, but the rough areas were draped by dense tree canopies. In a concession to the difficulty of the land (and perhaps out of respect for the maintenance budget), Ross's plan was unusually sparing in its use of fairway bunkers. The greens, which ranged from 5,000 to 10,0000 sq. ft., were built with much contouring. Sadly, the greens today betray the telltale signs of neglect. Their contours have been top-dressed too much, and the inevitable effects of years of careless maintenance have led to a loss of perimeter putting surface and with it, some interesting hole placements. Nor have the bunkers held up well, with too many of them having grown in, to the point where their intended shape has been lost.

By the 1970s, the George Wright Municipal Golf Course had fallen into decrepitude, its holes barely maintained, security at a minimum, and its finances, like those at other Boston municipal layouts, awash in a sea of red ink. Franklin Park was in even worse shape, with abandoned cars littering its (former) fairways and the holes serving as shooting galleries for druggies. A rare example of municipal vision by the Parks Commission managed to save these layouts and to breathe new life into Ponkapoag as well. But no one who treads these fairways today can fully sense the hope and excitement these layouts brought to golfers in Boston when they were built in the 1930s.

Northern links: Canada

Beyond his two courses in Cuba and his modest tinkering with Royal Dornoch in Scotland, the only country outside the U.S. where Ross made his mark was Canada. He worked on a total of 11 courses there, stretching from the original Banff Springs Hotel Golf Course at the famed Canadian Pacific hotel resort in Alberta's Rocky Mountains (1919) to Brightwood Golf Course in Dartmouth, Nova Scotia, and Riverside Golf Course near Saint John, New Brunswick in the mid-1930s. Record keeping on his work there is notoriously spotty, and only a handful of documented plans have survived to guide historians or designers interested in restoration. Ross's design work has also been heavily tinkered with. Only Essex Golf and Country Club in Windsor, Ontario, remains, in most respects, authentic Ross.

Banff

As with much of Ross's work, there are common misconceptions and rumors that have been so widely retold they seem to acquire a certain truth status. For example, in a 1985 *Golf Journal* article, "Donald Ross, A Man of Discovery," architect Brian Silva claims that Ross did the original design work in the Canadian Rockies for the Canadian Pacific Railway in 1910; CPR president Cornelis Van Horne reportedly turned down Ross's request for a $35 a day inspection fee and had his own railway engineers do the work. Unfortunately, they interpreted Ross's plans, which were drawn up in inches, to be feet. The result, reports Silva, were wildly undulating features, including 12-foot swales in the putting surface and 20-foot deep bunkers in the original 9-hole routing; a mistake only discovered—but never corrected— when German POWs began building a second nine.

Silva got the story from Canadian-born designer Geoffrey Cornish (Silva and Cornish have been partners since 1987), who himself was on the site in the 1920s and 1930s. Unfortunately, the story isn't quite true, although it's close. Van Horne, for example, retired from the presidency of Canadian Pacific Railway in 1899. The photographic evidence suggests broad, open features to the old holes rather than severe ones. Railway engineers, who lived and died with the accuracy of their measurements, would not likely have made such mistakes, and if they had, the experienced golfers on hand would surely have noticed. Besides, the point is moot since Ross never detailed his slopes and depths in inches alone but in feet and inches, as in 1 ft. - 6 in. or 2 ft. 6 in. The figure of $35 a day—in an era when Canadian and U.S. currencies were worth virtually the same when traded against one another—suggests the possibility that the arrangements were being negotiated very early in Ross's design career. It's possible, though there is no documentary evidence of such negotiations with Canadian Pacific Railway at that time. The subsequent correspondence concerning Ross's work there—it was 1919, not 1910—does not refer to an earlier phase.

For the record, Ross's work in the Canadian Rockies dates back "only" to 1919, when he was persuaded during a visit to Winnipeg to make the further trip by train to Banff Springs, Alberta. By then, Banff already had a 9-hole layout by resident golf professional William E. "Bill" Thomson, designed and built in 1910-1911. Efforts to build an additional nine on the basis of subsequent plans by Thomson were made in 1917-1918, with labor provided not by German POWs but by native Austro-Hungarians who were living legally in Canada but were interned during the war. The work languished and was then abandoned in lieu of Ross's plan.

Ross was already working in Winnipeg, having arrived there in April of 1919 to work on two courses. He had been brought there by David Finnie, a prominent local men's clothier and a force in the fledgling Western Golf Association (comprising Manitoba, Alberta and Saskatchewan). Ross completed a 9-hole routing for St. Charles Country Club that now comprises the South Nine. (Curiously, the North Nine was done by Alister MacKenzie in 1930. It would be the only time the two "collaborated" on a golf course, though in fact there is no evidence that they ever met, much less communicated.) While in Winnipeg, Ross also undertook a remodeling plan for the Tom Bendelow-designed Pine Ridge Country Club. For a fee of $508.20 (the club's notes do not say whether in Canadian or U.S. currency) Ross designed 11 new tees, 103 bunkers, six new greens, and four entirely new holes.

E.J. Hart's 1999 history of golf at Banff, *Golf on the Roof of the World*, provides helpful information on Ross's work there. According to Hart, the decision to bring Ross to Banff came at Finnie's suggestion, but ultimately had to be approved by the federal Minister of the Interior, whose Dominion Parks Branch had taken over the park in 1917. There was some public concern about Ross's $1,000 fee, but the parks branch head, James Bernard Harkin, thought otherwise. "I am advised," he wrote, "that in the United States expert golfers will travel thousands of miles to reach a course which they know has been laid out by this man."

Ross was on site at Banff making inspections by May 25. The site was at 5,000 feet above sea level, with the existing 9-hole course sitting along a floodplain on the south side of the Bow River. Mount Rundle towered over the course on the south, and the whole setting was framed by the Canadian Rockies. The ambiance

The setting for Banff Springs Golf Club, Alberta, Canada. "Golf on the roof of the world." (Bradley S. Klein)

Banff's 171-yard par-3 second, one of the few remaining Ross holes left relatively intact by architect Stanley Thompson. (Bradley S. Klein)

gave rise to a widely used phrase that came to be associated with Banff: "Golf on the roof of the world."

Ross's design for 18 holes called for a new nine to complement the original Thomson nine, part of which was ultimately revised in the process. Ross pushed the course out toward the east, but did not venture onto the rougher ground to the south, nor extend onto the densely wooded ground on the west side to the Spray River and the hotel building. Those changes would only take place in yet a subsequent phase of expansion. Not that the ground Ross had to work with was ideal. His instructions carried a note about this: "It will be found necessary to haul a great amount of soil to cover the rocky sections and a large quantity of Peat Humus and compost will also have to be hauled on to the greens."

A lack of funding led to construction delays for the Ross course. It also didn't help that Bill Thomson, who was to supervise the work, was on the road designing courses elsewhere in Canada. The Ross course, a par 73 of 6,402 yards, did not open until the summer of 1924. It was outfitted with an irrigation line, and it utilized fertilizer that was fashioned from powdered buffalo chips. Bunkers were designed to capture low-running shots, with many hazards placed within 125 yards of the tees and most approach bunkers located well short of the putting surfaces.

Turf growth was limited on the course. According to Hart, plans were made by late 1926 to upgrade the irrigation line and to spread up to half a foot of top-dressing on the course. But the combination of 18,000 cubic feet of soil and 100 carloads of manure would end up costing $25,000. With the opening of the Stanley Thompson-designed course at Jasper National Park in 1926, Banff now had serious competition 175 miles to the northwest. Nothing but a new course, this time with Thompson's imprimatur, would do. In 1927, Thompson went to work and incorporated holes from both the original Thomson and Ross layouts, while carving out very difficult terrain in two new areas: a 4-hole segment for the opening and closing of the course on wooded ground by the hotel at Spray River; and a dramatic 2-hole section across Loop Road to the south. It was here, under the stark upslope of Mount Rundle, that Thompson would create one of his most memorable holes, the downhill par-3 "Cauldron" over water.

Subsequent reroutings have complicated the story, but the remains of the Ross course can today be found as holes No. 2, 6, 17, and 18 of the Stanley Thompson course. Many of Ross's hole corridors, including tee and green sites, were thus incorporated by Thompson, though with considerably more depth and character to the bunkers and mounds. Some of Ross's abandoned work was subsequently occupied by the Tunnel Nine, a 1989 design by Cornish and Bill Robinson that, because of routing considerations, was unable to make more than partial use of old, overgrown corridors.

Ross never saw his completed, and short-lived, Banff course. There is, however, some evidence of a follow-up visit to Winnipeg in 1923, when he remodeled an existing nine and added nine of his own at Elmhurst Golf Links.

ROSELAND

Ross's other work in Canada came in Ontario and the Maritimes. Consider the case of Roseland Park Country Club in Windsor, Ontario. Ross made many visits to Detroit, just across the Detroit River, and so a side trip to Windsor could have been easily handled in a morning or afternoon. In a rather hasty letter to Walter Irving Johnson dated August 3, 1926, Ross asks his associate back in Pinehurst to send six blueprints of general plans, a black line print and a crayon colored plan to Mr. Percy R. Hoad of the Michigan Investment Co. of Detroit. Separate sheets bear Ross's rough-hewn drawings of greens plans. Johnson was to use them to prepare construction plans, evidently to be undertaken by a team not under Ross's direct control. "Show a cross section of each green from right to left and from front

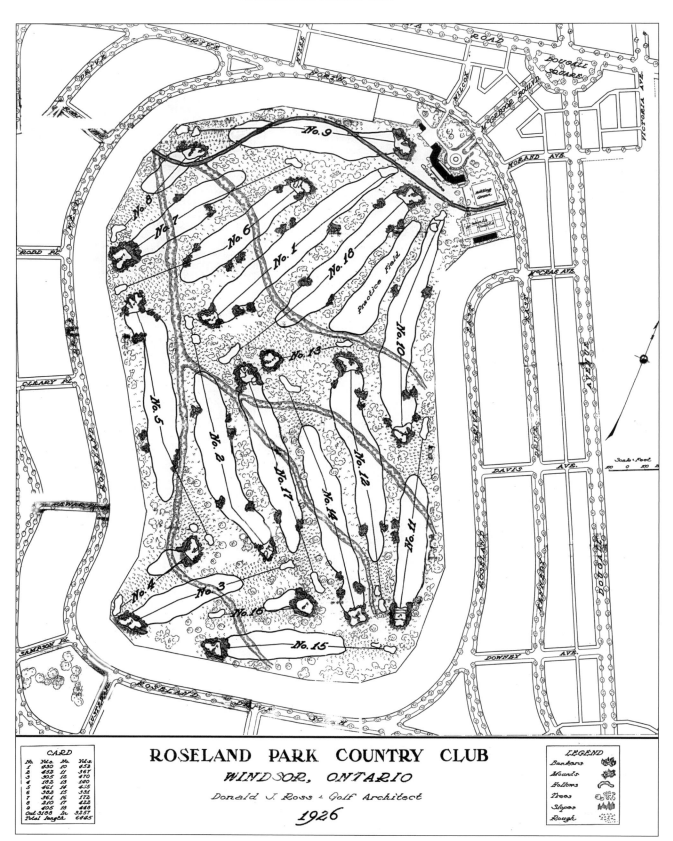

ROSELAND PARK COUNTRY CLUB

WINDSOR, ONTARIO

Donald J. Ross ~ Golf Architect

1926

to rear. This is very necessary as I do not believe we are going to have the construction of the course. You understand the ground is absolutely flat."

Hole-by-hole written instructions attest to the low-grade relief of the site: "Tee raised not more than 6 in. unless necessary for drainage purposes." Greenside bunker depths were all between 3 feet and 6 feet, with 4 ft. 6 in. the norm—depending upon site constraints, as "the depth to which the bed of the bunkers may be depressed, depends entirely on drainage." Mounds 4 to 5 feet high and 35 to 45 feet wide at their base were planned, with their mass shaped or floated out into the putting surface to create the green's surface flow. The mounds provided virtually the only topographic relief on the site. There is a wonderful economy of strategy, with the entrances on longer approaches left open, and the shorter par 3s and par 4s bunkered in front and demanding a precise lob shot in. Of the 88 bunkers planned for the course, 40 were around the greens. They were placed tight to the putting surfaces; only once was there sand behind the green. In subsequent years, Roseland, which is now run as a municipal facility, became heavily overplanted and overgrown with trees. However, its original routing remains.

MARITIMES

Ross also worked on four courses in the Maritime Provinces. It is not clear he ever made site visits to Nova Scotia, but in any case two layouts there bear his stamp: Liverpool Golf Course in Hunts Point along the Atlantic Ocean (1929); and a 9-hole addition in 1934 to a Willie Park Jr. course, Brightwood Golf and Country Club in Dartmouth, overlooking Halifax Harbor. He also prepared design plans for another Canadian Pacific Railway hotel project in St. Andrews, New Brunswick, this one called the Algonquin. The magnificent setting in the province's extreme southwest corner overlooked Passamaquoddy Bay and allowed glimpses of eastern Maine. Ross's plans for the Algonquin included a short 9-hole layout, but it was the 18-hole that claimed tourists' attention for its links-like playing character and its exposure to coastal winds.

In the mid-1930s, Ross journeyed up to New Brunswick to work on Riverside Country Club in Rothesay, eight miles northeast of Saint John. The client was a frequent guest at Pinehurst by the name of Percy W. Thomson. He was something of a self-appointed agronomist and, judged on the basis of his voluminous correspondence with Leonard Tufts, not shy to offer his advice on the golf courses. One particularly tedious exchange from March 1933 involves a series of detailed suggestions by Thomson: moving the 17th green on the Pinehurst No. 1 Course 65 yards closer to the tee ("Estimated cost $100. Work should be done in May to allow the bermuda to knit and the green to age."); moving the 14th tee back 65 yards ("Estimated cost $50."); and reworking the practice tee ("cut the topsoil off of the brow of the hill—take two feet of the hill off—carry thus cutting back 50

Opposite page: The 1926 routing plan for Roseland Park Country Club, Windsor, Ontario, Canada. The routing remains intact today. (Roseland Golf & Curling Club)

to 70 yards—replace the topsoil—plant in bermuda—plant the field also in bermuda. . . Estimated cost $350.") Further suggestions included a new fertilizer regimen for the No. 2 Course, raising dues, and a new green for the seventh hole on the No. 3 Course. He was also generous enough to propose advancing the funds to complete the work. Tufts tactfully turned down the kind offer.

If Thomson was not shy about offering advice, he also knew enough to hire a qualified architect when it came time to build a good layout. Riverside already had a rudimentary 12-hole course on a member-owned farm. In 1936 or 1937, Thomson got Ross to come up and oversee a proper 18-hole routing. The site was a broad, rolling plain overlooking a four-mile wide stretch of the Kennebecasis River. Ross planned a layout over open ground that incorporated the subtle swales and moguls of the native terrain. Not surprisingly, Thomson ruled the club like a loving patriarch.

Essex G&CC

The most famous Ross course in Canada is surely Essex County Golf & Country Club in LaSalle, a suburb of Windsor, directly across the Detroit River from the American city of that name. The course, which dropped the "County" from its name in the 1940s, has hosted prestigious Canadian professional events and was the venue for the PGA Tour's 1976 Canadian Open and the LPGA's 1998 du Maurier Classic. The club was founded in 1902, and its original golf course was located on a site five miles to the north and closer to the town center. Its membership included many golfers from Detroit, and when serious discussion arose as to expansion or relocation, attention turned to Detroit Golf Club, which in 1915 was in the process of building two new Ross-designed courses. Detroit GC's golf professional and greenkeeper, Ernest Way, was then supervising construction of the layout. Having just turned over his golf professional duties to Ross's younger brother Alex in order to concentrate on greenkeeping and construction, Way was now able to offer his services as a consultant to area clubs. Way proposed himself to modify and expand Essex's existing 9-hole layout for a sum of $300.

Essex chose to modify its existing layout rather than to break new ground. That would wait more than a decade, and this time Ross was brought on board. The club acquired a 126-acre parcel for $106,000 (Canadian). Starting in 1928, Ross made a handful of site visits, and his own surveyors shot the levels. Construction supervisor for the new layout was Essex's own greenkeeper, John Gray, a Scotsman by birth and, at 6'2", 250 lb., an imposing man. Gray would go on to a distinguished career at Essex, where he remained until 1958. In 1926, he had been among the 60 founding members of the National Association of Greenkeepers of America and, in 1941, was the only Canadian ever to serve as that group's president.

At Essex, Gray supervised a work crew of 135 men on a site of sandy loam

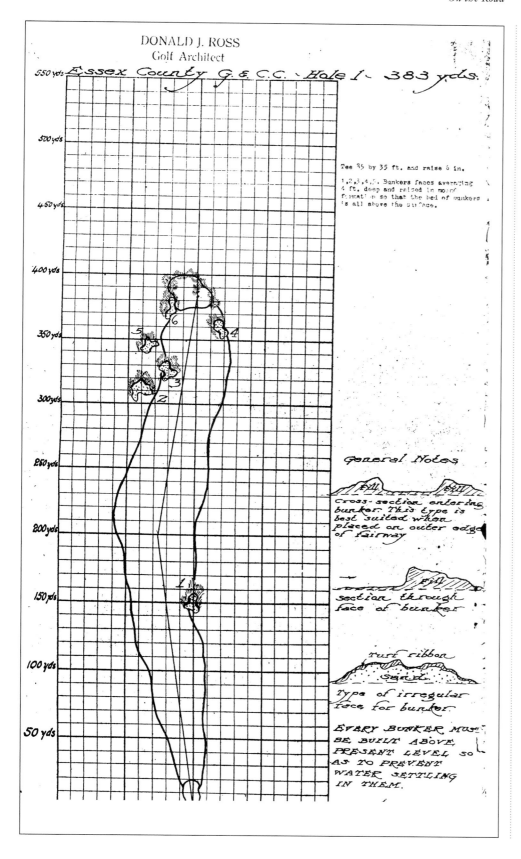

Essex (County) Golf & Country Club, Windsor, Ontario, Canada. This is the 383-yard par-4 first hole. Ross's plans called for a left-to-right tee shot and a right-to-left approach. In his "General Notes" for bunker construction, Ross included three-dimensional cross sections, plus a reminder that for such a flat site, "every bunker must be built above present level so as to prevent water settling in them." (Essex Golf & Country Club)

Essex Golf & Country Club aerial, c.1962, before trees had heavily overgrown the grounds. The first green is just above and to the left of the pond at lower center. Most of the original fairway bunkers were still there, though they have since been removed. (Essex Golf & Country Club)

packed tightly with trees. Stumps were blown away with dynamite, and a pair of steam shovels were deployed to lay 12-inch drainage tile. The natural topography was extremely flat; a series of swales and drainage ditches were manufactured to meander across the site. Total natural elevation change was under five feet. Most of the earthmoving involved cut and fills balanced on each hole to hive up enough dirt for greens. Gray also installed French drains around some of the push-up greens to supplement the surface flow of water. Construction and grow-in took a year, with the new course opening in July of 1929.

The par-72 layout, at 6,683 yards (par 70 and 6,085 yards from the short tees), was a masterpiece of routing on a rectangular site boxed in on three sides with roads or railway line. Each of the returning nines occupies contiguous ground and is sequenced; the graceful loop on each nine folds back in on itself and passes by the clubhouse at midpoint. For all the effort on the golf course, it was the club-house that absorbed the bulk of the club expenditure– some $190,000 (Canadian) in all. A celebratory article about the new facility in a March 1930 issue of *Canadian Golfer* devoted 12 paragraphs to the 310-foot-long clubhouse and one paragraph to the golf course.

Ross's design represented an elegant economy of hazards and ground features. The sole pond on site barely intruded into play on two holes: the eighth and ninth. The ditch also scarcely intruded. Four holes, however, deploy the shallow swale as a diagonal cross-feature, though it barely affects the strategy of the tee shot because so often the feature crosses diagonally within 50 yards of the teeing ground. Many of his fairway bunkers were set in the range of 160 to 200 yards from the back tees, allowing for relative comfort on the drive. Indeed, few Ross courses have ever been set up better than Essex as a "second-shot" layout—meaning the approach shots into the meticulously sculpted greens constitute the bulk of the challenge.

At Essex, there was also enough setback of trees for play to proceed in uncluttered fashion. No Ross course ever deployed trees as a central feature of the holes. It unduly limited playing options and made for bad agronomy.

Unfortunately, Essex has not fared well in this regard. Its green complexes have remained intact, and the basic routing has also been preserved. But when it comes to trees, few courses have been rendered as claustrophobic over the years as Essex. Nor has the overgrowth all been attributable to the trees left by Ross. Essex, like many courses, engaged in an aggressive tree-planting program, much of it in the name of "beautification" or "renovation" that has served to obscure rather than enhance its native ground features. In a case that is paradigmatic rather than exceptional, Essex undertook to eliminate much of its ingenious ground game, and the result has been a loss of the architectural style endowed by Ross. In 1999, the green committee devoted itself to a restoration program overseen by Tom Doak and Bruce Hepner that is designed to bring back the sensibility that had been lost.

Chapter Six
Life and Character

*T*he caddies called him "DJ," though not to his face. Not surprisingly, Ross enjoyed a comfortable relationship with the loopers at Pinehurst. He was, after all, one of their own social rank, in terms of social class, if not skin color and marginal status. One who still remembers him fondly is Robert "Hardrock" Robinson, a stooped, bald, yet energetic man spotted almost on a daily basis in Pinehurst center these days, years after he retired from the caddie ranks. "Hardrock," who says he was born on January 1, 1914, became "DJ's" regular bag toter sometime in the 1930s. Average pay in those days was 75 cents, and if you got a dollar—as "Hardrock" usually did from "DJ"—it was said you were "doing great." According to this witness, Ross was a stickler for keeping the caddie yard swept and clean. It was a habit of neatness that he adhered to personally as well, his playing attire always including knickers and a collared shirt and a tie, often with a jacket as well. Out on the golf course, says Hardrock, Ross was easy to work for because he didn't lose his temper. "A fine man, a Scotsman," Hardrock says. "He lectured me and I lectured him."

FAMILY MAN

"We were just a happy normal family," recalled Lillian Ross Pippitt. "I didn't know him as a famous golf course architect. I just knew him as Dad." Throughout her life, Lillian spoke with both sadness and admiration of her love for her father. One got the sense that she judged everyone she met by the lofty standard he set.

The Ross family remained close-knit despite Donald's frequent out-of-town traveling and their twice-a-year moves back and forth between Pinehurst and Massachusetts. The Ross family loved music. Janet had played the violin as young-ster, and though she did not play after coming to the States, she and her husband frequently sang when at home. Lillian learned to play the piano when she was seven

or eight years old, and on her 10th birthday Donald Ross bought her a Steinway baby grand piano. Her parents taught her a great many Scottish songs and the three of them would sing "Lizzie Lindsay," "Gray Sands," "White Sands," and "Hundred Pipers." Both parents were faithful churchgoers and the family attended Protestant services in the Pinehurst town chapel. For years, congregations used the meeting room in the town hall, a few yards south of the Holly Inn and across the street from the town green. In 1924, a smart colonial-style brick chapel opened on the south end of the wooded oval. Though the church was officially nondenominational, it followed Episcopalian form. Mr. Thaddeus A. Cheatham, the town minister, was for a time next-door neighbor to the Ross family and became a good friend of Donald. The Cheatham's daughter, Elizabeth, became a childhood friend of Lillian Ross.

Above: Ross and caddie. (Tufts Archives)

Opposite page: Robert "Hardrock" Robinson, erstwhile Ross caddie. (Tufts Archives)

Above right: Janet (center left) and Donald Ross, ca.1910. (Tufts Archives)

Opposite page, top: Ross and Lillian, ca.1912-13. (Elizabeth Pippitt Shapiro)

Opposite page, bottom: Mr. and Mrs. Ross and their daughter, Lillian, ca.1912-13. (Elizabeth Pippitt Shapiro)

Janet was an avid golfer and a member of the Silver Foils at Pinehurst Country Club, where she competed in tournaments with a handicap of 35. One of her scorecards from a round at Pinehurst No. 4 records a score of 67-65 =132. She and Donald frequently played rounds together at Pinehurst. Once, while playing golf with him on the old No. 1 Course, she pulled a drive on a dogleg left and landed in a massive gully. She insisted on hitting out and flailed away 19 times before extricating her golf ball. Donald watched her from the fairway, completely convulsed in laughter at the site of her futile attempts at recovery. He was so amused by the incident that for years he refused the suggestions of Pinehurst members to soften the offending hazard.

Janet was fluent in Gaelic; Donald wasn't, though he understood it well enough to be able to track conversations. Together, they raised Lillian with a stern but loving kind of discipline that was derived from their Scottish tradition. Lillian recalled being prohibited from whistling on Sundays, and the most profane expression she would ever utter was "h-e-double sticks." She was 18 years old before she was allowed to play poker with her mother at home. There was little extravagance about their life in Pinehurst. Young Lillian was an avid horse rider, and Donald was a frequent visitor to the stables where he would watch her ride. When a friend offered to buy her a fine Kentucky Walking Horse, Donald politely refused. Instead, he bought her a pony named Sheila.

Lillian enjoyed a mild streak of rebelliousness, though never to the point where she would lose her trust in her father's counsel. An early plan to run away from home on her bicycle was quickly thwarted when an employee from the Pinehurst Country Club hailed her down in town to give her a money bag to be delivered to her father.

Like so many other Scottish women, Janet was skilled at handwork, and during World War I she taught Lillian to knit. Together they made socks for the Red Cross. Lillian would knit them and Janet would turn the heel and finish the toe. They also knitted scarves. Janet loved children and was quite a storyteller. Mom and Dad both helped Lillian with spelling and her school work, and when it came to imparting the sterner aspects of Scots Presbyterian morality, it was Donald who conveyed the lessons. "I worshipped him and he worshipped me," she told me. There's no doubt that long after his passing the sentiments were sincere and abiding.

For all his success within the golf world, Ross remained a soft-spoken, modest person who never betrayed his religious roots or his humble origins as a

Scotsman. He lived in an era when sports heroes and celebrities were defined solely by their achievements on athletic fields. Journalists didn't inquire into the private lives of such people. And the extent to which sports was part of a larger business enterprise was of no concern to the public or the press. Ross, the preeminent course designer in his day, was scarcely known outside the golf world, and even within it was a figure recognizable only within a relatively small circle. When he walked the teeing grounds of "Maniac Hill" during the North and South Open, the country's best players readily engaged him in conversation. People of power in both the business world and politics knew him well and might be a guest at his house for tea. But none of this went to Ross's head and it never changed him from his modest, parsimonious ways. He remained stolid: self-contained, quietly confident, and never one to boast. Nor was he prone to worrying or delaying a decision because of self-doubt. "I never remember him agonizing over anything," said Lillian.

Ross's design career coexisted with a dramatic growth in golf's popularity, particularly in the United States. The game had only taken root in the New World a few years prior to his arrival in 1899, and it was to remain largely a private, exclusive amusement until Francis Ouimet's dramatic 1913 U.S. Open play-off win over Englishmen Harry Vardon and Ted Ray at The Country Club. The triumph by the 20-year-old former caddie quickly became the stuff of prototypical American legend: a working lad, a mere amateur, native to this country, fends off foreign professionals and thereby forges a national myth that gives the game newfound popularity.

The impressive achievements of Walter Hagen, Bobby Jones, Gene Sarazen, and others occupied the country's golf coverage. The pages of *Golf Illustrated, American Golfer,* and of the nation's daily newspapers all prominently featured women amateurs as much as they covered the male professional game. Coverage of architecture was limited to the occasional features about new layouts, tournament venues, or travel pieces promoting the virtues of a particular region or resort. Architects themselves were scarcely known as such. Ross produced his own promotional brochures, and his name was used to market turfgrass, golf equipment, and the Pinehurst Resort. But course design has always been the most esoteric of the game's interior domains, and Ross's world was no exception. The way to secure new assignments was to cultivate a reputation among a coterie of well-respected, powerful businessmen. At this, Ross was a quiet master rather than a self-promoting salesman.

A telling measure of his modest standing in the golf world can be discerned from his treatment at the hands of the club that spawned his golf career, Dornoch Golf Club. To be sure, he did little actual design work there. His intervention was limited to a brief visit in 1921 when he stretched the first hole into its present configuration, replete with a new green, and shortened the old second into the shape as a medium-length par 3 that remains as well. Ross wanted to make further changes in the second green, and club secretary John Sutherland apparently had to resist him. When asked a few years later about the hometown boy who had made good in the golf world, Sutherland's response was limited to a few terse words. "Aye, and he would have made the second green a saucer."

There may well have been a deeper underlying antipathy toward the local lad who made good in the world. In 1933, when Dornoch's John Sutherland gave a celebrated speech on the occasion of a testimonial to his 50 years as club secretary, he recited a litany of famous golf names that had helped establish Dornoch's reputation—Old Tom Morris, J.H. Taylor, and George Duncan among them. Yet in his 30-minute talk, which was widely reprinted at the time and is still regarded as a profound moment in the golf club's history, there was no mention of the local mason's son whom Sutherland had hired as greenkeeper and clubmaker. Donald Ross was no local hero. Is this owing to public scorn for the father who had become a town "character?" Or can the slight be attributed to the Ross family's lowly dual standing as artisans and Free Church adherents? The irony is that while the town did not acknowledge its native son, with even a plaque until 1999, Ross himself held dear the place that nurtured him. It was symptomatic of his love for his hometown that he was later to name his house in Pinehurst "Dornoch Cottage." He even left a provision in his will that would have enabled the town itself to inherit his wealth if other named beneficiaries predeceased him. For all the love he carried for Dornoch, it was an affection that remained unrequited. In the eyes of the townspeople he left behind, Donald Ross never escaped the status of a carpenter in overalls who had abandoned them.

Ross met many famous people and was comfortable without ever being carried away by the status he had quietly achieved. Pinehurst was a very famous resort in the 1920s. Many well-known people came to Pinehurst and most of them were eager to play golf with young Lillian's father. She recalls poet Edgar Guest and U.S. Secretary of State Frank Kellogg as regular golfing partners with Ross. One measure of his having made it as an emigrant came in the form of a gift from President Harding, an inveterate golfer and frequent visitor to Essex County Club, where he had first gotten to know Ross. In the early 1920s, he presented Ross with a signed black and white photograph. The personal inscription, mistake and all, reads as follows: "To Donald J. Ross With tribute to a great golpher an honored and outstanding figure in the golfing world Sincerely, Warren G. Harding." Luckily, the 29th president caught his mistake, crossed out the "ph" and overwrote them with an "f."

In those days, the Pinehurst resort operated during three seasons. Its doors would open in late October, and guests would continue coming in and staying through late April. The first two weeks of May were generally reserved for meetings and large groups. Then the resort would shut down for the summer. The time was used for repairs and improvements on the hotel grounds. One golf course, or sometimes 27 holes, would be maintained throughout the summer for local play. It was then that Ross and his associates would go to work making improvements and experiments upon the layout—especially on No. 2, which seems to have been in a perennial state of being tinkered upon.

During the summer months, the Ross family lived in New England. Mrs. Ross and Lillian lived together while Donald used his northern base for a torrent of train travel throughout the country. Ross did his work in this way from spring all the way through summer and into fall. Because he traveled so much by train, they summered in Worcester, Holyoke, and Newton, towns in eastern or central Massachusetts that were close to railroad stations. During World War I, they lived in Worcester at 821 Pleasant Street along a bustling road whose main advantage was that it was near the trolley line and thus provided easy transport to the downtown station two miles to the east.

From 1919 until 1925, he worked out of a home office at 1032 Beacon Street in Newton Centre. It was a comfortable eight-room house on a corner lot and it sat on a rise in the road just a mile east of the town center. In those days the location was considered "out in the country." Ross cultivated 11 different varieties of roses in his yard. There was a four-door black Packard sedan in the garage, but Ross preferred to travel around the country on trains.

During their Pinehurst years, the Ross family occupied three different houses. From 1914 until 1922, they lived in a gingerbread house called Hawthorne Cottage at 50 Magnolia Road, around the corner from the town center. In the backyard, Lillian and her playmates would construct cardboard houses out of packing cartons and dig tunnels in the backyard. Janet did most of the cooking, and prepared afternoon teas for Donald and his guests. A local fellow named John Womble served as house-helper; he and Lillian would catch squirrels and bake squirrel pie for the family.

Ross house, 1032 Beacon Street, Newton Centre, MA, where he worked and lived from 1919 to 1925. (Bradley S. Klein)

Opposite page, top: Ross and his Packard. (Tufts Archives)

Opposite page, bottom: Hawthorne Cottage, 50 Magnolia Road, Pinehurst, the Ross residence from 1914 until 1922. (Tufts Archives)

In 1919, Janet was diagnosed with breast cancer and underwent a mastectomy operation at the hands of a Dr. Carleton Potter in Cambridge. Though the surgery was said to be successful, her health soon began a noticeable slide. Although a small woman, barely 5-feet tall, she had been lively in tone and full of face. But she was in fading health. Her skin grew taut and her face sank, her hair turning completely gray as well. The last family trip back to Scotland took place in the summer of 1921. Donald, Janet, and Lillian set sail on Saturday, July 2 for Scotland on the *S.S. Cameronia*. The crossing took 10 days. Upon their arrival, they visited both families, at Moniaive and Dornoch. Ross looked over courses that had been built there in the two years since his last visit in 1919. It was during this six-week visit to Scotland that he did his only design work at Royal Dornoch—confined, as it was, to the first and second holes. On the return voyage in mid-August, Janet looked wistfully at the shoreline as their steamer departed from Glasgow.

Both Donald and Lillian saw that she was in tears so he put his arm around Janet to comfort her. "I just don't think I'll ever see Scotland again," she said.

The prophecy turned out to be right. Janet's health continued to deteriorate. Though she was not bedridden, she was slowed down. She and Donald managed a round of golf on Saturday, February 11, 1922. The next night, at 10:40 p.m., she died in their bedroom on the second floor of Hawthorne Cottage. The death certificate listed two causes: "myocarditis" (an inflammation of the heart) and gallstones. Ross publicly mourned her loss by wearing a black armband. Lillian, only 12 years old at the time, was tended to by the MacNabs, and for several months she moved in with them at the Pine Crest Inn.

Despite no turndown in the national golf market, Ross's productivity slowed down noticeably in 1922. His output was only half of what he'd done the year before, suggesting that the emotional burden of Janet's death had taken its toll on his career. Uncharacteristically, of him, he took a long journey out to the West coast during the summer of 1922, leaving Boston on July 19 and not returning from California until just after Labor Day. While he was out there, Lillian moved into the Pine Crest and was cared for by the MacNabs.

TEUGEGA

Ross spent the summer of 1923 in Rome, New York, where he was affianced to Susan Comstock Aldridge. Aunt Susie, as young Lillian fondly referred to Susie Aldridge, hailed from a moderately wealthy family in Rome. Evidence suggests she was born in 1877, making her about five years younger than Ross. A graduate of Rome Free Academy, she also held a music degree from Albany Business College and went on to become secretary to Mr. Barton Haselton, president of Rome Brass and Copper Co. Occasionally she went on family trips with Mr. and Mrs. Haselton, including winter visits to Pinehurst. It was there that she first met Donald and Janet Ross, at one point even attending a birthday party for young Lillian—with whom she developed and maintained genuine mutual affection. Aldridge had even corresponded with Mrs. Ross, and upon her death in 1922 she sent Donald Ross a condolence letter. Susie was an outstanding golfer who regularly won events at her home course, the Teugega Country Club in Rome, which Ross had designed and built in 1920. Indeed, Susie was Teugega's first women's champion in 1921.

Ross had received the Teugega commission through Haselton, who was a member at the original 9-hole Teugega facility before its move northeast of Rome onto a 250-acre site adjoining Lake Delta, including 3,000 feet of shoreline frontage. Ross had been unsparing in his judgment of the original layout. "Outside of one other course that was built out of a swamp," he told the board of directors, "this is the second worst course in the country." Unfortunately from the standpoint of planning golf holes, 81 prime acres of lakefront property was set aside for estate-like homes and the clubhouse. But the par-72, 6,366-yard inland course, which Ross (working with Hatch) designed for the site, would remain one of his most elegant, if least appreciated. The cost of the course, including land acquisition and construction, came to $73,946.23. Ross's share for design and supervision was $4,040.43.

In part drawn by his developing relationship with Susie Aldridge, Ross was a frequent visitor to Rome and Teugega. Barton Haselton's daughter, Joan Haselton Evans, born in 1913, is among those interviewed for this book who relishes her memories of Ross. She met Ross in Pinehurst around 1920 and saw him during his many visits to Rome, when he was a houseguest while working on Teugega. She remembers him as always being well dressed in a wool jacket and often in knickers.

Teugega Country Club, Rome, NY, ca.1940, looking east to Delta Dam, with Lake Delta on the north. Note the pronounced mounding around the two adjoining greens, the 18th (left) and 9th (right). The 136-yard, par-3 seventh green, easily identified by the eight bunkers that surround it, was the scene of Ross's first hole-in-one in 1923. The two-tiered green includes a bowled-out area at front-right. (Teugega Country Club)

She also enjoyed a friendship with young Lillian in the immediate aftermath of Janet's death. And when young Joan's family traveled away from Rome, it was Susie Aldridge—"Miss Susie"—who tended to Joan and her older sister at their house.

Ross was a frequent visitor to the Teugega course. He was 50 or 51 years old when he made his first hole-in-one, at the 136-yard seventh. The green, surrounded by eight deep bunkers, had (and still has) a punchbowl lower tier and an upper tier that fell off steeply behind.

Over the years, heavy plantings of cedars and firs have narrowed Ross's original links-style fairways at Teugega. The landing areas are also considerably more narrow owing to single-row irrigation. But the greens surfaces and surrounding bunkering have held up well. So, too, has the memory of Ross's considerable presence in Rome. Club members know they have something special in their unheralded upstate golf course.

Between the golf course and one another's company, Ross had much to share with Susie Aldridge. The two were engaged in late April of 1923. Writing from

Opposite page, top: Teugega's 136-yard par-3 seventh hole. (Bradley S. Klein)

Opposite page, bottom: The par-4 11th hole at Teugega. (Bradley S. Klein)

Above: The tee shot at Teugega's 432-yard par-4 17th hole. (Bradley S. Klein)

Detroit's Hotel Tuller on May 7, Ross sent an adoring letter to his daughter about the impending marriage. "Auntie Susie is longing so much to see you, she loves you, and can hardly wait until you get there. What a happy time we three will have together. Everyone is very happy to know Auntie is going to be with us forever."

A devout Presbyterian, Suzie lived with her brother and his wife and children in a gracious old home at 1006 North George Street in Rome, and it was there from which Ross maintained a steady correspondence from June 25 through August 1923. Sadly, however, there was to be no wedding. Susie died of cancer on the morning of August 31, with Ross at her bedside at home.

REMARRIAGE

The Ross family's final trip to Scotland in 1921 would prove fateful in more ways than one. It was not only Janet's last return visit to her homeland, it would also be the final time Donald Ross would see his parents. His mother, Lillian Campbell Ross, died in March of 1924, and his father, Murdoch, passed away 15 months later. Both were buried in the family plot at Dornoch Free Presbyterian Church.

Donald Ross finally remarried in 1924. It was to a wealthy widow, Mrs. Florence Sturgie Blackinton, whom Ross had met in 1922 while she was inspecting a two-story, wood frame house for sale at 120 Midland Road, Pinehurst. The house overlooked the third green of the No. 2 Course, and Donald, as representative of the Country Club, had some negotiations with her and a real estate agent regarding property boundaries along the golf course.

It would prove to be a fateful encounter. When Janet had died, Mrs. Blackinton sent along a condolence note but there was no contact between her and Donald for nearly a year. Then, after Susie Aldridge's death in 1923, Donald became an object of interest in Pinehurst social circles.

Florence Blackinton was a prosperous woman from Framingham, Massachusetts who was accustomed to a leisured life and not at all handy or skilled in the daily arts of life. In 1923, she became a widow. After she and Donald began to see each other socially, the relationship blossomed so quickly that his daughter was not the only one to be surprised about the betrothal. When they married in Framingham on November 7, 1924, there weren't any guests in attendance because Donald was suffering a serious case of throat ulcers. So prominent had the course designer become in Eastern social circles that the wedding was reported in the *New York Herald Tribune* of November 11 under the headline "Donald J. Ross, Golf Architect Wed on Sickbed." The ceremony was performed by the Rev. Walton H. Daggett in Florence's home, "where she was nursing her new husband back to health."

After the remarriage, Ross took up new residences in both Pinehurst and New England. In Pinehurst, it was Florence's house by the third green on No. 2. "Dornoch Cottage" he named it. Photographs from the early 1920s show it as a

substantial, two-story brick structure, surrounded by scrub and a few pines. A home like this passed for relatively prosperous in the Pinehurst of its era, making it appropriate for the town's most famous golf personality. There was room for a home office, and soon a garden area was opened up at the rear that looked out onto the third green. Ross grew roses here, along with azaleas, japonicas, and 13 types of holly trees.

Florence maintained her family residence at 55 Hunting Street in North Attleboro, Massachusetts, 20 miles northeast of Providence, and Ross continued to use it when he came north. This allowed him to sell his house in Newton Centre. On September 25, 1925 he moved his office into the Blackinton family's seaside property at Little Compton, Rhode Island. The 52-acre property, called Quaker Hill Farm, sits on a lovely, rock-strewn promontory at the point where Sakonnet Bay empties into Long Island Sound. At the house, Donald grew his prized rambling roses along a stone wall. He had a lovely garden there, and though he was skilled at cultivating flowers, vegetables, shrubs, and turfgrass, he left much of the

Donald Ross and Florence Blackinton were both widowed when they married in November of 1924. Ross, who had worn a wedding band during his first marriage, is not wearing one in this photo. The 1934 photo also shows that Ross had adapted to steel shafts in his golf clubs. (Tufts Archives)

*Right: Dornoch Cottage, 120 Midland Road,
Pinehurst, just to the left of the third green on the No. 2
Course, where Ross lived from 1925 until his death.
(Tufts Archives)*

*Below: Inside Dornoch Cottage. Ross and Florence in
the sitting room, ca.1940. (Tufts Archives)*

Above: Dornoch Cottage today. (Bradley S. Klein)

Left: Quaker Hill Farm, Little Compton, RI, looking out upon Rhode Island Sound. Ross and Florence spent summers here beginning in 1925. (Bradley S. Klein)

Opposite page, above: The view from Quaker Hill Farm. Opposite page, below: The cottage at Quaker Hill Farm where Ross and Eric Nelson did their design work and correspondence. (Bradley S. Klein)

Above: Sakonnet Golf Club, Little Compton, RI. The second hole is a 180-yard par 3 to a green set along the point where the Sakonnet River opens to Rhode Island Sound. Ross redesigned this unheralded gem in 1921 and maintained a golf membership at the club for years. Only 5,891 yards long, with a par of 69, the club remains a fascinating test of the windswept ground game. (Bradley S. Klein)

Left: Sakonnet Golf Club's sixth hole, a 213-yard par 3. Greenside features like these swales create interest that endures. (Bradley S. Klein)

day-to-day tending to the hired couple that helped around the house, Alfred and Jenny Glasspool. Jenny had come from Scotland when she was 18 and served as Mrs. Blackinton's cook. (It was also left to Alfred and Jenny to ferry Mrs. Blackinton's Packard back and forth between Little Compton and Pinehurst.) The house at Quaker Hill Farm was only two miles from Sakonnet Golf Club, a club Donald had reworked in 1921. He played many a summer round there and continually tinkered with the design of the layout.

Due to her upbringing, Florence was not accustomed to doing things with her hands, such as cooking, cleaning, and serving teas. She also wasn't comfortable at sea. In the summer of 1928, she and Donald set sail with 18-year old Lillian and Mrs. Blackinton's 22-year old son, John, for a two-month trip to Scotland. Florence was seasick the entire way. It would prove to be Donald's last visit to his homeland—the result of his wife's unease with such travel and the difficulties imposed first by the Depression and then by World War II.

Despite suffering from recurring throat abscesses, Ross persisted in his habit of one or two cigars daily. He stayed away from cigarettes and pipe tobacco, however, and his drinking did not go beyond a social whiskey in the afternoon or evening.

THE GOOD FATHER

For all his extended absences from home, Ross remained a loyal and doting father. Young Lillian greatly missed her mother and did not ever fully warm to her father's second wife. She had grown up with a stay-at-home mom while her father had been out traveling across the country. She was accustomed to seasonal residences, having switched homes—and schools—according to the same clock that governed her father's movements from Massachusetts to Pinehurst. With Janet gone and Donald's design practice requiring him to spend so much time on the road, the decision was made to send Lillian to prep school. So off she went in the fall of 1924 to the Emma Willard School in Troy, New York.

By Lillian's own account, she hated every minute of it. The girls were confined to uniforms, high boots in wintertime, laced up shoes otherwise, and absolute prohibitions on everything from silk underwear to silk stockings and high heels. Just before Christmas of 1924, she loaded up all her belongings for the train ride back to Pinehurst. Lillian was prepared to leave Emma Willard altogether, if she could only convince her father. After she arrived in Pinehurst, Donald and his daughter took a long walk out to the dairy farm. By the time they got back it had been decided that Lillian would return to school. "Because I was a Scots girl," she said, "and because if you started something you finished it. I suppose Dad was right about that." Lillian did take a small measure of revenge on her school, though. For her first reunion in 1928, Lillian, by then a freshman at college, returned to Emma Willard in an outfit entirely prohibited among the coeds enrolled there—silk underwear, a velvet suit, high heels, and her mouth plastered in lipstick.

Lillian attended Mount Holyoke College in South Hadley, Massachusetts. Her father had designed a golf course there called The Orchards adjacent to the campus; the first nine holes in 1922, the second nine five years later. Lillian applied to the school because the rustic New England campus in South Hadley allowed her easy access to good friends of her parents who lived in the adjoining town of Holyoke. Donald and Janet Ross had not only socialized with Mr. and Mrs. Lewis Wyckoff, Lewis had given Ross considerable impetus to start his full-time design business in 1913 and had remained a lifelong friend. In 1923, they hired Ross to design a new Mt. Tom Golf Course (now called Wyckoff Park). Lillian called Mrs. Wyckoff "Aunt Minnie" and treated her like a second mother—a feeling that, by all evidence, was reciprocated. Consequently, instead of making the long trek down to Pinehurst for holidays, Lillian often spent vacations in Holyoke. The close bonds would get tighter after Lillian met Richard Pippitt. He was Aunt Minnie's nephew, and eventually he would become Lillian Ross's husband.

Lillian graduated with a degree in French from Mount Holyoke College on June 17, 1932. The day before he attended the ceremony, Ross wrote to Leonard Tufts that "she has done very well, but we are glad it's over so that we can have her home for a while." Before Lillian would come home, however, there would be an extended trip abroad. Accompanied by Aeneas Ross, she set sail on the *Brittania* from Boston on Sunday, July 31 and landed in Liverpool a week later. She and her uncle spent two months together with the Ross clan at Dornoch before she headed down to visit her mother's family in Moniaive. Lillian would leave Scotland on November 6, but Aeneas had already decided to stay in his hometown. He ended up living a quiet, even poor life as an itinerant farmhand and remained something of a sad fixture of the town, his elder brother Donald having to rescue him from persistent if modest debt. He had never really been happy working for Donald in America. Perhaps he was a misfit who never quite adjusted wherever he went. Although he had worked as a construction supervisor for his brother on a number of golf course projects in the States, Aeneas never again got involved in the game after he returned to Scotland. In between jobs at area farms, his sisters would put him up. He died penniless in Dornoch in February of 1957, the last of his family to be buried under that one gravestone in Free Church cemetery.

FINAL YEARS

In the midst of the Depression, Ross accepted cutbacks in his own salary. In a June 17, 1932 letter to Leonard Tufts, for example, he acknowledges a pay cut of $1,000. "I am agreeable to this," he wrote, "as I feel that under present conditions it is fair for every one to bear their share of the burdens. My sincerest desire has always been for the success of Pinehurst—not only financially but in every other way."

Writing from Little Compton at another time, Ross also explains that he has recently taken on "interesting work as expert examiner" for the Massachusetts Civil Service Commission. Ross's job was to draw up exam questions for prospective club managers and greenkeepers at state and local municipal golf courses. The certification, such as it was, consisted of a written exam and oral interview. "When you know that all manner of men apply you can readily understand the fun I get," he added. One applicant, when asked how often the cup should be moved, responded that "once a year is enough." According to this aspiring superintendent, the greenkeeper can't be concerned that most golfers want the cup moved every time they putt.

The Depression era was not a kind time for any of the old famous Grand Hotel properties. Those that didn't close down limped through. The Pinehurst Resort, for all its fame as a golf property, was never especially profitable. Tight management by the Tufts family, coupled with the parsimonious ways of company treasurer I.C. Sledge, had characterized the resort's heady days. But as the economy slowed down and resort travel became affordable to a smaller sector of the population, additional measures were needed. Bank loans arranged through longstanding friends of the resort appear to have prevented Pinehurst Resort from falling onto even harder times during the 1930s. Yet hard decisions had to be made about maintenance. For years, Leonard Tufts's letters had been entirely preoccupied with fussing over details, new techniques for agronomy, or simply squeezing nickels. His successor, his son Richard, had a broader view than of mere day-to-day operations, especially when it concerned the quality of golf.

May 16th, 1938
Mr. Donald J. Ross
55 Hunting St.
North Attleboro, Mass.
Dear Mr. Ross:

I am might sorry you found it necessary to go north on account of your throat but without question this was the wise thing to do. I started several times to come by and say good bye to you but as there was nothing special to say I thought it better not to bother you as I know that the one thing you should not do at this time is to talk.

The only thing of any consequence we have to discuss at this time is the question of maintenance for the summer and I am sure we can cover this just as well by correspondence. I hope therefore you will not take any chances on coming down again unless your throat is fully recovered.

I have not yet received all the estimates for maintenance but it is quite apparent that we are going to have a very difficult time keeping the total figure down to the $70,000 fixed by the directors. I think it is going to be easy to keep the Carolina figure down but unfortunately the Carolina is the place that we really need to spend money on the most. As they say through the organization they are pretty well equipped now to compete for business *except in the bedrooms of the Carolina. However because it would take a lot of money to even start there I am afraid it is out of the question for this year. The reason the Carolina figure can be kept low is that what has been done there is now in pretty good shape.*

At the Holly Inn however, nothing has been done to the bedrooms since 1926, either for paint or furniture covering. Things are beginning to look pretty seedy and we have a lot that should be done there. Also their linen and china is about gone and we must make some replacements.

We also have a problem at the dairy. It is a question whether with the present condition of the buildings and the bottling equipment we can continue to pass the requirements for certified milk. If we cannot meet these we would have to put in a pasteurizing plant and this would be expensive.

The laundry does not require much unless we want to put in a dry cleaning plant. There has been very serious criticism of the service in this respect which, as you know, we have to go to Aberdeen for and we really ought to have this plant.

Frank [Maples] brought in today his figures on the golf courses but I have not yet seen the figures for the country club. There does not seem to be much that we can cut out of the golf course figures unless it be the work on the 10th hole of No. 2 course, building an approach green near the club house and putting down the wooden blocks in front of the work shop. The work on the fairways of No. 4 and No. 5 holes on No. 2 course, I think is very important as I have heard some criticism of the condition of these two holes. I also think it important to increase the fertilizer this year as the only criticism I heard of the golf courses was on the condition of the fairways.

Apparently Frank has to have a new tractor and nearly everything else he has listed is small. I would like to get your ideas on dropping out the three items I have mentioned above, if we find we are going to have difficulty sticking to the figures.

Incidentally, in connection with the changes on the 10th hole of No. 2, I suppose the principal reason for shortening the tee is to permit the short players to carry the top of the hill easily. I have heard criticism from short players that they are unable to get over the traps with their second shots. I have always felt that the hole would be weaker if they were able to and the way to make the hole easier for the short player would be to move the left hand trap back nearer to the green. This would enable the short player to play his second short of the trap and put his third down in front of the green or if he got an exceptionally good drive, to play over the right hand trap and gain the advantage of a better position to play his third shot. It has always seemed to me that this would also make the hole more attractive for the long player. As it is now, the left hand trap does not bother the long player in the least and the hole is uninteresting to him because all he has to do is hit two shots. I know the pros have criticized it to me for this reason, that the second shot was uninteresting. Moving the left hand trap nearer to the green would surely make the second shot more exacting for the long player.

I hope that you had a good trip north and that you will speedily recover from your throat ailment.

Sincerely,
Richard S. Tufts

By now the golf design business had slowed to a trickle. Ross's firm had all but dissolved, with Hatch and Johnson on their own and McGovern working only sporadically. Donald traveled only on occasion, spending his time between Pinehurst in the winters and Little Compton over the summer. The documentation for this phase of his life is thin. One letter, though, from his acquaintance, A.W. Tillinghast, conveys the sense of sadness and of the "lost world" that pervaded those who had achieved their fame and reputation in the headier days of golf's golden age.

A. W. Tillinghast
Golf Course Architect
Harrington Park, New Jersey
2444 Putnam Street
Toledo, Ohio
January 22nd 1942
Dear Donald:

Without a doubt these lines will come as a surprise to you for I have been buried away so long that very few know what has happened to me. But for the past two years I have been able to do little other than drop an occasional letter—to those old friends, whom I highly esteem such as O.B. Keeler et al and perusing their replies.

It has been six or seven years since Mrs. Tillinghast and myself called on you at Pinehurst. We hope that Mrs. Ross is still at your good right hand and that she is well. Please convey to her our best wishes. You may recall that at that time I was visiting courses throughout the country, sponsored by the P.G.A. and before finishing that work I critically examined more than six hundred in all parts. Naturally I enjoyed it and am sure I managed to accomplish some good. Then came the widespread, devastating and generally ridiculous efforts of the W.P.A. (And the P.W.A.) In mass production. Doubtless the idea had some merit but much real harm was a result. For, Good Lord, when I review it all I can only regret the waste of so much good money and the resultant amateur accomplishments. Thank God, I had sense enough to refuse to have anything to do with it at all. It really was criminal. Much could be revealed along these lines, but what's the use?

Then four years ago we removed to California, rather anticipating the ending of our days out there—and I nearly ended mine. I am chasing hard after 67 years, you know. I think we found that our ages were not far apart. Our Sun Kissed friends exhibited two widely divergent propensities. Either a singular reluctance to part with any real money or what was much worse the inclination to waste it on display with little understanding of creating golf holes as you and I understand them. It was rather discouraging work but after planning for the construction and reconstruction of a half dozen courses out there with some appreciation—I was laid low by a severe heart attack some two years since. For a time the doctors gave me but small chance but my reserve pulled me through eventually, but I received strict orders against continuing any sort of golf work. This was very tough on a man who had followed such from 1905, particularly one who loved it as much as I, but the warning was direct and unmistakable—"Continue and it will be curtains for you"! So that was that.

I was brought here last April and we have been living with the family of my eldest daughter ever since, while recovery has been slow and I am still confined to my room. As against my old normal weight of around 185 I just manage to move the scale beam at 134. However, while recovery has been discouragingly slow absolute rest is restoring me, but that is what is in store for me from now on—quiet and rest. It's hard though to give it all up— that is the golf. When I will be East again is a matter of conjecture. Before the bad weather settled on us, my daughter used to drive me around the country a bit. Quite a few golf courses but as far as I was able to observe, only one good one, old Inverness, which is much the same as ever. And it is good to find something in the game that suggests the good old days. So much has changed to the new tempo as to be a bit startling, even to the playing of the game.

I suppose Pinehurst is enjoying its measure of prosperity and that you see Bill Fownes now and then. Will you be so good as to remember me to him? I have known him and his family for a good many years now. And Bob Harlow? I presume he still is with you and doing good work. Speaking of Bill Fownes, I saw him . . . last at Pinehurst when I paid my one and only visit to you. I think he had an attack similar to mine. He was taking things mighty easy I do know. I hope he is getting along all right for one by one the old guard is moving on.

I wonder what ever became of Nipper Campbell. I used to have a letter from him now and then and he was out here in Ohio somewhere then. He had three brothers that I knew rather well—Jock, Matt and Andrew. I met his sister when out on the P.G.A. Tour, somewhere up in Connecticut, Hartford I think. They were a great lot and all thoroughly Scotch. Sandy Smith has gone to his reward, of course, and so many others, too.

And your good brother, Alec. He did not look like himself in the old days, when I saw him last. I think that one of the real joys of the P.G.A. tour was meeting up with so many of my old friends of the "Guttie" ball days. I am sure that this feeling will rather explain my lines to you. May you live long and prosper!

Very Sincerely
A.W. Tillinghast
When in the mood, with a bit of time on your hands, do drop me a line.
AWT.

On May 31, 1946, Ross resigned as "a director and officer or in a managerial capacity." Richard Tufts accepted the resignation, though he requested that Ross stay on with Pinehurst Inc. in an advisory capacity and that he serve as president of Pinehurst Country Club. His salary would remain at $2,400 for the winter season, plus concessions from the golf shop. Eric Nelson was to continue as manager of the country club while Frank Maples would stay on as manager of the golf courses.

Realizing the full weight of the transition, Richard Tufts added a personal note in which he conveyed with customary grace his appreciation for the years that Donald Ross had tendered to the company.

Above: Ross and two of his grandchildren, Susan (left) and Janet (right) Pippitt, November 1945. (Elizabeth Pippitt Shapiro)

Right: Ross's funeral service at Pinehurst Village Chapel, April 27, 1948. (Tufts Archives)

Below: Ross grave, Newton Centre Cemetery, MA. (Bradley S. Klein)

One of the happiest and most outstanding features of my work here at Pinehurst has been to know that you have always been at my side during the tough times we have gone through together. I am also mighty proud of the fact that we have worked together all these years under an unwritten understanding that really goes back to the agreements made with you by my grandfather in the early days of Pinehurst. In a sense I regret suggesting that our arrangements be reduced to writing, but as pointed out to you, I believe both Frank Maples and Eric Nelson would appreciate our doing so.

Of course as far as you and I are concerned there will be no change. I look on this new arrangement solely as a release for you from the burden of responsibility which you have so long carried and as providing you with the opportunity for greater leisure in which to enjoy the fruits of all your labors without interruption to the many happy associations of the past.

Ross's health seemed to decline slowly. A November 1945 photograph of Ross with his two grandchildren, Janet and Susan Pippitt, shows him in good spirits. But on the 22nd of that month, illness prevented him from attending the Detroit Country Club's tribute to his younger brother Alex for 30 years of service as head professional. By the time Ross served as host of the first annual meeting of the American Society of Golf Course Architects at Pinehurst in December of 1947, he was little more than a caretaker to a design shop whose work was entirely delegated to McGovern and Ellis Maples.

Donald Ross suffered a heart attack on Sunday evening, April 25, 1948. He was taken to Moore County Hospital, where he died the following morning at 9 a.m. at the age of 75. His daughter received the phone call a couple of hours later, but there was no time for her to get down to Pinehurst for the memorial service held the next day at the Pinehurst Village Chapel. Nor was she one to hold up such

a service until her arrival, though that was certainly her preference.

Later that week, Ross was buried next to his first wife, Janet Kennedy Conchie Ross, in Newton Centre Cemetery. Ross's second wife, Florence Blackinton, lived until 1955 and was buried with her first husband in North Attleboro. At the summer retreat in Little Compton, RI, home ownership at Quaker Hill Farm was subsequently divided, with both families continuing to enjoy use of the property through the 1990s.

On the day of the memorial service for Donald James Ross in Pinehurst Chapel, the *New York Times* ran a full column obituary, accompanied by his photograph. The article mistakenly credited him with "more than 600 golfing layouts, in this country, Canada and Cuba." A full-length, front-page piece in that week's *Pinehurst Outlook* went one better. Not only did the article repeat the figure of 600-plus, it embellished Ross's reputation with an account of him as "one of the world's greatest golfers."

The myth making had begun. Indeed, it had long been gathering momentum thanks to Ross's ingenious penchant for salesmanship. There was nothing disingenuous about it, however. His lifelong love of golf expressed itself in the kind of enthusiasm that always inspired people around him. Throughout his life, he was more devoted to promotion of the game than to his own career as a clubmaker, greenkeeper, and designer of courses. Nothing could quiet that spirited pursuit, and when he passed from these fairways there were many others eager to take up where he had left off. Not even for a day would his death stand in the way of the golf. The great masters' death would not shut down the links. This was made clear in the *Pinehurst Outlook* obituary:

"On the day Mr. Ross died two tournaments were scheduled at the Pinehurst Country Club. Play had already started when the news of his death reached the club house. Some thought that these tournaments should be cancelled or postponed. Some even suggested that the club house be closed. But others felt that as Mr. Ross had lived by and for golf all his life, that he would have wished for the tournaments to go on; for the golfers to continue to play the game. The flag at the club was lowered to half staff. The tournaments were completed."

Ross at Pinehurst in 1934. (Tufts Archives)

Chapter Seven
Reading A Ross Course

*F*ew people in the game of golf have been able to exercise as profound an influence as Donald Ross. During his 75 years, a sport originally confined to the untouched native linksland of the British Isles—which in the late nineteenth century included Ireland—spread throughout the world and took root on inland terrains that demanded considerable modification.

In his day, no one specifically trained for the craft. Yet few people have ever been better prepared to alter the game's landscapes. Yes, the greenkeeper in overalls from the far north of Scotland was a high school dropout, but he was also gifted in the ways of the earth. A half century after his death, we continue to be inspired by his work and have something to learn from it—providing we can properly read its intent. To do this requires that we identify the distinguishing elements of Ross's design work.

QUANTITY ALONE IS NO VIRTUE

It is, of course, easy to wonder about the supposed virtues of Ross and his 399 golf courses simply because he couldn't have spent much time refining very many of them. That's especially true for Ross because—as his record makes clear—he did not always personally supervise his plans in the field. He preferred, instead, to delegate authority to his longtime associates, or to a local crew. On that account alone, there is considerable variation in his work, often from one course to another in the same area.

A study of Ross's lifework shows that he didn't make as much as a single field inspection to nearly one-third of the courses he worked on. Instead he relied upon topographic maps and design sketches provided by his associates, as well as plans that he and his draftsman, Walter Irving Johnson, prepared back home in their design shop. In roughly another one-third of his projects he seems to have made a single visit, perhaps on an overnight basis and extending to several days.

Therefore, in only the remaining one-third of the projects attributed to Ross did he make follow-up or repeated visits.

The difficulty starts with the sheer volume of his work—certainly no virtue on its own accord. There are many architects working today with 15-20 courses on the drawing boards at any one time. And yet for all that volume (indeed, *because* of all that volume) their work likely will never be of any national significance, much less make a regional impact, in terms of design aesthetics and strategic intrigue. A very strong case can be made for adhering to a modest slate of work that allows a designer complete control and oversight of his projects. This is the preferred method for a number of creative architects whose work today appears to embody many of the traditional design values associated with the Golden Age of Architecture—the period between the two world wars. Only by keeping total control over a small number of projects can a designer ensure consistency of vision and quality. Otherwise, the work is handed over to a construction crew, whose bulldozer operators and feature shapers will have little organic connection to a particular architect's vision of land and of golf.

The pursuit of large volumes of production is surely the most unfortunate legacy of Ross's otherwise admirable design career. As he himself acknowledged toward the end of his life, he simply did too many courses and did not have enough control over them.

To be sure, the design profession has changed dramatically since Ross's day. Most designers today are required to prepare extensive design documentation, including hole-by-hole plans for every contour, bunker, and green as a precondition of design. Such an exhaustive paper trail facilitates a number of functions— including environmental permitting, wetlands mitigation, construction bidding, material cost estimates, and the detailed schedule of building in the field. To this extent, the golf architecture practice has been thoroughly subjected to bureaucratic and regulatory control, making innovation in the field an exception to the rule rather than the standard of the craft. It would appear that "the suits" (the businessmen and lawyers) have all but taken over a craft that was initially the product of creative and idiosyncratic minds.

A few designers today adhere to the old-fashioned method of design and building in the dirt—and they do so at some risk of recurring cost overruns. But this is also the only way to exercise control over a project's final form and to maximize the subtle ground contours inherent in a plot of land. Depending upon the advantages and features of a given parcel, the best way to preserve and utilize them may be by innovating in the field rather than proceeding by sophisticated plans and construction documents. Ironically, the more systematic and self-conscious design becomes as a profession, the less natural and the more affected it appears upon completion.

Not that Ross "winged it." On the contrary, his courses resulted from careful observation, sketches made in the field, and planning in terms of construction and

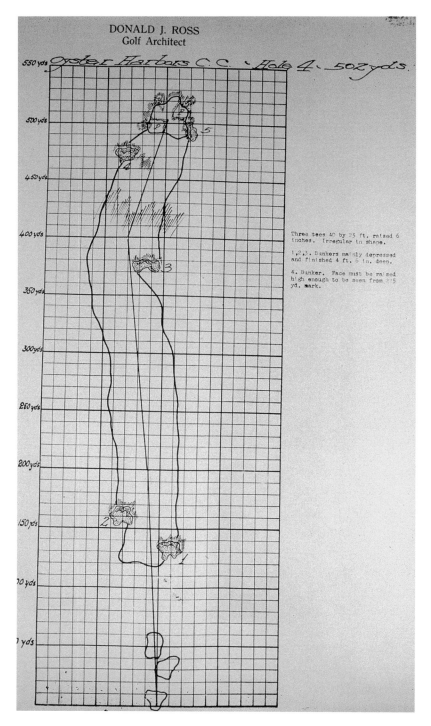

DONALD J. ROSS
Golf Architect

Three tees 40 by 25 ft. raised 6
inches. Irregular in shape.

1,2,3. Bunkers mainly depressed
and finished 4 ft. 6 in. deep.

4. Bunker. Face must be raised
high enough to be seen from 215
yd. mark.

seeding sequences. He was legendary for making notes on a hole-by-hole basis. Though Ross himself did not draw to perspective, he was not averse to putting tracing paper over a black and white photo of a (prospective) hole and penciling in the desired contours or features. The final drawings he and his associate, Walter Irving Johnson, produced remain today as examples of clarity and economy of expression. His green plans incorporated drainage and playing slopes. His hole sketches portrayed spatial relationships between open and closed ground, and his centerline depictions of vertical elevation changes down the centerline—or axis—of a hole from tee to fairway to green are elegant and revealing.

Ross was not a complicated man, and he did not occupy his life with frivolous or ostentatious pleasures. There was a devout humility and honesty of presentation in everything he did, whether in his family life, his business practice, or in his design work. Things were straightforward for him. Life demanded honesty and simplicity, but also sincerity. He was never one to offer an elaborate or deceiving image when basic truth would suffice. These character traits are evident in his design work

In a sense, he remained deeply indebted to his roots in the small town of Dornoch, a place where people knew one another and where a man's character spoke loudly even before one opened one's mouth. Add to this the sober virtues and level-headedness of a devout, Free Church Presbyterian upbringing and you have the elements of a sound if unadorned approach to life, to work, and to the rewards one would encounter during a round of golf. A sense of just rewards, of a reasonable balance between risk and punishments, was to characterize his design work.

The quirky, the unexpected, even the misleading if not the sudden and abrupt, also occupied a place in the game, as they did in life. The need to eliminate all such elements from golf results in a homogeneity of design and grooming that is anathema to a classic sensibility. Ross might not have shared Macdonald's or MacKenzie's penchant for the occasionally grandiose or extreme, but he surely believed, as they did, that there was no small element of luck involved, and that the better the player, the luckier he seemed to get.

Also evident in Ross's design work is his love of walking. His courses are a pleasure to stroll because they make use of—and allow one to experience—the

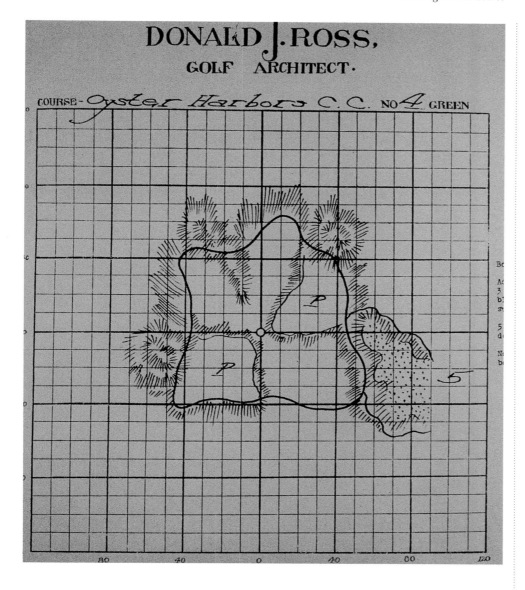

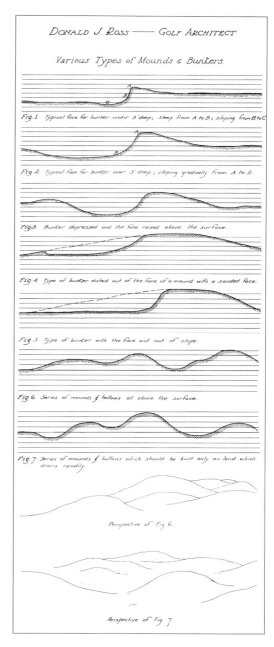

land. In this regard, there was nothing unique that might set him apart from his contemporaries. A man who grew up in a small town where everyone walked and who had an abiding love of flowers, plants, and the simple curve of natural ground would go on to design elegant if modest little parklands where golf could be pursued as a small but vital part of nature.

If he did not always build spectacular holes, he built very sound ones that cohered on the basis of efficient, elegant, and sometimes ingenious routings that left no ground wasted and no long walks between holes. Many designers today, armed with skilled shapers, cater to popular aesthetics and the flair for the dramatic by building big, bold, beautiful holes. What is often lacking among today's designers, even the most lauded ones, is a clearer sense of integration whereby the holes fit into a larger picture.

Opposite page and above left: Oyster Harbors Country Club, Osterville, MA. (Stephen Kay)

Above: "Various Types of Mounds & Bunkers." W.I. Johnson's drawings from the early 1920s depict bunkers in cross section and mounds in perspective. (Tufts Archives)

Ross kept this picture firmly in his mind as he worked. No one developed more economical routings. No one made better use of a rectangular or triangular parcel with golf holes that used up every corner without wasted space. The result is that most of his courses have an interior flow to them that makes them enjoyable as walks in the park—walks that can be enjoyed and managed without recourse to signage indicating where the next hole lies.

LESSONS OF LINKSLAND

From his days as a caddie Ross would have learned both the joys and the challenges that golf brings to people of every skill level. Dornoch was a particularly egalitarian town insofar as access to its links was open to virtually all of the citizenry. Although only better-off people could afford a caddie, the old Dornoch links was a place where golfers of all social classes met—and in Dornoch, that meant golfers of diverse religious sensibilities as well. What brought them together and humbled them equally was this very simple yet frustrating game. As a caddie and as a young player, Ross would have been both witness and participant in the game's democratic allure.

The firm, sandy character of both Dornoch and the Old Course at St. Andrews, where Ross apprenticed under Old Tom Morris, confirmed by virtue of their playing texture what the nature of the game made plain. Here was a sport that invited all players to develop an imagination. To be sure, there was tremendous skill required in getting the old "guttie" airborne with the help of those implements of yore—long, wooden-shafted clubs with handmade heads, devoid of weight balancing and with little consistency from one club to the next. Skill would be needed there. But imagination, too, in learning how to cultivate the kind of ground-game repertoire needed to circumvent the impending doom of a sandy hazard. The joy of golf in this purely naturalistic mode was seeing how tees, fairways, and greens were scarcely if at all distinguishable from raw, native turf and swales.

Ross's work as a designer is best understood as an early adaptation of links principles to the softer, lusher soil conditions of inland golf. The transition he undertook was aided by several technical factors that defined the practice of course architecture in his day. Earthmoving was out of the question, the manipulation of earth being limited to marginal scrapings and shavings of abrupt edges. Most of the ground features would reside where the native terrain dictated. Irrigation was limited, as well, assuring that firm turf conditions invariably prevailed. Where heavier clay and loam soil drained poorly or was prone to vast quantities of rain, Ross was a pioneer in creating drainage. Most of the time he used diagonal slopes to carry water away, but he also subtiled many of his bunkers, even some fairways as well, when he needed to get water off the course. The idea was simply to create via artifice the linksland character he had known so well at Dornoch and St. Andrews.

It is not possible to appreciate classic architecture without a thorough familiarity with the classic links layouts. To those, by contrast, who have never been back to the old country for golf, the work of a traditionalist like Ross will seem to be little more than a dull exercise—quaint, perhaps interesting in its heyday, but lacking the verve and visual excitement so readily found in the work of many modern marque "signature" architects.

Such are the conceits of those confined to the seductive imagery of contemporary design, with all of its dramatics and flair for the sensational and the densely carpeted, that they will basically find Ross's work on the tame side. They will look for forced carries over water hazards and bemoan the absence of thrill-a-rama shots. They wonder why more trees don't define a single path to the green, and so they overplant until they have transformed his golf courses into a straight-line arboretum. And they decry the appearance of tawny native grasses like fescues and knee-high blue stem, opting instead to plant it over with lush, dense green bentgrasses and bluegrass roughs that look as if they were color-copied from a television image of Augusta National Golf Club during Masters tournament week. Such turf is then maintained at near-saturation levels in the misguided belief that the only good golf course is one that is wall-to-wall green.

One doesn't need to spend as much time in Scotland as Ross did to appreciate classic links virtues—although an extended stay certainly helps. Even a century ago, The Old Course at St. Andrews stood out for its singularly striking imagery: all of 11 greens to accommodate 18 holes; fairways 120 yards wide, with the left side seemingly wide open off the tee, yet in most cases it was the tighter right side that opened up the better shot to the putting surface; and four or five distinct ways to play each hole, with the preferred route changing according to the fickle winds that howled, never predictably from any one direction, across the links. Most amazingly of all at St. Andrews was that here was a reversible golf course that was actually playable "backward" on certain weeks. Play today takes place on the "right-hand" course, with the holes looped in a predominantly counterclockwise loop as play proceeds on the right side of the double fairways. But in Ross's day, the "left-hand" course was also used: the first hole played from in front of the clubhouse down to the 17th green, and play then proceeded in clockwise fashion down the left side of the routing. The point, beyond historic interest, is that suddenly all of those quirky bunkers 50 yards in front of tees made sense as hazards that came into play from the other direction. Here was the genius of a routing and contours that made unsurpassed use of native twists and turns of earth. The vagaries of native humps and hollows were features to be negotiated, not decried as "unfair." To a strict Presbyterian moralist, life was too demanding and unpredictable to be classified ever as "unfair." It was a challenge to be confronted but not a pursuit that could be mastered.

As distinctive and memorable as pure links such as the Old Course and Dornoch are today, they were not quite so unique for their ground game qualities in

Ross's day. For one thing, all courses had a rough, unkempt look to them owing to precious little irrigation and to mowing patterns dictated not by reel blades capable of cropping fairways to three-eighths of an inch but to the peculiar eating habits of sheep.

Trees don't come into play at all at these aged links. This often strikes the modern player as a shocking indecency, tantamount to outright nudity. But a century ago, most golf courses were wide open fields that were scarcely graced with tree coverage. In Scotland, that was the unquestioned norm. In short, the courses that seem today so full of lessons about classic virtue were also considered in Ross's era to be intriguing, but they also shared much in common with other links layouts.

Golf at Dornoch to this day conveys much of this land-hewn sensibility. The ground is kept firm so that the ball runs, thus bringing bunkers into play that would not otherwise catch the attention of golfers. Soggy conditions promote an aerial-style power game in which the goal is to drop the ball into the green from a precise distance. But a firm ground game—along with the standard seaside wind conditions—makes it far more difficult to play a controlled aerial game. The ball rolls much more upon landing, bringing far bunkers and peripheral areas into play that would not normally be reached. Control is best secured under such conditions by low shots that are designed to run in along the ground. Dornoch, for instance, is to this day not tightly bunkered up front of its putting surfaces. There are open pathways into its greens that welcome creative shot making.

The complexity of the ground game is enhanced by the variety of playing textures. Instead of the dense, uniformly lush green swards of carpeting so familiar on U.S. parkland layouts, links golf conveys a feel of diverse surfaces: tight, rabbity fairways, patchy rough, tawny, and red knee-high fescues that wave in the wind, and denser marram grasses framing each play path. There are few inescapable hazards—ponds are all but unheard of, the only water hazard being the occasional cross ditch. Framing the tableau are those thickets of heavy plant life, whether low ferns, the densely surface-rooted heathers, or the larger, pricklier gorse plants. All of these come alive with colors, especially when they bloom yellow and red in the springtime.

More important for purposes of design than the beauty of these layouts is the democratic character of their turf and design. Anybody can play them, and there is no exclusion of higher handicappers for their lesser ability to hit the ball high and far. Not that skill is irrelevant. On the contrary, such conditions reward imaginative and controlled shot-making rather than sheer repetitive power.

Consider Dornoch's 14th, a 445-yard par 4 called "Foxy" that surely ranks among the world's great bunkerless holes. Ross would have no trouble recognizing this hole. It has remained largely as he knew it from his days as the club professional there.

One only needs to drop a ball 50 or so yards short of the plateau putting surface to revel in the complexities of a links ground game. The rock-hard green, some 4,500 sq. ft. in area, is perched up four feet above the putting surface and falls

away on every direction. Good luck trying to drop-kick a lob wedge onto this tiny target—or yet more delicately, trying to clip the ball just right without the leading edge of a lofted club bouncing off the turf and blading the ball. One of the jobs of local caddies is talking American players out of trying to hit such a shot. It takes folks on their first whirlwind tour of Scottish links some time to adjust, but instead of lofting the ball in, the preferred option is to run the ball along the ground with anything from a 5-iron to a putter. There is plenty of skill in judging such a shot— and a severe penalty for mis-hitting the line or, equally as consequential, hitting it too firmly. It is also common to see a ball not make it up the front slope and then roll 20 yards back down the fairway. In the face of all sorts of options like these, it takes some decisiveness to commit to a shot. Proper execution requires a different kind of skill than the acumen cultivated on a practice tee. This is talent honed only

Royal Dornoch's 14th hole, a 445-yard par 5. (Larry Lambrecht)

Misquamicut Golf Club, Westerly, RI, a 1923 Ross design over gnarly ground with clear influences of Scottish linksland. This is the tenth hole. (Larry Lambrecht)

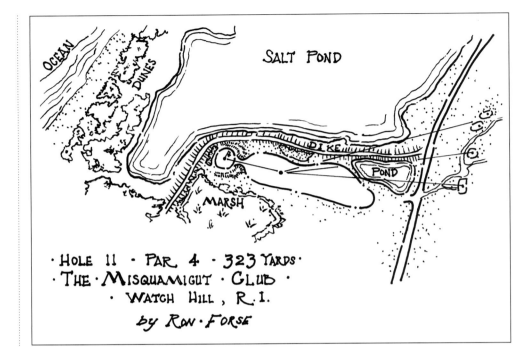

Right: Misquamicut's 11th hole, a 323-yard par 4 as sketched by Ron Forse. (Ron Forse)

Below: Newport (RI) Country Club, remodeled by Ross in 1915. A strong links character is evident on the front nine. This is the sixth hole, a 356-yard par 4, with Rhode Island Sound in the background. (Bradley S. Klein)

in the field, and a good case can be made that it requires far more mental and physical talent than conducting an aerial assault via a lobbed wedge shot.

Ross didn't design the greens at Dornoch, but that he was *influenced* by the style of golf they sustained and then imported the idea to the United States. In this sense his work bears the legacy of classic links golf, but it was adapted to the different landforms and agronomy found (inland) in North America.

THE PINEHURST ADAPTATION

The wonder of his involvement with Pinehurst is that here in the firm, sandy uplands of central North Carolina, 3,500 miles from his homeland, Ross found virtually ideal turf conditions with which to emulate his native game. As he wrote in the program of the 1936 PGA Championship at Pinehurst No.2, "...the Pinehurst conditions offered a really exceptional opportunity. Only in a sandy soil would the drainage problem permit construction of the rolling contours and hollows natural to the Scottish seaside courses where golf was born."

To be sure, the native plants were very different, but love grass and wire grass would serve as far more attractive—and far less punitive—substitutes for heather and gorse. Far more suitable was the firm, gently rolling terrain—ideal for linksland golf. In the early days of golf, a creative architect like Ross had all but a free hand in fashioning golf ground as he saw fit. There were no established standards with which to measure or judge golf holes. There were no serious critics of the craft who might take these artists to task for certain shortcomings. And no one knew whether or not an architect repeated himself from site to site. There wasn't any television coverage of tournament events, no opportunity to hop quickly from one course to the next to compare works by the same designer, and no quality (color) photography in magazines by which to see whether a particular designer had developed a unique style from site to site or was repeating himself. In short, it was an open field, and at Pinehurst, Ross had ideal conditions for creating his own version of the ground game. The result was a style that would transform the face of American golf and set the tone for a democratic style of play that would endure long after his death.

There aren't any water hazards in play, either. The sole spot of water today, fronting the 16th tee, only affects those who completely top their drives, but can be cleared with a tee shot of only 120 yards (from the middle markers). That's it for any frontal assault of hazards. Out-of-bounds is equally insignificant as a factor. A golfer has to hit the ball a long way, and a long way off line, in order to even spot a white stake. The point, briefly stated, is that most golfers, of whatever skill level, can play and finish the golf course with the very same ball they started with. Hit the ball 88 times and you score an 88, not a 91 for the three penalty strokes you incurred thanks to lateral hazards.

I can recall a number of rounds at No. 2 where my foursome, comprising golfers who were all thrilled if we broke 90, completed the round without losing a single ball. The rough is difficult to escape at Pinehurst, but at least you can always get your ball on the club. Controlling it is another matter, but finding it in the first place is easy. The wire grass and the dense underbrush of pine straw make for a nasty playing surface from which to approach a green. But you can play the ball, and so golfers at Pinehurst No. 2 can readily find their ball, hit it, and move on without having to spend hours in the woods looking about.

Despite all too many efforts of lesser talented designers to alter, revise, fix, and modernize that approach to the game, the Ross style is still discernible today in a number of his courses, and that spirit has animated the informed efforts of a small group of architects—not all of them well-known—to revive that traditional style.

Technically, the elements were quite basic. Ross's detailed drawings—of greens, approaches, and entire holes—show a consistency that borders on repetition. His greens consisted of raised fill pads, the dirt drawn in slightly from the surrounding grade and hived up to create a modest little mound that was then fattened or contoured with gentle but discernible slope. Bunkers were cut into this fill pad, whether tight to the front of the putting surface or at the base of the upslope, several yards in front of the green. The result, seen repeatedly at Pinehurst No. 2, among many other courses, is a visible target that presents itself readily to the fairway but which is most accessible along a particular axis or line of approach through the fairway.

His bunkers were not severe—generally 3 to 4½ feet deep, with the sand kept low, if not exactly flat, and the upslope to the green generally grassed rather than flashed up with sand. In keeping with his understanding that there should be a certain proportional relationship of challenge and recovery, Ross did not build inescapable bunkers. His fairway bunkers are much broader, with shallower surfaces and lower leading edges, generally about two feet deep. The closer one got to the green, however, the deeper the surface and the steeper the greenside wall—though never to the point where he built sheer parapet walls that required heroic escape efforts, like Charles Blair Macdonald in his interwar heyday or Pete Dye in his more contemporary heyday.

Ross, ever mindful of all aspects of the game, had in mind here not only strategic considerations but agronomy as well. The execution here was intended to ease maintenance. The same could be said of his greens, where a greenkeeper's interest in proper surface drainage required that the green slope outward so that it would carry water away along at least two points on every putting surface. Such was the surface contour—visually sensible because it tied into the surrounding landforms, and yet certain enough to make golfers think about particular angles of approach.

His detailed instructions to his field hands ensured a certain consistency. Whether the plan was fulfilled was then due to the local oversight, the skill of builders and shapers, and to the budget at hand for each project. Even Pinehurst was undertaken within severe budget considerations. But in those days there was no need or idea of moving heaven and earth to build great golf holes. In this sense, Pinehurst epitomizes the craft in its purest form. It took years of careful, quiet nudging and massaging to get the holes just right. Bunkers were moved, new holes occasionally cut, and slopes adjusted to steer surface water one way or the next. The point was that Ross was on hand throughout the entire process. What evolved, therefore, can be said to embody—more than any of his other courses—his approach to the game.

Perhaps more than anything else, Ross's attention to the lay of the land and his understanding of the basic principles of agronomy distinguish him from his peers and his contemporaries. His work embodies a close adherence to the most elemental rules of good drainage and thereby, to strategic shotmaking. The golf ball, like water, will run along a slope. A builder sensitive to native slopes will be aware of how the land will play. The firm, sandy, well-draining soils and features needed for sound agronomy also make for sound golf. Ross, ever the greenkeeper, saw it as more central to golf than the more ornamental function of the golf professional: "Greenkeeping is destined to be a very important and lucrative profession, of really far greater importance to a golf club than the services of a club professional. . . . We haven't realized this sufficiently here yet, but already some of the universities in the east have started special courses of greenkeeping and course maintenance."

Strategic Elements

Reducing anything in golf to a formula or checklist is likely to prove misleading. All the more problematic is an approach to course design that imposes undue standards where the lay of the land suggests something else. There is nonetheless some value in making the effort—much as Alister MacKenzie did when he came up with his famous list of 13 principles. The result is less a formula than a set of basic guidelines that orient the design process and that constitute what might be called a design philosophy. In Ross's case, the elements can be discerned from the body of his work.

1. Efficient Routings.

Veteran club professional John Gerring, most recently at Greenville (S.C.) Country Club, has observed that "the mark of a good routing is that you can stand on a tee and hear the ball land on the green you've just played." In other words, a comfortable routing is one with little distance between holes. There's no need for cart paths or signage posts indicating the way. A well-routed course suggests the path from hole to hole much as one might take a stroll, so that instead of having to stop and gaze for the next arbitrary marker or signpost, golfers can simply follow the natural flow of the land. In today's litigious society, however, the desire for intimacy sometimes seems to give way to expansiveness for the sake of safety margins.

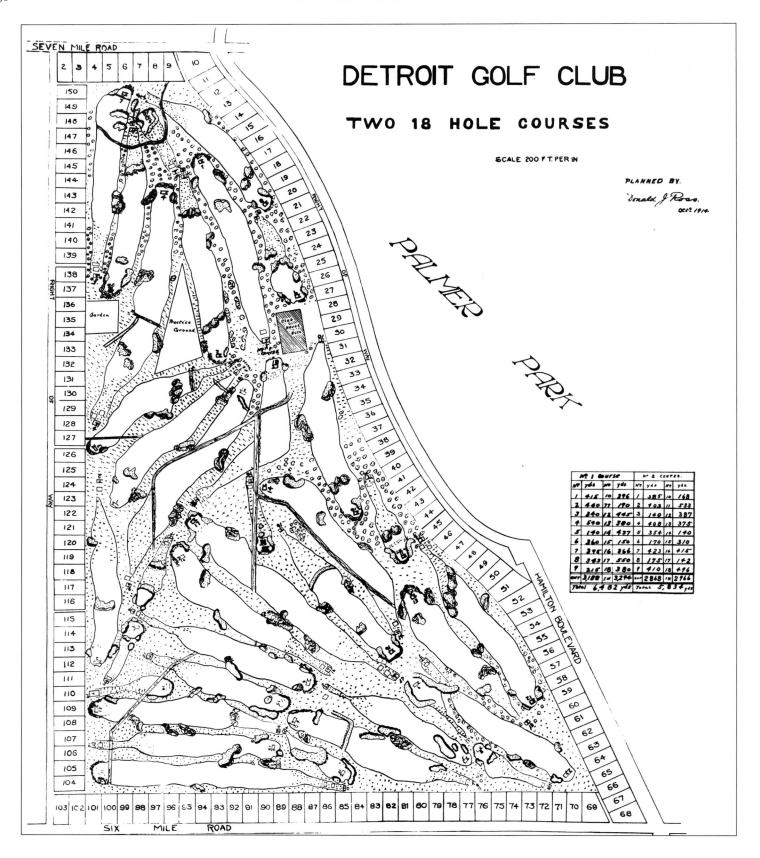

DETROIT GOLF CLUB

TWO 18 HOLE COURSES

SCALE 200 FT. PER IN

PLANNED BY.

Donald J. Ross.
Oct? 1914.

SEVEN MILE ROAD

PALMER PARK

HAMILTON BOULEVARD

SIX MILE ROAD

Nº 1 Course				Nº 2 Course.			
Nº	yds	Nº	yds	Nº	yds	Nº	yds
1	415	10	396	1	385	10	168
2	440	11	190	2	703	11	533
3	240	12	445	3	140	12	387
4	540	13	380	4	400	13	375
5	140	14	437	5	354	14	140
6	360	15	150	6	170	15	310
7	395	16	366	7	423	16	415
8	343	17	550	8	175	17	142
9	215	18	380	9	410	18	476
out	3,188	in	3,274	out	2868	in	2966
Total	6,482 yds			Total	5,834 yds		

Moreover, the classic designers were free to culvert wet areas or to drain swamps in search of playable golf ground. Today's designers enjoy less creative freedom owing to the regulatory process. Or have they become so spoiled by reliance upon cart paths to bridge basic routing problems and to overcome awkward hikes from greens to tees?

Ross courses generally have a seamless flow to them, with an enormous economy of design in terms of the use of land and the absence of wasted space. Whether the out-and-back style exemplified at Waterbury Country Club or the more conventional routing of returning nines found at the majority of his layouts, Ross was able to place holes in a way that displayed compositional unity. He generally reserved uphill ground for shorter par 4s, while relying upon broader and gently descending ground for longer par 4s.

2. Modest Getaway Holes.

The major exception to short uphill par 4s came on his opening holes, which usually—but not always—were modest par 4s that tended to have generous

Opposite page: Detroit Golf Club, 1914. This is Ross's earliest plan for a new 36-hole facility. The No. 1 Course, at 6,482 yards, has contiguous returning nines; the No. 2 Course, at 5,834 yards, offers neither contiguous nor returning nines. (Detroit Golf Club)

Above: The 459-yard par-4 second hole at Scioto Country Club, Columbus, OH. A perfect use of an upslope to create demands on a tee shot. This is the course where Jack Nicklaus honed his game. (Bradley S. Klein)

landing room off the tee and would flow out, often from an elevated tee. The object here, as epitomized with Worcester Country Club's first hole, was to give golfers a sense of security and ease without overtaxing their abilities.

3. Generous Fairways.

Ross's clearing plan always called for corridors at least 40 yards wide on short holes, with fairway and adjoining rough ground 60-90 yards wide on longer holes. Straight cuts should be avoided, since the slightly irregular clearing line generated a more interesting path of play.

His bunkering patterns tended to punish poorly struck low shots and to help establish lines of play off the tee. The point was to define different paths to the green. As he wrote in *Golf Has Never Failed Me*, "If rightly bunkered, the high-handicap man can always find his way to the hole with but little difficulty, provided he uses his brain a bit. But the type of player who depends all on brawn rather than some on brain will find any bunkered course difficult." The fairway bunkering was

Opposite page, top: Whitinsville (MA) Golf Club's 446-yard par-4 ninth, the finishing hole to one of the country's most highly regarded nine-hole courses. (Bradley S. Klein)

Opposite page, bottom: The 14th at Cedar Rapids Country Club. Ross's 1915 design for this 360-yard par 4 placed the green atop an old Indian burial mound – a perfect use of existing contours. (Bradley S. Klein)

Below: Worcester (MA) Country Club's first hole, a 380-yard par 4. A gentle starting hole, but with steeper elevations to come. The course hosted the 1925 U.S. Open, the 1927 Ryder Cup, and the 1960 U. S. Women's Open. (Bradley S. Klein)

usually 2½ to 3½ feet deep. Bunkers built on clay sites were generally shallow, while bunkers built on sand loam or sand were usually deep because they could be drained more readily. Advancing the ball out was not meant to be impossible—thus the avoidance of deep-faced pot bunkers in fairway landing areas. But it would require only the most spectacular second shot to get home in regulation from a fairway bunker. As he wrote in the program for the 1936 PGA Championship at Pinehurst No. 2, "... those penalties should not be unduly severe nor of a nature that would prohibit a full recovery by the execution of an unusually well-played shot."

4. Angles of Play.

Ross did not enjoy a reputation for the bold, angular drama of design features that were more common in the hands of his Golden Age colleagues. His work was more craftsman-like: subtler in its reliance upon architectural features and more difficult to discern as well. A casual golfer might easily miss their depth of character. His courses required a golfer's attention strategically even if at first they did not compel it aesthetically.

His genius was in the offset or echelon style of bunkering. His earlier work tended to rely more upon cross bunkering off the tee, though even these were placed alongside the dominant line of play rather than directly in front. He was not making the mistake of crude, turn-of-the-century designers who tended to aggregate their hazards across the middle and thereby punish for the sake of punishing. But as Ross's work matured, so did the lightness of his touch. His bunkers were as much signals as hazards, designed to indicate to the intelligent player that a choice needed to be made between the bold and the safer (if longer) path of play.

The result was the shifting-gear rhythms of classical shot-making rather than a gun-the-motor version of the game. A left-to-right tee shot would be followed by a right-to-left approach, and then the demands would be reversed at the very next hole. Shifting hole placements on the green of a par 4 might also necessitate an entirely different way of playing the tee shot. Here is Ross' account of the eighth hole at Pinehurst No. 2:

> "Here there is a ridge in front of the green which throws a ball played on the right side still further to the right and vice-versa. If the pin is on the right of this green, a player who wishes to avoid the effects of this slope must place his tee shot on the right side of the fairway, and conversely, on the left side of the fairway when the pin is on the left. A majority of the two-shot holes on Number Two are of this general type."

5. Offset Tees/S-Shaped Fairways.

A careful look at a Ross course shows that a remarkable degree of apparent complexity can be designed into a par 4 or par 5 simply by offsetting the tee slightly from the centerline and then creating a modest S-curve in the fairway. Rare is a Ross hole with a straightaway fairway and a tee complex down the center. The ideal

Opposite page: Plainfield (NJ) Country Club's 18th hole. A par 4 of 384 yards with well-defined angles of play around or over diagonally arrayed hazards. (Larry Lambrecht)

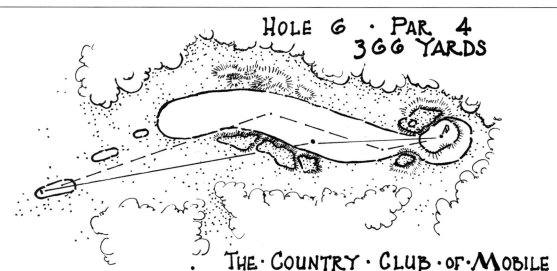

HOLE 6 · PAR 4
366 YARDS

THE · COUNTRY · CLUB · OF · MOBILE ·
· ALABAMA ·

by RON · FORSE

APPROX. 1" = 200'   JULY, 2000

AS OF FEB — JUNE, 2001 — THE "NEW", D.J. ROSS
REINSTATED HOLE 6 @ C.C. OF MOBILE, ALABAMA.
PAR 4, 366 YDS.
ALTERNATE LINE(S) OF PLAY (DASHED LINES) GIVES
"BOGEY" WAY TO PLAY HOLE THUS CREATING AN
"S" CURVED SHAPE TO THE HOLE. MAXIMUM
REWARD LINE OF PLAY IS STRAIGHTEST &
RISKIEST OF ALL CHOICES. BUNKERS(S) SET UP

REWARD & STRATEGY, BUT ALSO THE GENTLE
FALL-OFF SURROUNDS OF PUTTING GREEN
GIVE INCENTIVE TO CARRY THE FAIRWAY
BUNKERS AT THE TURN. BUNKER SHORT RIGHT
OF GREEN SERVES TO KEEP THE HOLE INTERESTING
FOR THE BOGEY PLAYER (WE CALL THESE
SO-POSITIONED BUNKERS, "BOGEY BUNKERS". OBJECTS
OUTSIDE DOGLEG ARE AN UNDULATING MASS ON
GROUND SLIGHTLY HIGHER THAN THE RIGHT.

RON FORSE

configuration was to place the tee on one side and have the fairway start on the other, only to cross over and then bend gently back. With a little tilt to the land for added slope, the resulting effect would be a graceful curvilinear flow and multiple angles of play. The formation was easier to achieve before tree canopies enclosed linear paths of play and before the widespread adoption of single-row irrigation lines down the middle of the fairway. Too often, Ross's graceful flow would be narrowed and straightened up for the sake of easy maintenance. But this is to sacrifice a distinctive design element for the wrong reason. Ross's flair for strategy and angles enabled golfers of different classes to feel comfortable aiming for different parts of the fairway. High-handicappers could aim short of the center point for safety, moderate golfers could aim for the crossover point, and bold golfers could target a farther landing spot down the inside of the curved fairway that left a much shorter shot into the green.

6. Demanding Iron Play.

Ross always emphasized solid, imaginative shot making. In his day, good scoring was not a matter of sinking many putts. The spotty turf conditions of even the best putting surfaces simply did not allow for frequent holing on the greens. But as someone raised on courses that demanded imaginative shot making, Ross incorporated into his design a sense of working the ball and playing the angles. It was less a matter of rote technique than adapting to the ground conditions presented by each stroke. As he wrote in *Golf Has Never Failed Me*,

> *You know, it is one thing to go out and hit every shot the same, merely using a different club for the various distances, and still another to play the shot as it should be played. In the old days we did not have the dozen different irons the present golfer carries. We played with one wooden club, a mid-iron, a mashie, a niblick and a putter. The exact distance from the green did not always determine the club to use. We all learned to play several types of shots with each of these clubs. We had no matched set with numbers determining the club to use . . .*
>
> *The golfer with one shot in his bag will go nowhere in the future . . .*
>
> *The game is easier now. We never used to find two greens on a course that putted alike. No attempt was made in the old days to build a green so that it would hold an approach shot. We never had more than seven clubs, and they were crude compared with the clubs used today.*

Ross paid particular attention to varying the length and demands of his par 4s. He was meticulous in creating short yet demanding par 4s, usually no more than one such hole per nine, and invariably—where there was any slope on the site at all—the short par 4 would be placed on upsloping terrain. Often the fairway would be generously wide, but then the green would be small and/or crowned. It was invariably also sharply bunkered to make the demands of the second shot all the more intense.

His 14th at Oak Hill Country Club's East Course, called "Bunker Hill," is a model of such a hole. His design plans from 1923-1924 show a 324-yard par 4, the

Opposite page: The sixth hole at the Country Club of Mobile (AL). A 366-yard par 4 with an S-shaped fairway and diagonal hazards. Notice how Ross shifts the shot-making demands: a left-to-right drive is required, followed by a right-to-left approach. (Ron Forse)

The 14th hole on Oak Hills' East Course, Pittsford, NY, a par 4 of 323 yards. (Bradley S. Klein)

tee shot slightly downhill to a broad fairway nearly 50 yards wide with only a few trees scattered beyond and outside of the landing area. Placement of the tee shot and coordinating it with the cup placement were more important than length. Indeed, the longer the tee shot, the harder the approach because of the sharp upslope and the difficulty of judging a light wedge. The green was perched high above the fairway—the last 60 yards or so sweep dramatically uphill. The green, fronted by a trio of steeped-faced bunkers, cants noticeably left to right and the fill pad falls off sharply all around—especially behind. The green, about 80 x 60 ft., had more depth than width and left no margin of error for what amounted to a short-iron approach shot.

Subsequent versions of the hole have wandered from Ross's basic genius.

Trees were planted to the point of squeezing the landing area, and in 1955 Robert Trent Jones Sr.—who was rebuffed by the club in his attempt to make the hole a left-to-right dogleg—added a fairway bunker on the left side that has since come to be fronted by a leaning tree.

History, and the home club, have been far more kind to a lesser-known Ross gem in metropolitan Detroit: Franklin Hills Country Club. There, Ross's ingenious plans for a very short par 4 have been left intact since the course debuted in 1926. The 298-yard par-4 13th is one of Ross's shortest holes, played down a bunker-free but tree-lined fairway to a tiny putting surface (no more than 1,900 sq. ft.) perched on a natural rise. The concept is elegant, uncluttered, and timeless. Yet, unlike other equally short par 4s today, there is no pretense of it being driveable because the available greenside landing area is minuscule and lacks support to the rear.

For all his inventiveness with the terrain for short par 4s, however, it was the long, demanding two-shot hole that most embodied Ross's strategic genius.

"I consider the ability to play the longer irons as the supreme test of a great golfer," he wrote in the program to the 1936 PGA Championship. He rightly pointed to the tournament venue, Pinehurst No. 2, as embodying this principle. But he could well have pointed to dozens of other courses characterized by long, demanding par 4s.

7. Slightly Raised Putting Surfaces with Bunkers Built into the Fillpad.

Ross's work on greens was guided as much by sound agronomics and drainage as by strategic considerations. He was not one simply to hive up dirt and call it a "push-up green." All of his projects were concerned with percolation through the putting surface as well as surface runoff. The need to provide both out-flow and a stable growing medium led him to devote careful attention to his greens—not simply so that they would hold a shot but also to make sure they would cultivate and sustain a good crop of putting turf.

Nor did he rely, as is often claimed, upon crowned greens. That would have been too demanding from a shot-making standpoint. The claim also assumes that his only method of drainage was surface runoff. But as we have seen, he was meticulous about building layers of rock, gravel, sand, and topsoil in a growing medium that is an early version of the post-1960 model of a USGA-specified suspended water table. While his greens would have retained far less internal moisture than modern USGA greens, they certainly percolated well and were built with enough drainage tile that they could drain without simply relying upon surface slopes of 6-7% to repel the water.

The resulting structure was of a slightly perched or elevated target area, usually built up from dirt "hived in" by scrapers or pans that brought the dirt in from the immediate surrounds. The dirt would be carefully shaped, and underground piping in the form of clay-pipe drainage tiles would carry the water away.

Unfortunately, many of his greens have been revamped over the years to accommodate the lowered mowing heights and increased putting speeds of greens. In Ross's day, reel mowers could simply not clip the putting turfs to heights tighter than ¼ inch. It is even doubtful whether the greens could have survived at lower heights given the limitations of available irrigation systems. As result, bermuda-grass greens in Southern climates would have been very grainy, and in northern climates bentgrass and ryegrasses would not have rolled faster than 5 or 6 on today's Stimpmeter. Greens with 4-5 feet of vertical fall over the course of 100 feet from back to front were not uncommon. So what was easily workable in his day threatens to become out of control with modern green speeds of 10 to 11.

Softening greens is not a simple matter. Taking a foot out of back slope and adding a foot to the front in order to create a more level green is an extremely complex process. It can dramatically alter (ruin) drainage patterns, and it can also have a marked effect on playability from the approach area since it means the green's front has to be raised. To get even marginal adjustments of a green's contour done correctly, the surrounding area has to be graded out 20-50 feet in order to tie the slopes in properly. And the green itself has to be cored out, rebuilt, and outfitted with properly built subgrades of gravel, peat, and sand.

One alternative, of course, is to keep green speeds around 9 and to simply enjoy the contours that Ross built. Another alternative is to close the course on August 1st for eight months and spend $800,000 in the hopes of getting acceptable new putting surfaces. In the face of such an option, most facilities would be better off simply letting do with more moderate green speeds.

The temptation to modernize or to renovate has been a powerful one over the years. It has also led to the demise of many classic golf course features.

Franklin Hills Country Club, Franklin, MI. The 298-yard par-4 13th with its domed, postage-stamp-sized putting surface. (Dave Richards)

Opposite page: Franklin Hills is not as well-known to the public as other Ross layouts, but most major golf publications include it in their annual "Top 100" lists. (Tom Gray)

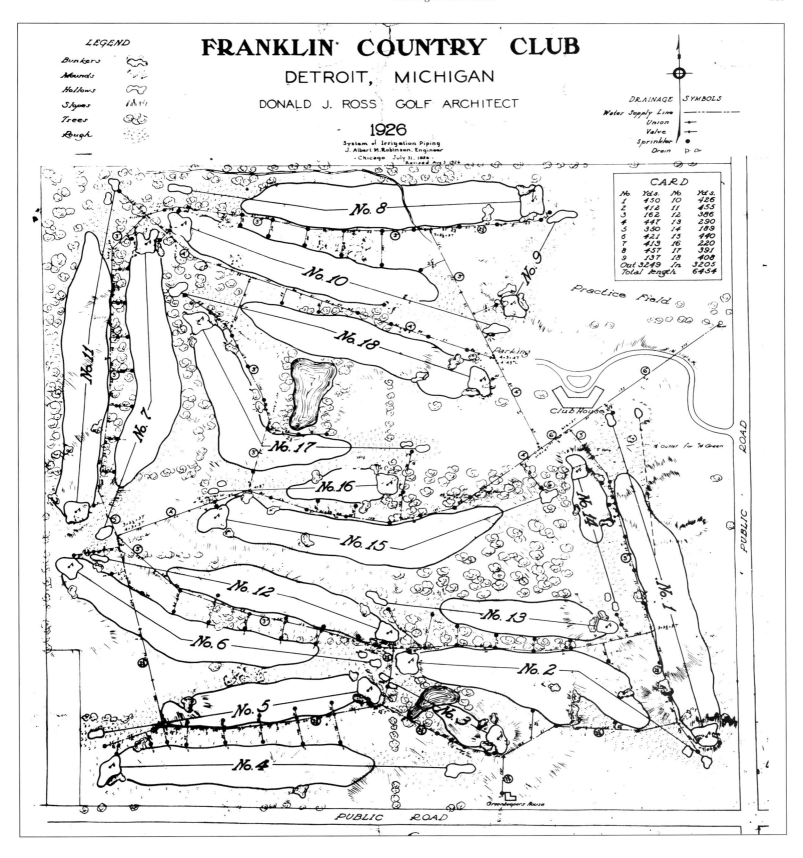

FRANKLIN COUNTRY CLUB
DETROIT, MICHIGAN
DONALD J. ROSS GOLF ARCHITECT
1926

System of Irrigation Piping
J. Albert M. Robinson, Engineer
Chicago July 31, 1926
Revised Aug 3 1926

LEGEND

Bunkers
Mounds
Hollows
Slopes
Trees
Rough

DRAINAGE SYMBOLS

Water Supply Line
Union
Valve
Sprinkler
Drain ▷ Dr

CARD

No.	Yds.	No	Yds.
1	150	10	426
2	112	11	455
3	162	12	386
4	447	13	290
5	350	14	189
6	421	15	440
7	413	16	220
8	457	17	391
9	137	18	408
Out	3249	In	3205
Total length			6454

Practice Field

Parking

Club House

Outlet for 14 Green

Greenkeepers house

PUBLIC ROAD

PUBLIC ROAD

Chapter Eight
Rescuing Ross: The Fine Art of Restoration

A HOME COURSE

*S*even miles from my front door, in the adjoining town of West Hartford, Connecticut, is a wonderful old Ross course, Wampanoag Country Club, where I am lucky enough to regularly play golf. The 18-hole layout sits just behind a moderately busy road that bisects the town. The houses along this well-trafficked, two-lane road are larger than average for a suburban community, and their appearance is enhanced considerably by mature hardwood trees that give the area an established look. Indeed, many of the houses in this area predate the post-World War II era of suburban sprawl that so dramatically converted this countryside. This section of West Hartford is the kind of imposing, leafy community that began to burgeon in the 1920s, just as successful business people in places like downtown Hartford were beginning to discover the advantages of life on the frontier of farmland.

Aerial photographs of the Wampanoag course a quarter century after Donald Ross designed it in 1924 and built it in 1926 reveal scattered houses, an unpaved road, and an image of genteel, country life very different from the inner city only five miles away. Such was the ideal of the country club—a place for the newly wealthy to escape, if only for a few hours, but not so far away that it would take one away from home.

I'm reminded of this every time I run out for an "emergency nine" during the week. Not that Wampanoag is really a country club anymore in the full-blown sense of an active tennis crowd, clubhouse life, and a dining room that dominates the members' social calendar. Like many once well-established clubs, members only reluctantly spend their monthly dining minimum here—a problem unbeknown in the late 1950s and early 1960s when dinner every weekend and a steady barrage of social events helped make "the club" the focus of one's life outside of work. As life inside the clubhouse has receded in importance, attention has focused more and more on the quality of the major attraction that brings most people to the facility.

In this sense we are no different than most other clubs. What counts is the quality of the golf course. Throughout the country, attention is increasingly being paid to the condition of the turfgrass and the design of its layout. Fifty years ago, few people bothered to notice that their home course was a "Donald Ross." Nowadays, that's the start of any conversation into which the name Wampanoag is introduced.

Not that Wampanoag is some unheralded masterpiece. But it is a really good golf course at the core that needs considerable dusting off and tweaking. The course lacks definition in its bunkering. It has far too many trees. Drainage lines do not work as well as they used to. The green contours are phenomenal, but the surfaces have become rounded off and the result is that certain pin-able areas have been abandoned. And yet the par-72 course—all of 6,610 yards—with its four par 5s all in the 463-509 yard range, retains its compelling charm as a very solid layout.

The routing remains original. The front nine makes a large counterclockwise loop, and the back nine is sequenced in a series of elegant little interior shifts and turns, with both sides returning to the clubhouse via uphill approaches. The surrounding uplands frame a central area of wetlands and low-lying native grass spots—though much of the latter has been overplanted with evergreens. Both nines start with modest downhill par 4s. From then on, all the short par 4s are uphill and all the long ones are downhill—with the exception of the 427-yard 18th, a dramatic and demanding par 4 with the green perched atop a long fronting slope that runs into a large water hazard. The par 3s at Wampanoag require everything from a short iron to a fairway wood. And the par 5s offer tempting targets for bold,

The first green at Wampanoag Country Club, West Hartford, CT, during construction in 1925. The notion of "soil push-up greens" understates the complexity of putting surface construction during the classical era of course design. Note the rock assembled here as the base of the fill pad – an early version of the subgrade later specified as the basis for modern, sand-based greens built on the principle of a suspended water table. (Wampanoag Country Club)

long hitters. The course lacks length to test the modern tournament professional but is ideal for member golf. The real challenge of a round at Wampanoag lies in the chipping and putting. The old rule about trying to avoid hitting past the hole is a truism here. Golfers might find themselves hitting many greens in regulation, but the real excitement of a round at Wampanoag is making recovery shots from behind the hole and in tricky comeback putts.

In recent years, Wampanoag has become less of a country club and more of a golf club. Whether that's because the course is so good or the clubhouse so limited is a matter I can't decide. In any case, I have suggested that they change the name to Wampanoag Golf Club to reflect this more modest reality. But on this, as on most matters regarding the place, nobody listens to my advice. And why not, since I'm just one of 400 members? If the club management company that runs the facility or the superintendent, Greg Stent, listened to me they'd have to listen to dozens of others. As Ross wrote on October 10, 1927: "It is the usual thing for a golfer to have some pet scheme for the changing of a green or tee but I find that very few of their schemes are practical or desirable and I usually convince them of that fact."

Actually, I cannot decide if my love for this facility is because it is a Donald Ross golf course or because it is simply a golf course. Not that it really matters. What counts — to me and to visitors who come to play — is that Wampanoag continually evokes a special sensibility that distinguishes it from all other layouts in the region. So perhaps it is Ross after all whom we can thank. Or perhaps we can simply be grateful that the course sits on such a fine, rolling piece of contiguous ground and that despite some regrettable tinkering the original hole corridors remain intact. Thus credit must go to the original architect who had the wisdom to hew the course so closely to the native contours of this parcel.

And yet I also feel a sadness each time I play. This is not, after all, the same Ross golf course that he designed. Too much of it has changed. And too much of its original design remains discernible in the form of abandoned bunkers whose contours can still be seen. There are also far too many little conifers stuck into the ground like darts from outer space. All they seem to do is block the eye's flow across the landscape and make it impossible to gain a full sweeping vista of the site. And it is a beautiful site, all 130 acres. There's a stream that runs lazily across the southern side of the property, a veranda on the clubhouse that looks out over the 1st, 10th, and 18th fairways, and a ridge line from Talcott Mountain (it's not really a "mountain") presiding over the far northern end of the property. There are courses in the region that are better groomed, but none better routed and none more naturally fitted to the land and to the setting.

Occasionally, upon returning to the area by airplane, I'll get a good birds-eye view of the course (Wampanoag sits under one of the approaches to the nearby airport). During these precious flyovers I end up pressing my nose to the window, much as a child does when flying over the Grand Canyon or New York City. There's a certain skill involved in the aerial interpretation of the land that frequent flyers

are very adept at, especially those well-traveled golfers who like to practice "course spotting." Frequently, I will spot the hollowed remains of an abandoned bunker at Wampanoag. Upon returning to the course, I'll go out and check the site to see if it confirms my observation from above.

Maps on the clubhouse wall and the memories of veteran members provide a continuing historical narrative of the glory that—I am convinced—has been lost over the years. Consequently, I feel a sadness almost every round—and not because my 15 handicap bespeaks a game of perpetual frustration. For all the beauty and joy of a round here, the experience could be all the more compelling if only the original layout were restored.

Wampanoag, ca.1930s, with first green at lower left. (Wampanoag Country Club)

DONALD ROSS SOCIETY

The story is repeated throughout the country: an original plan, somewhat diverse construction methods, then the course is subjected to ongoing intervention, to some extent at the hand of nature, plus well-intentioned (and too often, badly-intentioned) green committees. In the face of such frequently seen examples of managed decline, the alternative mode of administration (usually led by an all-powerful patriarch) at least holds out the possibility of controlling the architecture. If the price of democratic management is a golf course that is frequently altered to suit successive visions of the game, it is far more advisable to leave a single person in charge, even if the membership resents such tyranny. Who said a golf course needs to be run like a democracy?

The continual ebbing away of architectural integrity is a fate that has befallen many courses. The only thing sadder than seeing a decaying MacKenzie, Tillinghast, Raynor, or Ross layout is to see it hacked up in the name of "modernization" or "renovation."

To prevent this, the Donald Ross Society was organized in order to educate the golfing public. Curiously enough, the group was founded at precisely the club where I now play my golf: Wampanoag. Its headquarters—such as they are—are located in my adopted hometown, though I had nothing to do with the society's creation and only heard about it a year or two after its founding in 1988. For the sake of truth in journalism, I must also admit to having been elected to its Board in 2000.

The Society's original name, the Donald Ross Touring Society, sounded elitist, so the itinerant dimension was abandoned. At one time, some 1,400 people have been members; today the active list includes about 700 names, and what brings them together is an interest in promoting the appreciation of classic courses. The nonprofit group also recognizes the importance of traditional designers other than Ross and provides informal consultation to clubs interested in redoing (the actual buzz word is "restoring") their layouts.

The Society has developed a nationwide network of architecture aficionados. Its membership has included nearly a dozen course designers, some of whom have landed restoration contracts through their affiliation and commitment to the cause. In mid-April of each year, the Donald Ross Society holds a rabble-rousing meeting. Often it has been at Pinehurst, and when there, the meeting has included a Friday night cocktail party at Dornoch Cottage, Ross's old residence adjacent to the third green on the No. 2 Course. There is much golf during the weekend, plus a gala dinner Saturday night. Following the meal, keynoters take the floor, though they are always encouraged to keep their remarks brief. At one legendary meeting in 1995, secretary-treasurer Michael Fay's opening comments, through a cloud of smoke and over a din of clanking ice, went as follows: "Welcome to Pinehurst. Speakers at Ross meetings keep their remarks brief." Then he sat down.

It's easy to identify Ross Society members. They walk rather than ride golf carts, take caddies, have lots of bag tags, play quickly, and are not deterred by wind or rain. In short, they love

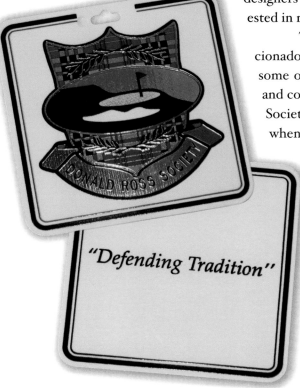

Donald Ross Society bag tag, with Ross tartan plaid around the short par-3 third at Wannamoisett. (Donald Ross Society)

traditional golf. In case the message is lost, the society's bag tag contains no shortage of symbolism: Ross tartan plaid around an image of the 127-yard, par-3 third hole at Wannamoisett on one side, and the words "Defending Tradition" on the other.

The group traces its start back to 1988, when some members at Wampanoag expressed concerns about changes in their design's layout that had been overseen in 1986-1987 by a young Massachusetts-based architect named Brian Silva. The renovations were initially undertaken to address some agronomic problems and gradually expanded. Silva did not have the benefit of Ross's original plans. At the time, however, he was only asked by the club to do a renovation, not a restoration. On a number of occasions, the work was implemented after Silva left, and upon his return he would find that the work had not only been shaped but turfed over as well. Some of this, as it turns out, was shaping work undertaken by a crew member working under the promise of extra days off if he did the work requested by a committeeman. When the work was done, the green committee and its chairman expressed their satisfaction.

The resulting changes at Wampanoag, however, were awkward and ill-suited to the course. Five holes in particular, involving the 4th, 5th, 7th, and 14th green complexes and a fairway bunker on the tenth hole, bore the brunt of the intervention. Even a decade later, they stood out like sore thumbs. Bunkers were underscaled while their surrounding mounds were oversized. Mounding behind

The 465-yard par-5 fourth hole at Wampanoag, following 1986-1987 renovations. Greenside mounding and bunkering are underscaled and overdone. (Bradley S. Klein)

greens that was apparently intended to create definition looks lunar and highly artificial. And instead of greens built to complement the existing surfaces, Wampanoag was saddled on a few holes with low-slung, nearly flat putting surfaces or surrounds which simply looked contrived and out of character.

When a handful of members began seeing other Ross layouts in nearby Massachusetts, including The Orchards in South Hadley, Worcester Country Club, or the nine-hole gem at Whitinsville just south of Worcester, they began to see the need for preserving those courses and others and organized themselves into what amounted to a Donald Ross defense group. The founders were all from Wampanoag: Steve Edwards, Michael Fay, Barry Palm, and Bruce Taylor.

Wampanoag was by no means Silva's only New England renovation work. He had been involved in several older, established courses around the time the Ross Society was created.

Some time after Wampanoag and the creation of the Ross Society, Silva found it increasingly difficult to obtain renovation work on classic New England courses. Some close observers of the regional architecture scene suggested that Silva's reputation was being undermined by insiders tied to the Ross Society who were essentially condemning him for his earlier indiscretions and were conspiring with club officials to keep him from getting redesign work. Or was it independent judgment by superintendents and green committees that led to the frustrations Silva encountered? There can be no question that when course officials solicited representatives of the Ross Society, they expressed themselves frankly and critically.

The subject of Silva and the Ross Society burst into public view in the June 14, 1999 issue of *Sports Illustrated*. An article by Ivan Maizel, "Keepers of the Flame," focused on the Ross Society and its outspoken head, Fay. The article portrayed Fay as a self-appointed zealot, one who was unrestrained and undiplomatic in condemning Silva's work. Fay's intemperate words—"He [Silva] can sue me if he wants because I exposed him for the horse's ass that he is"—overshadowed the magazine's account of the Society's efforts in promoting awareness of Ross's work. If the point of the article was to create a controversy, it succeeded—to the point of nearly costing Fay his titular role as executive secretary of the Ross Society.

Four months later, *Golf Digest/Golf World* architecture editor Ron Whitten weighed in with a riposte that properly focused attention on Silva's work at a number of courses, both original and restoration-oriented. "Success by Design: Architect of the Year Brian Silva answers his critics" announced the Golf World cover of October 15, 1999. Besides reviewing the case of Wampanoag, Whitten went on to show that Silva's work on new courses was heavily inspired by his experience with classic layouts. While Silva had clearly moved on and continued to grow, the article and the whole episode revealed the degree to which a small number of ideologically charged golfers could take simplistic ideas about design and appoint themselves as experts. Renovation and restoration are never politically innocent. There's much explanation and education required as part of the process. In the case of Wampanoag, the anger directed at one designer should properly have been focused on a misguided process of internal club planning.

Indeed, recurring mismanagement and improper financing had led to a cycle of dues assessments and frustration, to the point where the club was on the verge of bankruptcy before it was rescued from oblivion through a deal by which day-to-day operations were taken over in 1994 by a management company, International Golf Group, based in Fairfield, Connecticut.

For all the controversy about Silva, however, the design compromises at Wampanog had a longer history—perhaps dating to the outset of the club when, in all likelihood, the course was not quite built to Ross's original plans. For example, a number of Ross-proposed short carry bunkers were never installed. Also, evidence from an aerial photograph taken around 1950—before the present clubhouse site was developed for the building in 1953—show bunkers on the map that were never on the Ross plan.

It can never be known how much of the course was built to plan and how much of it evolved over the next 30 years through maintenance and/or deliberate intervention. What is clear is the influence of a nationally regarded golfer and many-time Wampanoag club champion named Frank Ross (no relation to the

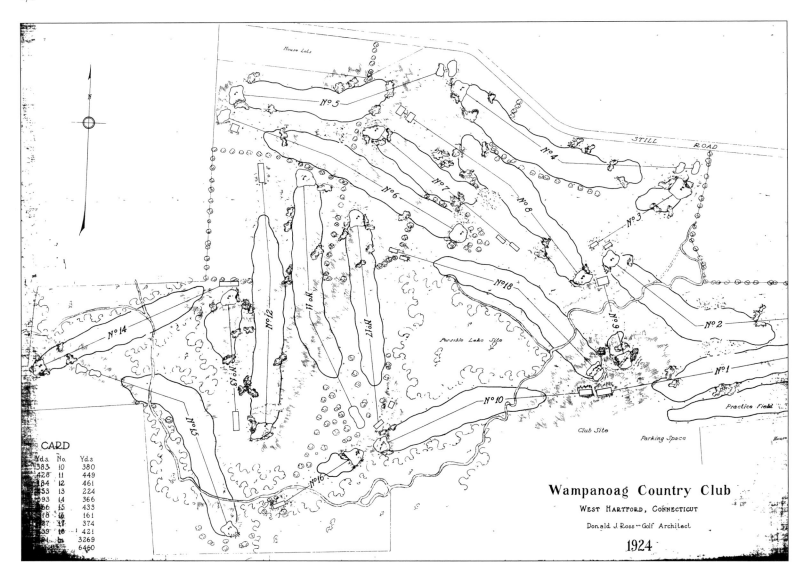

Wampanoag routing plan, 1924. (Wampanoag Country Club)

designer) with a penchant for hooking the ball. Because of this tendency—legend has it—the left side of many greens were either cleared of their bunkers or the sand was pulled short to leave plenty of room for both mishit approaches to the left (Frank Ross's) and gang-mowers trying to get through. Then, also at Frank Ross's behest, an Indianapolis-based designer named Bill Diddel came to Wampanoag in 1958 to redesign the greens. The detailed blueprints and plans he drew up that year lay quietly for decades in the superintendent's office.

Diddel's drawings of his proposed new greens lay over the circular outlines of the putting surfaces that he found during his site visit. As he made clear in his notes, Wampanoag's putting greens by 1958 were little more than circles or ovals, averaging 3,000 to 3,500 sq. ft. He also wrote that, "All greens have gradually been changed in their cutting until your greens as shown in the dotted lines of these

maps are in very regular patterns, either circles or slightly elongated rectangles, with even curves at all corners."

Diddel then made an interesting suggestion for ensuring that the greens reconstruction proceed without trouble:

> *I strongly advise making a flat box approximately 3 feet square and filling this with sand, and modeling each of these greens before actual work is started, so your superintendent will have a visual model to guide him as well as the contour lines on these blueprints. When this has been done, wet down the sand thoroughly and check it to see that flatter portions of the green are as indicated on the prints and that there is plenty of cup setting area.*

Wampanoag's 18th hole, a 427-yard par 4. The view is from behind the elevated green, with Talcott "Mountain" in the background. Note the proximity of the cedars to the fairway. (Bradley S. Klein)

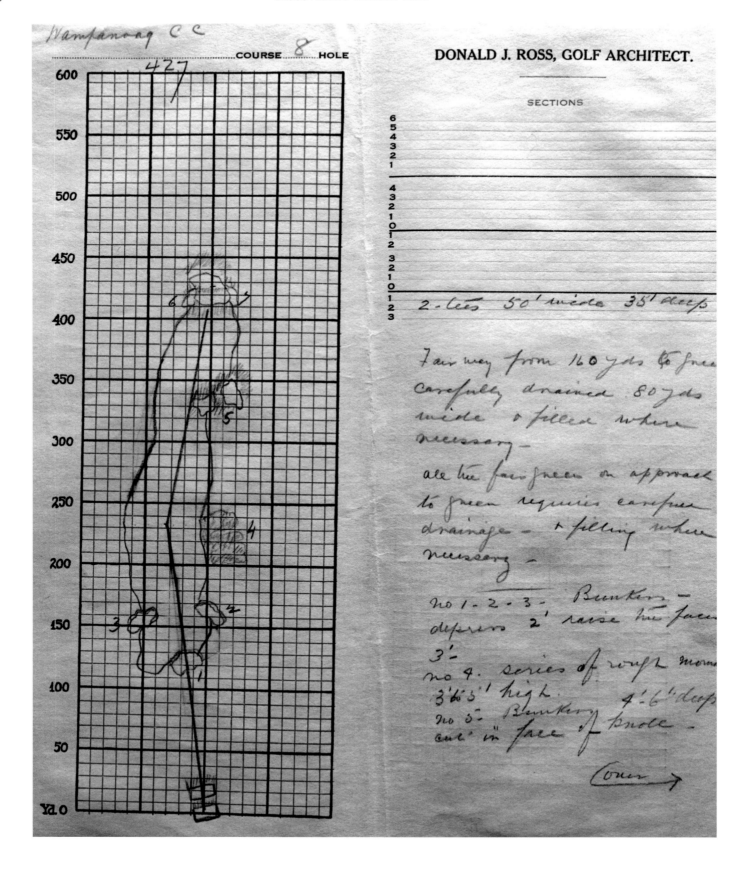

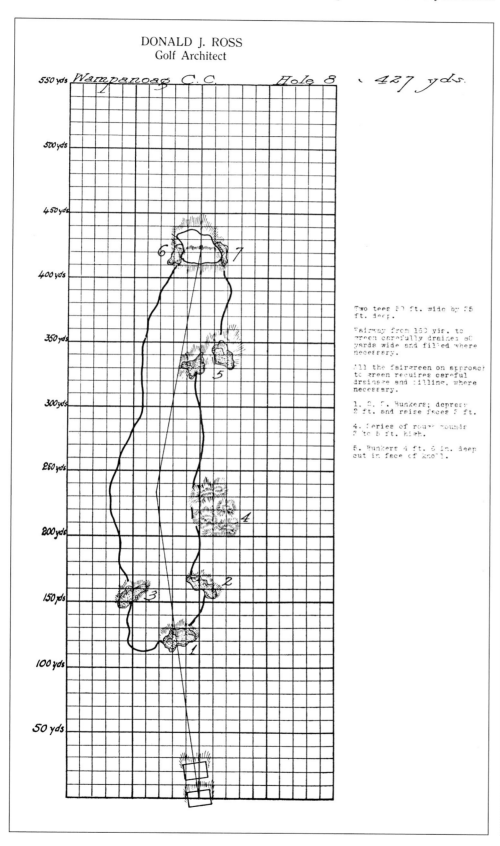

DONALD J. ROSS
Golf Architect

Wampanoag C. C. Hole 8 . *427 yds.*

Two tees 50 ft. wide by 35 ft. deep.

Fairway from 160 yds. to green carefully drained 80 yards wide and filled where necessary.

All the fairgreen on approach to green requires careful drainage and filling, where necessary.

1. 2. 3. Bunkers; depress 2 ft. and raise faces 3 ft.

4. Series of rough mounds 3 to 5 ft. high.

5. Bunkers 4 ft. 6 in. deep cut in face of knoll.

Opposite page: Evolution of a golf hole: Wampanoag's 427-yard par-4 eighth hole, as sketched by Ross in 1924. (Tufts Archives)

Left: Ross's plan for Wampanoag's eighth as formalized by Walter Irving Johnson. "Fairway from 160 yards to green carefully drained 80 yds wide & filled where necessary." Note the three short carry bunkers ("depress 2 ft. and raise faces 3 ft."). Also indicated at "4" is a "Series of rough mounds 3 to 5 ft. high." (Wampanoag Country Club)

Page 274: Ross's green plan for Wampanoag's eighth hole. The green sat on a gentle two-foot upslope, with flanking bunkers that were 4 to 5 feet deep. The rear level of the green was 1 foot 6 inches above the lower tier. (Wampanoag Country Club)

Page 275: Bill Diddel's 1958 green plan for Wampanoag's eighth. "The present green ... is too small. It also has too much pitch." Ross's green, planned at 80 feet by 80 feet with squared front corners, had become rounded into a 53 foot by 80 foot oval (indicated by dashed lines). Diddel eliminated the right bunker and increased the putting surface by 2 to 3 yards. His softened slope yielded a green that fell exactly 3 feet 6 inches in the 100 feet from back-left to front-right, a slope of 3.5 percent. (Wampanoag Country Club)

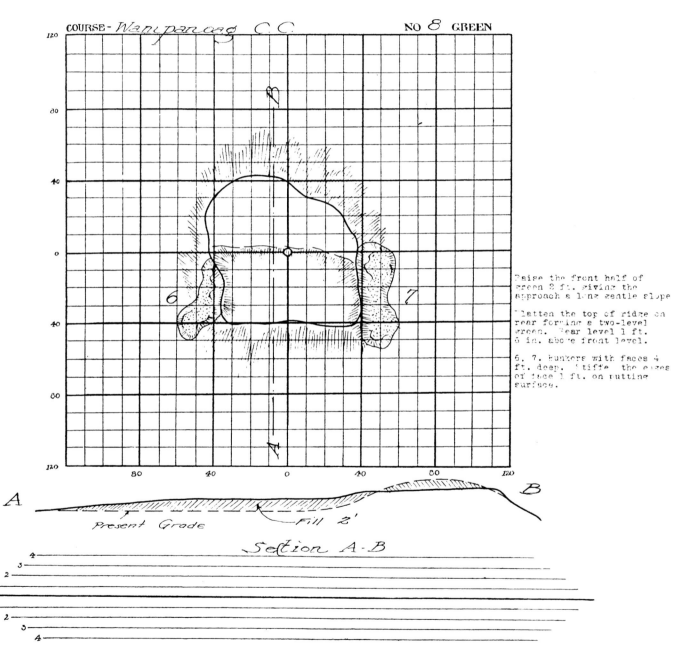

DONALD J. ROSS,
GOLF ARCHITECT·

COURSE - *Wanipanoag C.C.*   NO 8 GREEN

Raise the front half of
green 2 ft. giving the
approach a long gentle slope

Flatten the top of ridge on
rear forming a two-level
green. Rear level 1 ft.
6 in. above front level.

6, 7. bunkers with faces 4
ft. deep. Stiffe the eyes
of face 1 ft. on putting
surface.

Present Grade   Fill 2'

Section A-B

WILLIAM H. DIDDEL–GOLF ARCHITECT
INDIANAPOLIS

COURSE .... GREEN No. .... 2 .... SQ. FT. .... 200 ....

SCALE: 1 INCH .... 20 .... FEET

ENLARGE AT SAME DEPTH

Wampanoag's eighth hole, 2000. The series of mounds to
the right of the fairway remains. Trees behind the green
to the left have since been removed. (Bradley S. Klein)

The surprising aspect of the discovery of these plans in the summer of 2000 for those of us who have enjoyed Wampanoag's holes all these years is that many of the most vexing greens that we assumed belonged to Ross's genius in fact turn out to have been redesigned and built by Diddell, who expanded the putting surfaces he found, recaptured or created many peripheral hole placements, and moved the center of two greens as much as 10-20 yards.

However, that's assuming that Diddel's plans were followed, which in a few cases cannot be determined, especially given the fact that it was Frank Ross who ruled the club and determined what would be built. An aerial photograph from the mid-1960s suggests that some of Diddell's proposals for greens and surrounding bunkers were not implemented. Further complicating matters was the fact that sometime in the 1970s, a New England designer named Al Zikorus rounded out and flashed up many of Wampanoag's bunkers to the point where what had been conceived as low-lying hazards with turf mounds on the escape side had been relegated to large, curvilinear forms. By then, many cross-bunkers and diagonal bunkers had also been eliminated. It was still a Donald Ross course because the routing was never tinkered with. But by the mid-1980s, the course had already been heavily compromised—including extensive tree plantings and the narrowing of fairways.

BRIAN SILVA

As for Silva, it must be said that he has gone on to some sensitive and detailed restoration work on Ross courses elsewhere. At Seminole in 1996, he returfed the bunkers and saw that the sand, which had come to be flashed up far too boldly, was brought back into form. Ross's bunkers there had already been heavily changed by Dick Wilson in the late-1940s into a more ornate, almost rococo form than they had been. In the process, golf balls were plugging into the faces of the bunkers and the sand was frequently washing out during rainstorms. Silva, working closely with superintendent Harold H. Hicks, achieved an impressive synthesis, with the sand brought back down somewhat and the grass rolled partway over and down.

Having good photographic evidence of what holes used to look like is an invaluable tool in restoration. Witness Silva's 1998 effort at Biltmore Forest Golf Club in Asheville, North Carolina. The club was fortunate to have an unusually complete set of old black and white photographs: every tee box and every green complex, all of them photographed at ground level so that surface contours could be discerned. Silva reclaimed lost cupping areas on the greens by pushing the surfaces back out to their original extent—often at the edge or breakpoint of the fill pad. He also took down the flashed-up sand and restored a low-profile look to the bunkers. According to Silva, "Biltmore had gone through the usual cycles of changes, everything from removal of cross-bunkers to placing greenside bunkers on the high side of the approach area, right where a player might be tempted to land the ball if trying to run the ball in." Silva eliminated such hazards from the high right side of the 9th, 13th and 16th greens. Many trees were also peeled back, revealing a gracious routing over land that rolls rather sternly, although with little awkward movement to the holes. The restoration has been so well received that Biltmore Forest Country Club is considering a subsequent round of restorations under Silva's supervision, including a return of those fairway cross-hazards.

At Charlotte Country Club, Silva undid the flashed-up sand and forced-carry style of Robert Trent Jones Sr. from the early 1960s and rolled the turf down onto concave bunkers. Not all of Ross's features were brought back into play. The 391-yard par-4 15th hole, for example, originally presented golfers with two short-carry bunkers and a string of five small traps on the outside (right) of the dogleg left. Silva's work thus made some concessions to modern strategic sensibilities with respect to bunker placement. But if the modern aerial game has rendered obsolete some of the older preferences for hazards, it still has to deal with the vexing nature of a ground game that has increased in tempo over the years thanks to tighter mowing heights and improved bentgrass cultivars like the G-2 used in Charlotte Country Club's newly rebuilt putting surfaces (the same kind used at Pinehurst No. 2).

Mention should also be made of another fine restoration under Silva's supervision: Old Elm Club in Highland Park, Illinois, the 1913 Colt design built by "Douglas" Ross. Very few vintage courses in the Northeast and Midwest have with-

Top: Biltmore Forest Golf Club, Asheville, NC. This is the ninth hole soon after the course opened in 1925. (Biltmore Forest Golf Club)

Middle: Biltmore Forest's ninth hole in 1992, before restoration. (Brian Silva)

Bottom: The ninth hole at Biltmore Forest in 1998, following restoration by Brian Silva. (Brian Silva)

held the onslaught of conifers, but Old Elm is that rarity. Its 6,435-yard, par-73 layout might be deemed out-of-date for modern tournament play, but the members at this isolated private club obviously don't worry about such vanities and prefer to enjoy the run of an other-worldly layout where none of the bunkering is where a modern golfer would expect it to be. Wisely, Silva's work has held true to this sensibility, and the result is gracious bunkering, with the sand lifted up just enough to present itself to an oncoming player and the grass rolled down the side about halfway. The green surfaces remain very much in vintage form, though modern green speeds do create far more kick to the contours and outslopes than classic designers imagined.

The difficulties of recreating classic features in a modern milieu are problematic enough; far more demanding is building new holes to match or complement

Charlotte Country Club, 1933, with the 14th green at lower right. Note the string of five fairway bunkers on the right side of the adjoining 15th hole, a dogleg left. (Charlotte Country Club)

Charlotte CC's 391-yard par-4 15th, following Silva's 1998 restoration. Note the rolled-down turfed faces on the bunkers. (Bradley S. Klein)

Opposite page: Shennecosset Golf Course, Groton, CT. The 400-yard par-4 16th hole is a fine hole in its own right, but mismatched with the older existing holes. (Larry Lambrecht)

long-established ones. The subtle earth movements of an earlier day are hard to emulate with modern bulldozers and back hoes. Handwork is hard to reproduce mechanically. Consider some work done by Mark Mungeam, a principal in the design firm of Cornish, Silva and Mungeam, Inc.

The case of Shennecossett Golf Club in Groton, Connecticut illustrates how hard it is to match old holes with new ones. In 1916, at a spot called Avery Point where the Thames River empties into Long Island Sound, Ross reworked an existing layout into one of the Eastern seaboard's grandest coastal golf resorts, with guests staying at the palatial Griswold Inn. Unfortunately, a long, sad history of neglect set in and it led to the demise of the once-grand Inn and the deterioration of the golf course. But conditioning issues aside, daily-fee visitors to Shennecossett (which was eventually taken over by the town of Groton) were always treated to some fascinating ground features that included gun-platform tees, diagonal fairway bunkering, green surfaces not only pushed to the edge of the fill pad but tumbling off into bunkers, and perfect little Ross/Hatch swales that nosed into the putting surfaces.

When a late-1990s expansion plan by Pfizer Industries, Inc. claimed the land on which three of Shennecossett's holes sat, town officials negotiated the

rights to the waterfront land formerly occupied by the old Griswold Inn. Pfizer, which owned the land, gave it to the town for golf holes in exchange for the land occupied by the existing three holes (Numbers 5, 6, & 7).

Mungeam, working on behalf of his firm, designed three new holes on prime coastal frontage. To clear up some routing problems and to provide for newfound continuity, he also added two other holes and another green. The holes he built—the 8th, 9th, 15th, 16th 17th—are perfectly fine (or would be anywhere else) except that their flat greens and surrounds prove mild on a course otherwise brimming with visual and strategic interest. Even a novice can spot their discrepant character. The one exception to his out-of-place work is the new 18th green, which fits perfectly well in terms of contours and bunker shaping. But the other holes suggest that in terms of emulating Ross, the design work at Shennecossett is somewhat disappointing.

The problem, of course, is that restoration is hard work—probably harder than original design work. Matching holes without getting to redo all the others is just about impossible. The historical record is loaded with examples by many different designers and at many fine courses. The introduction of clamshell-edged, flashed-up bunkers at Scioto Country Club (OH); the symmetrical greenside mounding at Southern Pines Country Club and Cape Fear Country Club (NC); the reliance upon ungainly, anachronistic mounding at Exmoor Country Club, Skokie Country Club (IL), and Cedar Rapids Country Club (IA); the removal of ground-game subtlety at Charlotte Country Club; the aggressive rebunkering work that was done at Aronimink in the mid-1980s; and the work at both Inverness Golf Club (OH) and Oak Hill Country Club's East Course (NY) in the late-1970s (see upcoming explanation). Perhaps most stylized was the aggressive restyling of the West Course at The Country Club of Birmingham (AL). Robert Trent Jones had been there in the early 1960s and introduced modern elements of forced carries into some of the greens. In the process of undoing that work, an attempt was made to recapture of Ross's original shot-making; the left-to-right and right-to-left shots are again there, but the playing surface was intensified through a kind of vertical amplification. The effect was to situate Ross's original shot-making demands on a far more dramatic three-dimensional scale.

In virtually all of the above-named cases, a sensativity to tradition has gained a foothold. So, too, at Wampanoag, which recently hired Steve Smyers to bring back its basic character.

WHY EVEN BOTHER?

There are often good reasons for a club to consider reconstruction and to call upon an architect. First of all, a golf course is an organic composition that naturally undergoes changes. Trees grow in. Bunker faces erode. Silt builds up in drainage pipes. Modern maintenance techniques also exact a toll: the use of triplex mowers on the greens often leads to a rounding off of playing surfaces, and riding bunker rakes wear down edges at the point where they enter and exit the sand.

Now add some other factors. Many of these courses were built before they had complete irrigation systems; their original fairways tended to be wide—40-50 yards—and elaborately curved. Only after the widespread adoption of full-length irigation systems in the 1950s did fairways acquire their linear, bowling alley look. When they did, their width was reduced to 30 yards, basically the extent of irrigation coverage that could be provided by a single row of sprinkers down the middle. The straightening of courses led to a loss of intricacy in design and to a subsequent loss of appreciation by golfers of the width and strategic variety of golf holes. Trees were then planted in the lateral playing area of light rough that could not be irrigated, leading to the narrow, tree-lined look of parkland golf. Bunkers that might have been in play on a wider playing field were now abandoned, covered over, or overgrown by trees.

Next, a green committee, in the interest of labor-saving innovations, decides to take out those old cross bunkers 130 yards in front of a tee. These same high-handicappers, many of them in search of lower scores, decide to cut down the rough that had normally been knee-high. Other members, impressed by the championship courses they see on television, decide to emulate the "all green" look by overwatering everything in the areas covered by their (limited, single-row) irrigation system. This softens the course and removes the ground game by requiring all shots to be flown to the green rather than bumped and run up. Any bunkers 30 yards short of the green now lose their bite. Add in a green chairman all too willing to "make his mark" on the golf course, and you've got a pretty standard formula for the loss of design integrity. At some point, it becomes necessary to make amends for these transgressions. The question is whether to renovate or to restore.

Complicating the matter is the belief that many traditional courses are considered obsolete today because of a lack of length, imperfect turfgrass, or the absence of cart paths. And who can blame the well-intentioned superintendent or green chairman (or finance chairman) for wanting to update and modernize the golf course? Often the reason is to attract new members or, in some cases, to attract major tournaments.

It's unfortunate that clubs are forced, in effect, to shoulder the responsibility for adapting to the modern game. The burden wouldn't be so great, of course, if the USGA cracked down on all those equipment changes in golf that have rendered obsolete so many classic 6,500-yard championship courses. Until the USGA steps in, course officials will have to fend for themselves. But as the hypothetical history (above) suggests, length is not the only matter that leads clubs to reexamine their design.

The shame of it is that few architects take the trouble to educate their clients on the virtues of a classic design. Indeed, all too many designers today are looking for work and are willing to comply when the honest answer to the club's wishes would be a resounding "No." The club or its green chairman is the client, and many architects adhere to the view that their job is to serve the client's wants and not to impose their own agenda.

In a 1999 interview, architect John Lafoy, then the president of the American Society of Golf Course Architects, explained the dilemma in which some find themselves when faced with a proposed renovation.

"I've run into this a number of times, where the client was not particularly interested in putting it back, and ultimately your work is for the people you are working for— they're the ones who are paying you. You're obligated either to say you're not interested in doing it, or you do it the kind of way they want. Sometimes architects are given too much credit for having the power to tell the client what to do.

. . . If you just don't feel like it ought to be done, I think you ought to tell them that. I think you may have a responsibility to walk away. One architect told me once that if a client wanted you to build a green upside down and purple, it's your duty to do that if they're paying you. I think it just depends on the architect."

Even when needed work is undertaken, few designers bother to search out old plans. Fewer yet are interested in a master plan for redesign that would essentially restore the course. The problem is that many architects are headstrong and persuasive. If given any latitude, they are often able to use their persuasive powers to create considerable freedom for themselves.

What is it about the designer/builder that leads to, and rewards, such determination? Surely it has much to do with the pure act of planning and creating a structure anew, imposing a vision upon land and thereby transforming nature into artifice. The very nature of designing and building requires a measure of arrogance and boldness. The incredible maze of financiers, lawyers, and regulatory boards can only be navigated with a kind of single-focus willfulness. The problem is surely greater today than in Ross's day, yet there is every reason to believe that he had a measure of confidence (bordering on professional arrogance) that allowed him to create the design empire he did. Ross was surely different from such colleagues as Macdonald, Tillinghast, and MacKenzie in that his external confidence was not bombastic and ego-driven. It was more sober. And so was he.

Competition plays a role, as well. It is a tough business, subject to cyclical variation, often with considerable lead times that delay payment schedules. Financial pressures are evident, especially during the early phases of a career, when the need to make a mark leads designers into developing a unique style that would differentiate themselves from the competition. Such trademark styles are good for marketing purposes, and they may help differentiate a finished product from another course down the road created by another architect. But the reliance upon style is more a function of market pressures than a method of correct engineering procedure. Much of architecture, after all, is a matter of style. When one designer goes to work on another designer's golf course, the result is usually a clash of approaches that can have stylistically confusing effects.

It is no simple matter, then, for an architect to be true to the original approach and design philosophy of Ross. Nor is it always clear that there even existed some pristine, original condition—pure "Ross" to go back to. The irony may well be that what is today called "restoration" is largely a matter of evoking a state of design that may never have actually existed. Indeed, the very best examples of architectural restoration do not duplicate the past so much as emulate it under somewhat altered circumstances. The standard of achievement is less a recreation of what actually existed than an interpretation of Ross's intent adapted to very different contemporary standards of turfgrass and shot-making.

BROOKSIDE

This is the issue facing Brookside Country Club in Canton, Ohio, a private club that is keen to preserve and reclaim its Donald Ross-design character. The club has maintained its original putting surfaces, which are among the bolder and more compelling that Ross ever built. The key to any golf course ultimately resides in its putting surfaces; not the mere quality and cut of its turfgrass, but in the nature of its ground contours.

Brookside Country Club was originally called Lakeside Country Club and it came to its present site in 1920, under the new name. Ross, who was on site for the design, had extensive ground to work; over 200 acres, with no need to save any of it for real estate. The bold, dramatic putting surfaces he created were beautifully tied into ground contours. They display careful integration of shaping with the surrounding areas. Ross's layout was liberally sprinkled with fairway bunkers in the primary and secondary landing areas (especially the par 5s). The property was virtually treeless and, when opened, without irrigation lines. Green construction was designed to facilitate surface drainage but also to create moisture retention in the fill pad, whether through heavy organic soil composition or by a green built in a slightly bowled-out fashion that would hold moisture in the middle. These needs help to account for the nature of the greens at Brookside: steeply sloped at the back but softened toward the front. The fairways also provided plenty of roll and kick owing to their being kept dry.

From the standpoint of design integrity, however, Brookside has endured two major changes. The first was the removal of its fairway bunkers. The second alteration was a series of heavy tree planting. The results were: (1) a loss of strategic variety and lateral playing area; and (2) Brookside's original wide, curvy fairways became narrow paths of play.

Despite these architectural compromises, Brookside had much to be proud of when I saw it in November of 2000. Chief among these is a well-managed

Brookside Country Club, Canton, OH, ca.1925. Note the proliferation of bunkers—the ninth hole, far right, has over 10. The 18th hole, with its green to the front of the clubhouse, is treeless (like most of the golf course). (Brookside Country Club)

club, with highly respected veterans in key posts for long periods of time: PGA golf professional Jim Logue (since 1969) and superintendent Bob Figurella (since 1971). Seniority and wisdom in these two key positions are enormous assets to a club and contribute to a sense of collegiality and stability. This tone is also evident at the committee level. In an era when many private clubs are torn apart by contending factions, Brookside offered an admirable tone of civility and mutual respect in which members shared a common pride in their facility regardless of their capabilities as golfers. This provides an important reservoir of goodwill on which to build an effort of restoration and heritage retrieval.

Besides the standard obvious issues of tree management and bunker restoration, Brookside in late 2000 faced a complex issue of what to do with greens that in some cases sloped at 4 to 6 percent. The ideal agronomic/design solution

would be to soften every green by one or two feet in the rear and a foot in the front. But this is virtually impossible without very complex reconstruction in which the entire green surface is laser-measured, the fill pad taken down, and the surrounding grades contoured out 30 to 50 feet in order to tie in all the contours. Simply taking down the putting surface alone doesn't work because drainage would be destroyed and the outflow would never work with the existing surrounds. So expertly did Ross and his associates build the original course that the contour lines are perfectly tied in, making any adjustment difficult and costly to achieve. Marginal adjustments of a few inches here and there are possible without such complex landscape measures, but this would achieve very little, if anything, given the prevailing slopes at Brookside. An attempt to reclaim lost putting surface area would also prove marginally effective. Perhaps the simplest way to proceed is to continue living with

Brookside, 1979. Dozens of bunkers have been removed—the ninth hole, to the lower left center, only has one. Note the symmetrical tree planting down the length of the 18th hole. Fairways have been narrowed and straightened, owing to irrigation patterns. The putting surfaces, however, remain intact. (Brookside Country Club)

green speeds in the range of 9 on the Stimpmeter rather than risking major alterations to the greens.

Brookside is not rushing headlong into a decision. The green committee and club officials are proceeding cautiously, all the while knowing that they have a valuable heritage worth preserving and cultivating. Decisions here will follow the guidelines of a long-term master plan rather than the short-term considerations of a green chairman's whim or the desire to host a major tournament.

OAKLAND HILLS

In the 1950s and 1960s, it was standard for architects to renovate older courses by lengthening holes and fortifying greens. The paradigm case for this modernization was Robert Trent Jones Sr.'s recasting of Donald Ross's Oakland Hills Country Club (South Course) outside of Detroit for the 1951 U.S. Open. (Jones undertook a similar, if somewhat less grandiose, project at Baltusrol Golf Club's Lower Course prior to the 1954 U.S. Open.)

It only takes a glance down the first fairway to realize that this is one tough golf course. Yes, the land is lovely, the trees graceful, and the two-story colonial clubhouse just behind the first tee makes it all look so inviting. But then there's that green 433 yards away, and all those bunkers in between. Worse yet is the narrow fairway—almost as if somebody had strangled it. In a way, somebody had.

Welcome to the South Course at Oakland Hills Country Club, 18 miles northwest of downtown Detroit. It was here in 1916 that transplanted Scotsman Donald Ross transformed 250 acres of farmland into a wondrous test. In fact, OHCC was good enough to hold the U.S. Open in 1924 and 1937. It was also—at 6,850 yards or so for both events—among the longest championship golf course of its era. Par back then was 72, with the par-5 8th and 18th holes both playing under 500 yards, as was Ross's wont.

Following World War II, however, came the era of modern golf—and with it, a vision of power jointly championed by the USGA (and its Executive Director Joe Dey) and the man who would quickly become its architectural poster boy, Robert Trent Jones Sr. In redoing the course for the 1951 U.S. Open, Jones touched neither the routing nor the green sites. But what he did to the bunkers and to the target areas helped brutalize not only that Open's competitors, but two generations of Motown golfers as well. Jones pushed back all of Ross's fairway bunkers, created miniscule targets off the tees, and performed a similar shrink-wrapping of the greens. Goodbye ground game, hello aerial golf. In addition, the 8th and 18th holes were converted into par 4s that played from tees only a few steps forward of the back markers. This changed these holes entirely (some thought unfairly). Originally designed for par 5s, the greens were contoured to receive short, high third-shot approaches. For the 1951 Open, players had to hit their second shots with long-irons and fairway woods, and that would make it more difficult to hold the putting surface.

Add a few hundred trees to what used to be a wide-open site and those landing areas get even scarier. Not that Oakland Hills could be described as claustrophobic. Intelligent tree management over the years has given the course room to breathe. But there is a clear sense during a round here that a missed shot will be heavily taxed—if not by a tree or two, then by the 5-inch bluegrass rough.

The original design by Ross offered diagonal bunkering throughout the golf course, which at least afforded optional angles of play. Trent Jones, by contrast, removed all the strategy when he placed sand on both sides of the targets. You either hit it straight or you suffered. The tone is set on the first hole, where the ball must land in a fairway that's chock-a-block with bunkers. This was golf as a forced march, hardley a Ross approach to the game.

As demanding as the front is, the back nine is even more impressive. The 10th is a roller-coaster of a par 4 that plays every inch of its 450 yards—uphill, to a green with a mound in the middle that creates maddening breaks. The dogleg-right 11th, at 399 yards, plays much harder than its distance suggests. This is due in part to a fairway that kicks dead left, and to a long, narrow, saddle-shaped green flanked by sand.

The most renowned hole at Oakland Hills is the 401-yard 16th, where a large right-side lake—reachable off the tee with a driver and also in play on the approach—is the key problem. The water, by the way, was on the original property and the hole today plays very much as Ross had intended. Jones sharpened the turn on this dogleg-right but most of the hole was created by Ross, including the forced-carry approach over what was then a former farm pond.

The pattern of bringing championship courses up-to-date was set at Oakland Hills, although it was not always executed with the relentless consistency Jones showed as he ripped up the old course and rebuilt its playing character (all the while using the exact same routing). It was modernization of the most arrogant and ambitious sort—precisely what was expected of Jones. The USGA was announcing to the golf world that the classic game was now obsolete. In place of the old would be a new style of golf: power oriented, disallowing alternative paths, reducing the rough to a penalty that forced golfers to play the golf hole single file down the fairway, and less concerned with angles and diagonals than with sheer power and the aerial game. Even recovery shots around the green were reduced to the monotony of the lofted wedge shot.

Oakland Hills Country Club's South Course, Birmingham, MI. This photo of the 401-yard par-4 16th hole was taken in 1937. Note the green's steep fall from back to front. (Oakland Hills Country Club)

*The 16th on the South Course at Oakland Hills in
1996. (Bradley S. Klein)*

Inverness

With all too many designers, heavy-handed surgery became standard operating procedure—not only for clubs hosting national championships, but also for private country clubs and municipal layouts seeking to stay competitive. All too often, however, clubs tried to improve what they *perceived* were their weakest holes. In many cases, these were the club's shorter but strategically interesting holes, often the only ones that mid-handicap members could reach in regulation.

There was a price paid along the way. A certain charm in the ground game and in the native flow of landforms was threatened. The shortcomings of such reconstruction were evident in the work done at Inverness prior to the 1979 U.S. Open and at Oak Hill for the 1980 PGA. The work was simply out of character with established features, and traditionalists rightly groaned. At least Trent Jones had a distinct vision of how the new power game should be played. In the work to prep these courses for majors, what was shown was an absence of any vision by which their new holes would match or even complement the old.

As with any historic tournament tract, Inverness has gone through many revisions. In preparation for the 1931 U.S. Open, A.W. Tillinghast made numerous adjustments, including new or expanded greenside bunkering at the present 10th, 15th, 17th and 18th holes. A quarter of a century later, prior to the 1957 U.S. Open, Dick Wilson altered or created 28 bunkers, in the process flashing them up somewhat and making them more conspicuous, if less well-integrated into the green fill pads, than they were under Ross's plan. It should also be said that the character of bunkering and putting surfaces at Inverness also owes much to the innovative maintenance practices of superintendent Wilbert Waters, who presided from 1949 through 1979. It was he who cultivated Inverness's hearty strain of Poa annua and German bentgrass.

But of all the refinements on Ross's design of Inverness, none has been more conspicuous—or controversial—than those made for the 1979 U.S. Open. Originally, the design team of George and Tom Fazio was asked to tame an overly steep slope of 6 percent at the back of the 17th green. It quickly became apparent that the course suffered limitations in terms of modern tournament conditions. The biggest problem was cramped golfing grounds. The green at the par-4 seventh, reachable for some off the tee, was perilously close to the 17th green and 18th tee. Moreover, two par 3s—the 8th and 13th—were shoehorned into adjacent areas that created an impasse for spectators and players alike. The need to open up space created an opportunity to rectify another problem, namely that the sixth and seventh holes, both of them short par-4s, had become outdated for championship play. When it was all over, the architects had created four new holes. The current third, fifth, and sixth holes were built on new land to the southwest, while the current par-5 eighth was fashioned out of features that had comprised parts of the old sixth, seventh and eighth.

The new holes were ill-adapted. Two new ponds, for example, were alien to Ross's style. And much of the feature work on the new holes was more abrupt than had previously existed. To its credit, the club has subsequently softened some of this heavy-handedness. Course designer Arthur Hills, a member at Inverness, has attempted to weave a closer pattern between the new and the old holes. A harsh, ungainly pond at the par-4 fifth was removed, for instance, and the green made more amenable to approach shots.

There are many varieties of history at Inverness, as touring pro Lon Hinkle discovered during the first round of the 1979 U.S. Open. He had fashioned a shortcut to the 528-yard par-5 eighth hole by playing his drive down the adjoining 17th fairway. The USGA went into emergency session, and early the next day planted a scraggly looking Black Hill spruce to obstruct the alternative path. Though the tree today is 25 feet tall, it looks no more appropriate than it did that Friday morning. There it stands, a strange monument to tinkering.

The "Hinkle tree" near the eighth tee at Inverness Golf Club, Toledo, OH. (Bradley S. Klein)

OAK HILL

Oak Hill Country Club in Pittsford, New York was originally a Donald Ross design. Substantial architectural modifications that were made to the championship-venue East Course in 1976 never fit right and still don't. The revisions simply did not complement the original design and feel of the course. Despite some refinements to the original alterations over the years, discordant elements at odds with the look and feel of the rest of Oak Hill are evident in the 1976 work.

Ross featured lightly mounded greens that tipped forward about three feet from back to front. Over the green was death, and chipping from either side required utmost delicacy. Most importantly, his greens rolled continuously and were not composed of distinct sections. The greens, by contrast, are forced and artificial—as if someone set about self-consciously to construct distinct pin placements and then stitched together the plateaus in the hope they would cohere.

Why did Oak Hill alter its layout in the first place? Prior to the 1956 U.S. Open, Robert Trent Jones, Sr. rebuilt a number of tees, added substantial length to the course, and removed some two dozen short-carry and orientation bunkers in favor of hazards in much longer landing zones. It was a typical modernization of the mid-1950s, but it did not resolve some issues of a tight routing. For the 1968 U.S. Open, traffic congestion between the par-4 fifth and the old par-3 sixth hole led to removal of the shorter hole. A new 3-par, designed in-house, was put in adjacent to the present fourth. But the consensus on the new 3-par was that it was no challenge to play. The short par-3 15th was equally inadequate because of the out-of-bounds close on the left side, spectator traffic congestion, and a general lack of challenge so late in the round.

After 1968, officials at Oak Hill were told (in so many words) that the USGA was not planning to return because the course was lacking in certain championship qualities. At this point, club officials decided to revamp the course and bring it up to U.S. Open standards. They hired George and Tom Fazio. The par-4 fifth was rebuilt, in the process, replacing what most members considered the loveliest hole on the course. A new par-3 sixth was built. The tee and green at the 15th were relocated (replete with a new pond, itself out of character with the course). The long par-4 17th was rebunkered, the driving area on 18 was toughened, and the green was brought down some thirty yards so that it sat atop a precipice and required a long uphill approach shot.

By everyone's reckoning, these changes enabled Oak Hill to return to major championship status (it was the site for the 1980 PGA, the 1984 U. S. Senior Open, the 1989 U.S. Open, and the 1995 Ryder Cup). But in the process, the gentle integration of bunker forms and hole styles was sacrificed. A layout of championship caliber had lost some of its compositional unity. It was Jones's dramatic modernization that had eliminated much of the old ground-game character, but at least he had the freedom to rework the entire course in this guise. The latest

Opposite page: Evolution of the second hole on Oak Hill Country Club's East Course, Pittsford, NY. (Oak Hill Country Club)

"The Breather"

PAR 4

#2 EAST -401 Yards
1924 DONALD J. ROSS, 356Yards

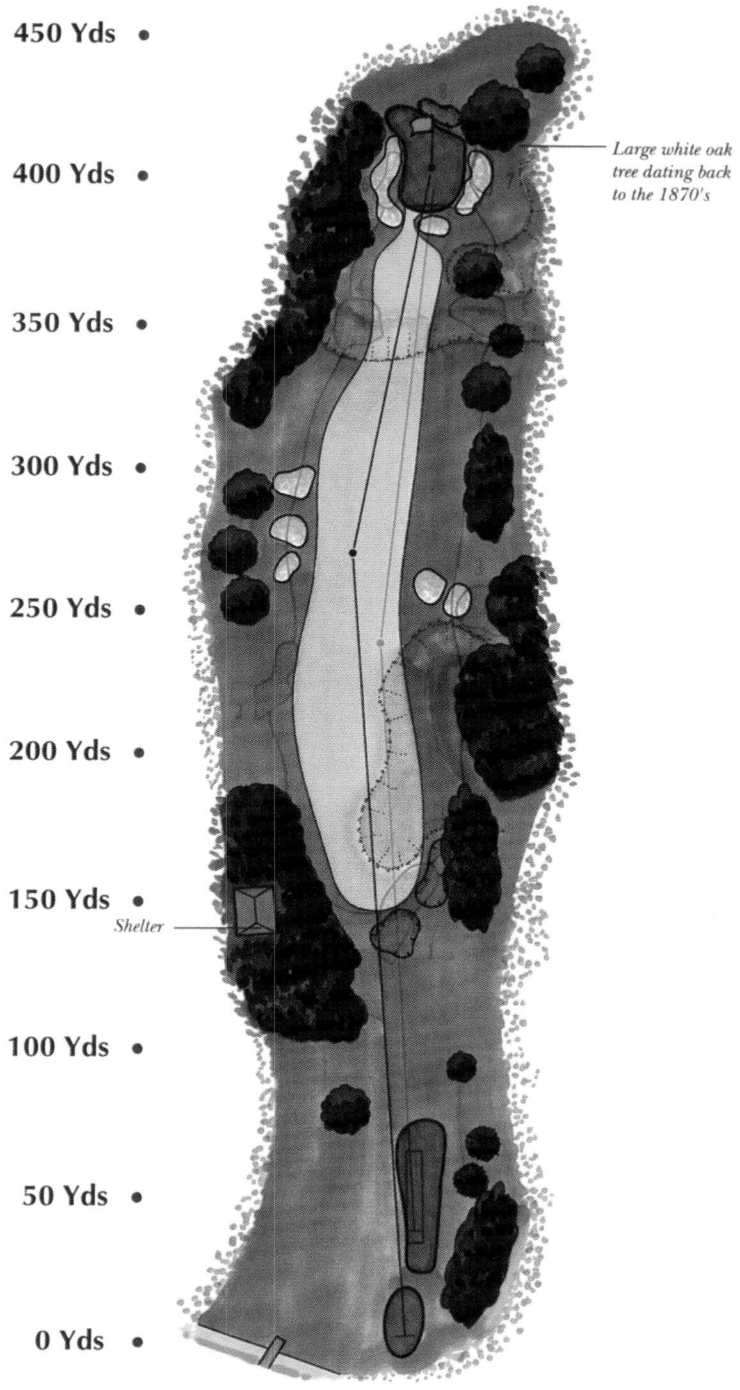

450 Yds •

400 Yds •

350 Yds •

300 Yds •

250 Yds •

200 Yds •

150 Yds •

*Large white oak
tree dating back
to the 1870's*

Shelter

100 Yds •

50 Yds •

0 Yds •

DONALD ROSS DESIGN NOTES

Tee 90 by 20 feet. Raise 1 foot 6 inches.

1. Bunker finished 4 feet deep. Keep face low so as not to obstruct view of fairgreen beyond.

Lower the ridge between bunkers 4 and 5 sufficient to open a view of the green; cut to have a natural valley formation.

2,3,4,5. Bunkers dished out of face of slope.

Ridge on center line of play at 300 yards must be lowered so as to open a view of green.

EVOLUTION

Bunker 8 was specified by D.J. Ross and shaped during original construction but there is no evidence that sand was ever placed. It has remained a grass hollow since the course opened.

Bunker 1 eliminated. R.T. Jones - 1955.

Bunker 3 reshaped. R.T. Jones - 1955.

Bunker 4 and 5 eliminated. R.T. Jones - 1955.

Back tee extended. R.T. Jones - 1955.

Greenside bunker 7 was reshaped which reduced the front right portion of the green. R.T. Jones - 1955.

Left fairway bunker added. R.T. Jones - 1955.

Back left pin placement restored during regrassing. W.C. Schreiner - 1993.

Above: 1995: The 401-yard par-4 second hole on Oak Hill's East Course. (Bradley S. Klein)

Opposite page: Oak Hill, East Course. Evolution of the 15th hole. (Oak Hill Country Club)

changes, by contrast, created a few new green placements and hole corridors, so the work, if more limited, was also more jarring. Subsequent efforts to redress the loss of design coherence at Oak Hill have not fully succeeded. Craig Schreiner's work prior to the 1995 Ryder Cup restored some lost cupping areas on the putting surfaces. He also attempted to bring back the scratchy, uneven look of Ross's bunkers, but this did not fit well with the easily trimmed edges and flashed-up sand that prevailed on the rest of the course.

These results, without critical commentary, are documented in an excellent design history of the club, *The Evolution of a Legacy*, written by Donald M. Kladstrup and published by the club.

Interestingly, the West Course, which has never been subjected to such ambitious architectural intervention, retains much of its original charm, particularly in its greens.

"The Plateau"
PAR 3

#15 EAST -177 Yards
1924 DONALD J. ROSS, 125 Yards

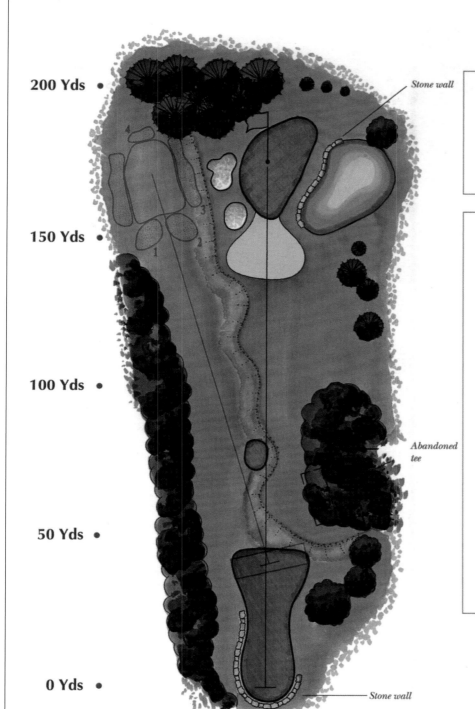

200 Yds •

150 Yds •

100 Yds •

50 Yds •

0 Yds •

Stone wall

Abandoned tee

Stone wall

DONALD ROSS DESIGN NOTES

Tee 70 feet wide by 20 feet deep. Use material taken from cut on #14 green to build up tee; take base of tee stake as grade.

EVOLUTION

New tee added to increase visibility to the green. R.T. Jones - 1955.

Bunkers renovated at green. R.T. Jones - 1955.

New bunker added at back left of green. R.T. Jones - 1955.

Slight undulation placed in the center of green by R.T. Jones - 1955.

Hole abandoned when new green was constructed. Pond built and fairway graded to improve drainage and visibility. G. & T. Fazio - 1976.

Stone wall erected along pond to support green edge. Oak Hill grounds crew-1986.

Wall and tee expansion completed. W.C. Schreiner - 1995.

EAST LAKE

Occasionally, a restoration effort can spark an entirely new interest in the golf course. In the case of East Lake Golf Club, the heart and soul of an Atlanta neighborhood has been revived in the process.

Back in 1908, the Atlanta Athletic Club built a course on wooded parkland at what was then the end of an electric streetcar line. The original layout by Tom Bendelow was rerouted by Ross in 1913. In 1925, Ross added a second course. However, because he was never able to cultivate reliable two-season grass there, the course had double greens for each hole—one for summer play and one for use during winter months. The consolidation of these greens into one set of putting surfaces only took place long after Ross was gone from the scene. In 1959, George Cobb performed a "modernization" of the main 18-hole layout in preparation for the 1963 Ryder Cup matches. It was not until 1994, however—following a masterful reconstruction of the championship course by Rees Jones—that East Lake reached real grandeur.

East Lake has enjoyed a glorious history, in large measure because it was the home course of Bobby Jones for many years (his family spent summers in a cottage on the property). It also had a distinguished membership that made extensive use of the 36-hole layout and its vast, Tudor-style clubhouse. Gradually, however, the club's fortunes waned. This was due in part to demographic factors and the deterioration of the surrounding neighborhood (a situation not unknown in other American cities). The courses remained busy, but use of the club's dining and other social facilities slowed down as members feared venturing through the nearby streets to reach the club. In an emotionally contentious decision in 1966, the AAC sold off the second golf course and applied the proceeds as down payment on a new 600-acre site along the Chattahoochee River in Duluth, a northeast suburb of Atlanta.

The remaining course became part of a newly formed East Lake Golf Club. Across the street, on the land where the second layout once stood, sprawled one of those ridiculously ill-conceived housing projects of the 1960s: 650 low-income units stuffed onto a 55-acre parcel. Not surprisingly, East Lake Meadows, as it was dubbed, soon became a shooting gallery (not golf, but a crack cocaine distribution center) that further contributed to the area's decline. Sadly but inevitably, East Lake Golf Club also deteriorated.

Businessman Tom Cousins came along in 1993 and set out to salvage East Lake. Under the aegis of the East Lake Community Foundation, a subsidiary of his own C.F. Foundation, Cousins proposed a partnership with the federal government's Housing and Urban Development agency (HUD) and private developers to invest about $100 million to rehabilitate the golf course and the surrounding community. He then hired Rees Jones as his golf course architect.

Whatever charm the older incarnations of the course might have had, the new version is simply stunning. Strictly speaking, this was not a pure restoration

Opposite page, top: 1995: The 177-yard par-3 15th on Oak Hill's East Course. (Bradley S. Klein)

Opposite page, bottom: Oak Hills East Course, East: the 458-yard par-4 17th in 1995. (Bradley S. Klein)

164-yard par-3 sixth hole at East Lake Golf Club, Atlanta, as redesigned by Rees Jones. (Larry Lambrecht)

because there was no chance of going back to Ross's double greens. There weren't any detailed Ross maps or blueprints to go by either—only old aerial and ground photography. This meant that Jones had to make crucial decisions about resiting greens and adding contours. Along the way, he stripped the course, reworked the slopes, reconstructed every bunker, put in new irrigation and drainage, and then sodded the fairways with Meyer zoysia grass. The greens were seeded with Crenshaw bent grass; 419 bermudagrass forms the rough. The only significant routing tweak was swinging the old 17th fairway and green to the left so that they now sit astride the shore of 27-acre East Lake. The result has been an impressive revival, not only of the golf course but also of the club and surrounding community. The project, which culminated in the club hosting the 1998 Tour Championship to rave reviews from the public and the players, shows that in today's golf market, heritage and tradition are valuable commodities that make good economic sense.

RENOVATION OR RESTORATION?

Throughout the United States, clubs are taking a serious look at their architectural heritage. A generation ago, the buzzwords were "renovation" and "modernization."

Opposite page: East Lake's seventh hole, a 394-yard par 4. (Larry Lambrecht)

Below: East Lake's ninth, a par 5 of 551 yards. (Larry Lambrecht)

Today, the trend is toward classic restoration. It's part of an effort to preserve traditional values. Decisive in this is a generation of lesser-known architects whose primary concern is less to impose their signature on a course than to bring out its native subtlety and charm.

Ron Prichard, based in suburban Philadelphia, styles himself as a purist when it comes to preservation. He's designed his share of new courses, including the TPC at Southwinds near Memphis. But his real love is for the traditional layouts. His portfolio today of Ross renovation projects includes Metacomet, Point

Above, right: Restoring a Ross bunker: Wilmington (NC) Municipal Golf Course, sixth hole, before Ron Prichard's work in 1998. Note outline in white of bunker shape to be restored. (Ron Prichard)

Right: Completed bunker. (Ron Prichard)

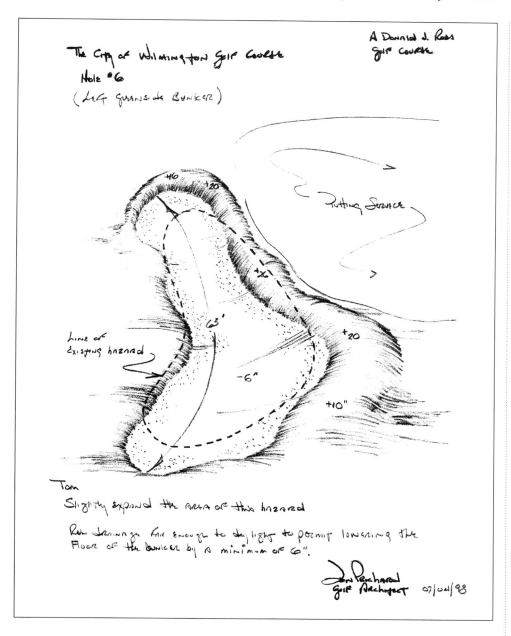

The City of Wilmington Golf Course
Hole #6
(Left greenside Bunker)

A Donald J. Ross
golf Course

Putting Surface

+6
+20
+26
63'
+20
Line of
Existing hazard
-6"
+10"

Tom
Slightly expand the area of this hazard

Run drainage far enough to daylight to permit lowering the
Floor of the bunker by a minimum of 6".

Ron Prichard
Golf Architect 07/04/98

Judith, and Wannamoisett in Rhode Island; Charles River Country Club, Longmeadow Country Club, and The Orchards in Massachusetts; Aronimink Golf Club in Pennsylvania; Wilmington Municipal Golf Course in North Carolina; and Beverly Country Club and Skokie Country Club in Illinois.

For Prichard, the allure of classic courses is that their creators knew how to utilize good land. "These people had a very special perception of the game," says Prichard, "and they were much more generous than architects today in establishing playing areas. There was only one set of tees, and par was really meaningless. There was never a full shot penalty, and they created intricate greens. They worked with

Ron Prichard's perspective sketch of the proposed bunker, including existing bunker shape in dashed line. (Ron Prichard)

a certain sense of freedom and were not out to embarrass or humiliate players."

The toughest aspect of course renovation is not the dirt work, it's the in-house politics. Clubs that are wracked by factions and competing agendas are notoriously difficult to work with. The ideal situation, says Ben Crenshaw, is "a club that's proud of its course, that has accurate archives, and where the people in charge are in concert with each other."

There is always the fear that such enthusiasm can reach the level of dogma. Was every Ross feature brilliant? Can a debate today about placement of bunkers be settled by referring to Ross's plans?

These are important questions. The game, in some respects, is not quite the same one that was being played when Ross was designing courses. Many architects express regret about the distances the golf ball can now travel. PGA Tour pros regularly *fly* the ball farther than the best players hit it 75 years ago. Average players also hit the ball much farther—and much more in the air—than was the case when Ross worked. Prichard is not alone in singling out the game's governing body on this. "Because the USGA hasn't had enough courage to review its criteria on equipment, and perhaps to turn a few pages back," he said, "most of our brilliant classical courses are becoming museum pieces for championship play."

In the face of such challenges to the design and strategic integrity of classic courses today, architects face many difficulties of interpretation. Was every classic course worth saving? Do hazards placed 140 yards from the tee deserve to be preserved, or having been removed, returned, or would their strategic value be more suited for placement 230 yards off the tee?

Such work is time-consuming and requires continual adjustment in the field. This is not work that pays well, however. And it rarely garners the national media attention that a sparkling new layout might attract. In the past, renovation work fell between the cracks, often picked up by aspiring designers or as an effort by otherwise middle-range architects to get their hands on top quality courses. The rare high-profile "doctoring" for a major championship has its rewards in terms of publicity. But for the most part, renovation work is more technical: agronomy, drainage, traffic flow, cart paths, etc. Most of this type of work is contrary to classic design principles, as the intent of the new work has often been to expedite play, toughen the golf course, and minimize maintenance, usually facilitating use of riding bunker rakes rather than hand-raking.

Restoration is a more disciplined craft and it demands more of a facility. It asks of golfers that they accept certain quirks and ground features not as design flaws but as stylistic traits unique to a certain vision (and/or era) of the game. And it usually requires costlier handwork in terms of subsequent bunker raking and greens mowing.

Restoration as a more esoteric, more traditional practice, has fallen to a coterie of design connoisseurs willing to devote time to tracking down archives and interviewing senior members in order to get a clearer sense of what the course used to look like and what the designer intended. It is also mandatory that long hours be spent on-site accompanying the shaper, massaging each roll and twist of earth. In most cases, the spadework of restoration is not as lucrative as new course assignments. But it is nonetheless important as a way of preserving the game's traditions. It is also crucial that members, owners, committee members, and golfers understand what is going on. Forty years ago (even 20), restoration was dismissed as anachronistic. Now, as in so much of contemporary culture, retrofitting is seen as trendy and good business. It also makes more agronomic sense, producing healthier turf with less reliance upon chemicals and other pesticides.

LONGMEADOW AND THE ORCHARDS

It also makes for more interesting golf. Consider the case of Longmeadow Country Club in Massachusetts, a 1921 Ross design five miles southeast of Springfield, where Prichard, with the blessing of the membership, started on a meticulous restoration project. The site is unusual: 120 acres, bisected by a moderately traveled road, with holes 1 and 10-18 on the clubhouse side and holes 2-8 across Mill Street. A number of water courses and dry creek beds run through the property. Ross put them to brilliant strategic use by arraying his holes so that they brought these features into play diagonally, creating multiple angles of play. The best of these is the par-4 fifth (only 318 yards from the back tee) where dramatic natural folds help define the landing areas and the green sits on a little plateau on the far side of a ravine. Prichard's plan here is to expand the teeing ground slightly, elevate it to make the landing area more visible, then remove trees that are crowding the landing area. He also plans to expand the green to its original size, thereby regaining pin placements (behind greenside bunkers) that had been lost over the years.

Little earthmoving was needed at Longmeadow; besides, not much was possible in those days. The elegance of the routing is assured by the natural settings of the putting surfaces. The lines of approach into the greens always seem to traverse ground that slopes on a diagonal curve. The par-70 layout, at 6,549 yards from the back tees, commands attention because there is rarely a level lie in the fairway.

The greens bear a modest crowned slope at back-center, a feature characteristic of the work of Ross's associate, Walter Hatch, who, as a resident just up the road in North Amherst, was on-site during construction. The resulting greens are what Geoffrey Cornish calls "more Ross than Ross," meaning that Hatch's style became indistinguishable from his mentor's.

Trees, not surprisingly, had heavily overgrown the Longmeadow site—hardwoods and conifers planted in the 1960s and 1970s in the name of beautification. The 11th green, redesigned in the 1970s, looked mechanical in form thanks to a less-than-perfectly-executed cross slope through the putting surface. But Longmeadow is luckier than most New England courses that have been tinkered with in that it retains its original routing.

Prichard's master plan, underway since the fall of 1999 and slated for completion for the 2002 golf season, calls for removal of nearly 1,000 trees. This will help reclaim angles of play and open up lost views. About 30 fairway bunkers will also be reestablished, nearly half of them well short of standard landing areas but nonetheless helpful for orienting shots. Prichard is more of a purist than most restorationists in insisting that such bunkers be put back precisely where they were. He also tends to place them in areas of fescue for a drier, tawnier look that's at odds with the all-green aesthetic.

As is typical of Ross courses, many of Longmeadow's greens (originally about 6,000 sq. ft.) had become rounded out and had lost vital areas on the flanks and rears of fill pads. Prichard plans to bring these back as well. The result will be the recapture of some fascinating potential hole locations that will enable the course to play in a more challenging manner than it has in decades.

Below: Longmeadow (MA) Country Club's 18th hole, a 374-yard par 4. (Bradley S. Klein)

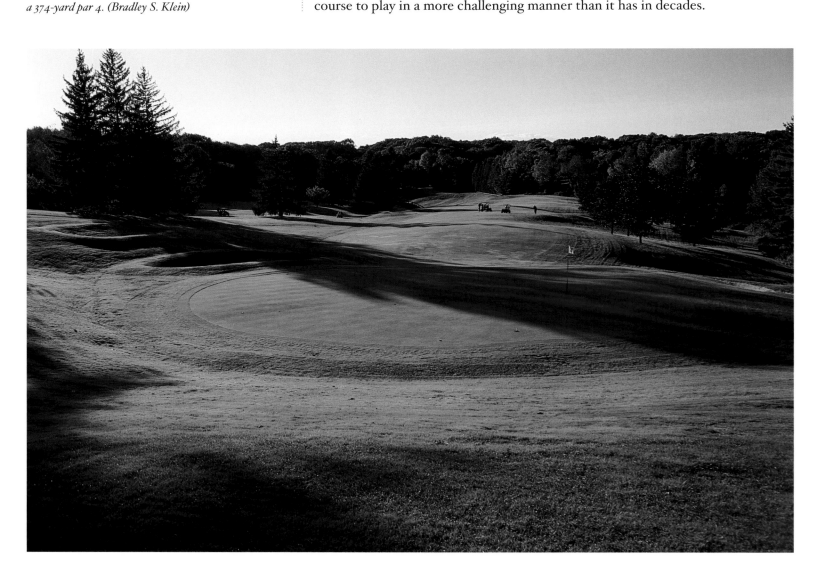

The beauty of such a plan is that it will make the course more enjoyable for average golfers as they will have a wider berth to play and maneuver the ball. At the same time the course will become more demanding for crack golfers, thanks to the regained hole placements that are precariously near bunkers and falloffs. The tree removal plan will also enable the turf to dry, thus allowing for firmer, faster playing conditions. This also benefits higher handicappers because their golf ball rolls farther. On the other hand, the tighter turf conditions will be challenging for better players because they will no longer be able to play darts with their golf shots and will have more trouble controlling the ground game.

Prichard is also under contract to complete a restoration program at The Orchards, 16 miles north of Longmeadow in South Hadley. The Orchards is another Ross/Hatch collaboration from the 1920s that has been gradually nursed back from neglect to become a widely admired gem.

The restoration of The Orchards dates to the mid-1980s, when then-superintendent Paul Jamrog undertook to reclaim a faded design heritage. When Jamrog first got there in 1983, the course at the base of the Holyoke Range in west central Massachusetts was unkempt. Poa annua and crabgrass had infested the course. The putting surfaces all appeared rounded off. Many of the bunker faces were in disrepair and the sand had been so carelessly raked that it spilled over the edges. The course drained so poorly that at times it looked like a bog. In addition, the natural contours of the rolling land were scarcely visible because all of the fairways were being mowed in a straight line from tee to green.

Jamrog figured that the first thing to do was get some good grasses back onto the course. He began with a massive seeding of rye, a grass that, if not ideal, would at least "take" quickly. Once the rye had spread, he began the full conversion to bentgrass fairways. Jamrog began to cut the greens and tees with walking mowers in order to control the shaping. Eventually, greens were brought out to include mounds and rolls that had become overgrown with rough. Jamrog also stopped cutting the rough and allowed the fescues to come back. As he explained it, "What had been seeded into the golf course when Donald Ross designed and built it was mainly fescues, and they were everywhere. At that time they didn't have the variety of grasses that we have available now. Really, the look of the golf course should be to let those fescues grow up and then to let them go dormant in the summer months. That's the type of look, the Scottish look, that had been intended for the golf course."

Jamrog combined his regrassing and mowing plans with a reworking of the drainage system for the layout, including clearing out areas that had silted over. Luckily, The Orchards had been a shoestring operation over the years so the club never had a lot of money to spend on ambitious renovation projects. The one attempt to build new greens for the third and eighth holes resulted in rock-hard surfaces that looked and played out of character with the rest of the course. But only a few bunkers had been added or removed since the course opened, and the native charm of the layout was such that Jamrog's success brought the club new-found attention—including the 1987 U.S. Girls' Junior Championship and rave reviews from the likes of former USGA Executive Director Frank Hannigan and Ben Crenshaw.

Jamrog eventually ran into budgetary limitations, as well as the resistance of certain members (many of them seniors) who wanted to be able to play seven days a week for fees that were well below what the southern New England market would bear for such a vintage facility. Jamrog eventually left for another Ross course, Metacomet in Rhode Island. With his departure, further plans for restoration of The Orchards were delayed for several years. In 1998, Prichard was hired to move the work forward.

His plans included further drainage improvements and water course management, refacing and regrassing the bunkers with fescue turfgrass, and rebuilding the problematic second green. It was bad enough that the green sloped some 3 to 4 percent and that it was less than 2,500 sq. ft. in size. But it also suffered excess

The Orchards, South Hadley, MA. The 14th hole is a 408-yard par 4. (Bradley S. Klein)

surface water that was running off the nearby road to the rear.

In the middle of Prichard's restoration efforts, The Orchards, which was nominally owned and controlled by Mount Holyoke College, made a major move. It shifted its operations from a quasi-independent board to the tutelage of Arnold Palmer Golf Management, effective January 1, 2000. The new management pledged itself to continue with Prichard's plans. In line with the regional market, a new fee schedule for new members of The Orchards has been announced, one that called for an increase. The Orchards' vintage Ross character turned out to be a much-vaunted selling point. Ross and Hatch's orignal hole-by-hole sketches adorn the hallways of the cottage-style clubhouse and add a traditional sensibility to the club. In short, heritage pays.

TIMUQUANA

Any work done on a Ross course can be controversial, no matter how decayed the original design may be. The task is made even more difficult if Ross's efforts were not well documented. Such was the case at Timuquana Country Club, a 1923 Ross design along the St. Johns River in Jacksonville, Florida, with views of the downtown skyline behind the plantation-style clubhouse. Over the years, the course (and with it, the club's reputation) had deteriorated. In 1994, local regulatory agencies mandated that Timuquana begin irrigating with treated wastewater, a shift from its freshwater wells that required a new irrigation system. The mandated revisions provided an occasion for more extensive work. Along the way, as superintendent Bill Griffith found out, meeting members' expectations about a layout they were long familiar with would prove to be a complicated challenge. "They're used to a quality golf course," he said, "and after closing it down for half a year we were asking them to adapt to a different version of their home layout."

Ross's original drainage plan had relied on an extensive ditch system that ran through the woods on the 120-acre site. These ditches had become clogged with vegetation, to the point where water was backing up rather than drawing down. The course also suffered agronomically. The traditional, native soil greens had consisted of an obsolete bermudagrass species that had mutated over the years, rendering turf delineation between greens and collars, or between collars and surrounding rough, all but indistinguishable—except by virtue of mowing height. A zealous pine tree planting program by members was choking out light and air from the course, rendering the turf both wetter (because it didn't dry out as well) and more stressed (owing to inadequate sunlight) than it should have been.

Club officials turned to Jacksonville-based architect Bobby Weed, a former golf course superintendent who became an architect for Tournament Players Club properties before heading off on his own in 1995. Armed only with an aerial photograph taken in 1943, Weed was forced to approach each hole individually, making his own interpretations of Ross's intentions. By keeping his own ego in check, Weed showed that a modern course architect can breathe new life into the work of an old master.

On the morning of May 1, 1996, nearby residents awoke to the sounds of a giant Caterpillar rototiller (called a "soil stabilizer") that is normally used for road construction. This one, though, was ripping up every square foot of turf inside Timuquana's tree lines. After seven decades of growth, a thick organic layer had covered the native soil and it had to be tilled under.

Griffith didn't want to be left with lots of steep slopes that had to be maintained with time-consuming (and dangerous) handheld fly-mowers. Sometimes, these concerns entail a battle with architects who are more interested in flashy imagery and steep slopes than in sound construction for maintenance. Not so with Weed, whose years as a greenkeeper provide a reminder that one test of a good design is whether it can be maintained. His plans for Ross-style contours called for soft rather than hard edges. The same consideration governed bunker shaping; Timuquana's new bunkers would not require hand-raking; they'd hold up well with ride-raking.

Triple-row irrigation was installed, some 800 trees were removed, the entire golf course was reshaped, and the tees and fairways were sprigged with 419 bermudagrass. The old pop-up, native soil greens were also rebuilt, this time to modified USGA standards: rock, drainage, sand—but no pea-gravel choker layer. The whole operation took under six months to complete and the golf course reopened on October 21, 1996.

The remodeled fourth hole is indicative of the care taken to restore Ross's strategic design. The 1943 drawing shows the fourth hole as a 473-yard par 5. As with the entire golf course, there was virtually no elevation change. A cluster of bunkers guarded the left side of the fairway about 200 yards off of the tee. Farther on up the right side, another group of bunkers challenged the second shot. The green angled from front-right to back-left and was protected by two flanking bunkers.

By 1996, the fourth hole had been extended 30 yards, and the bunkering had evolved significantly. Only two fairway bunkers remained along the left side, and a single bunker sat to the right to guard the second shot. The green had eroded into a nondescript circle. Maturing trees along the perimeter of the hole were overgrowing the corridor and producing inferior turf while reducing strategy and playability. The fairway had also become straighter, further reducing strategy and angles of play.

"We could never be entirely sure what the hole had looked like on opening day," Weed reported. "So we concentrated our efforts on determining Ross's strategic intention, and then bringing that strategy into a modern context."

The 1943 aerial of Timuquana's fourth hole suggested that Ross intended players to flirt with the left-hand bunkers on the tee shot, thereby affording a better angle to skirt the right-side group on the second shot. From there, players would be pitching down the long axis of the green. Clearly, golfers who hugged the

Opposite page: Evolution of a golf hole: Timuquana Country Club, Jacksonville, FL. The fourth hole, a 473-yard par 4 that Ross designed in 1923, as it appeared in 1943. (Bobby Weed)

Page 312: The 503-yard par-5 fourth at Timuquana in 1996, just before restoration. Note tree incursion, fairway straightening, lost bunkers, and rounding out of green surface. (Bobby Weed)

Page 313: Timuquana's fourth hole, following restoration. (Bobby Weed)

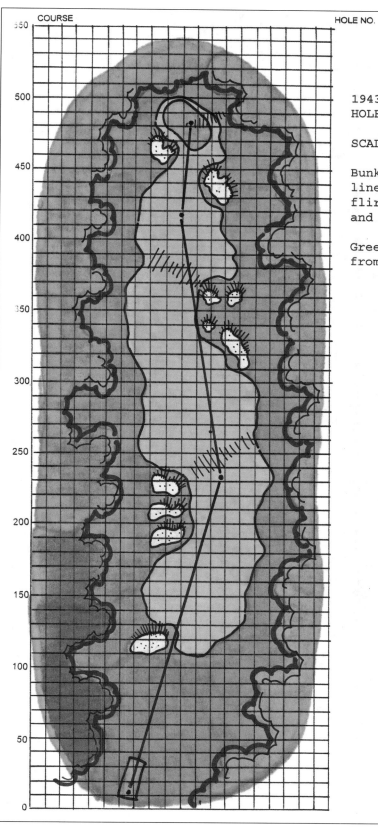

COURSE

HOLE NO.

1943 -- EARLIEST RECORD OF HOLE

SCALED DISTANCE: 473 yards

Bunker positioning gives best line into green to players who flirt with sand on their first and second shots.

Green strategically angled from right to left.

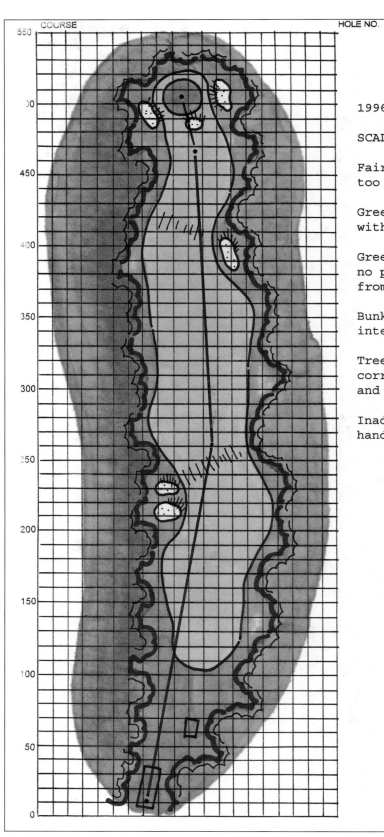

COURSE   HOLE NO.

1996 -- PRIOR TO RENOVATION

SCALED DISTANCE: 503 yards

Fairway bunkering off of tee
too short for modern players.

Green reduced to simple shape
with no strategic interest.

Greenside bunkering presents
no preferred angle to pitch
from.

Bunkering has no visual
interest.

Trees crowding out golf
corridor, reducing visibility
and playability.

Inadequate teeing space
handicaps weaker players.

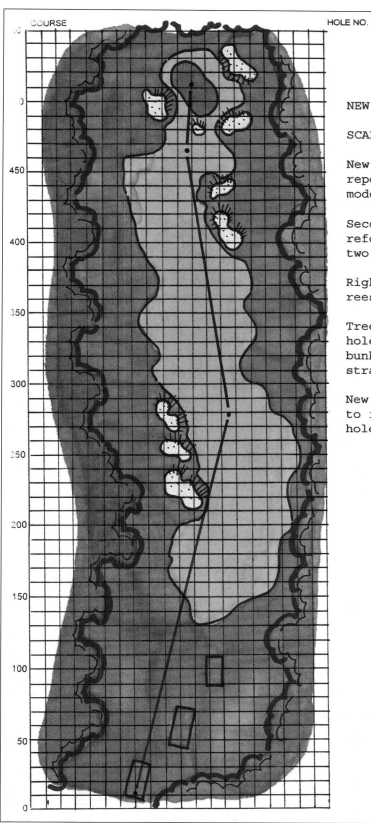

COURSE   HOLE NO.

NEW HOLE FOLLOWING RENOVATION

SCALED DISTANCE: 503 yards

New left-hand fairway bunkers
repositioned to challenge
modern players from the tee.

Second shot fairway bunkers
reformed into a cluster of
two.

Right to left green angle
reestablished for strategy.

Trees cleared away from golf
hole, opening up views to
bunkers and increasing
strategic interest.

New forward tees constructed
to increase flexibility of
hole.

bunkers along the length of the hole would be rewarded with an easier third into the green—and in those days a 473-yard par 5 did, in fact, virtually guarantee that even for strong players it would take a third shot to get to the green.

During the renovation, Weed formed the bunkers into groups again, although he repositioned them at distances more relevant to modern players. The left-side fairway bunkers were set at 220 to 275 yards from the back tee. Weed reshaped a group of two fairway bunkers to challenge the second shot, and a third one was added some 20 yards further along. At the green, Weed altered the putting surface in order to recapture its original sharp angle. He also tinkered with the greenside bunkering. Clearing work took place along both sides of the hole, exposing worthy specimen trees to be preserved.

The new hole, like so much of the new course, once again favors the shot maker. Golfers who challenge the bunkers on the tee shot at the fourth, and again with a second shot up the right side, are rewarded with a short pitch along the length of the green—the best opportunity to put the ball close. To allow golfers of all abilities to confront similar strategic options on the hole, Weed added two new forward tees that made the hole more playable.

The best renovation work moves beyond two dimensions. Even though it was easy to see that there was virtually no elevation change on site, Weed was unclear about the subtler forms of surface contouring that steered the ball in gentler ways. The 1943 aerial photograph showed where the bunkers had been placed, along with the depth and width of surface features. But Weed had no indication as to the topography of the golf course. "So much of a good Ross design depends on subtle contouring," observes Weed. "We were very careful to introduce features in keeping with Ross's style."

The fairways were reshaped with softer, gentler rolls. Subtle ridges now extend from the bunker faces, steering mishits in the sand while adding distance to well-struck drives. The bunkers were also given an older-looking character: simple, low-profile shapes. There are no turf capes or sand bays. Smooth grass banks flow easily around the edges, and the occasional flash of sand peeks back down the fairway.

In keeping with Ross's preference for plateau putting surfaces (raised fill pad, with bunkers installed at the base), Weed was adamant about bringing back many of the classic short game options. (Superintendent Griffith concurred and agreed to maintain the rebuilt course accordingly.) With this in mind, one of the things Weed did was elevate the fourth green several feet above the level of the fairway. Gentle falloffs are now located around the edges, and the putting surface has been extended to the very downturn point of the fill pad so that the surface edge rolls over the sides.

Strictly speaking, the transformation at Timuquana is not so much a pure restoration as an empathetic recreation in which classic principles are relied upon but adapted to the somewhat stronger modern game. The efforts of Weed and Griffith suggest a new approach to restoration. It is possible to bring back an older character that has been long lost—all the while keeping in mind modern expectations of the game. "Restoration" in this sense thereby becomes more an act of modern interpretation than a pure throwback to some pristine past.

PENINSULA

A parallel effort at restoration is taking place at Peninsula Golf and Country Club, in San Mateo, California. This 1922 design, which Ross laid out but didn't build (see Chapter 5) has been changed dramatically. Trees have become overgrown. Bunkers have been flashed up. Distinctive holes have been altered (if not removed outright). And the heavy clay soil profile does not allow for the kind of firm, linksland ground game that typified Ross's work. Yet with the impetus of Michael Jamieson—member, club historian, and architecture afficionado—and the input of architecture restoration specialist Ron Forse, Peninsula has now undertaken plans for a dramatic renaissance. The plan includes steps to firm-up fairways by "sand-capping" them.

Peninsula Golf & Country Club, San Mateo, CA. The 15th hole, a 151-yard par 3, was redesigned by Robert Trent Jones Sr. in 1964. Note flashed up sand, incursion of trees, and loss of putting surface on the right. (Bradley S. Klein)

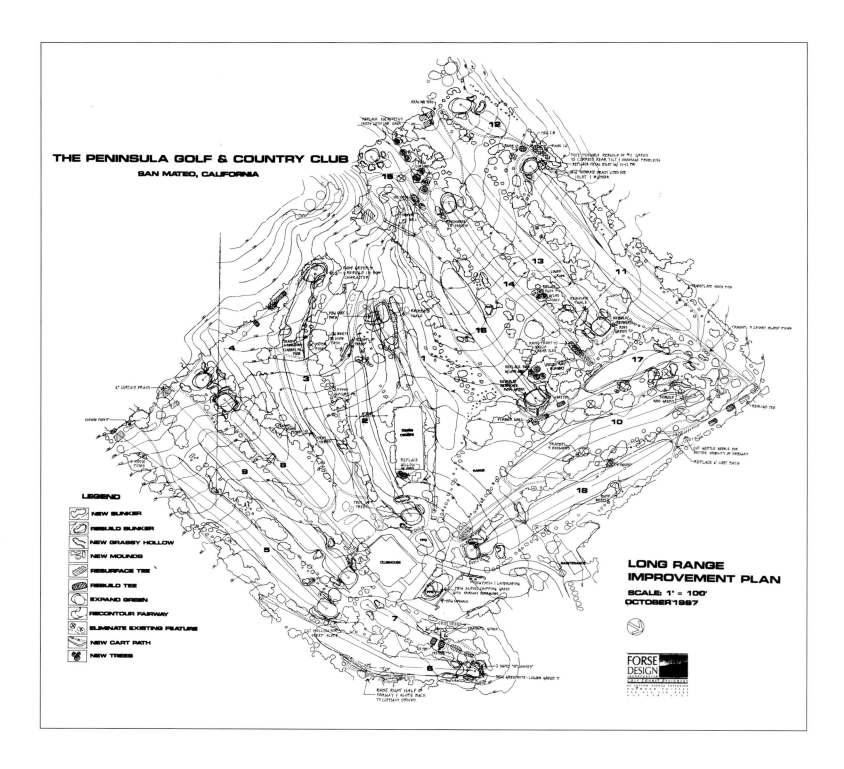

To prepare his plan, Forse relied upon an early general sketch of the golf course as well as historic photography. He also has the Robert Trent Jones, Sr. blueprint from 1964 that documents the already much changed state of the golf course and includes Jones's plans for further alterations. Forse was also able to document subsequent changes made by a number of regional architects. Unfortunately, what Forse and officials from Peninsula don't have are the hole-by-hole sketches that Ross made. Most of the existing Ross drawings, as it turned out, are on file at the Tufts Archive in Pinehurst. The library presides over some 220 sets of plans, both partial and complete, of Ross's 399 courses. Many of the other sets of plans have probably been lost for good.

The case points out the importance of having complete plans, as well as the need for a repository or clearinghouse for such information. The world of golf course architecture is, however, thoroughly decentralized, almost to the point of anarchy, so that access to historic plans is largely a matter of good or bad luck, as the case may be.

At Peninsula, Forse has overseen an ambitious plan of tree management: removal, cutting and transplanting, especially the elimination of an inferior species of eucalyptus tree that drops debris and prevents turf growth for a considerable area around its trunk. In terms of landforms, Forse will recreate lost swales. Much of the original putting surfaces has been lost over time through the rounding out of green perimeters. The bunkers will also be rebuilt because their walls have eroded to the point where the original demarcation between sand and turfed areas was lost. Forse will also try to recreate the sense of fairway contours and rough lines that have been eliminated over the years to indifferent mowing patterns and saturation irrigation practices.

Not that Forse will uncritically go back to all of Ross's original plans. Even though Ross was fully aware of the variety of golfers playing the game, he, like other designers of his day, did not build into his courses the strategic flexibility of multiple sets of tees that is commonplace today. Most of his courses had only two sets of tee markers—scarcely adequate for a wide differentiation of skills. In Ross's defense, it must be noted that he learned architecture in an era when the basic difference between players was not so much the distance they hit the ball as the control they exhibited from tee to green. Today's players show much greater variation in distance, and so multiple tees—three or four sets—are now standard.

Another distinguishing mark of Ross in his pure form was the presence of fore bunkers or carry bunkers 150 to 200 yards from the tee. All through the 1920s, Ross deployed them liberally. They stared a golfer in the face, so to speak, and frequently punished the less-than-well-struck shot. From a strictly strategic point of view they could be said to have punished the "wrong kind of player," namely, the high handicapper. What need, a critic might say, of punishing the high handicapper with additional sand when such a player is punished every time he or she plays golf? And yet they had—and have—their proper place, to define angles of play and to

Opposite page: Peninsula master plan. (Ron Forse)

create among high- to mid-handicappers a sense of exhilaration when they successfully carry the hazard.

BACK TO ESSEX

Perhaps the best way to ensure a faithful restoration is to not stray too far from the original in the first place. That's the philosophy that superintendent Patrick Kriksceonaitis believes at Essex County Club, one of Ross's earliest designs.

In the course's early days the ground was kept firm, owing to the absence of any automatic irrigation system and to the presence of native seaside grasses that grew tall, hearty, and brown. Many of the bunkers were deep, and there was little that could be done to keep grass on the green-side walls of these hazards. Finally, the green contours were all perfectly formfitted to the native terrain; surrounding mounds and hillocks were blended into the contours of the putting surfaces so that each green seemed a natural extension of its surrounds.

It helped matters that the club was too parsimonious to undertake an ambitious "modernization" program. Too many of Ross's layouts in New England have been ruined that way and many others that retained the original layout have been treed or turfed over beyond any form that Ross would have recognized. A visitor lucky enough to play Essex today finds a golf course with trees that do not intrude. Fescue and native field grasses pervade. The bunkers are bony, almost scratched out rather than uniformly manicured. Yardage markers are nowhere to be found.

Kriksceonaitis, a 1981 graduate of the University of Massachusetts' Stockbridge School in Agronomy, works out of an old wooden barn between the clubhouse and the 10th tee and loves the classic feel of his 160-acre office. "We walk-mow the greens, hand-rake the bunkers, and keep the water off," said the lanky superintendent. "The members want it that way, and frankly, the turf here is a lot healthier for it."

During a typical morning walk-through, Kriksceonaitis inspects the greens as he cuts new cup placements. "You learn a lot about the quality of your greens by walking the greens and looking at the plugs," he says. "It's like watching your kids carefully. You can tell when they're healthy, or when there's a problem."

At Essex, Kriksceonaitis has the full support of his members, thanks in large part to the guidance of a green committee that favors tradition and stability over innovation. Such is the point of the club's mission statement of classic design principles that ensures that Donald Ross's legacy remains well-entrenched.

ESSEX COUNTY CLUB: A MISSION STATEMENT
One of the missions of the Essex County Club is to preserve and protect the legacy and character of its Donald Ross designed golf course. All of his courses contain highly iden-

tifiable and enduring characteristics that have survived both the test of time and equipment enhancements. Many of these features are reflected within the 18 holes at Essex. Essex is committed to maintaining these distinctive architectural characteristics for the enjoyment of present and future generations of members.

The following represents the basic precepts of golf course care and maintenance which Essex intends to follow to preserve both the Ross features and the links personality of the course:

1. Minimal reconfiguration or restructuring of hole designs and only on a very exceptional basis.

2. Design enhancements or reconditioning will be dominated by ground structure (mounds, bunkers, contours), not trees which were a minimal part of the original Ross course layout.

3. Fairways to be wide and landing areas for both tee shots and approach shots will be maintained to preserve the firmness characteristic of links courses.

4. Green approaches will be maintained to retain the option of run-up shots which are major features of links design and are classic Ross characteristics.

5. Existing bunkering will be retained, particularly with respect to the open landing areas in front of most greens. Some variety in bunker surface and depth characteristics is desirable and will also be retained.

6. Greens will be firm and fast, a characteristic of links course conditioning. Typical Ross greens have many undulations and contours that repel a poor approach and provide subtle breaks which are enhanced by firm turf and the speed of the greens.

7. Penalty areas will reflect natural hazards (grasses, brooks, hay, mounds), but will not be placed so as to eliminate lower risk strategic options for the play of each hole, which was typical of Ross designs.

The expected result of the proposed maintenance guidelines is a more natural course that offers greater seasonal variety of shot making because conditioning will more closely reflect the characteristics of the weather pattern—soft and green during the spring, firm with some brown spots during the summer, and green and firm during the fall. Little effort will be made to artificially maintain playing characteristics throughout the season.

The overall objectives are to maintain Essex so that the course will be fair, playable, and enjoyable for golfers of all skill levels, and to ensure that the Ross design characteristics endure for the enjoyment of future generations.

A Manifesto for Masterplanning Ross Restoration

Establishing a need for a complete restoration is one thing. Implementing it is quite another. One prestigious mid-Atlantic Ross layout recently spent nearly $1 million on a new irrigation system. Members were informed about it when they opened their lockers and found a letter announcing the plan, along with notifica-

Essex County Club, Manchester-by-the-Sea, MA. The third hole is a 617-yard par 5 to the oldest green in the United States, with tall fescue rough and grassed mounds to the right. (Larry Lambrecht)

Essex County Club 10th (left) and 18 hole (right) holes.
(Bradley S. Klein)

tion of a $5,000 assessment. No sooner was the new irrigation system up and running than the club patriarchs decided it was time to evaluate its bunkering, trees, tee placement, and grassing plan.

This is backward planning—or no planning at all.

Golf courses whose management teams don't develop a long-term master plan are asking for trouble. The design integrity and aesthetic structure of layouts are all too easily undermined by years of ad hoc changes. The only way to create a consistent and distinctive quality that brings out the features of the land is to adhere to a farsighted program.

How many Ross layouts have been ruined by wave upon wave of indiscriminate tree planting, all in the name of beautification, even when it betrayed the original intent of the architect? Ross was not alone among designers from the Golden Age of Course Design (between World War I and II) in arguing that a tree should not be a central feature of a golf hole. He tolerated the occasional hardwood behind a tee, near the inside of a dogleg, or behind a putting surface. But the idea that a golf hole should be organized around such a specimen struck him as bad strategy and worse agronomics.

Over the years, trees have done more damage to design integrity and healthy turf than any other single factor. Trees, after all, have a peculiar habit of growing, which means that their canopies extend out into the space intended for golf balls. Far more invasive are those armies of little wooden soldiers, invariably cheap white pines and other conifers that some benighted green chairman planted in the name of "beautification" and which now stand chock-a-block around the grounds, impeding air movement, sunlight, and shot-making options. A tree is 90% air, you say? So is a screen door.

Topiary and ornamental gardens might look pretty to members of the Tuesday afternoon bridge club, but lacking a coherent plan for the entire grounds they can simply clutter up the land and be at odds with the flow of the golf holes. No wonder people don't appreciate Ross—they can hardly see his work anymore.

Design integrity also suffers when scratch golfers, eager to toughen up the courses for championship play, convince committees to add length by building new back tees or moving greens back. The effect, is to erase intentionally designed features and homogenize the holes. As previously mentioned, Ross often routed his short par 4s uphill and incorporated smaller, more undulating putting surfaces. Add 30 to 40 yards to the tee shot and now that green is no longer receptive to the approach shot. Invariably, that meant it gets rebuilt and its contours flattened and its character sacrificed.

Superintendents can also be faulted, especially when they flatten interesting ground features or pull greenside bunkers back from putting surfaces merely to facilitate ease of maintenance. Seemingly minor alterations that are made this way can lead to a loss of design character. Thousands of Ross's characteristically squared putting surfaces have been shrunken and rounded off in this manner. Then, to make matters worse, they have become encircled by two-inch thick blue grass rough, thereby separating the green from the surrounding chipping areas and greenside bunkers.

Of course, not all changes affecting (or afflicting) play are attributable to direct human decision. Consider a golf course 10 miles from downtown that was once out in a rural or undeveloped area but gradually has become surrounded by suburban sprawl. The change in local drainage and runoff patterns can lead to considerable siltation being dumped on the golf grounds. This can fill in streams, ponds, or low-lying areas that once served as water courses or runoff areas.

As new turf grasses are developed and as new courses in the area devise successful programs for improved conditioning, established facilities will often feel the need to upgrade their grassing plan, maintenance expectations and course setup. None of these factors occurs in isolation. The drive for ever-faster green speeds can lead to a sense that older, more contoured greens need to be toned down or flattened. These are not decisions that should be made on a casual basis.

With the growth of the game, many more women and juniors are availing themselves of the course, and that creates a need for well thought-out sets of tees. Practice habits have also changed dramatically. Whereas many Ross courses were designed with a small corner or quadrant of the grounds set aside for practice, golfers today tend to work on their games more. The requirements of teaching have also grown, rendering many practice facilities in need of expansion.

All of this makes for a powerful case that change is a constant when it comes to golf course operations. The point is to anticipate such changes and to plan for the long term rather than simply responding to the whims of this or that individual.

Golf facilities that have determined that they need an overall guide or master plan—as they all do—have no easy task before them. The game itself is supposed to be a leisurely activity, but overseeing it and managing the future of any course requires many evening meetings and the occasional butting of heads. How, then, to ensure that restoration projects can proceed with modern technology and methods while remaining true to Ross's basic design strategy?

Organization. It's best to proceed through a tight committee structure in which a few interested golfers take the lead. Playing skill should be less important as a criterion for participation than interest, knowledge, and the ability to communicate. Any project monopolized by low or high handicappers or by a certain class of golfers is sure to arouse the enmity of others and create undue friction. In short, any central grouping ought to be representative of the skills, genders, and needs of all of those who use the course.

Openness. There's nothing wrong with having closed discussions that allow committee members to discuss in detail. But any decisions involving a substantial commitment of monies and disruption in facility use should always be subject to evaluation and vote by the membership at large. Privately owned daily-fee facilities don't have to worry about this, but municipally owned and operated courses should at least make the occasional effort to inform the citizenry of what plans are afoot.

Education. The single most important factor in galvanizing support is educating members as to the value of the property. In recent years, a spate of older private courses have turned to producing their own commemorative history books. There is no better way to reclaim local traditions, but this requires strenuous efforts of research and writing. Catacombs need to be searched, newspapers dusted off, and county records need to be uncovered. Many towns did aerial photography in the 1930s, and these are an invaluable resource. Photography and drawings comparing "then" and "now" are very powerful evidence. It also helps to post historic golf photography, drawings, and memorabilia around the clubhouse and to celebrate the traditions of the facility. Clubs that adorn their walls with prints of English hunting hounds are incapable of appreciating—much less reclaiming—their own golf legacy.

Selectivity. Put out a call for architectural services and invite competition for the contract. There are many qualified designers out there willing and able to do the laborious work of restoration or master planning. Cast the net widely. Don't just rely upon personal contacts or inside candidates. Invite them in to make presentations and to share their thoughts about the golf course. It's surprising what you'll learn about your own course in the company of an expert—which is not to say that all architects are equally inspiring or even respectful of the past.

Evaluation. It can be difficult for committees to distinguish among proposals. Cost should only be one consideration; quality is far more important. Don't be snowed by the "shmooze factor" of having a chance to meet and greet some celebrity. Master planning, especially restoration, is detailed, time-consuming work. It cannot be accomplished well by someone airmailing in the plans or just making two afternoon visits.

One good rule of thumb is to make sure the architect in question shows respect and reverence for the course you have. There is nothing more destructive to an established faculty than someone with a narrow engineering or landscape approach who is not in awe of the classic art form and who doesn't at least take a long look at the special features your course has to offer. Far too many distinctive features have been effaced by second-rate hacks more concerned with technical considerations or to make their own mark than in allowing the unique elements of a property to (re)emerge.

Make field visits to other properties the architect has worked on. Don't take the architects' word for how great they are. Most architects are master showmen. The problem is that some are nothing more than that. Make phone calls. Make field visits. Ask superintendents at those facilities how the changes have held up.

A healthy dose of skepticism goes a long way. Look behind the facade of those who claim a "signature name" and investigate carefully. It may turn out that lesser-known designers with an interest in building a solid reputation for their work may well be a reliable choice. At the end of the process, the most important thing is to have a golf course that looks, feels, and can be maintained in a way that complements the natural site and surrounds.

The ultimate goal, after the architect has left, is for golfers to revel at the layout and to have the sense, however ironic, that the course is more like it used to be than it ever was before.

Chapter Nine
A Consulting Report

Hyde Park Golf & Country Club
Cincinnati, Ohio,
consulting report - final draft
Oct. 8, 1999

1. SUMMARY

Hyde Park Golf and Country Club is in an excellent position to draw upon the strengths of its course, its traditions, and its leadership. To a degree that has largely gone neglected, the holes are, for the most part, structurally sound, with enough interesting and worthy ground features to offer a very interesting challenge for decades to come if properly renovated.

The golf course presents a surprising number of very strong and memorable holes, including a fascinating uphill par 4 (No. 4) and a long par 3 (No. 12). The strengths of the course are a group of distinct par 3s, shot-making demands off the tee, greens that call for (and accommodate) artful shot-making, and a wonderful piece of ground whose dominant feature—a gracefully sloped ravine—is beautifully integrated into eight holes as a perpendicular cross-slope. The zoysia fairways provide a firm, dense playing turf that is ideally suited for a club membership of diverse playing abilities because it encourages low-running shots while providing excellent lies for those who play the game in the air and can spin the ball.

Curiously, however, the overall experience of the course does not add up collectively to the strengths represented by many of the holes and by so many of the course's features. Something is missing. Some things need to be enhanced, others reduced, so that the golf course presents a more aesthetically coherent, thematically clear experience.

Key weakness to be addressed include: an awkward first green; tree clutter

Opposite page: Aerial photo of Hyde Park Golf and Country Club, ca.1930. Natural ravines, not trees, dominate the scene, including (from left to right) the 1st, 18th, 17th, 9th, and 12th holes. (Hyde Park Golf and Country Club)

that strangles turf generation on the tees, fairways, and roughs; inadequate differentiation of teeing grounds; poorly established rough grasses; and not enough use of alternative textures and turf media such as fescues, tall native grasses and flowering plants. The course is also both too hard for high-handicappers and too easy for low-handicappers.

Areas of immediate upgrading to be addressed include (in order): the quality of rough grasses, a determined tree management program, tee expansion, and the introduction of low-maintenance native grass areas beyond immediate paths of play.

Longer-term planning needs to address fairway bunker renovation, greenside bunker renovation, pond and watercourse development, and the adequacy of the irrigation system.

The golf course is in the hands of very capable people at the levels of course maintenance, golf operations, and overall club management. They share a common and strong commitment to enhancing the experience of member golf at the club while cultivating a more interesting, more beautiful, and more traditional course. This is a welcome working relationship, especially because many of the undertakings suggested below can and ought to be done in-house.

2. COURSE PROFILE

- ► Hyde Park Golf & Country Club
- ► Cincinnati, Ohio
- ► Par-71; 6,449 yards
- ► Rating: 71.7; Slope: 126
- ► Rounds per year: 23,000: 80% cart / 10% caddies / 10% walk & carry
- ► Soil conditions: clay loam
- ► Cart paths: discontinuous, asphalt
- ► Greens: Poa annua and bentgrass; 4,500 sq. ft. avg.
- ► Green cut/speed: 5/32-inch. Stimpmeter reading of 9
- ► Greens construction: push-up, with No 1 green USGA spec.
- ► Elevation change on site: 60 ft.
- ► Tees: Poa/bentgrass, 3,000 sq.ft. ; cut to ½-inch
- ► Fairways: Zoysia; 26-33 yards wide; 21 acres; cut to 11/16-inch
- ► Rough: mixed; 80 acres; 1-inch first cut, 3.5-inches primary
- ► Bunker faces: mixed grass
- ► Bunkers: 42
- ► Water Hazards: ravine in play on many holes, creek bed on 6
- ► Practice area: 1-acre tee, 8 acre range
- ► Irrigation: Toro double-row, two-speed heads on fairways; BT3&4, will be Toro LTC; 550 heads
- ► Water source: city water

Opposite page: Aerial photograph of Hyde Park Golf and Country Club during the summer of 1994. Extensive tree growth has dramatically changed the course. Note construction of new first green beyond existing putting surface at top left. (Hyde Park Golf and Country Club)

Below: Hyde Park's fourth hole, a 389-yard dogleg-left par 4 to a dramatic plateau green. (Dr. David C. Bell)

Opposite page, top: The 225-yard par-3 12th hole at Hyde Park, ca.1945. A small, natural landing area sits between two arms of a ravine that crosses between the tee and the green. (Hyde Park G&CC)

Opposite page, bottom: Hyde Park's 12th hole in 1999. Note secondary line of trees, most of them conifers, to left and rear of green. (Dr. David C. Bell)

- Trees: pin oaks, maples, tulip, white pines
- Turf vehicles: Toro
- Architects: Tom Bendelow (1909), unknown (1911), Donald Ross (1920-21), Dick Wilson (early 1950s), Arthur Hills (1986, 1994-95)
- Superintendent: Joe Kaczmarek, CGCS, Purdue (1977)
- Asst. superintendents: Tony Ross and Mark Zahn
- Staff: fulltime - 6 / 10 fulltime seasonal; 3 part-time seasonal
- Golf Professional: Larry Drehs

3. ARCHITECTURAL HISTORY

The Hyde Park course dates to an 9-hole design in 1909 by Scottish-born designer Tom Bendelow (1872-1936) and includes what remains today (basically) as the 1st, 3rd, 11th, 12th, 17th and 18th holes.

The current course derives from a dramatic transformation rendered in 1920-21 by Donald J. Ross (1872-1948), in part on additional new land acquired by the club. While there are no design plans in the Tufts Archive at Pinehurst, N.C. documenting his work there, that is also the case for well over of the 399 courses Ross did during his design career. The 1930 edition of a small pamphlet that Ross had prepared listing his courses includes "Hyde Park Golf Course, Cincinnati." Moreover, unlike other layouts he did, which he lists as "remodeled," the reference to Hyde Park makes it clear that Ross's work was considerable enough for him to have classified it as an original layout.

Ross, an inveterate train traveler, made repeated visits to the Midwest, both from his summer office in the Boston area and from his winter residence in Pinehurst. The circumstantial evidence suggests that Ross's visit to Hyde Park was of a limited duration, and that he did not have on site either of his most trusted construction superintendents, J.B. McGovern or Walter B. Hatch. Still, there remains today enough evidence, including features of the course itself, to be able

say with full confidence that Hyde Park is a Ross course.

As with all layouts, there have been many subsequent changes. Some of them are the result of tree growth, changes in the water flow through the site owing to residential/commercial, development, and changes in turf cover. Others are of a more architectural sort, having to do with steady dramatic tree planting and growth, bunker removal, and the work of at least two architects.

In the early 1950's, Dick Wilson undertook some changes in the shape and size of the third and 14th greens, both of which betray his trademark of being elongated and angular rather than more rounded, as was Ross's metier. He also lengthened the 15th hole and created the present 15th green. The 16th tee was also lengthened.

Subsequent work was undertaken by Arthur Hills. His records for the course are dated 1986-87, though it appears the work was done in 1994-95. It is not clear who actually undertook the construction work—whether in-house or whether an outside shaper was used. The resulting design works include a number of fairway bunker complexes and, most significantly, a rebuilt first hole, essentially from new tees west of the old first tee utilizing the same fairway corridor, and to a new green site some 65 yards west of the old green. This helped relieve congestion around the practice putting green as well as reduced wayward shots from the practice tee reaching the first fairway. However, the bunker work and new first green are out of character with the rest of the course; the putting surface, which falls away from the line of play, rejects shots rather than accepts them and is framed by three uncharacteristic mounds.

Despite these changes, Hyde Park is lucky to have what remains a Ross course insofar as all 18 holes conform to his routing. Moreover, most of the putting surfaces retain their original shape and contour, as well as the character of their fill pad and surrounds (to the sides and rear).

4. STRENGTHS

► Facility combines an unusually well-balanced combination of family/social activities and serious golf. Zoysia fairways are outstanding. Bent/Poa greens are in very good shape, with interesting contours. The caddie program is widely regarded and fairly well utilized.

► Native land form is fascinating, with ravine/water course traversing half a dozen holes. It is particularly lovely in late afternoon as low-angle sun casts long shadows across holes.

► The ravine is a dominant strategic feature on several holes. Excellent routing insofar as most holes are proximate, with relatively short walks from green to next tee.

▸ The golf course presents a shifting rhythm of short/long par 4s, with the 2nd, 10th, & 17th holes easily the most sophisticated in terms of strategy and challenge. Par-4 fourth hole is among most memorable par 4s Ross ever built in terms of deceptive difficulty.

▸ Excellent mix of par 3s, running the gamut from medium-short (7th, 15th) to very long (12th). Twelfth hole is an unusual and memorable long par 3, with two cross-ravines and an optional path to hole (although it is doubtful that enough people intentionally use it).

▸ To a degree unusual in most Ross-designed courses today, Hyde Park has retained much of its original character in the greens. This is esp. evident with the contours and features in and around the 4th, 8th, 9th, 12th, and 17th greens. Recent sodding of these areas has helped considerably.

5. PROBLEM AREAS

▸ Rough grasses are uneven and poorly established, offering inadequate playing surface and capricious lies.

▸ Course is overstuffed with trees, many of them planted within last 30 years in competition with established, worthy deciduous trees which are worth preserving. White pines are especially cumbersome in their placement and appearance. Chinese Elm are in obvious stress. The major results of such largely arbitrary tree-plantings are inadequate air circulation, delayed or inadequate sunlight on fairways and green, and loss of strategic flexibility in that the layout becomes far too difficult for higher handicappers.

▸ There is not enough separation between various tees (blue, white, gold, and red). The insufficient differentiation/placement of intermediate and forward tees leads to too many players proceeding from wrong sets of tees. The existing gold tees are not appropriately utilized, and the existing forward (red) tees are all too often sited in areas that frustrate play by placing people directly in line with hazards or upslopes.

▸ Fairway bunkering is uninspired, with the contours out of character with the golf course and offering no penalty to lower-handicap players.

▸ First hole is out of character, esp. the green, which repels rather than accepts shots.

► Approach shots into the par-5 5th and 13th holes are without character or interest, esp. for low-handicap player.

► 16th hole is very weak.

► Given high percentage of high-handicappers at club, all changes undertaken on the course should provide an easier way to play many of the holes, while enabling long hitters to get themselves into more trouble than before.

6. RECOMMENDATIONS

► Undertake a prudent but sustained tree management program consistent with preservation and health of mature specimen trees while promoting growth of turf, both in fairways and roughs.

► Revegetate rough areas with turfgrasses, as determined by superintendent..

► Reconfigure teeing grounds by moving up some forward tees, and reclassifying tees into a differently colored system such as gold (back), blue, white, green (forward). This will eliminate stigma of red and gold, and get people to move up, esp. to white tees, so that they can play from proper markers.

► Rebuild fairway bunkers into style more consistent with, though shallower than, greenside bunkering.

► Make the entire golf course more consistent with Ross philosophy of promoting the possibility of playing recovery shots from rough.

► Have civil engineer inspect safety, adequacy of existing paved service roads/cart paths on course and determine whether they are adequate to handle combined cart traffic and maintenance vehicle traffic.

► Determine long-term viability of current irrigation/control system.

► Cultivate in-house heritage program designed to promote and enhance traditional character and heritage of the golf course. Among the undertakings would be the development of a Donald Ross room with memorabilia, historic photography, maps, sketches; name the golf holes on the scorecard, including such long-established names as First (1st), Burn (3rd), The Glen (14th), "Devil's Own (15th), Highball (17th) and Home (18th); cultivate membership in the Donald Ross Society.

7. ACTION PLAN

▸ Secure detailed topographic map (2-foot contours) of golf course on 1 in. = 100 ft. scale. The ideal would be a GPS-generated aerial photograph with accompanying software package to facilitate a range of long-term design/maintenance functions.

▸ Hire qualified restoration specialist architect to oversee drafting and implementation of a 5-year restoration plan to cover these and other proposed changes. Fee will vary, plus construction costs.

▸ Develop priority list of desirable projects, proposed timetables and budgets so that sound planning can proceed.

Conclusion

Hyde Park is a lovely, modest layout that is ideally suited to serve its membership well into the next century. Its character and strength lie close at hand and will flourish if given the proper attention. The main thing is to preserve and enhance existing natural ground features and to work with the Ross routing.

Chapter Ten
Postscript: the U.S. Open at Pinehurst No. 2

*I*t took nearly a century for Pinehurst No. 2 to host its first U.S. Open in 1999, but the next one has already been scheduled for 2005. Meanwhile, tournament officials, superintendents, and architects everywhere have something to learn from the experience—about the ideal way to set up a golf course.

Golfers, whether contestants or spectators, might have been surprised when they first got to Pinehurst No. 2 for the U.S. Open and didn't see knee-high rough. They didn't see fairways that were single file in width, either. Or any ponds sitting smack in front of greens. Even more surprising, the USGA and the maintenance staff at the Pinehurst Resort had the insight during practice rounds to go out and cut down the thick bermudagrass rough from four inches to three. It was a decision that allowed the golfers to play the course and to experience—and suffer—its special ground features.

For one of those rare times, the original architectural genius of a golf course was thus able to come to the fore during a national championship. It has taken the USGA decades to recover from the overly penal approach it devised at the 1951 U.S. Open at Oakland Hills. There, Robert Trent Jones Sr. eliminated most of Ross's original ground strategy. That course simply played brutally hard. In subsequent decades, difficulty was mistaken for a virtue, and toughness was sought by growing deep rough. Not until 1972 at Pebble Beach did the USGA at least get back to the virtues of seaside golf. In 1986 at Shinnecock Hills, an Open venue finally allowed players to run the ball in. And it was not until 1988 at The Country Club in Brookline, that the fully restored virtues of classic shot making were put on full display; the layout that was not a monochromatic green lawn but rather a wavy, tawny field of fescues.

Now the Open has experienced something really radical: a back-to-basics focus on the short game and chipping areas, made possible, as it turns out, because for the first time the tournament was held on a full set of well-constructed, USGA-specification greens. Their excellent drainage enabled them to withstand the

Opposite page, top: Paul Jett, CGCS, superintendent at Pinehurst No. 2 since 1996. (Bradley S. Klein)

Opposite page, bottom: The 330-yard par-4 third at Pinehurst No. 2. (Bradley S. Klein)

unseasonable rains. And when they did fully dry out, as they did on Friday and Saturday after a one-inch rain before Thursday's first round, their fury terrorized the field.

For all the speculation during that week about Ross's original design intent, there was something deeply ironic about seeing this tournament played on bentgrass greens when Ross was actually unwilling (or unable) to break with Pinehurst's tradition of sand greens until 1935. In the 1970s and 1980s there were various permutations of turfgrass on the greens. The putting surfaces reverted back and forth between bentgrass and bermudagrass until a solution was found in the mid-1990s: high quality G-2 bentgrass was finally available for adoption. Pinehurst No. 2 superintendent Paul Jett worked closely with architect Rees Jones in rebuilding the greens and making sure that the outer edges flowed imperceptively into the surrounding areas of tightly cut bermudagrass.

Ross could never have envisioned greens, much less bentgrass ones, cut as they were for the 1999 U.S. Open at Pinehurst No. 2, to 135/1000th of an inch; nor collars and approach areas trimmed to exactly 225/1000ths. The combination of

hump-backed contours and closely cropped turf meant a perfect integration of putting surfaces and surrounds. In many ways, Ross's vision had finally been realized.

The firm, sandy soil and the domed, well-draining bentgrass greens that ran off into surrounding humps and hollows conspired to create some of the most exciting and demanding shot-making ever seen at a U.S. Open. Ross has long been known for elevating his green platforms and putting his bunkers into the base of the resulting fill pad. Pinehurst No. 2 is unique, even among his own courses, for its convex, turtle-backed shaped greens. As we have seen, these greens evolve over time through top-dressing beyond Ross's original plans, but they also tied in well to the surronds. As he wrote in the 1936 program to the PGA Championship on this golf course," [t]his contouring around a green makes possible an infinite variety in the requirements for short shots that no other form of hazard can call for."

The same could be said about the long par 4s, which included three of the five longest par 4s in U.S. Open history—the 482 yard fifth, the 485-yard eighth, and the 489-yard 16th. On the eve of that '36 PGA, Ross wrote, that "I consider the ability to play the longer irons as the supreme test of a great golfer." Back then, the

Pinehurst No. 2's 569-yard par-5 tenth hole. (Bradley S. Klein)

eighth hole played as a 466-yard par 4. Today it does not seem unduly strenuous for world-class players to hit middle-and long-irons into par 4s. If it takes holes in the 480-yard range to test their ability, so be it.

There is much to be learned in terms of architecture from the 1999 U.S. Open. There is no need for trees to impede the line of play. There is no need for hard edges and all-or-nothing heroic shots over water hazards or cross bunkers in front of greens. Nor does golf have to be turned into a putting contest over dull, flat greens measuring 14 on the Stimpmeter. Golf does require the freedom to play the driver, and it also requires finding the correct angles of approach. Patience, not mere power, is the defining virtue—to know when to fire at pins and when to be satisfied playing to the front third of a putting surface.

The beauty of the way the course was set up is that it allowed the best golfers in the world to hit every club in the bag. That included the driver—normally a club that stays under wraps during the U.S. Open. The fairway widths were modest, 28-32 yards, and there weren't any trees overhanging the landing areas, as there are on all too many tournament courses. The relatively light rough did not

The 13th hole at Pinehurst No. 2, a 370-yard par 4.
(Bradley S. Klein)

177-yard par-3 17th at Pinehurst No. 2. (Bradley S. Klein)

require an automatic pitch-out; it enabled golfers to go for the greens. Yet, it allowed them to get into trouble because it was so difficult to control the ball around the domed putting surfaces.

Golfers could choose to shoot for flagsticks, but if they veered away from the relatively flatter spots of each green putting surface they found themselves in big trouble. What a pleasure to see players thinking their way around, with options running the gamut from the lob wedge to middle-irons and even fairway woods or putters. Donald Ross designed the course to play hard and firm, and the course setup, which included no rough around any of the greens, enabled the architect's intentions to come through. A golf course completed in 1907, which only got its grass greens in 1935, thus showed its relevance. Par stood up for four days, with only winner Payne Stewart finishing under par—by a single stroke.

All week, the players raved, even during Saturday's windswept round, when the ball was especially hard to control. When John Daly is your only critic, as he was after the final round, you know you've done things correctly. If it takes holes of 482, 485, or 489 yards to make these fellows hit middle- and long-irons to par 4s, then that's fine. The beauty of the course setup was that an average golfer could have gone out on the same day—from the middle tees—and enjoyed the round and played the whole way with only one golf ball.

For years, the USGA set up dull, wedge-out courses with knee-high rough around the greens. Now they finally got it perfect. There's no need to trick up a golf course. The best equalizer, and the best defense of par, is a firm, fast golf course with interesting ground contours. The fact that this layout held up even in wet weather attests to its timelessness. It also attests to the genius of its design and to the foresight of the USGA and Pinehurst maintenance staff. May it become a model for future Opens.

These are lessons that the classic architects knew and that too many today have forgotten. After the 1999 U.S. Open at Pinehurst No. 2, it will be harder than ever to pretend that there is nothing to learn from dead architects.

A century after its inception, the spirit of Pinehurst No. 2 lives on, and with it, the genius of its mastermind: Donald J. Ross.

Robert "Hardrock" Robinson, former Ross caddie, at Pinehurst Resort & Country Club, 1999. (Thomas Toohey Brown)

Courses Designed by Donald J. Ross

	Course	City	Holes	Year	New Course	Remodel	Plan	On Site Confirmed	Note:
Alabama									
1	Country Club of Birmingham (East)	Birmingham	18	1927	X		X	X	
2	Country Club of Birmingham (West)	Birmingham	18	1929	X		X	X	
3	Country Club of Mobile	Mobile	18	1928	X			X	
4	Mountain Brook Country Club	Birmingham	18	1929	X			X	
California									
5	Peninsula Golf & Country Club	San Mateo	18	1923		X	X	X	was Beresford
Colorado									
6	Broadmoor Golf Club	Colorado Springs	18	1918	X			X	
7	Lakewood Golf Club	Lakewood	18	1916		X			
8	Wellshire Golf Club	Denver	18	1926	X		X		
Connecticut									
9	Country Club of Waterbury	Waterbury	18	1926	X		X	X	
10	Greenwich Country Club	Greenwich	18	1946		X			
11	Hartford Golf Club	West Hartford	14	1914		X	X	X	
	Hartford Golf Club	West Hartford	14	1946	X	X	X	X	
12	Shennecossett Golf Club	Groton	18	1916	X			X	
	Shennecossett Golf Club	Groton	3	1919		X			
13	Wampanoag Country Club	West Hartford	18	1924	X		X	X	
Florida									
14	Belleair Country Club (East)	Belleair	18	1925	X				
15	Belleair Country Club (West)	Belleair	18	1915		X	X	X	
	Belleair Country Club (West)	Belleair	9	1915	X			X	
16	Belleview Biltmore	Belleair	18	1925	X			X	was Belleview Mido
17	Biltmore Country Club	Coral Gables	18	1924	X		X	X	
18	Bobby Jones Golf Course -British	Sarasota	18	1927	X				
19	Boca Raton - Cloisters	Boca Raton	18	1925	X		X	X	
20	Bradenton Country Club	Bradenton	18	1924	X		X	X	was Palma Sola
21	Brentwood Golf Club	Jacksonville	18	1923	X		X	X	closed
22	Country Club of Orlando	Orlando	18	1918	X				
23	Daytona Beach Golf & Country Club - North	Daytona Beach	18	1946	X				
24	Daytona Beach Golf & Country Club - South	Daytona Beach	18	1922	X				
25	Delray Beach Golf Course	Delray Beach	18	1923	X		X	X	
26	Dunedin Country Club	Dunedin	18	1926	X		X	X	
27	Florida Country Club	Jacksonville	18	1922	X			X	
28	Fort George	Jacksonville	18	1927	X				

	Course	City	Holes	Year	New Course	Remodel	Plan	On Site Confirmed	Note:
Florida (continued)									
29	Fort Meyers Golf & Country Club	Fort Meyers	18	1928	X				
30	Gulf Stream Golf Club	Delray Beach	18	1923	X		X	X	
31	Handley Park Golf Club	New Smyrna Beach	9	1922	X				closed
32	Hyde Park Golf Club	Jacksonville	18	1925	X			X	
33	Keystone Golf & Country Club	Keystone Heights	9	1928	X				
34	Lake Wales Country Club	Lake Wales	18	1925	X		X		
35	Melbourne Golf Club	Melbourne	18	1926	X		X		
36	Miami Country Club	Miami	18	1919	X	X		X	closed
37	New Smyrna Beach Municipal Golf Club	New Smyrna Beach	18	1922	X				
38	Palatka Municipal Golf Course	Palatka	18	1925	X				
39	Palm Beach Country Club	Palm Beach	18	1917	X			X	
40	Palma Ceia Golf Club	Tampa	18	1923		X			
41	Palma Sola Golf Club	Bradenton	18	1924	X				
42	Panama Country Club	Lynn Haven	18	1927	X				
43	Pinecrest on Lotela	Avon	18	1926	X			X	
44	Ponce de Leon Resort & Country Club	St. Augustine	18	1916	X				was St. Augustine's
45	Puntra Gorda Country Club	Puntra Gorda	18	1927		X			
46	Riviera C. C. (Miami Biltmore)	Riviera	18	1924		X			was S. course of Biltmore Hotel
47	San Jose Country Club	Jacksonville	18	1925	X		X		
48	Sara Bay Country Club	Sarasota	18	1925		X?	X		was Whitfield
49	Seminole Country Club	North Palm Beach	18	1929	X		X	X	
50	St. Augustine Links (South)	St. Augustine	18	1916	X		X	X	closed
51	Timuquana Country Club	Jacksonville	18	1923	X		X	X	
52	University of Florida Golf Club	Gainesville	18	1921		X			was Gainesville
Georgia									
53	Athens Country Club	Athens	18	1926	X		X	X	
54	Augusta Country Club	Augusta	18	1927		X	X	X	
55	Bacon Park Golf Course #1	Savannah	18	1926	X			X	
56	Bacon Park Golf Course #2	Savannah	18	1926	X			X	closed
57	Bon-Air-Vanderbilt	Atlanta	18	1927		X			
58	Brunswick Country Club	Brunswick	9	1938	X				
59	Country Club of Columbus	Columbus	18	1925		X	X		
60	East Lake Golf Club #1	Atlanta	18	1914		X	X	X	
61	East Lake Golf Club #2	Atlanta	18	1925	X			X	closed
62	Forest Hills Golf Club	Augusta	18	1926	X		X	X	
63	Gainesville Municipal Golf Course	Gainesville	9	1920	X				closed
64	Highland Country Club	La Grange	9	1922	X			X	
65	Roosevelt Memorial Golf Course	Warm Springs	18	1926	X				
66	Savannah Golf Club	Savannah	18	1927	X			X	
67	Sheraton Savannah Resort & Country Club	Savannah	18	1929	X		X		was General Oglethorpe Hotel
68	Walthour Golf Club	Savannah	18	1928	X				closed
69	Washington Wilkes Country Club	Washington	9	1925	X				

	Course	City	Holes	Year	New Course	Remodel	Plan	On Site Confirmed	Note:
Ilinois									
70	Beverly Country Club	Chicago	18	1916	X			X	
71	Bob O'Link Golf Club	Highland Park	18	1916	X		X	X	
72	Calumet Country Club	Homewood	18	1917	X			X	
73	Evanston Golf Club	Skokie	18	1917	X		X	X	
74	Exmoor Country Club	Highland Park	18	1914		X		X	
75	Hinsdale Golf Club	Clarendon Hills	18	1913	X	X			9 new
76	Indian Hill Club	Winnetka	18	1914	X			X	
77	La Grange Country Club	La Grange	18	1921		X			
78	Northmoor Country Club	Highland Park	18	1918	X			X	
79	Oak Park Country Club	Oak Park	18	1916	X			X	
80	Ravisloe Country Club	Homewood	18	1915		X		X	
81	Skokie Country Club	Glencoe	18	1915		X		X	
Indiana									
82	Broadmoor Country Club	Indianapolis	18	1921	X			X	
83	Fairview Golf Club	Fort Wayne	9	1927	X				
84	French Lick Springs Resort	French Lick	18	1922	X			X	
Iowa									
85	Cedar Rapids Country Club	Cedar Rapids	18	1915	X			X	
Kansas									
86	Shawnee Country Club	Topeka	18	1924	X	X		X	9 new
Kentucky									
87	Idle Hour Country Club	Lexington	18	1924	X		X		was Ashland
Maine									
88	Augusta Country Club	Manchester	9	1916	X				
89	Biddeford-Saco Club	Saco	9	1927	X				
90	Cape Neddick Country Club	Cape Neddick	9	1919	X				
	Cape Neddick Country Club	Cape Neddick	9	1920		X			
91	Kebo Valley Club	Bar Harbor	18	1926	X				
92	Lake Kezar Country Club	Lovell	9	1924	X				
93	Lucerne Hills Golf Club	Lucerne	9	1926	X		X		
94	Northeast Harbor Golf Club	Northeast Harbor	9	1922	X				
95	Penobscot Valley Country Club	Orono	18	1924	X		X	X	
96	Poland Springs	Poland Springs	9	1913		X			
	Poland Springs	Poland Springs	9	1913	X				
97	Portland Country Club	Falmouth	18	1923	X		X	X	
98	York Golf & Tennis Club	York	18	1923	X			X	
	York Golf & Tennis Club	York	9	1930	X				

	Course	City	Holes	Year	New Course	Remodel	Plan	On Site Confirmed	Note:
Maryland									
99	Bannockburn	Glen Echo	18	1924	X				closed
100	Chevy Chase Club	Chevy Chase	18	1910		X			
101	Congressional Country Club	Bethesda	18	1930		X			Blue Course
102	Fountain Head Country Club	Hagerstown	18	1926	X				
103	Indian Spring Golf Club	Silver Spring	18	1922	X		X	X	closed
104	Price Georges Country Club	Landover	18	1921	X				closed
105	Silver Spring Country Club	Silver Spring	18	1921	X				closed
Massachusetts									
106	Bass River Golf Course	South Yarmouth	18	1914	X	X			9 new
107	Belmont Country Club	Belmont	18	1918	X			X	
108	Brae Burn Country Club	West Newton	18	1912	X			X	
	Brae Burn Country Club	West Newton	18	1947		X		X	
109	Charles River Country Club	Newton Centre	18	1921	X			X	
110	Cohasse Country Club	Southbridge	9	1916	X				
	Cohasse Country Club	Southbridge	4	1927		X			
	Cohasse Country Club	Southbridge	4	1930		X			
111	Cohasset Golf Club	Cohasset	9	1922	X			X	
112	Commonwealth Golf Course (Newton)	Newton	18	1921	X				
113	Concord Country Club	Concord	18	1915	X		X	X	
114	Country Club of New Bedford	North Dartmouth	9	1924	X				
	Country Club of New Bedford	North Dartmouth	9	1924		X			
115	Country Club of Pittsfield	Pittsfield	18	1921	X				
116	Ellinwood Country Club	Athol	9	1920	X		X		
117	Essex County Club	Manchester-By-Sea	18	1909	X			X	
118	Franklin Park Golf Course	Boston	18	1922	X				was William J. Devine
119	George Wright Golf Course	Hyde Park	18	1938	X		X	X	
120	Greenock Country Club	Lee	9	1927	X		X		
121	Hyannisport Club	Hyannis Port	9	1936		X			
	Hyannisport Club	Hyannis Port	9	1936		X			
122	Island Country Club	Martha's Vineyard	18	1913	X				closed
123	Kernwood Country Club	Salem	18	1914	X		X	X	
124	Longmeadow Country Club	Longmeadow	18	1921	X		X	X	
125	Ludlow Country Club	Ludlow	18	1920	X				
126	Merrimack Valley Golf Club	Methuen	18	1906	X				
127	Nantucket Golf Links	Nantucket	9	1917	X		X		closed
128	North Andover Country Club	North Andover	9	1920	X				
129	Oak Hill Country Club	Fitchburg	18	1921		X	X	X	
130	Oakley Country Club	Watertown	18	1900	X	X		X	9 new
131	Orchards Golf Club	South Hadley	9	1922	X		X	X	
	Orchards Golf Club	South Hadley	9	1927	X		X	X	
132	Oyster Harbors Golf Club	Osterville	18	1927	X		X	X	
133	Petersham Country Club	Petersham	9	1922	X				
134	Plymouth Country Club	Plymouth Center	18	1929	X			X	
	Plymouth Country Club	Plymouth Center	3	1934	X				
135	Pocasset Golf Club	Pocasset	18	1916	X				
136	Ponkapoag Golf Club-1	Canton	18	1931	X				
137	Ponkapoag Golf Club-2	Canton	18	1939		X			

	Course	City	Holes	Year	New Course	Remodel	Plan	On Site Confirmed	Note:
	Massachusetts (continued)								
138	Salem Country Club	Peabody	18	1925	X		X	X	
139	Sandy Burr Country Club	Wayland	18	1925	X			X	
140	Springfield Country Club	West Springfield	18	1924	X		X		
141	Tatnuck Country Club	Worcester	18	1930	X				
142	Tedesco Country Club	Marblehead	1	1937	X				
143	Tekoa Country Club	Westfield	9	1923	X		X		
144	ToyTown Tavern Club Glub	Winchendon	18	1924	X		X	X	closed
145	Vesper Country Club	Tyngsboro	9	1919		X			
	Vesper Country Club	Tyngsboro	9	1919	X				
	Vesper Country Club	Tyngsboro	9	1947					
146	Wachusett Country Club	West Boylston	9	1911	X		X		
147	Waltham Country Club	West Boylston	9	1921	X				closed
148	Wellesley Country Club	Wellesley	9	1911	X				
149	Weston Golf Club	Weston	9	1916	X			X	
	Weston Golf Club	Weston	9	1923	X				
150	Whaling City Golf Club	New Bedford	9	1920	X				
151	Whitinsville Golf Club	Whitinsville	9	1925	X		X		
152	Wianno Golf Club	Osterville	9	19133		X			
	Wianno Golf Club	Osterville	9	1920	X				
153	Winchester Country Club	Winchester	18	1903	X			X	
	Winchester Country Club	Winchester	18	1928		X			
154	Woodland Golf Club	Auburndale	18	1928		X			
155	Worcester Country Club	Worcester	18	1913	X			X	
156	Wyckoff Park Golf Course	Holyoke	18	1923	X			X	
	Michigan								
157	Barton Hills Country Club	Ann Arbor	18	1920	X			X	
158	Bloomfield Hills Country Club	Bloomfield Hills	18	1936		X			
159	Dearborn Country Club	Dearborn	18	1925	X		X	X	
160	Detroit Golf Club – North	Detroit	18	1916	X		X	X	
	Detroit Golf Club – North	Detroit	18	1936		X	X	X	
161	Detroit Golf Club – South	Detroit	18	1916	X		X	X	
	Detroit Golf Club – South	Detroit	18	1934		X		X	
162	Elk Rapids Golf Club	Elk Rapids	9	1923	X		X		
163	Franklin Hills Country Club	Franklin	18	1926	X		X	X	
164	Fred Wardell Country Club	Detroit	9	1920	X				closed
165	Grosse Ile Golf & Country Club	Grosse Ile	18	1920	X				
	Grosse Ile Golf & Country Club	Grosse Ile	9	1920		X			
166	Hawthorne Valley Golf Club – Brightmoor	Dearborn	27	1925	X				closed
167	Highland Park Golf Club	Grand Rapids	9	1922	X				
168	Highlands Country Club	Grand Rapids	9	1927	X				closed
169	Kent Country Club	Grand Rapids	9	1921		X		X	
	Kent Country Club	Grand Rapids	9	1921	X				
170	Monroe Golf & Country Club	Monroe	18	1919	X			X	
171	Muskegon Country Club	Muskegon	18	1911	X			X	
172	Oakland Hills Country Club – North	Bloomfield Hills	18	1923	X			X	
173	Oakland Hills Country Club – South	Bloomfield Hills	18	1917	X			X	
174	Rackham Golf Course	Huntington Woods	18	1925	X		X	X	
175	Rogell Golf Course	Detroit	18	1921	X				

	Course	City	Holes	Year	New Course	Remodel	Plan	On Site Confirmed	Note:
Michigan (continued)									
176	Shadow Ridge Golf Club	Ionia	9	1916	X				
177	St. Claire River Country Club	St. Claire	18	1923	X				
178	Warren Valley Golf Club - East	Wayne	18	1927	X				
179	Warren Valley Golf Club - West	Wayne	18	1927	X				
180	Western Golf & Country Club	Redford	18	1926	X				
Minnesota									
181	Interlachen Country Club	Edina	18	1921		X	X	X	
182	Minikahda Club	Minneapolis	18	1917		X	X	X	
183	Northland Country Club	Duluth	18	1927	X			X	
184	White Bear Yacht Club	White Bear Lake	9	1912	X		X		
	White Bear Yacht Club	White Bear Lake	9	1915	X		X		
185	Woodhill Country Club	Wayzata	18	1917	X			X	
	Woodhill Country Club	Wayzata	18	1934	X				
Missouri									
186	Hillcrest Country Club	Kansas City	18	1917	X			X	
187	Midland Valley Country Club	Overland	18	1919	X				closed
New Hampshire									
188	Bald Peak Colony	Moultonboro	18	1922	X			X	
189	Balsams Grand Resort Hotel	Dixville Notch	18	1915	X			X	Panorama
190	Bethlehem Country Club	Bethlehem	9	1912		X			
	Bethlehem Country Club	Bethlehem	9	1912	X				
191	Carter CC	Lebanon	9	1923	X				was Farnum Hill
192	Kingswood Country Club	Wolfeboro	18	1926	X		X		
193	Lake Sunapee Country Club	New London	18	1928	X		X		
194	Lake Tarleton Club	Pike	18	1916	X				closed
195	Manchester Country Club	Bedford	18	1923	X			X	
196	Maplewood Country Club	Bethlehem	9	1914	X				
	Maplewood Country Club	Bethlehem	9	1914		X			
197	Mount Crotched CC	Francestown	9	1929	X				closed
198	Mount Washington Golf Club	Bretton Woods	18	1915		X	X	X	
	Mount Washington Golf Club	Bretton Woods	9	1915	X		X		
199	Wentworth-by-the-Sea Golf Club	Portsmouth	9	1910	X				
New Jersey									
200	Crestmont Country Club	West Orange	18	1923	X				
201	Deal Golf & Country Club	Deal	3	1915	X	X			
202	Echo Lake Country Club	Westfield	18	1919	X				
203	Englewood Country Club	Englewood	18	1916		X		X	closed
204	Essex County Country Club	West Orange	18	1924		X			
205	Homestead Country Club	Spring Lake	18	1920	X		X	X	closed

Course	City	Holes	Year	New Course	Remodel	Plan	On Site Confirmed	Note:
New Jersey (continued)								
206 Knickerbocker Country Club	Tenafly	18	1915	X			X	
207 Lone Pine Country Club	New Brunswick	18	1925	X		X		closed
208 Montclair Golf Club	Montclair	27	1919	X		X	X	
209 Mountain Ridge Country Club	West Caldwell	18	1930	X		X	X	
210 Plainfield Country Club	Plainfield	18	1921	X		X	X	
Plainfield Country Club	Plainfield	15	1928		X			
Plainfield Country Club	Plainfield	3	1928	X				
211 Ridgewood Country Golf	Ridgewood	18	1916			X		closed
212 Riverton Country Golf	Riverton	18	1916	X		X	X	
213 Seaview Resort (Bay)	Absecon	18	1918	X		X	X	
New York								
214 Apawamis Club	Rye	3	1930	X				
215 Belleview Country Club	Syracuse	18	1914	X			X	
216 Brook Lea Country Club	Rochester	18	1926	X		X	X	
217 Chappequa Country Club	Mount Kisko	18	1929	X				closed
218 Chautauqua Golf Club	Chautauqua	9	1921		X			
Chautauqua Golf Club	Chautauqua	9	1921	X				
219 Country Club of Buffalo	Williamsville	18	1926	X			X	
220 Country Club of Rochester	Rochester	18	1913	X			X	
221 Elmsford Country Club	Elmsford	18	1919	X				closed
222 Fairview Country Club	Elmsford	18	1912	X			X	closed
223 Fox Hills Country Club	Staten Island	18	1928		X		X	closed
224 Glenburnie Golf Course	Lake George	18	1915	X	X			closed
225 Glens Falls Country Club	Glens Falls	18	1923	X			X	
226 Hudson River Country Club	Yonkers	18	1916	X			X	closed
227 Irondequoit Country Club	Rochester	9	1916	X		X	X	
Irondequoit Country Club	Rochester	9	1916	X			X	
228 Mark Twain Golf Course	Elmira	18	1940	X		X		
229 Monroe Country Club	Pittsford	18	1923	X		X	X	
230 North Fork Country Club	Cutchogue	9	1912	X				
North Fork Country Club	Cutchogue	9	1922	X				
231 Oak Hill Country Club - East	Rochester	18	1924	X		X	X	
232 Oak Hill Country Club - West	Rochester	18	1924	X			X	
233 Sagamore Resort & Golf Club	Bolton Landing	18	1928	X		X	X	
234 Siwanoy Country Club	Bronxville	18	1914	X				
235 Teugega Country Club	Rome	18	1920	X			X	
236 Thendara Golf Club	Thendara	9	1921	X				
237 Tupper Lake Country Club	Tupper Lake	118	1915	X				
238 Whipporwill Country Club	Armonk	18	1925	X		X	X	
239 Wykagyl Country Club	New Rochelle	18	1920	X			X	
North Carolina								
240 Alamance Country Club	Burlington	18	1947	X				
241 Benvenue Country Club	Rocky Mount	18	1922	X		X	X	
Benvenue Country Club	Rocky Mount	18	1946		X			
242 Biltmore Forest Country Club	Asheville	18	1925	X			X	

	Course	City	Holes	Year	New Course	Remodel	Plan	On Site Confirmed	Note:
North Carolina (continued)									
243	Blowing Rock Country Club	Blowing Rock	9	1922		X		X	
	Blowing Rock Country Club	Blowing Rock	9	1922	X			X	
244	Buncombe Country Golf Course	Asheville	18	1927	X		X	X	
245	Cape Fear Country Club	Wilmington	18	1926	X	X	X	X	7 new
	Cape Fear Country Club	Wilmington	18	1946		X			
246	Carolina Golf & Country Club	Charlotte	18	1928	X				
247	Carolina Pines Golf Club	Raleigh	18	1932	X				closed
248	Catawba Country Club	Newton	18	1946	X		X	X	
249	Charlotte Country Club	Newton	18	1925		X	X	X	
	Charlotte Country Club	Newton	18	1942		X			
250	Country Club of Asheville	Asheville	18	1928	X			X	
251	Country Club of Salisbury	Salisbury	18	1927	X		X		
252	Forsyth Country Club (#2 Course)	Winston-Salem	18	1929	X				
253	Forsyth Country Club (Twin City)	Winston-Salem	18	1911	X			X	
254	Greensboro Country Club, Irving Park	Greensboro	18	1911	X		X		
255	Grove Park Inn & Country Club	Asheville	18	1926		X		X	
256	Hendersonville Country Club	Hendersonville	18	1927	X				
257	Highland Country Club	Fayetteville	18	1945	X		X		
258	Highlands Country Club	Highlands	18	1928	X		X	X	
259	Hope Valley Country Club	Durham	18	1927	X		X	X	
260	Lenoir Golf Club	Lenoir	9	1928	X		X		
261	Linville Golf Club	Linville	18	1928	X			X	
262	Mid Pines Golf Club	Southern Pines	18	1921	X		X	X	
263	Mimosa Hills Golf Club	Morganton	18	1928	X		X		
264	Monroe Country Club	Monroe	9	1927	X				
265	Mooresville Golf Club	Mooresville	9	1948		X			
266	Myers Park Country Club	Charlotte	18	1930		X	X		9 new
	Myers Park Country Club	Charlotte	18	1945		X			
267	Overhills Golf Club	Overhills	9	1910	X		X		
	Overhills Golf Club	Overhills	9	1918	X				
268	Penrose Park Country Club	Reidsville	9	1928	X		X		
269	Pine Needles Country Club	Southern Pines	18	1927	X			X	
270	Pinehurst #1	Pinehurst	18	1900-1946	X	X		X	
271	Pinehurst #2	Pinehurst	18	1903-1946	X	X		X	
272	Pinehurst #4	Pinehurst	18	1912-1937	X			X	abandoned
273	Pinehurst #5	Pinehurst	9	1928	X			X	
	Pinehurst #5	Pinehurst	9	1935	X			X	abandoned
274	Raleigh	Raleigh	18	1947	X		X	X	
275	Richmond Pines Country Club	Rockingham	9	1926	X				
276	Roaring Gap Club	Roaring Gap	18	1926	X		X	X	
277	Ryder Golf Club	Fort Bragg	9	1922	X				
278	Sedgefield Country Club #1	Greensboro	18	1926	X			X	
279	Sedgefield Country Club #2	Greensboro	18	1929	X				
280	Southern Pines Country Club	Southern Pines	18	1923	X			X	
	Southern Pines Country Club	Southern Pines	18	1928	X			X	
281	Stryker	Fayetteville	18	1946	X				
282	Tryon Country Club	Tryon	9	1916	X				
283	Waynesville Country Club	Waynesville	9	1924	X				
284	Wilmington Golf Course	Wilmington	18	1926	X		X	X	

	Course	City	Holes	Year	New Course	Remodel	Plan	On Site Confirmed	Note:
Ohio									
285	Acacia Country Club	Lyndhurst	18	1923	X		X		
286	Arlington Golf Club	Columbus	18	1921	X				closed
287	Athens Country Club	Athens	9	1921	X				
288	Brookside Country Club	Canton	18	1922	X			X	
289	Columbus Country Club	Columbus	18	1914	X	X			9 new
	Columbus Country Club	Columbus	18	1920		X			
290	Congress Lake Club	Hartville	18	1926		X	X	X	
291	Dayton Country Club	Dayton	18	1919	X				
292	Delaware Golf Club	Delaware	9	1925	X				was Odevene
293	Elks Country Club	Worthington	18	1923	X				closed
294	Elks Country Club (Portsmouth)	McDermott	18	1920	X			X	
295	Granville Golf Club	Granville	18	1924	X			X	
296	Hamilton Elks Country Club	Hamilton	18	1925	X		X	X	
297	Hawthorne Valley Country Club	Solon	18	1926	X		X		
298	Hyde Park Golf & Country Club	Cincinnati	18	1926	X			X	
299	Inverness Club	Toledo	9	1920		X	X	X	
	Inverness Club	Toledo	9	1920	X		X	X	
300	Lancaster Country Club	Lancaster	9	1926		X			
301	Maketewah Country Club	Cincinnati	18	1929		X			2 new
302	Manakiki Country Club	Willoughby	18	1928	X			X	
303	Mayfield Country Club	Euclid	18	1935	X				
304	Miami Shores Golf Club	Troy	18	1947	X		X		
305	Miami Valley Golf Club	Dayton	18	1919	X			X	
306	Mill Creek Park Golf Club - North	Youngstown	18	1928	X		X	X	
307	Mill Creek Park Golf Club - South	Youngstown	18	1928	X			X	
308	Mohawk Golf Club	Tiffin	9	1917	X		X		
309	Oakwood Club	Cleveland	18	1915		X		X	
	Oakwood Club	Cleveland	18	1920		X		X	
310	Piqua Country Club	Piqua	9	1920	X			X	
311	Scioto Country Club	Columbus	18	1916	X			X	
312	Shaker Heights Country Club	Shaker Heights	18	1916	X			X	
313	Springfield Country Club	Springfield	18	1921	X			X	
314	Westbrook Country Club	Mansfield	18	1920	X		X		
315	Willowick Country Club	Willoughby	18	1917	X	X	X		closed
316	Wyandot Golf Course	Centerburg	18	1922	X				
317	Youngstown Country Club	Youngstown	18	1924		X		X	
318	Zanesville Country Club	Zanesville	18	1932	X				
Pennslyvania									
319	Allegheny Country Club	Sewickley	3	1933		X	X	X	
320	Aronimink Golf Club	Newtown Square	18	1928	X		X	X	
	Aronimink Golf Club	Newtown Square	9	1928		X		X	
	Aronimink Golf Club	Newtown Square	18	1930		X		X	
321	Bedford Springs Golf Club	Bedford	18	1924		X		X	
322	Buck Hill Golf Club	Buck Hill Falls	27	1922	X		X		
323	Cedarbrook Country Club	Blue Bell	18	1921		X	X	X	closed
324	Chester Valley Country Club	Malvern	18	1928	X				
325	Country Club of York	York	18	1928	X		X	X	
326	Edgewood Country Club	Pittsburgh	18	1921	X		X	X	

	Course	City	Holes	Year	New Course	Remodel	Plan	On Site Confirmed	Note:
Pennslyvania (continued)									
327	Elkview Country Club	Carbondale	9	1925	X		X		
328	Green Oaks Country Club (West)	Verona	18	1921	X				
329	Gulph Mills Country Club	King of Prussia	18	1919	X			X	
330	Kahkwa Club	Erie	18	1918	X		X	X	
331	Kennett Square Golf & Country Club	Kennett Square	9	1923	X				
332	Lewistown Country Club	Lewistown	9	1945	X			X	
333	Lu Lu Country Club	North Hills	18	1912	X			X	
334	Overbrook Country Club	Overbrook	18	1922	X			X	closed
335	Philadelphia Country Club - Flourtown	Philadelphia	18	1914		X			
336	Pocono Manor Golf Club	Pocono Manor	18	1919	X				
337	Rolling Rock Club	Ligonier	9	1917	X		X	X	
	Rolling Rock Club	Ligonier	9	1947		X			
338	Schuylkill Country Club	Orwegsburg	9	1945	X				
339	Silver Creek Country Club	Hellertown	18	1947	X			X	
340	St. Davids Golf Club	Wayne	18	1927	X		X	X	
341	Sunnybrook Country Club	Flourtown	18	1921	X			X	closed
342	Torresdale-Frankford Country Club	Philadelphia	9	1930	X			X	
	Torresdale-Frankford Country Club	Philadelphia	9	1930		X		X	
343	Tumblebrook Golf Club	Coopersburg	9	1931	X				
344	Wanango Golf Club	Reno	9	1913	X				
345	Whitemarsh Valley Country Club	Lafayette Hill	18	1930		X		X	
Rhode Island									
346	Agawam Hunt Club	Rumford	18	1931		X		X	
347	Metacomet Country Club	East Providence	18	1921	X		X	X	
348	Misquamicut Country Club	Westerly	18	1923		X	X	X	
349	Newport Country Club	Newport	18	1915		X	X	X	
350	Point Judith Country Club	Narragansett	9	1927	X		X		
	Point Judith Country Club	Narragansett	9	1927		X	X		
351	Rhode Island Country Club	West Barrington	18	1912	X		X		
352	Sakonnet Golf Club	Little Compton	18	1921	X		X	X	
353	Triggs Memorial Golf Club	Providence	18	1932	X		X	X	
354	Wannamoisett Country Club	Rumford	18	1914	X		X	X	
	Wannamoisett Country Club	Rumford	18	1926	X	X	X		
355	Warwick Country Club	Warwick	9	1924	X		X	X	
356	Winnapaug Country Club	Westerly	18	1921		X	X		
	Winnapaug Country Club	Westerly	9	1928	X	9			9 new
South Carolina									
357	Camden Country Club	Camden	18	1939		X	X	X	
358	Cheraw Country Club	Cheraw	9	1924	X				
359	Fort Mill Golf Club	Fort Mill	9	1947	X		X		
360	Lancaster Golf Course	Lancaster	9	1935	X				

	Course	City	Holes	Year	New Course	Remodel	Plan	On Site Confirmed	Note:
Tennessee									
361	Belle Meade Country Club	Nashville	18	1921	X			X	
362	Brainerd Municipal	Chattanooga	9	1925	X				
363	Chattanooga Golf and Country Club	Chattanooga	18	1920	X				
364	Cherokee Country Club	Knoxville	18	1910	X			X	
	Cherokee Country Club	Knoxville	18	1925	X	X		X	3 new
365	Holston Hills Country Club	Knoxville	18	1928	X		X	X	
366	Memphis Country Club	Memphis	18	1910	X			X	
367	Richland Country Club	Nashville	18	1920	X		X		closed
368	Ridgefields Country Club	Kingsport	18	1947	X				
369	Tate Springs Golf Club	Tate Springs	18	1924	X		X	X	closed
Texas									
370	Galveston Municipal Golf Course	Galveston	18	1921	X			X	closed
371	River Oaks Country Club	Houston	9	1924	X			X	
	River Oaks Country Club	Houston	9	1927	X			X	
372	Sunset Grove Country Club	Orange	18	1923	X				
Vermont									
373	Burlington Country Club	Burlington	18	1930	X			X	
374	Woodstock Country Club	Woodstock	18	1938		X			
Virginia									
375	Army-Navy Country Club	Arlington	18	1944	X				
376	Belmont Park Golf Course	Richmond	18	1940		X		X	was Hermitage
377	Country Club of Petersburg	Petersburg	18	1922	X		X	X	closed
378	Hampton Golf Club	Hampton	18	1921	X			X	was Hampton Rhodes
379	Jefferson-Lakeside Club	Richmond	18	1921	X			X	
380	The Homestead Golf Club	Hot Springs	18	1912	X	X		X	12 new
381	Washington Golf & Country Club	Arlington	18	1915	X				
382	Westwood Golf Club	Richmond	18	1916		X	X		closed
383	Woodberry Forest Golf Club	Woodberry Forest	9	1910	X				
Wisconsin									
384	Kenosha Country Club	Kenosha	18	1922	X			X	
385	Oconomowoc Golf Club	Oconomowoc	18	1915	X		X	X	
Canada									
386	Algonquin	New Brunswick	27	1927	X		X		
387	Banff	Banff Springs	18	1917	X			X	
388	Brightwood	Dartmouth, NS	9	1934	X				
389	Elmhurst	Winnipeg, Manitoba	9	1923		X		X	

	Course	City	Holes	Year	New Course	Remodel	Plan	On Site Confirmed	Note:
Canada (continued)									
	Elmhurst	Winnipeg, Manitoba	9	1923	X				
390	Essex	LaSalle, Ontario	18	1929	X		X	X	
391	Liverpool (White Point)	Hunts Point, NS	18	1929	X		X		
392	Pine Ridge	Winnipeg, Manitoba	18	1919		X	X		
393	Riverside	New Brunswick	18	1937	X				
394	Roseland	Toronto	18	1919		X		X	
395	Roseland	Windsor, Ontario	27	1921	X		X		
	Roseland	Windsor, Ontario	9	1924		X		X	
396	St. Charles	Winnipeg, Manitoba	9	1920	X			X	
Cuba									
397	Havana Biltmore	Havana	18	1927	X				closed
398	Havana Country Club	Havana	18	1911	X			X	closed
Scotland									
399	Royal Dornoch	Dornoch	2	1921	X			X	2 new

Donald J. Ross Designed Courses Hosting Major Championships (108)

	U.S. Open (23)	PGA (15)	Women's Open (13)	Senior Open (8)	Amateur (19)	Women's Amateur (27)	Ryder Cup (6)
1916		Siwanoy					
1917							
1918							
1919	Brae Burn						
1920	Inverness						
1921							
1922	Skokie						
1923							
1924	Oakland Hills	French Lick				Rhode Island	
1925	Worcester						
1926	Scioto						
1927					Minikahda		Worcester
1928					Brae Burn		
1929						Oakland Hills	
1930	Interlachen						
1931	Inverness	Wannamoisett			Beverly	CC of Buffalo	Scioto
1932						Salem	
1933						Exmoor	
1934						Whitemarsh Valley	
1935						Interlachen	
1936		Pinehurst No. 2					
1937	Oakland Hills					Memphis	
1938							
1939							
1940							
1941							
1942		Seaview					
1943							
1944							
1945							

	U.S. Open (23)	PGA (15)	Women's Open (13)	Senior Open (8)	Amateur (19)	Women's Amateur (27)	Ryder Cup (6)
1946							
1947						Franklin Hills	
1948					Memphis		
1949			Prince Georges		Oak Hill		
1950					Minneapolis	East Lake	
1951	Oakland Hills						Pinehurst No. 2
1952							
1953			CC of Rochester			Rhode Island	
1954			Salem			Allegheny	
1955					CC of Virginia	Myers Park	
1956	Oak Hill		Northland				
1957	Inverness	Miami Valley					
1958							
1959		Minneapolis			Broadmoor	Congressional	
1960			Worcester				
1961	Oakland Hills						
1962		Aronimink			Pinehurst No. 2	CC of Rochester	
1963							East Lake
1964	Congressional	Columbus					
1965						Lakewood	
1966							
1967					Broadmoor		
1968	Oak Hill				Scioto		
1969							
1970							
1971			Kahkwa				
1972		Oakland Hills			Charlotte		
1973			CC of Rochester		Inverness	Montclair	
1974							
1975					CC of Virginia	Brae Burn	

	U.S. Open (23)	PGA (15)	Women's Open (13)	Senior Open (8)	Amateur (19)	Women's Amateur (27)	Ryder Cup (6)
1976		Congressional					
1977					Aronimink		
1978					Plainfield	Sunnybrook	
1979	Inverness	Oakland Hills				Memphis	
1980	Oak Hill						
1981				Oakland Hills			
1982							
1983							
1984			Salem	Oak Hill			
1985	Oakland Hills				Montclair		
1986		Inverness		Scioto			
1987			Plainfield			Rhode Island	
1988						Minikahda	
1989	Oak Hill					Pinehurst No 2	
1990							
1991				Oakland Hills			
1992							
1993		Inverness					
1994				Pinehurst No.2	Newport		
1995			Broadmoor	Congressional			Oak Hill
1996	Oakland Hills		Pine Needles				
1997	Congressional						
1998						Barton Hills	
1999	Pinehurst No.2					Biltmore Forest	
2000							
2001			Pine Needles	Salem			
2002					Oakland Hills		
2003		Oak Hill		Inverness		Philadelphia	
2004			Orchards			Kahkwa	Oakland Hills
2005	Pinehurst No.2						

BIBLIOGRAPHIC ESSAY

This biography has been based upon a variety of primary archival sources. A crucial repository for Ross material now exists and is publicly available at the Tufts Archives of the Given Memorial Library in Pinehurst, North Carolina. The existence in one place of Ross letters, maps, and contemporary newspaper accounts is largely due to the painstaking efforts of the late W. Pete Jones of Raleigh, North Carolina, and to the management skills of archivist Khristine Januszik. The collection represents the only substantial gathering of such material pertaining to any single golf course architect's work. It also stands as a model of the kind of archival work needed to preserve the records of classic golf course architecture.

The design maps alone are a treasure for any Ross-designed course seeking to recapture its original design heritage. At the same time, the archive is eager to accept materials from facilities and collectors who may have material of their own that they are willing to share.

The documentary record on Ross's life in Dornoch is extremely limited. Two booklets by Donald Grant provided informative looks at the golf communities there: *Donald Ross of Pinehurst and Royal Dornoch* (Golspie: The Sutherland Press, 1973) and *Personal Matters of Royal Dornoch Golf Club, 1900-1925* (no publication information given). Both suffer numerous minor factual errors but are nonetheless helpful guides to the local golf culture. Dornoch secretary John Sutherland's testimonial speech, which praises all of those who helped to create the golf community there without ever mentioning Ross, supposedly his star pupil, is reprinted in *The Northern Times* (Golspie) of September 7, 1933.

The general culture of Scottish golf finds its most sophisticated treatment in David Hamilton's *Golf: Scotland's Game* (Kilmacolm: The Partick Press, 1998). The lifework of Old Tom Morris is found in two accounts: *The Life of Tom Morris* by W.W. Tulloch (London: T. Werner Laurie, 1908) and Robert Kroeger's *The Golf Courses of Old Tom Morris* (Cincinnati: Heritage Communications, 1995).

The story of golf in Pinehurst and Ross's role in that development is best covered in several manuscripts by Richard S. Tufts. *The Scottish Invasion* (Pinehurst: Pinehurst Publishers, 1962) provides a helpful overview. Far more detailed on the early days of the resort are two of the author's unpublished drafts: *The First Seventy-five Years: A History of the Village of Pinehurst* and *Pinehurst*, both of them to be found in the Tufts Archive. A useful summary of these developments with considerable updating can be found in Raymond E. North's *The Pinehurst Story: June 1895-June 1984* (Pinehurst: Resorts of Pinehurst, Inc., 1985). An attractively illustrated volume combining personal recollections by key figures with revealing character portraits is *Pinehurst Stories* by Lee Pace (Pinehurst: Resorts of Pinehurst, Inc, 1991).

The starting point for any student of course architecture is the classical literature. Among the indispensable volumes are *Some Essays on Golf Course Architecture* by H.S. Colt and C.H. Alison (New York: Charles Scribner's Sons, 1920); Robert Hunter's *The Links* (New York: Charles Scribner's Sons, 1926); Charles Blair Macdonald's *Scotland's Gift: Golf* (New York: Charles Scribner's Sons, 1928); *Golf Architecture* by Alister MacKenzie (London: Simpkin, Marshall, Hamilton, Kent & Co., 1920); *Golf Has Never Failed Me* by Donald J. Ross, (Ann Arbor, MI. Clock Tower Press, 1996); *Golf Architecture in America* by George C. Thomas Jr., (Los Angeles: Times-Mirror Press, 1927); A.W. Tillinghast's *The Course Beautiful* (Warren, NJ: TreeWolf Productions, 1996); and *The Architectural Side of Golf* by H.N. Wethered and T. Simpson (London: Longmans, Green & Co., 1929). *The Architects of Golf* by Geoffrey S. Cornish and Ronald E. Whitten (New York: HarperCollins, 1993) remains the single indispensable introduction to the master designers. Geoff Shackelford's *The Golden Age of Golf Design* (Ann Arbor, MI. Clock Tower Press, 1999) summarizes the interwar architects and provides an unsurpassed collection of photographic evidence documenting their brilliant work. Michael Fay's *Golf as it was Meant to be Played* (New York: Universe Publishing, 2000) celebrates Ross's work in the form of a tour of 18 of his exemplary holes.

A detailed contemporary account of design techniques can be found in a previously overlooked 10-part series, Conrad Moser's "Golf Course Design and Construction," *American Landscape Architect*, March-December 1931, which contains dozens of photographs of New England layouts. Fred Hawtree, Ed., *Aspects of Golf Course Architecture I, 1889-1924* (Worcestershire: Grant Books, 1998) makes available more than a dozen neglected historical pieces by British architects/writers. Geoff Shackelford, Ed., *Masters of the Links* (Ann Arbor, MI. Clock Tower Press, 1997) combines classical essays with accounts of their enduring relevance to modern architecture. Herbert Warren Wind's *Following Through* (New York: Ticknor & Fields, 1985) includes many of his classic profiles in *The New Yorker*, including the famous 1951 essay on Robert Trent Jones Sr. For book-length studies linking traditional strategic principles with contemporary design, see *The Anatomy of a Golf Course* by Tom Doak, (New York: Lyons & Burford, 1992) and my own *Rough Meditations* (Ann Arbor, MI. Clock Tower Press, 1997).

Michael J. Hurdzan's *Golf Course Architecture: Design, Construction & Restoration* (New York, NY John Wiley & Sons, 1996) presents a detailed view of golf course development linking strategy and construction techniques. *Golf Course Design* by Robert Muir Graves and Geoffrey S. Cornish (New York: John Wiley & Sons, 1998) locates these design considerations within the framework of modern real estate and financing considerations. The status of agronomy in Ross's day is covered in *Turf for Golf Courses* by Charles V. Piper and Russell A. Oakley (New York: Macmillan, 1923). The evolution of maintenance, including a look at Ross and Frank Maples, is the subject of a special issue of *Golfweek's Superintendent News: A*

Century of Greenkeeping, December 10/24, 1999.

Club histories provided an indispensable source of material for this biography, though here, as in all cases, they cannot be taken at face value. Too little of the original history remains a matter of speculation and lore, and many of these books neglect their own golf course architectural history. Their quality ranges wildly, from the picture-book genre, to those that seem to detail excessively (and exhaustingly) nearly every shot played at annual club events, to the truly scholarly and thoughtful. Nevertheless, no serious student of the game can overlook this genre of evidence for the clues and glimpses it affords.

Oakley Golf Club: The First Fifty Years (no publication information given) provides fascinating insights into the early life of Ross's first U.S. posting. The club kindly allowed me access to its extensive archival records, where I was able to determine that Ross was not paid enough to enable him, as he claimed, to send $2,000 home after his first year.

No club history is more detailed than George C. Caner Jr.'s *History of the Essex County Club, 1893-1993* (Manchester-by-the-Sea, MA: Essex County Club, 1995). He admirably documents, among many matters, Ross's role on the redesign of the golf grounds. The history is an invaluable guide to golf at one of the country's most historic (if overlooked) layouts.

Chris Rawson's *Where Stone Walls Meet the Sea: Sakonnet Golf Club, 1899-1999* (Little Compton, RI: Sakonnet Books, 1999) is a wonderfully researched and well-written narrative of life at the club where Ross summered during the last third of his life. The loving attention paid to the club's history is reflected in the Sakonnet's attitude toward its own Ross-designed golf course. Two books proved helpful on Oak Hill Golf Course outside Rochester, NY. Howard C. Hosmer's *From Little Acorns: The Story of Oak Hill, 1901-1976* (Pittsford, NY: Oak Hill Country Club, 1977) never mentions Ross and devotes not a single sentence to either of his two courses there, though it does lavish much attention on the many trees on site and the club's early history. Donald H. Kladstrup, *The Evolution of a Legacy* (Pittsford, NY: Oak Hill Country Club) provides an exemplary design history, including hole-by-hole sketches of all major changes.

Carolyn Green Smithfield's *The Country Club of Birmingham* (Birmingham, AL: The Country Club of Birmingham, 1999) a social history of the club, with precious little about the facility's twin Ross courses. Ray W. Rancourt's *Shennecossett: The History of a Golf Course* (Groton, CT: Town of Groton Department of Parks & Recreation, 1989) is only slightly more forthcoming on design details at what used to be one of the East Coast's grandest seaside golf resorts. Two other club histories are essentially photo-documentaries. Although it concentrates on the club's impressive history of major tournaments, *75 Years at Oakland Hills* (Warren, MI: Perry and White, 1991) does have some fleeting but tantalizing glimpses of the original design work. Plainfield (NJ) Country Club's *The First Hundred Years* (no publishing data given) is a brief but attractive album-style book that offers a look at one of Ross's most distinctive sets of putting surfaces. *The Detroit Golf Club: 100 Years* (Detroit: Detroit Golf Club, 1998) is far more mindful of its design heritage, as is Robert D.B. Carlisle's *The Montclair Golf Club* (Montclair, NJ: Montclair Golf Club, 1984). Patricia Condon Johnson's *Reflections: The White Bear Yacht Club, 1889-1989* (White Bear Lake, MN: White Bear Yacht Club, 1989) concentrated on the culture of the club rather than on the inception or evolution of the golf course. R. Milton Lynnes's *Exmoor Country Club, the First Hundred Years* (Highland Park, IL: Exmoor Country Club, 1996) was more helpful on the layout. In part because of a glorious tournament history that culminated in the 1922 U.S. Open, Michael Bartlett's *Celebrating One Hundred Years: Skokie Country Club, 1897-1997* (Glencoe, IL: Skokie Country Club, 1997) provides fine details and illustrations, both historical and contemporary.

Gary Larrabee's *Salem Country Club: One Hundred Years, 1895-1995* (Peabody, MA: Salem Country Club, 1995) benefits from an ideal combination of a thoughtful narrative and excellent photography, including hole-by-hole comparisons that juxtapose vintage black and white construction images with contemporary color views. *Wannamoisett Country Club* (Rumford, RI: Wannamoisett Country Club, 1998) displays a powerful historical sensibility supported by hole-by-hole photography, as does *Brae Burn Country Club, 1897-1997, Centenary* (West Newton, MA: Brae Burn Country Club, 1997). The story of half a dozen designers working on a golf course for more than half-century as it literally migrated from one side of a road to the other is the subject of *The Hartford Golf Club 1896-1996* (West Hartford, CT: Hartford Golf Club, 1995); thankfully, superintendent Herb Watson has in his possession a rare set of two complete design plans by Ross, circa 1915-1919, the other dating to a 1946 plan that was among Ross's last projects.

Mitchell P. Postel's *The History of the Peninsula Golf and Country Club* (San Mateo, CA: Peninsula Golf and Country Club, 1993) did much to focus attention on Ross's only work west of the Rocky Mountains and along the way sparked membership interest in a restoration plan, undertaken by architect Ron Forse. When it comes to research detail and photographic drama of Ross work in remote sites, nothing surpasses the accounts of his work in the Canadian Rockies found in companion volumes by E. J. Hart, *Golf on the Roof of the World* (Banff: EJH Literary Enterprises Ltd., 1999) and *Banff Springs Golf* (Banff: EJH Literary Enterprises Ltd., 1999).

Only very late in the research and writing of this book did I come across an idiosyncratic work, as yet unpublished, concerning a fictional meeting and collaboration among Ross, Tillinghast, and MacKenzie that manages to convey their respective characters: Warner Bott Berry's *Scotland's Dream*. The enduring power of their work, along with that of other classical masters, occupies a lively internet discussion group, "golfclubatlas.com.

INDEX